ELECTIONS IN DANGEROUS PLACES

Elections in Dangerous Places

Democracy and the Paradoxes of Peacebuilding

Edited by
DAVID GILLIES

Published for
The North-South Institute
by
McGill-Queen's University Press
Montreal & Kingston • London • Ithaca

© McGill-Queen's University Press 2011
ISBN 978-0-7735-3935-8 (cloth)
ISBN 978-0-7735-3936-5 (paper)

Legal deposit third quarter 2011
Bibliothèque nationale du Québec

Printed in the United States on acid-free paper that is 100% ancient forest free, processed chlorine free.

McGill-Queen's University Press acknowledges the support of the Canada Council for the Arts for our publishing program. We also acknowledge the financial support of the Government of Canada through the Canada Book Fund for our publishing activities.

Library and Archives Canada Cataloguing in Publication

Elections in dangerous places : democracy and the paradoxes of peacebuilding / edited by David Gillies.

Co-published by: North-South Institute.
Includes bibliographical references.
ISBN 978-0-7735-3935-8 (bound). – ISBN 978-0-7735-3936-5 (pbk.)

1. Elections. 2. Political violence. 3. Conflict management. 4. Democracy. . I. Gillies, David, 1952– II. North-South Institute (Ottawa, Ont.)

JC328.6.E54 2011   303.6'2   C2011-902447-0

This book was typeset by True to Type in 10.5/13 Sabon

For Malcolm and Hannah

Contents

Acknowledgments ix

Contributors xi

Introduction: Electoral Democracy and the Paradoxes of Peacebuilding xix
David Gillies

PART ONE   ELECTIONS IN CONFLICT SITUATIONS: AN OVERVIEW

1 Understanding Elections in Conflict Situations 3
   Benjamin Reilly

PART TWO   LESSONS LEARNED FROM COUNTRY SITUATIONS

2 Elections and the Future of Afghanistan 21
   Francesc Vendrell

3 Iraq's Conflicted Transition to Democracy: Analyzing Elections in a Violent Society 32
   Marc. A. Lemieux

4 Democracy in Africa: Rumours of Its Demise Have Been Greatly Exaggerated 53
   Christian R. Hennemeyer

5 Elections, Governance, and Secession in Sudan 71
   Khalid Mustafa Medani

6 Election-Related Conflict Resolution Mechanisms:
The 2006 Elections in the Democratic Republic of the Congo   90
Eugenia Zorbas and Vincent Tohbi

7 Dying to Win: Elections, Political Violence,
and Institutional Decay in Kenya   105
Susanne D. Mueller

8 Lessons Learned and Forgotten: The International
Community and Electoral Conflict Management in Kenya   127
Stephen Brown

PART THREE   POLICY AND PRACTICE IN ELECTORAL
CONFLICT MANAGEMENT

9 Merging Conflict Management with Electoral Practice:
The IFES Experience   147
Lisa Kammerud

10 Preventing and Mitigating Election-Related Conflict
and Violence: The Role of Electoral Justice   171
Sara Staino

11 Electoral Dispute Resolution: A Personal Perspective   190
Johann Kriegler

PART FOUR   CANADA'S ROLE IN INTERNATIONAL
DEMOCRACY PROMOTION

12 Is Democracy Promotion "Globaloney" or a Categorical
Imperative?   209
Thomas S. Axworthy

13 Ongoing Dilemmas of Democratization:
Canada and Afghanistan   220
Gerald J. Schmitz

Conclusion: An Ounce of Prevention:
Preliminary Implications for Policy and Practice   246
David Gillies and Gerald J. Schmitz

Notes   263

Acknowledgments

Each passing year brings new examples of flawed, conflicted, and sometimes violent elections that compromise peace and stability. As we enter a new decade, unresolved conflicts in Haiti and Côte d'Ivoire underscore the need for more systematic attention to anticipating, managing, and resolving election-related conflicts. Notwithstanding the instability that can accompany political transitions, uprisings across the Middle East and North Africa, sparked first in Tunisia and then set ablaze in Egypt, confirm the pent-up demand for greater political openness, including through genuinely competitive elections.

The idea for this book began when the editor was an election observer in Zimbabwe's deeply flawed and conflicted 2002 presidential election; it was nurtured by discussion with colleagues at the North-South Institute and the Canadian International Development Agency (CIDA), and notably with Linda Maguire at the United Nations Development Programme (UNDP). The North-South Institute thanks the CIDA Afghanistan-Pakistan Task Force and UNDP for their support. The editor wishes to thank Gerald Schmitz, Ben Reilly, Grant Kippen, Nana Marcus Kwamie, Susanne Mueller, Stephen Brown, and Eugenia Zorbas for their support and critical thinking at various stages of this project. Copyediting and editorial support from Ruth Bradley-St-Cyr and Nicolas Levesque, and from Joan McGilvray and Kyla Madden at McGill-Queen's University Press has been invaluable. The views expressed here are those of individual authors and do not necessarily reflect those of the North-South Institute or other institutions. The Canadian International Development Agency enabled me to take a sabbatical and The North-South Institute provided a stimulating research environment. Finally, I would like to thank my friends and family for their support, especially Malcolm and Hannah. This book is dedicated to those many citizens across the Middle East and North Africa who, with remarkable courage, have awoken to the possibilities of their own emancipation, a struggle for human dignity as noble and ancient as the idea of democracy itself.

David Gillies
Ottawa
March 2011

Contributors

THOMAS S. AXWORTHY is the president and CEO of the Walter & Duncan Gordon Foundation. He served as senior policy adviser and principal secretary to Prime Minister Pierre Elliott Trudeau. In 1984, Axworthy became a fellow of the Harvard University's Institute of Politics at the John F. Kennedy School of Government and appointed William Lyon Mackenzie King Visiting Professor of Canadian Studies. In 1999, Axworthy helped to create the Historica Foundation to improve the teaching and learning of Canadian history. To recognize these achievements – including the *Heritage Minutes*, which he initiated – he was given the Order of Canada. In 2003, he became chair of the Centre for the Study of Democracy, School of Policy Studies, Queen's University, pursuing the themes of expanded human rights and responsibilities, democratic reform, Canadian-American relations, and modern liberalism that have characterized his research, teaching, and advocacy career. He has edited several publications, including *Bridging the Divide: Religious Dialogue and Universal Ethics* (School of Policy Studies, Queen's University, 2008). He was awarded the Public Affairs Association Award of Distinction in 2008.

STEPHEN BROWN is associate professor of political science at the University of Ottawa. His research focuses on foreign aid, democratization, political violence, peacebuilding, and transitional justice – mainly in relation to Sub-Saharan Africa. He has published on democratization, political violence, peacebuilding, and transitional justice/rule of law in Angola, Kenya, Malawi, Mozambique, and Rwanda. Recently he has been visiting researcher at the German Development Institute, Bonn, and visiting Professor at the Centre de recherche et d'étude sur les pays d'Afrique orientale (CREPAO), Université de Pau et des Pays de l'Adour, Pau, France. He is currently working on two projects: the first examines Canadian aid policy in comparative perspective; the second analyzes accountability mechanisms for the 2007-08 post-election violence in Kenya. He is also editing a book on Canadian development assistance and the Canadian International Development Agency, and co-editing a volume on security and foreign aid with Jörn Grävingholt of the German Development Institute.

DAVID GILLIES was until recently the principal researcher in Fragile and Conflict-Affected States at The North-South Institute in Ottawa. Gillies is now based at the Canadian International Development Agency. He has also worked in England as a probation officer, at the Canadian Department of Foreign Affairs, the Aga Khan Foundation Canada, and Rights and Democracy. Gillies was educated at Oxford and McGill and has taught at Carleton University. His publications include *Between Principle and Practice: Human Rights in North-South Relations* (McGill-Queen's University Press, 1997) and *The Challenge of Democratic Development: Sustaining Democratization in Developing Societies*, with Gerald Schmitz (North-South Institute, 1992).

CHRISTIAN R. HENNEMEYER is currently vice-president for external relations of the Washington, DC–based Bridging the Divide (BTD), a new NGO dedicated to using new technologies to overcome dangerous social, religious, and political schisms in Africa and the Middle East. Prior to joining BTD, Hennemeyer held senior positions with the International Foundation for Electoral Systems (IFES). During his five years with IFES, Hennemeyer worked on a number of crucial elections, including those of Liberia, Burundi, the Democratic Republic of the Congo, and Kenya. Hennemeyer began his international career as a Peace Corps volunteer in Ghana and went on to serve for nineteen years with Catholic Relief Services in a variety of field positions, including country representative for Senegal, Benin, Ghana, Haiti, Rwanda during the genocide, and the DRC during its first war. He also ran major relief operations in Liberia, Sierra Leone, Macedonia, and Burundi.

LISA KAMMERUD is a research officer at the F. Clifton White Applied Research Center for Democracy and Elections at the International

Foundation for Electoral Systems in Washington, DC. She is involved in a variety of research and programs related to elections and conflict and election dispute resolution. She manages the development and implementation of the Election Violence Education and Resolution (EVER) project, and has led field projects in Bangladesh, East Timor, Guyana, Kyrgyzstan, Nepal, and Nigeria. Kammerud holds an MA in International Affairs (concentration in Conflict Resolution and International law) from George Washington University and a BA in International Relations and History from the University of Tennessee-Knoxville.

JOHANN KRIEGLER, a former judge of the South African Constitutional Court, led his country's first democratic elections in 1994 and the subsequent establishment of a permanent electoral agency. Since then he has been involved in electoral preparation, administration, or evaluation in more than a dozen emerging democracies, ranging from Timor-Leste (1999) through Pakistan, Afghanistan, and Iraq to Sierra Leone, Liberia, and Kenya (2008), where he headed a six-month commission of inquiry into that country's failed presidential and parliamentary elections. He is currently one of two foreign commissioners serving on the Electoral Complaints Commission of Afghanistan dealing with cases arising from the country's parliamentary elections. He is a member of the International Foundation for Electoral Systems Executive Advisory Council and has lectured extensively on electoral, judicial, and human rights topics. Justice Kriegler has also led a number of international missions inquiring into human rights issues and threats to judicial independence.

MARC A. LEMIEUX is visiting professor in the Master's seminar "Democracy Promotion: Theory and Practice" at the School for International and Public Affairs at the University of Ottawa. From 2006 to 2009, he was director of the Iraq program at the Forum of Federations, having served two years in Iraq as regional civic education coordinator with the International Foundation for Election Systems (IFES). The IFES Election Violence, Education and Resolution (EVER) program trained local civic groups on methods to monitor and corroborate political and election violence. In 1993, Lemieux worked with the United Nations Transitional Authority in Cambodia (UNTAC) to organize elections there and has since monitored elections for the United

Nations, Organization for Security and Co-operation in Europe, Organization of African States, IFES, and Canadian International Development Agency in Haiti, Bosnia, Serbia, Ukraine, Russia, Georgia, and the Democratic Republic of the Congo. He has worked for Elections Canada and was most recently managing the Forum of Federations' Pakistan program. His article "The Politics of Identity: Comparing Iraq's Local 2005 and 2009 Elections" was published in the July 2010 issue of the *International Journal of Contemporary Iraqi Studies*. Lemieux holds an MA in International Relations from McGill University.

KHALID MUSTAFA MEDANI is assistant professor of political science and Islamic studies at McGill University. Medani has published extensively on the political economy of Islamic fundamentalism and civil war in Sudan, the war on terrorist finance and informal banking in Somalia, and the recruitment of Islamist militants in Egypt. He has also conducted extensive research on globalization, informal networks, and political Islam in Egypt, Sudan, and Somalia. Medani holds a BA in development studies from Brown University, an MA in Arab studies from Georgetown University, and a PhD in political science from the University of California, Berkeley. He has worked as a researcher with the Brookings Institution and was a research fellow at Stanford University's Center for International Security and Cooperation. His publications include "Financing Terrorism or Survival? Informal Finance, State Collapse in Somalia, and the War on Terror" and "State Building in Reverse: The Neo-Liberal 'Reconstruction' of Iraq," both published in *Middle East Report* in 2002 and 2004 respectively. In 2007 Medani was named Carnegie Scholar on Islam and awarded a research grant from the Carnegie Endowment of New York.

SUSANNE D. MUELLER is a visiting researcher at Boston University's African Studies Center and consults with the World Bank and the United Nations. Mueller has a PhD from Princeton University and has taught there and at the University of Nairobi. She lived and worked in Kenya for twenty years, initially as an academic and later as a consultant, working in most of the countries of Eastern and Southern Africa. She also has resided in Tanzania and Uganda, and outside Africa has worked in Ukraine, Moldova, India, and the Maldives. Mueller has published articles on economic and agricultural development, political parties, democracy and governance, human rights, repression, conflict, and violence in Kenya and Tanzania. She has participated in numerous policy and project field missions and has written many reports and working papers for various United Nations agencies, including the food agencies, and the World Bank.

BENJAMIN REILLY is director of the Centre for Democratic Institutions and professor of Political Science in the Crawford School of Economics and Government at the Australian National University, Canberra. Reilly is the author of six books and more than sixty journal articles and book chapters on issues of democratization, constitutional reform, party politics, electoral system design, and conflict management, and has advised governments and international organizations on these subjects. His latest books are a study of democratization and political reform, *Democracy and Diversity: Political Engineering in the Asia-Pacific* (Oxford University Press, 2006), and an edited volume, *Political Parties in Conflict-Prone Societies* (United Nations University Press, 2008). He is currently a visiting professor at Johns Hopkins University's School of Advanced International Studies in Washington, DC.

GERALD J. SCHMITZ holds an MA from the University of Saskatchewan and a PhD in political science from Carleton University in Ottawa. Schmitz has been director of the Library of Parliament's Political and Social Affairs Division and its principal analyst for international affairs. From 1994-2008 he was research director of the House of Commons Standing Committee on Foreign Affairs and International Development, involved with its major reports on Canada's international role in democracy promotion and in Afghanistan. He was also adviser to the Canada-Europe Parliamentary Association. From 1991 to 1993, Schmitz was program director at the North-South Institute and co-authored *The Challenge of Democratic Development: Sustaining Democratization in Developing Societies* (1992) with David Gillies. In 2003, he was an adviser to Canada's minister of foreign affairs. He has addressed international conferences on Canada's role in Afghanistan and the Central Asia region, and is the author of many books and articles.

SARA STAINO, currently working as a capacity building and training specialist for the International Foundation for Electoral Systems (IFES) in Southern Sudan and as a BRIDGE trainer in the Middle East and North Africa, is a former program officer for the Electoral

Processes Programme at International Institute for Democracy and Electoral Assistance (IDEA). Staino is co-author and editorial anchor of the IDEA handbook *Electoral Management Design,* published in 2006, and for the past seven years has collaborated closely with the European Commission and United Nations Development Programme on the conceptualization and development of the ACE Electoral Knowledge Network and the Effective Electoral Assistance program. She has also taught international politics, international election observation, and democratic elections and international electoral support in the Department of Political Science at the University of Örebro in Sweden.

VINCENT TOHBI is a graduate of the National Administration School, Abidjan, Côte d'Ivoire. He worked for the Ivoirian Ministry of Interior before joining the Electoral Commission in 2000, where he was in charge of the issues related to the budget, logistics, and voter education and registration. At the United Nations Development Programme he managed projects supporting the NGOs involved in resolving the conflict in Côte d'Ivoire. He has electoral experience in several countries in Africa and beyond, where he has observed elections, trained independent electoral commissions staff, supported civil society organizations and political parties, and carried out assessments and consulting. Since February 2004, Tohbi has been country-director at the Electoral Institute for the Sustainability of Democracy in Africa in the Democratic Republic of the Congo. In 2005, along with the DRC IEC, he conceptualized "conflict management panels," a model now applied in Sudan and Lesotho and proposed to Mozambique and Côte d'Ivoire.

FRANCESC VENDRELL is adjunct professor at SAIS, Johns Hopkins University, Bologna campus, and spent a year as diplomat-in-residence and visiting professor at the Woodrow Wilson School of Public and International Affairs at Princeton University. From 2002 to 2008, he was special representative of the European Union for Afghanistan, and from 2000 to 2002, he was the personal representative of the UN secretary-general for Afghanistan. He has been a UN civil servant, mediator, and adviser on East Timor, Cambodia, Papua New Guinea, Myanmar (Burma), Haiti, Guatemala, El Salvador, Nicaragua, Cuba, Namibia, and Chile.

EUGENIA ZORBAS earned her PhD from the London School of Economics and Political Science for her thesis entitled "Reconciliation in Post-genocide Rwanda: Discourse and Practice." Eugenia has worked on or in the African Great Lakes region for several years, most recently for Human Rights Watch during the 2010 Rwandan presidential elections. She was the lead political affairs officer in Goma, North Kivu, for the UN peacekeeping mission in DRC, MONUC (now MONUSCO), during the height of the 2008 Goma crisis. She has also worked as a policy adviser for the Canadian Department of Foreign Affairs and International Trade, and for the Canadian International Development Agency.

INTRODUCTION

Electoral Democracy and the Paradoxes of Peacebuilding

DAVID GILLIES

Election-related conflict and violence have risen to the forefront of the international agenda in the aftermath of turbulent elections in Côte d'Ivoire, Haiti, Iran, Iraq, Afghanistan, Pakistan, and Kenya. Egypt's recent "Facebook revolution" was also driven by frustration, demonstrations, and riots over flawed parliamentary elections. The UN estimates that up to 1,500 people may have died in election-related violence in Côte d'Ivoire. Thousands of people have been internally displaced or fled as refugees to neighbouring countries. In Kenya more than 1,200 people may have died and up to 350,000 were internally displaced after the December 2007 election. Up to 300 Nigerians lost their lives in the 2007 election in that country. The surge of global interest[1] in these conflicted elections has now filtered into international human rights law. Philip Alston, the UN special rapporteur on extrajudicial, summary, or arbitrary executions has, for the first time, addressed election-related killings. And in December 2010 Luis Moreno-Ocampo, chief prosecutor at the International Criminal Court, released a list of six Kenyans, including the deputy prime minister, senior civil servants, and an opposition figure, suspected of organizing violence after the 2007 election.

This collection of essays from an expert group of scholars and practitioners is about elections in dangerous places.[2] Drawing on an analysis of elections in conflict-prone societies, such as Afghanistan, Sudan, the Democratic Republic of the Congo, Iraq, and Kenya, as well as on thematic issues, such as mediation and dispute resolution, the book examines:

- the contexts and root causes of election-related conflict;

- the lessons learned from managing elections in conflict situations; and
- the practical action that can be taken to mitigate or prevent conflict.

The contributors consider significant questions of policy and practice, such as:

- Where does electoral democracy promotion fit in the sequencing of international support in war-torn or post-conflict societies?
- Are there minimal standards for "good enough" elections in conflict-prone situations? Can these be agreed on internationally?
- What is the role of international actors in election management and how can conflict prevention approaches be mainstreamed into international electoral assistance?
- What institutional and legal practices help to mitigate election-related conflict, and what are the limitations of a technical approach?
- What are the incentive structures for politicians and political parties to use illegal strategies or play by agreed rules of the game?
- Where are the gaps in knowledge and practice that may benefit from more investigation and innovation?

Elections serve three key purposes in a society: choosing representatives, choosing governments, and conferring legitimacy. In countries emerging from conflict, additional international expectations are placed on elections. They are seen as key to the consolidation of fragile peace settlements intended to help societies navigate war-to-peace transitions. However, following a catalogue of poorly conducted and violent elections from Bosnia, Liberia, and Angola in the 1990s to Iraq and Afghanistan more recently, there is no longer agreement about the centrality of elections to post-conflict state building (see Ben Reilly's chapter in this volume). There is also growing recognition that unrealistic expectations can be placed on elections that are sometimes held too early in war-torn societies. In countries with protracted and deep-rooted conflicts, elections alone can rarely, if ever, confer legitimacy on a particular government.

ELECTIONS IN CONFLICT-PRONE SOCIETIES

Support for democratic development has been a pillar of the international relations of advanced democracies in the post–Cold War era. The establishment of durable democratic regimes has been regarded as key for achieving economic development in low-income countries, for building stable government in fragile states, and for the general promotion of peace. Each year, an estimated US$6 billion to $8 billion is spent on democracy assistance.[3] Today, more than two decades after the fall of the Berlin Wall, which prompted another wave of democratization, the mood of the times is much more pessimistic about international democracy promotion. Nowhere is this pessimism more acute than regarding the state-building project of major powers in so-called "failed and fragile states."[4] These conflict-affected countries share three common problems: deficits of political legitimacy, deficits of governance, and dysfunctional social systems with their own incentives and logic. Elections in such dangerous contexts can magnify each of these deficits.[5] The promotion of democratic governance is a central pillar in the masonry of peacebuilding at war's end.[6] In this architecture, the "liberal peace" is to be constructed by the simultaneous pursuit of markets and democracy. However, after nearly a full generation of experimentation and a spectrum of international engagement, ranging from UN transitional administrations in East Timor and Kosovo; robust Chapter VII enforcement in Bosnia, the DRC, and Sierra Leone; and armed nation building in Iraq and Afghanistan, there is growing recognition that many war-torn societies continue to be conflict-prone and that a durable peace is, in most cases, an elusive goal. This has prompted a view among some scholars that to "fix" fragile states, peacebuilders should sequence their efforts, focusing first on the basics of public order and building capable institutions before taking on the lofty and complex goal of political liberalization.[7]

However, despite the accumulating evidence that "all good things" (security, markets, democracy) may not go together, the business model for international engagement in fragile states continues to emphasize procedural democracy. Elections, which are at the heart of this agenda, are a paradox of peacebuilding. When they are well designed and well managed, elections are a key to the peaceful management of political competition in a democracy. When they are poorly managed, or perceived as stolen, they can be a lightning rod for social discord. Poorly conducted elections further discredit the idea of democracy and should be seen in the light of growing concern about backsliding in some parts of the world, notably in Africa.

Elections in deeply divided societies can bring out both the noblest human ideals and the darkest behaviours. In Harare, long, dignified queues of voters snake into the gathering gloom of a city slum alongside the menacing glare of youth militia linked to the ruling party. In rural Sierra Leone, the public appearance of a masked dancer from a secret (male) society dissuades women from venturing out to cast a ballot. Elsewhere, ghost voters are mysteriously spirited onto voter rolls. And ballots are stuffed in situ or in transit from the polling station to a central counting centre. The opportunities for procedural shenanigans are legion: from not making public the voter roll or gerrymandering electoral boundaries to manipulating the census or setting down draconian laws that restrict media coverage, political campaigning, or civic and voter education by civil society organizations. And outright violence is always an option when other approaches have not succeeded.

A closer look at Zimbabwe – although not one of the case studies in this collection – underlines why elections need to be set against the wider canvas of struggles for democracy and pluralism in closed, authoritarian, or conflict-prone societies. It provides a cautionary tale for those who see in the emergence of multiparty elections the beginnings of a transition to democracy or the transformation of liberation movements into democratic political parties. While reality is often Janus-faced, one feature of Zimbabwe's last decade is that as elections have become more closely contested they have been especially vulnerable to irregularities and intensified, politically manipulated violence.[8]

Electoral manipulation in Zimbabwe rests on a deep foundation. Through a close reading of elections in Zimbabwe's first two decades, Norma Kriger shows that the onset of real political competition began with the vote against a new constitution proposed by the ruling ZANU-PF in the 2000 referendum.[9] This event galvanized the political opposition and raised the potential for regime change through democratic elections in 2002 and 2005. The presidential election of 2008 intensified longstanding practices of intimidation, violence, internal displacement, and other human rights abuses used by the ruling party to win elections and maintain its grip on power. As Kriger underlines, despite their different contexts, the four general elections between 1980 and 2000 reveal the same ZANU-PF discourse and coercive tactics. The ruling party repeatedly created the conditions for electoral violence by casting opponents as enemies of the nation or puppets of the whites and imperial forces.

The 2008 presidential election was played out using many of the tools and strategies of the past. No candidate received an absolute majority in the 29 March first round. Considerable pre-election violence had the desired effect of prompting Morgan Tsvangirai, the principal opposition presidential candidate, to withdraw from the second round runoff. Facing no opposition, incumbent Robert Mugabe could claim a pyrrhic victory with 85 per cent of the vote from a much-reduced electorate.

As Bratton and Masunungure explain, the recourse to violence in 2008 was "new only in its desperation."[10] The violence was efficiently carried out because the security chiefs were put in charge of logistics and operations for the 2008 runoff. As in the 2002 election, the violence was substantially outsourced to youth militia, called Green Bombers, who were trained by the army in rural camps and instructed to burn houses, invade farms, and incite violence. These youth militia also conducted political education campaigns or *pungwes*, a liberation war tactic, to intimidate and coerce regime opponents. The sum of these tactics was a strategy of electoral cleansing to kill, harass, and displace MDC officials and their supporters and to create "no go" zones, particularly in swing vote districts where ZANU-PF had become increasingly vulnerable.

What is especially bleak about the case of Zimbabwe is the resilience of anti-democratic forces, notwithstanding the important gain of more closely contested elections. Bratton and Masunungure dub this style of politics "electoral authoritarianism." Over time, the ruling ZANU-PF has sustained an anti-democratic identity marked by an ideological belief in the right to rule; control of the key state organs; reliance on corruption as a patronage tool; strong military influence on policy; and recourse to violence and intimidation, often "outsourced" to militia.

Although an African outlier in the low quality of its democratic institutions, Zimbabwe must be considered here because personal rule remains a "lurking danger that lies perennially in wait for nearly all African regimes."[11] Zimbabwe's recent history shows that elections can be a poor reflection of the overall quality of a country's democracy. The regularity of elections can be deceptive. On the other hand, the opposition in Zimbabwe has doggedly organized around electoral politics and, notwithstanding intimidation and procedural shenanigans by the ruling party, has made electoral gains leading to a power sharing arrangement. That is no small victory. The tension between elections read as a potential mode of transition and elections as a destabilizing force in conflict-prone societies will reappear in several of the country cases considered in this collection.

IMPLICATIONS FOR RESEARCH

Situated at the meeting place of scholarship, policy, and practice, this collection fills an important gap in the literature. Good practice "grey literature" is slowly emerging.[12] There is also a small case-study literature examining elections and conflict.[13] There appears to be few book-length efforts that brings these two approaches together. De Zeeuw and Kumar's collection looks at three facets of democracy promotion: human rights, the media, and post-conflict elections and political party development.[14] These authors have a broadly positive view of international assistance in the conduct of elections, noting that in all the post-conflict countries studied (Guatemala, Cambodia, Mozambique) successive elections have been held without a return to war.

Mansfield and Snyder challenge the liberal peace theory that democracies do not go to war against each other.[15] That may be true for the relatively small group of well-established democracies. Using statistical evidence over two centuries they show that in a "transitional phase of democracy, countries become more aggressive and war-prone, not less."[16] The big policy message is that support to enlarge the zone of stable democracies is worthwhile, but practitioners must realize that "in the short run, much work remains to be done to minimize the dangers of turbulent transition."[17] Paul Collier, in *Wars, Guns and Votes*, takes a statistical look at the linkages among elections, conflict, and economic performance. His findings are at odds with the received wisdom about elections as Collier finds that democracy increases political violence in low-income countries. Elections can become part of the conflict trap in many "bottom billion" societies. Electoral competition is not producing accountable governance and the risk of reversion to conflict in the year after an election "explodes upwards. The net effect of the election is to make the society more dangerous."[18] All this happens because integrity and competence are not rewarded; "crooks will replace the honest as candidates."[19] In these circumstances, elections do not produce accountable governments.[20]

By contrast, Staffan Lindberg examines the proposition that successive elections can provide a new mode for democratic transition.[21] Democratization is a gradual process through which transitional societies come to recognize that the costs of continued oppression outweigh the costs of toleration. Elections can be manipulated but only at the cost of decreased legitimacy. The decline in legitimacy can function to decrease the costs of toleration. Seen this way, successive multiparty elections can "trick, lure, and cajole" leaders to act in more democratic ways. In Ghana's transition from military rule through a series of transitional regimes to a more liberal democracy since 2004, elections have been key milestones of democratization. Elsewhere in Africa, Sierra Leone and – in a more qualified sense – Mozambique represent positive scenarios for the constructive role of multiparty elections in post-conflict societies.

Although overriding trends may not be easily discernible, Lindberg asks whether more elections are always good for democratization or if flawed elections only serve to institutionalize facade regimes. He "strongly believe[s] that the struggle over regime change and stability is going to be played out to a significant degree through electoral processes for the foreseeable future."[22] An important consideration for practitioners and policy-makers is the emphasis placed by both Lindberg and Collier on how the incentives and disincentives for power holders and elites impact the prospects for democratic transition.

Taken together the essays in this collection address a "central dilemma facing peacebuilders," namely, how to avoid the "pathologies of liberalization" while helping put conflict-prone societies on a long-term path toward stable, market democracies.[23] It should be underscored that there is no prior assumption that elections are ipso facto a pathology of liberalization. The influence of external actors, even in conditions of combat and militarized occupation, is quite limited. As President Karzai's high stakes manoeuvring for the date of the 2010 election illustrates, the timing of an election is an intrinsically domestic political act as incumbents and opposition jockey for position.

Instead, much more attention needs to be given by international actors to the strategic role of an election in a conflict situation or a complex war-to-peace transition, including the need to help demilitarize politics as far as possible.[24]

The country studies and essays on dispute resolution in this collection also shed some light on whether electoral support and democracy promotion works, and how it can be improved. As George Perlin underlines, "the need for better information about the effectiveness of assistance has become a major concern. At issue is how program activities affect the complex and system-wide processes of long-term change that are required to produce enduring political reform."[25] There is, in short, a pressing need for evaluative research that can contribute to improved democracy promotion strategies. A key requirement is for research that deepens understanding of how democratic regimes consolidate or decay, and how democratic processes may be affected by external intervention. These building blocks can in turn help build a more convincing theory of change, one that sets out a credible framework for assessment, an account of the dynamics of democratic development, and the relationships among the many moving parts: elections, legislatures, political parties, rule of law, civil society, and human rights.[26]

IMPLICATIONS FOR POLICY AND PRACTICE

There is growing demand for international support of elections in fragile states and conflict-affected societies.[27] This interest may be because elections are a formal milestone of a peace agreement, as in Sudan, or because elections are seen as one more marker of progress toward a democratic transition, as in Sierra Leone. A successful election may be a benchmark for a peacekeeping exit plan or a recalibration of the aid relationship from stabilization to long-term development.

Providing timely and effective electoral assistance is a complex matter, requiring good technical knowledge, sound coordination, and detailed understanding of the political environment. On the face of it, election support in conflict situations has some distinct challenges, such as:

HIGH RISK: Planning in conditions of uncertainty regarding timing, changing levels of security, and preparedness; speed and nimbleness is of the essence.

COMPLEX POLITICS: Technical success may be overshadowed by political manipulation, discord, or violence; security issues loom large.
IDENTIFYING NICHE: Determining value added requires whole-of-aid agency, whole-of-government coordination, and harmonization with other donors.

Getting elections in conflict situations right is important not only because they are central to the democratic idea but also because elections are the stuff of high politics and drama, engage considerable financial and human resources, and can affect economic performance, impact stability, and undermine social cohesion – even at the cost of human life. The financial costs alone can be staggering, particularly in countries with vast geographies, daunting climates, and very limited infrastructure. About US$450 million was required to administer elections in the DRC in 2006, about US$500 million in Afghanistan in 2009 and 2010, and about US$315 million[28] in the Sudan in 2010. Even a small state like Burundi required US$43 million for its most recent election. The lion's share of these costs is borne by international aid donors, often through pooled funding arrangements managed by the United Nations Development Programme.

Despite the high costs and often-complex technical demands, there is relatively little practical guidance on how to provide effective election support in conflict-prone societies. Policy makers and planners could gain from a closer understanding of the security challenges and mitigating actions that can be taken to reduce the likelihood of election processes and outcomes perceived as illegitimate, that undermine stability, or set back transitions to democracy. An enhanced understanding of the potential for conflict in the electoral environment and strategies to defuse that conflict should in turn help improve donor election-support activities. These may include pre-election conflict mapping, conflict prevention training and activities with communities, security providers, election management bodies, and political parties, civic and voter education, and traditional and alternative dispute-resolution mechanisms.

Anticipating and mitigating conflict is the responsibility of many stakeholders, from the security, judicial, and electoral institutions of national governments to civil society monitors, international peacekeepers, election observer missions, and development aid donors.

Unfortunately, as events in Iran and Kenya underline, domestic security institutions may be ill prepared or not impartial and may fuel further conflict by reacting violently against mass protest at election results. The Commission of Inquiry into Post-Election Violence (CIPEV) in Kenya, for example, found that "state security agencies ... failed institutionally to anticipate, prepare for, and contain the violence." The report goes on to note that "the effectiveness of the Kenya Police Service ... was also negatively affected by the lack clear of policing operational procedures and by political expediency's adverse impact on their policing priorities." Donors and host governments thus have a considerable stake in ensuring that candidates, voters, vulnerable groups, and election materials are protected and that the overall integrity of an election is affirmed in an environment in which citizens can choose their leaders without fear or favour.

At the level of practice, *Elections in Dangerous Places* should help encourage a more holistic view of election-related conflict and a more realistic understanding of what can and cannot be achieved in conflict mitigation. What clearly emerges is that scholars, policy makers, and practitioners have until recently faced considerable uncertainty on how best to manage electoral violence in countries at risk of instability. However, this also presents a tremendous opportunity to strengthen international coordination and good practice in electoral conflict mitigation.

Using the "electoral cycle approach"[29] as an organizing framework, the book focuses on the causes, signposts, and consequences of electoral discord and violence, and on the prevention or mitigation of conflict before, during, and after elections. A key purpose is to link the analysis of root causes and consideration of specific country cases to good practice in mitigating and managing election-related conflict. More understanding of the contributory or causal links between elections and conflict is the basis for organizing new responses for bilateral aid agencies, such as USAID, DFID, or CIDA, and multilateral organizations, such as the United Nations or the African Union.

The book tries to bring the worlds of scholarship, policy, and practice into closer dialogue. A distinctive feature is to bring in the views of a variety of professionals working on the front lines of democracy and election support. Several bring an insider's view of the dynamics affecting the role of the international community before, during, and after elections in dangerous places. Legal expert Johann Kriegler has played a pivotal role in addressing electoral disputes in Kenya. Thomas Axworthy, now at the Walter & Duncan Gordon Foundation, was appointed by the Canadian Government to chair a panel looking at the potential creation of a Canadian democracy support organization. Francesc Vendrell is a former senior UN official and EU special representative to Afghanistan. Some contributors, such as Marc Lemieux (Iraq), Susanne Mueller and Stephen Brown (Kenya), and Khalid Medani (Sudan), have lived in the countries they write about. Three other contributors, Vincent Tohbi, Lisa Kammerud, and Sara Staino, add the perspectives of international or regional democracy support organizations, such as the Electoral Institute for the Sustainability of Democracy in Africa, the International Foundation for Electoral Systems, and the International Institute for Democracy and Electoral Assistance. Finally, Ben Reilly, Chris Hennemeyer, and Canadians Eugenia Zorbas and Gerald Schmitz have all been on the front lines of democracy promotion as thinkers, practitioners or policy makers.

The collection will thus appeal to a wide range of interests. Scholars of democratization and political development will find interesting case study and comparative material. Elections and democracy promotion professionals in civil society and in aid agencies and multilateral organizations will find the discussions of good practices and tools, such as mediation or electoral dispute mechanisms, of interest. Students of politics and international development will be immersed in the scholarly thinking and practical responses to the real world challenges of democratic development in fragile states. Inevitably, a diverse set of backgrounds and skills also means some variation in style, which ranges from scholarship, to personal observation, to institutional experience, and journalism. The editor has judged it important not to impose a uniform style but rather to encourage the authors to speak in their own voice.

The collection is organized into four sections framed by an introduction and short conclusion. In part 1, Ben Reilly provides a framework for thinking about elections in conflict-prone societies. He is interested in understanding how variations in five parameters – timing, scope, voting system, national versus sub-national voting, and the role of parties and civil society – affect "the shape of post electoral politics."

The contributions in part 2 examine some of complex contexts for elections in conflict prone situations. These include combat and armed occupation (Iraq), insurgency and weak, corrupt governance (Afghanistan), and elections as milestones in UN-backed peace agreements (DRC and Sudan). Given the histories of these states under autocratic, military, or warlord rule, the prospects for democratically organized elections face almost insuperable hurdles. How these challenges, including the risk of insecurity and violence, have been met is at the heart of the essays on Afghanistan, Iraq, Sudan, and the DRC.

In Afghanistan, a flawed, poorly managed, wartime presidential election in 2009 has shown that a democracy cannot grow roots without addressing other social and political problems, particularly the rule of law. In one view, elections in failed states such as Afghanistan are a waste of time because the pre-conditions for free and fair competition are simply not present. These must include basic security, an enabling constitution and election laws, functioning civil liberties, an independent election management body with the logistical ability to run an election, a functioning civil society, and timely electoral dispute resolution.

The actions of two election bodies, the Independent Election Commission (IEC) and the Electoral Complaints Commission (ECC) underscored the tension between local ownership and international supervision of the Afghan election. The IEC was appointed by the incumbent, President Karzai. The ECC was composed of three international representatives nominated by the UN and two Afghans with credentials for impartiality. As Francesc Vendrell, a former EU special representative to Afghanistan, explains, the impact of the ECC investigation of fraud allegations was to cast aside over one million ballot papers, effectively overturning the IEC's earlier announcement of a Karzai victory. While local ownership of the elections is endorsed by donors as good international engagement in fragile states, this value should never be achieved at the expense of international standards. There is now widespread doubt about the independence of the IEC and suspicion about the subsequent "indigenization" of the ECC with a reduced number of UN-backed representatives in the five-person body appointed by the president. In the absence of reforms, it is not clear how the IEC's legitimacy can be restored. Vendrell is particularly trenchant in his critique of the NATO allies. The US, EU, and UN, in successive elections, repeatedly missed opportunities to insist on electoral reform as a condition of their support for elections in

Afghanistan. Western governments having in practice "given up on the need for credible elections," the upshot has been a fundamental loss of trust among citizens disenfranchised by allegations of fraud, and a crisis of legitimacy for the UN.

The chapter by Marc Lemieux on Iraq represents the sharp end of the spectrum of election environments addressed in this collection. Lemieux poses three questions: Have elections meeting international standards been possible during a militarized occupation? Have elections overcome or deepened sectarian divisions? Has electoral design helped to mitigate conflict? Paradoxically, Lemieux's analysis of local, regional (Kurdish), and national elections held since the 2003 US invasion leads to the most positive interpretation among the country cases considered of the beneficial role of elections in peacebuilding and nation building. He challenges the position of some critics that Iraq's democracy remains "unconsolidated, violence-plagued, foreign-directed, and temporary." Elections in Iraq have been possible because most Iraqis wanted them and have accepted their results as legitimate, as supported by UN endorsements and by the latest Supreme Court decision confirming the 2010 results. Lemieux finds that the Iraqi experience with democracy during five years of public policy debate has, although slowly and amid moments of violence, channelled tensions into the formation of coalitions while mitigating concerns about the long-term viability of the state, a governing system that will continue to mature after the withdrawal of American combat troops. In sum, democratic practices have laid the foundations for a return to coexistence among Iraq's communities and political parties. Leaders are required to be more pragmatic and flexible about party platforms and policies to attract larger pools of voters.

In January 2011, the people of the southern provinces of Sudan voted overwhelmingly to declare independence from the North. The referendum is the culmination of an armistice in the longest running civil conflict in Africa. The impending emergence of two new nation-states, argues Khalid Medani, has been greatly influenced by two developments: the failure of democratization in the country and structural flaws associated with the nature and implementation of the peace agreement brokered by the international community in 2005. The overriding question Medani addresses is whether, having failed to build unity out of diversity, Sudan will plunge into conflict or even a new round of civil war. Drawing on the literature on secession and conflict resolution, Medani focuses on the probability of renewed conflict following the impending partition of Africa's largest country. He outlines a framework for identifying the potential for future conflict and offers an analysis of potential scenarios in the aftermath of the referendum.

The 2006 elections in the DRC were meant to signal the country's transition from war to peace, leaving behind a decade of violent conflict and the Mobutu legacy of "kleptocracy," combining corruption, authoritarianism, and state decay. Congolese citizens underscored this sense of history by participating en masse in presidential as well as national and provincial legislative elections: voter turnout was estimated at between 77 to 81 percent. Ultimately, the incumbent, President Joseph Kabila, won the presidential runoff and the elections were declared a success by Congolese authorities and the international community, which had become heavily invested both financially and diplomatically in the exercise. Indeed, the elections were organized with significant international financial and logistical support, including the presence of the largest and most expensive United Nations peacekeeping mission in the world. As Eugenia Zorbas and Vincent Tohbi show, the international community was active in coordinated, on-the-ground mediation efforts led by ambassadors in Kinshasa operating as the Comité international d'accompagnement de la transition and by African elder statesmen operating as a *comité des sages*. This international, often daily, coordination helped keep the electoral process on track even as tensions at the national level mounted. No such international attention was mobilized around the management of equally critical local conflicts, however, such as the latent secessionist sentiments in Katanga Province and unresolved land and citizenship questions in the Kivus. Non-governmental organizations such as the Electoral Institute for the Sustainability of Democracy in Africa (EISA), spotting these and other potential impediments to the electoral process, intervened by training and deploying Congolese conflict management panels to various areas in the country. Zorbas and Tohbi conclude that mounting the 2006 elections was in itself a significant achievement, which holds some lessons applicable to other conflict settings. However, this achievement was marred by instances of violent repression of political opponents (both during and after the polls) and by insufficient attention to local conflicts that have since resurged. Furthermore, since 2006, the now-elected government has failed to break from the authoritarianism, impunity, and state failure that characterized the Mobutu regime. This underscores perhaps the most important lesson of the 2006 electoral exercise in the DRC: the importance of not conflating elections with democracy, or with good governance.

By contrast, the case of Kenya is something of an outlier. Long viewed as a relatively stable African polity, both Susanne Mueller and Stephen Brown underscore that while violence has been associated with several Kenyan elections since the onset of multiparty politics in the early 1990s, the scope, severity, and links between semi-organized crime and politicians caught the international community off guard and poorly prepared. The spectre of electoral violence in Kenya has sent a chill throughout the democracy support community. It demonstrates that the preconditions for electoral conflict are present in many societies and that aid agencies and election management bodies should vigorously invest in conflict prevention activities.

The 2007 Kenyan election highlights some of the root causes of election-related violence, such as the diffusion of violence and growth of criminal gangs, a deliberate weakening of democratic institutions, the personalization of power, and an elite political culture of winner-takes-all and zero-sum competition. In one view, the international community did not sufficiently anticipate the likelihood of violence or adequately plan to mitigate conflict. Contrary to popular belief, Kenyan elections have been marked by varying degrees of ethnic voting and violence since the onset of multiparty politics in 1991. Stephen Brown asserts that there has been "no large-scale conflict in Kenya that has not been associated with electoral violence." He also chides the donor community for a collective amnesia, only partial comprehension of the lessons from previous elections, and a failure to anticipate fully the potential scale or severity of the ensuing violence. The continued uncritical support of donors for an increasingly partisan and ineffective election commission proved to be a grave mistake.

Notwithstanding a peaceful 2010 constitutional referendum, the prognosis drawn by Mueller and Brown for future elections in Kenya is quite negative. Despite a mediated interim government (Grand Coalition) and elite agreements for independent investigation of the violence and processes to manage grievances (Constitutional Review Committee; Truth, Justice and Reconciliation Commission; National Cohesion Commission; Electoral Dispute Court), donors should plan for worst-case scenarios and help support a societal coalition against violence. Institution building or technical fixes alone cannot alter the climate of zero-sum competition and illegal election strategies in the absence of changed incentive structures among Kenyan political elites.

Finally, Christian Hennemeyer, a long-time election monitor, provides an overview of democratic progress and backsliding in Africa, a vast crucible in which histories of ossified, autocratic rule or illegal regime change increasingly confront the demand for pluralism, accountability, and political participation. On balance, he discerns much that is positive, if not yet conclusively durable, in the relative demise of the "strong man" and the military coup as a mode of succession, and in the movement toward democracy in Africa.

The essays in part 3 focus on thematic issues and contributions from election professionals. Two papers focus exclusively on electoral dispute resolution (EDR): Sara Staino examines different forms of EDR drawing on the *International IDEA Handbook of Electoral Justice*; by combining the electoral cycle with the conflict cycle of analysis, prevention, mitigation, and resolution, Lisa Kammerud describes a toolbox of practical interventions to address conflict in a variety of volatile elections. Johann Kriegler shares his practical wisdom in handling election disputes. Recognizing that elections are "political enterprises," that justice delayed is justice denied, and that EDR must be "firmly rooted" in specific contexts, Kriegler emphasizes the importance of timeliness and flexibility to resolve the dispute and craft an appropriate remedy in a dynamic and rapidly changing context. Disputes must be dealt with "as and when they arise" because an early EDR intervention can have important moderating effects on later events through its educative, deterrent, or exemplary functions. In Kriegler's view, the Kenyan crisis of December 2007 "was in large measure ascribable to the absence of an effective EDR mechanism."

Finally, in part 4, essays by Canadians Thomas Axworthy and Gerald Schmitz help draw a link between the technical challenges of election support and democracy promotion as a strand in Canadian foreign policy and international cooperation, a timely comparison that will interest Canadian policy makers in view of the Harper government's announced (but not realized) intention to establish a democracy promotion entity with an international remit. Schmitz applies critical issues surrounding Canadian support for democracy building to questions about the Afghanistan conflict, which has dominated Canadian foreign policy priorities since 2001. The failure of that country's recent, externally subsidized elections to advance either stabilization or democratization goals – indeed quite the contrary has occurred – presents acute dilemmas for policy and practice.

As Schmitz suggests, this is a case where, rhetoric aside, a pre- to post-electoral agenda capable of producing more sustainable democratic outcomes has never been adequately, or resolutely, articulated, much less implemented. We should not then be surprised when the hopes of the Demos remain largely unfulfilled in the wake of internationally supported electoral episodes – adding to the questions for which satisfactory answers are lacking.

This is neither a counsel of despair nor an argument to wait for the emergence of some ideal theoretical model of electoral transition to stable liberal democracy. There may be few iron laws or predictable paths on the road to democratization. The Middle East and North Africa were not on the radar screen as a locus of imminent change. Beyond recognition that a revolution in expectations may lead to early disillusionment and backsliding, we are all riding the tiger of unpredictable change. Whatever the differences among the cases and the critical stances adopted by the authors in this volume, the analysis cumulatively points to a series of observations elaborated in the conclusion as a basis for further research and theorization. At a time when the democratic spirit is simultaneously under siege, on trial, and breaking out in unlikely places, a lot of assumptions can be challenged. It is that same spirit which runs through the contributions that follow. The road to electoral democracy is usually long, often rocky, and always unfinished. But it *is* a road worth taking.

PART ONE

Elections in Conflict Situations
An Overview

1

Understanding Elections in Conflict Situations

BENJAMIN REILLY

Elections have three main functions in a democracy. First, they are means of choosing the people's representatives to a legislature, congress, or other representative forum, or to a single office such as the presidency. Second, elections are not just a means of choosing representatives but also of choosing governments. Indeed, in practice, elections are primarily a contest between competing political parties to see who will control the government. Finally, elections are a means of conferring legitimacy on the political system. Especially since the end of the Cold War and the third wave of democracy around the world, elections have become an essential element in constituting a legitimate government. Today, very few states in the world do not conduct elections, although the competitiveness and quality of these vary enormously.

In conflict-prone societies, elections serve all these purposes, but also some others. In particular, elections held in the midst of violent conflict are one of the instruments used not only to promote democracy but also to consolidate a fragile peace. By enshrining a new political order focused on rule-based competition for office, elections can also play a key role in transforming the expression of societal conflicts so that they take place within the boundaries of a democratic political system rather than through armed violence. In this way, elections are a key step on the road from war to peace. In cases of outright state failure, internationally supervised elections also provide a clear signal that legitimate domestic authority has been returned – and hence that the role of the international community may be coming to an end. For all of these reasons, elections have become central to the process of state reform and rebuilding following a period of violent conflict in the contemporary world.

In practice, however, there has been considerable variation in the relative success of elections in meeting these goals. One problem is that the goals themselves are often unrealistic. Elections in zones of conflict tend to be saddled with multiple and sometimes incompatible objectives, being expected simultaneously to bring an end to armed violence and usher in a new era of democratic peace, but also to enable a sustainable expression of societal cleavages via a competitive but non-violent political process. Similarly, there is a tension between the massive international support lavished upon key post-conflict elections by the United Nations and other international actors, which often builds up the capacity of election administrations to unsustainable levels, and the reality that a successful election process has become part of an "exit strategy" for the international community from worst-case situations.

Given these basic dilemmas, what are the key elements of successful post-conflict elections? In terms of the electoral process itself, at least five main areas of variation have a crucial influence on the shape of post-conflict electoral politics in most countries:

FIRST, there is the question of election timing: should elections be held immediately after a conflict to take advantage of a peace deal and quickly introduce the new democratic order? Or is it better to wait for a year or two to allow the political routines and issues or peacetime politics to come to prominence? This area has a marked gap between "theory" and actual practice.

SECOND is the matter of the scheduling of national versus sub-national elections. Is it better to hold national elections before local ones, as some scholars have argued? Or should local-level elections be held in advance of national ones, in the hope of gradually inculcating voters in the rights and responsibilities of representative democracy? As with the question of election timing, there is a range of opinions on this issue.

THIRD, there is the question of the electoral system, which determines how votes cast at the elections are translated into seats in a representative body. The choice of electoral system is seen by political scientists as a particularly crucial institutional choice because it influences not just who gets represented and who does not but also the behavioural incentives facing campaigning politicians, the kind of appeals they make to voters, the nature of the emerging political party system, and many other aspects of post-conflict politics.

FOURTH, there is the administration of the elections themselves: Who runs the elections? How are voters enrolled? How are electoral boundaries demarcated? How are electoral disputes dealt with? All of these decisions have a profound impact upon the development of post-conflict politics, as we are seeing in Afghanistan with internal disputes within the UN (which reflect a broader division within the international community) about the way accusations of electoral fraud should be investigated and adjudicated.

FIFTH, there is the often underestimated issue of the effect of post-conflict elections on the development of civil society and political parties. In post-conflict situations, many civil society organizations are weak or non-existent. Politics is often personalized around identity ties to ethnicity, region, tribe, or language group. This makes the interaction between civil society, political parties, and the electoral process highly fraught, as demonstrated in cases such as Kenya, where flawed elections became the catalyst for large-scale ethnic violence.

More generally, there is the overarching issue of under what circumstances elections can help to build a new democratic order, and under what circumstances they can undermine democracy and pave the way for a return to conflict. As one survey of post-conflict elections notes, the high expectations often placed upon post-conflict elections tend to be accompanied by a weakness in the preconditions for their success: "Most war-torn societies lack the political climate, social and economic stability, institutional infrastructure, and even political will to mount successful elections."[1] Despite progress in recent years, the international community remains insufficiently cognizant of the dangers of conflict-zone elections, particularly in countries that have recently emerged from civil war, where the logic of electoral competition typically leads to mobilization of the electorate by appeals to social cleavages and ethnic identities.

In order to develop and improve the accuracy, efficiency, and legitimacy of such elections, and in the hope of building sustainable democratic practices in transitional states, the international community has become involved in a wide range of activities in the electoral field

Table 1
Areas of International Electoral Assistance

Area	Description
Support for first-time elections	A central element of most international electoral assistance programs, support for free and fair elections can take many forms. Typically assistance is focused on election planning, monitoring, and budgeting. An increasing focus is on the use of low-cost, sustainable practices that will not require ongoing international assistance.
Assistance for constitutional and legal reforms	Often involves issues of political institutions and institutional reform (design and reform of electoral systems, legislative structures, promoting links of accountability between the government and the governed, and so on).
Assistance to electoral management bodies	Can be focused on a range of areas, including voter registration, boundary delimitation, computerization, dispute resolution, and so on. A recent focus has been on the need to build independent and permanent electoral management bodies.
Voter registration	The quality and usability of the voter register is a perennial concern in post-conflict elections. Assistance with voter registration is often focused on the need for a permanent and continuous electoral register that is constantly updated to reflect population movements, new voters, births and deaths, and so on.
Civic and voter education programs	Activities whose main goal is to expand democratic participation, particularly for women, the poor, indigenous groups, and other under-represented segments of society. Includes awareness-raising activities to highlight the rights and responsibilities of citizens inherent in a democratic society.
International monitoring and observation	Includes election observation, monitoring, and supervision. After placing huge resources on electoral observation for most of the 1990s, there is now more focus on the need to professionalize the process of international electoral observation and to place more emphasis on building domestic capacity in this area.
Strengthening of political parties	Activities that focus on strengthening a country's emerging party system, building parties' internal capacity, and training parties to function effectively in the legislature. An emerging area in electoral assistance likely to increase in importance in future.

over the past decade. These include technical assistance for constitutional and legal reforms; advice on electoral systems, legislative structure and other political choices; assistance for the establishment and functioning of electoral management bodies; support for voter registration and education initiatives; financial, technical, and strategic advice to political parties; support for civil society groups; provision of international monitors and observer groups; and so on. Table 1 sets out the major sub-areas within the field of electoral assistance in which support is usually focused.

EXPERIENCES AND LESSONS LEARNED

The intense international involvement in many post-conflict elections over the past decade is testament to the importance placed on the electoral process by the UN and other international organizations. However, the new challenge is to build sustainable procedures that function effectively without external assistance. In this area, progress has been slow. There is still a tendency to pay considerably more attention to a nation's first election than subsequent ones, and many countries have been left with a legacy of expensive procedures and equipment after an internationally supported transitional election that they cannot hope to replicate. Similarly, subsequent elections beyond the first often fail to attract the intense international involvement that accompanies first-time elections in the shape of observer missions, monitoring, and support.

There has also been a significant change in the way the oft-heard demand for "free and fair" elections are treated by observers, the media, and the international community. In general, a "free" election is one in which contestation for office is open and competitive, and free from electoral violence, while "fair" usually refers to features such as a level playing field, equal rights to participation, and acceptance of outcomes by all parties. In practice, however, there is great variation in the meaning attached to this term, and considerable variation in what a "free and fair" election constitutes, although some attempts have been made to define it.[2] In recent externally driven attempts at democratization by force, such as Iraq and Afghanistan, the international community has steadily lowered the bar for what is considered an "acceptable" or "credible" outcome, to the point that genuinely free and fair elections, once the litmus test of successful democratization, are today seldom mentioned, let alone advanced as threshold criteria for success. This represents a profound rhetorical and substantive shift from just a few years earlier.

Nonetheless, the electoral process in high-profile cases of external intervention such as these does appear to follow a kind of standard operating procedure. Once a minimum level of peace has been obtained (which does not necessarily mean a full ceasefire agreement), and a basic level of infrastructure is in place, the next step is usually to hold national elections – often within a year or two of the start of the mission – followed by a rapid hand-over to the newly elected authorities and an even more rapid departure of international troops and personnel. One recurrent criticism of this approach to elections in post-conflict scenarios is that, if held too early, they can undermine the nascent democratic order. In fact, this has been a fundamental problem of many UN-supervised elections: they have been held too soon and too quickly after peace has been restored.

ELECTION TIMING AND SEQUENCING

International (and sometimes domestic) pressure on the post-conflict election timetable and frequently leads to elections being held as early as possible in the life of a peacekeeping mission in order to create some kind of legitimate authority. In Iraq, for instance, there was strong political pressure to hold first-time elections after the US-led invasion for a range of reasons, both substantive (the need for a constituent assembly to draft a new constitution) and symbolic (to demonstrate the validity of the prevailing US policy of transforming Iraq into a bastion of democracy in the Middle East). This led to elections being held in early 2005 in the absence of popular security and in the face of a boycott from one of the country's main ethnic groups, the Sunni, which arguably hindered rather than helped the longer-term process of democratization.

Such "premature elections" can also create multiple ongoing problems for the development of peacetime politics in deeply divided societies even years after the war has ended – as demonstrated by the regular re-election of hard-line nationalist leaders in post-conflict Bosnia at successive elections since 1996, where nationalist parties and elites have not only continued to be elected by the voters but have used the democratic political process to continue to press their sectarian aims. In most cases, the early application of elections immediately following a conflict almost guarantees a de facto contest between the former warring armies masquerading as political parties. By contrast, an extended process of consultation and local-level peace building, in which some of the real interests and concerns that provoked the conflict are addressed in a step-by-step fashion before national elections are held, may offer better prospects for a peaceful transition in post-conflict societies.

A related issue is the coordination of national and sub-national elections. Some scholars argue that, in a new democracy, holding national elections before regional elections generates incentives for the creation of national, rather than regional, political parties – and hence that the ideal process of election timing is to start at the national level and work one's way down.[3] Others believe that simultaneous national and local elections "can facilitate the mutual dependence of regional and national leaders. The more posts that are filled at the regional and local level ... the greater the incentive for regional politicians to coordinate their election activities by developing an integrated party system."[4] This was the approach used at Indonesia's transitional 1999 elections, with identical party-based ballots being presented to voters at simultaneous elections for national, provincial, and local assemblies, which greatly strengthened the nascent party system. While this has real advantages in terms of party building, there are also strong arguments for the opposite sequence – that is, starting with municipal elections and working up. This approach is particularly suited to "state building" elections, which can help develop party politics from the ground up.

There is some evidence of genuine learning over time by the UN and other international actors on most of these issues. There is more recognition now of the need for sustained international involvement for several years after a conflict rather than the rushed in-and-out approach of former years. Aid donors have increasingly realized that second and third elections in transitional states can be as important as the first, while scholars have shown that repeated elections seem to boost democratic rights and processes, particularly in Africa.[5]

Moreover, the experience of major UN assistance operations such as Kosovo, East Timor, and Afghanistan suggests that pressure to hold "instant" national elections was resisted to some degree. Instead, a two-year period of political development was used to prepare the ground for elections as part of the much longer process of democratization. In both Kosovo and East Timor, for instance, relatively peaceful post-conflict elections were held in 2001, some two years after the peak of the conflict. In Afghanistan, presidential elections were held in 2004 and parliamentary elections in 2005, several years after the 2002 Loya Jirga that chose the country's transitional administration. Although questions remain as to whether even two years is time enough to develop the routines of peacetime politics, there is now little doubt about the benefits of this more gradual approach as opposed to the instant election model of earlier years.

THE CHOICE OF ELECTORAL SYSTEMS

Legal and constitutional issues, particularly the choice of electoral system, have long been recognized as one of the most important institutional choices for any political system. These choices can also influence other aspects of the political system, such as the development of the party system, linkages between citizens and their leaders, political accountability, representation, and responsiveness. Because of such impacts, constitutional and electoral system choices have many long-term consequences for the process of democratic governance and the choice of electoral system is one of the most important political decisions for any country.

Electoral systems are the rules and procedures via which votes cast in an election are translated into seats won in the parliament or some other office (e.g., a presidency). An electoral system is designed to do three main jobs. First, it translates the votes cast into seats or offices won. Second, electoral systems act as the conduit through which the people can hold their elected representatives accountable. Third, different electoral systems give incentives for those competing for power to couch their appeals to the electorate in distinct ways. In divided societies, for example, where language, religion, race, or other forms of ethnicity represent a fundamental political cleavage, particular electoral systems can reward candidates and parties who act in a cooperative, accommodating manner toward rival groups, or they can punish these candidates and instead reward those who appeal only to their own group.

Electoral systems are often categorized according to how they operate in terms of translating votes cast by electors into seats won by parties. A typical three-way structure divides such systems into plurality-majority, semi-proportional, and proportional representation systems. Plurality-majority systems typically give more emphasis to local representation, via the use of small, single-member electoral districts, than to proportionality. Among such systems are plurality (first-past-the-post), runoff, block, and alternative vote systems. By contrast, proportional representation (PR) systems – which typically use larger multi-member districts and deliver more proportional outcomes – include "open" and "closed" versions of party list PR, as well as "mixed-member" and "single transferable vote" systems. Semi-proportional systems offer yet other approaches, as well as various mixtures of plurality and proportional models – such as the "mixed" models by which part of the parliament is elected via PR and part via local districts, a common choice in many new democracies in recent years.[6]

One of the great political science debates of the past decade has concerned which electoral systems are most appropriate for promoting peaceful politics in divided societies. Two schools of thought predominate. The scholarly orthodoxy has long argued that some form of PR is all but essential if democracy is to survive the travails of deep-rooted divisions. The tendency of PR to produce multiparty systems and hence multiparty parliaments, in which all significant segments of the population can be represented, is especially important in post-conflict elections, where consensual or "consociational" solutions are often favoured. In contrast to this orthodoxy, an alternative approach argues for electoral systems that work to break down the political salience of social divisions rather than foster their representation. Drawing on theories of bargaining and cooperation, such "centripetal" approaches emphasize the need for cross-ethnic incentives and multi-ethnic parties. One way to achieve this is to use distribution systems such as those employed for presidential elections in Indonesia, Nigeria, and Kenya, which require winning candidates to gain a broad spread of votes from across the country in order to claim victory. Another is to use electoral models such as the alternative vote (as in Fiji) or the single transferable vote (as in Northern Ireland) which permit or require voters to declare not only their first choice of candidate on a ballot but also their second, third, and subsequent choices amongst all candidates standing. A third centripetal mechanism is for political parties to put forward multi-ethnic candidate lists to the electorate, or to ensure parties are organizationally plural, with offices and members spread across the country. Post-Suharto Indonesia is a successful example of this strategy in operation.

In contrast to these kinds of domestic reform initiatives that have come from third wave democracies themselves, elections conducted under UN auspices have almost all favoured proportional representation elections. In fact, major transitional elections in Namibia (1989), Nicaragua (1990), Cambodia (1993), South Africa (1994), Mozambique (1994), Liberia (1997), Bosnia (1996), Kosovo (2001), East Timor (2001), Iraq (2005), and the Democratic Republic of the Congo (2006) were all conducted under the simplest form of party-list PR, often with the entire country forming one electoral district.[7] This has strengths and weaknesses. On one hand, such systems can play an important role in ensuring that the voices of minorities and marginal groups can be heard and their genuine power enhanced. On the other hand, large-district PR systems also allow ethnic parties to form and compete freely, and have often featured parties that are thinly veiled versions of former warring armies.

Regardless of these political strengths and weaknesses, in practice the adoption of such systems for post-conflict elections has usually been dictated more by administrative concerns, such as the need to avoid demarcating individual electoral districts and to produce separate ballot papers for each district, than deeper concerns about political development. In many post-conflict elections, using national PR systems is the only feasible way to hold an election quickly, as a uniform national ballot can be used, no electoral districts need be demarcated, and the process of voter registration, vote counting, and the calculation of results is consequently simplified. In Liberia in 1997, for example, population displacement and the lack of accurate census data led to the abandonment of the old system of single-member majoritarian constituencies for parliamentary elections in favour of a proportional system with a single national constituency.[8]

Unfortunately, national PR systems also have some real disadvantages. They provide no geographic link between voters and their representatives and thus create difficulties in terms of political accountability and responsiveness between elected politicians and the electorate. Many new democracies – particularly those in agrarian societies[9] – have much higher demands for constituency service at the local level than they do for representation of all shades of ideological opinion in the legislature. In addition, PR systems such as those used in Iraq, where the whole country was effectively one constituency, tend to reward political fragmentation and encourage political fractionalization rather than aggregation. The result is often an excessive number of parties and a deeply polarized, often unworkable legislature.

It has therefore increasingly been argued that the UN's model of systems used at transitional elections should also be modified to encourage a higher degree of geographic and personal accountability – such as by having members of parliament represent territorially defined districts, or at least by allowing voters to choose between candidates and not just parties. Such a debate is taking place in Iraq in response to the flawed electoral model used in 2005. A popular choice in many transitional democracies in recent years has been for mixed electoral systems, in which part of the legislature is elected on a national level by proportional representation and part is elected at a local level from single-member districts, so that both proportionality and accountability are maximized. This was the system used for the 2006 elections for the Palestinian National Authority, which was intended to favour the incumbent Fatah party but instead resulted in a victory for Hamas. A final option, widely criticized by most experts, is the single non-transferable vote system currently used in Afghanistan, which not only tends to fragment the vote but also rewards minority victors and fosters intra- (rather than inter) party competition.

MODELS OF ELECTION ADMINISTRATION

While electoral systems have attracted a voluminous academic literature, issues of electoral administration remain under-studied by scholars and underrated in terms of their effect on post-conflict polities. There are several models of election administration used around the world. Some countries locate responsibility for the administration of elections within a government portfolio such as the interior or home affairs ministry. Other countries situate the responsibility for administration of elections within other agencies, such as the public records office, the tax department, or even the postal service. In some cases, the body responsible for running elections is created anew before each electoral event. And in some cases, the international community itself takes responsibility for running the elections. Probably the most important administrative decision concerns the composition of the electoral management body, and specifically whether elections are run by the government of the day or by some form of independent electoral commission.

Comparative experience to date, as well as a global study of electoral management bodies,[10] leaves little doubt that independent and permanent electoral commissions represent a clear best practice in terms of global electoral administration. Their perceived neutrality and independence from political interference lends credibility to the electoral process, which is a crucial determinant of the success of any election. A truly independent commission is one that is able to operate effectively without direct ministerial control, including in its financial and administrative functions, and is (ideally) comprised of non-partisan appointees. In practice, many independent commissions around the world do not have complete financial independence and may be comprised of party representatives rather than non-partisan appointments, but are still able to operate free from government interference.

Particularly in conflict-zone elections, the internal composition of electoral management bodies is also important. In some countries, electoral management bodies are comprised not of independent civil servants, judges, or other officials but by the political parties contesting the elections themselves. This practice is widespread in some areas, and can provide a form of non-partisan independence if the composition of party representation is balanced in such a way as to ensure genuine neutrality. However, problems with this model in some important transitional elections (e.g., the 1999 elections in Indonesia) as well as established democracies (e.g., the 2000 elections in the United States) highlight the propensity for politicization and deadlock that such structural arrangements can have, underlining the importance of careful composition of electoral management bodies.

The worldwide trend is definitely toward independent electoral commissions staffed by non-partisan civil servants; indeed, since the world's largest democracy, India, adopted this model at independence it has been widely adopted around the world. However, the influence of the United States is important here, as the American form of electoral administration is based on political appointees and party representatives, and many post-conflict democracies, particularly in Latin America, have also adopted this model. Rafael López-Pintor argues that, when there is no better tradition or an existing body of widely respected independent civil servants, a party-based electoral authority may be the only realistic choice.[11]

The comparative evidence, however, suggests that independent commissions run by apolitical civil servants are definitely preferable. Party-based commissions have an almost inevitable tendency to split along party lines. In Haiti, for example, the Provisional Electoral Council was made up of representatives of the political parties but was also deeply divided along party lines and internal mistrust and divisions prevented it from working efficiently.[12] In Cambodia, by contrast, a non-partisan electoral commission was widely seen as one of the outstanding elements of the entire UN mission. Non-partisan commissions were also a prominent and successful part of UN missions in Namibia and East Timor.

VOTER REGISTRATION

Elections are a unique area of public governance, being large-scale events that need to be organized and coordinated on a national basis so that virtually all adult citizens are able to take part. Because of this factor, and the need to collect, collate, and manage data on all eligible voters – that is, virtually the entire adult population in most countries – the issue of voter registration is a key aspect of election administration and a common source of requests for assistance.

Voter registration is a perennial area of concern in post-conflict elections. Because nearly all post-conflict elections take place in an environment where basic census and other records are missing, workable voter registers assume even greater importance than usual. The construction of a comprehensive register of voters is often a first step in the bureaucratic process of state building. It is also an enormously time-consuming, logistically challenging, and resource-intensive process: in Cambodia's 1993 UN-run elections, for example, the voter registration period took almost a full year and demanded huge investments in time, personnel, and money. In Côte d'Ivoire, citizenship and ethnic considerations became embroiled in the voter registration debate.

Another perennial issue for post-conflict elections is how to handle internally displaced people and refugees. Because electoral districts and polling places are often drawn and allocated based on voter registration records, this process usually affects these individuals too.

Finally, because in many countries the voter's roll represents the only form of civil register in existence, it is often used for wider purposes than the electoral event itself (for example, the voter register in East Timor was used to identify missing persons following the militia attacks that followed the 1999 plebiscite on independence).

Voter registration by its nature involves collecting specific information in a standardized format from a vast number of people, and then collating and distributing this data in a form that can be used at election time to ensure that only eligible electors vote and to guard against multiple voting, impersonation, and the like. The political sensitivity of these issues, and the laborious nature of the task itself, means that voter registration is often one of the most expensive, time consuming, and sometimes controversial parts of the entire electoral process.

Best practice with regard to voter registration is often focused on the need for a permanent and continuous electoral register that is constantly updated to reflect population movements, new voters, births and deaths, and so on. Because of the issues noted above, the computerization of the voter roll and other related aspects of new technology are commonly requested forms of electoral assistance. The compilation and maintenance of an effective voter register (as with many other areas of electoral administration) lends itself readily to the application of new technology, particularly the issue of computerization of the electoral roll in countries that have not yet moved in that direction.

However, computerization of electoral registers and other related databases has to be balanced against the reality, particularly in the poorest countries, that optimum use of new technology may not always be the most effective way to ensure a workable and cost-effective register of voters. For example, opportunities for electoral fraud via computer hacking and other manipulation of electronic data can actually increase with computerization. Due consideration of both the possibilities as well as the limitations of information technology is thus central to understanding best practice in relation to voter registration.

CIVIL SOCIETY AND POLITICAL PARTY DEVELOPMENT

Because of the underdeveloped and deeply divided nature of post-conflict societies, elections often have the effect of highlighting societal fault-lines and hence laying bare very deep social divisions. In such circumstances, the easiest way to mobilize voter support at election time is often to appeal to the very same insecurities that generated the original conflict. This means that parties have a strong incentive to "play the ethnic card" or to take hard-line positions on key identity-related issues, with predictable consequences for the wider process of democratization. Post-communist elections in Yugoslavia in the early 1990s, for example, resulted in the victory of extremist nationalist parties, committed to (and eventually achieving) the break-up of the federation. The 1993 elections in Burundi, which were supposed to elect a power-sharing government, instead mobilized population groups along ethnic lines and served as a catalyst for ethnic genocide a few months later. Similarly, Bosnia's post-Dayton elections effectively served as ethnic censuses, with parties campaigning on ethnic lines and voters reacting to heightened perceptions of ethnic insecurity by electing hard-line nationalists to power, greatly undermining the process of democracy-building.

For this reason, there is an increasing focus by policy-makers on the need to build broad-based, programmatic political parties in new democracies and to avoid the narrow, personalized, and sectarian parties and party systems that have undermined so many new democracies. Particularly in societies split along ethnic lines, cross-regional and multi-ethnic parties that compete for the centre ground appear to be a – and perhaps *the* – crucial determinant of broader democratic consolidation and peace building. While studies of this issue are surprisingly limited, in practice a great deal of innovation has occurred in many new democracies seeking to influence the shape of their emerging party systems.[13] Spurred on by a growing recognition of the crucial governance role that parties can play in new democracies, political party assistance has become an increasingly prominent aspect of international electoral assistance.

CONCLUSION

Despite the vast amount of attention given to electoral support and democracy promotion over the past decade, the international community today finds itself in something of an intellectual cul-de-sac regarding the value of elections as a method of conflict management.

One the one hand, enormous international resources have been spent organizing, assisting, and monitoring post-conflict elections in pivotal states around the world. In almost all cases, international assistance and other democracy-building efforts have provided the basis for higher-quality elections, with greater oversight and scrutiny, than would otherwise have been held. However, increasingly these post-conflict elections have also been overloaded both with too much assistance (rarely continued for second or third elections) and with unrealistic expectations (particularly the liberal fallacy that democratic procedures will in and of themselves ensure democratic victors).

By reifying the significance of post-conflict elections in this manner, the international community has no fall-back position when elections deliver what is determined to be the "wrong" result, such as the Hamas victory in Palestine in 2006, or in which the "right" result is arrived at by patently fraudulent processes, such as the 2009 Afghanistan presidential election. In response to these unwelcome developments, Western leaders have progressively moved the rhetorical goalposts, so that "success" in cases such as Afghanistan and Iraq is now defined largely in terms of attainment of basic security, state capacity, or other outcomes distinct from genuine democracy.

This may constitute a return to reality (as Barack Obama noted in 2006, "the notion that Iraq would quickly and easily become a bulwark of flourishing democracy in the Middle East was ... an ideological fantasy"). But it creates problems for those who actually believe in the substantive importance of electoral democracy. While they are certainly one part of a broader strategy of state building, elections themselves cannot build state capacity: indeed, competitive elections by their nature tend to highlight social cleavages and emphasize areas of difference rather than commonality. More broadly, the messy business of genuine democracy can actually make the basic tasks of government more difficult, particularly in transitional states. Given recent events, it may therefore be increasingly difficult to sustain arguments about the centrality of elections to post-conflict peace building.

PART TWO

Lessons Learned from Country Situations

2

Elections and the Future of Afghanistan

FRANCESC VENDRELL

I have always been a firm believer in elections, provided that these are what used to be called "free and fair" or more recently "according to international standards." Elections are not synonymous with democracy of course, but they constitute an important step towards it. I use the adjective "firm" because I spent the first twenty years of my life in a country where the only elections were to fill a portion of seats to a rubber-stamp "parliament" that was for the most part either appointed or indirectly elected. I was thirty-seven when, following Franco's death, I cast my first vote in the first free elections held in Spain since 1936.

During those long years of fascist autocracy, it was common for the partisans of the regime to claim that liberal-democratic elections, flawed and meaningless as they were portrayed, were really only suited to North American and northern European countries. The Iberian character, it was said, was too prone to intolerance and violence and thus not suited to a system of regular confrontations through the ballot box. I never accepted what was simply an excuse to perpetuate the regime in power. Based on my experience of thirty-four years working for the United Nations, followed by another six with the European Union in a variety of countries in conflict or where gross violations of human rights were taking place, I am as convinced as ever that peoples, regardless of their culture, religion or history, want their human rights respected, including the ability to periodically decide who should govern them. And so far no better system than elections between competing candidates, imperfect as it may be, has emerged to provide citizens with this opportunity.

Latin America, long regarded as the preserve of authoritarian military rule, has over the past twenty-five years become accustomed to periodic, credible elections. In Africa, it was once fashionable in certain "progressive" circles to accept the argument, put forward by newly independent African strongmen, that in their countries, saddled with artificial borders and divided by ethnicity and tribalism, the best system of government was the one-party state. But even there it became all too apparent, particularly when the end of the Cold War removed the last excuse for supporting dictatorial regimes, that most one-party regimes were characterized by corruption, repression, impunity, and underdevelopment. The popular revolts across much of the Arab world since the beginning of 2011 are a further reminder that peoples yearning for freedom and genuinely representative institutions know no geographic, cultural, or religious barriers.

On a professional level, I was involved in the decision taken in early 1990 by Secretary-General Javier Perez de Cuellar to send, for the first time in the UN's history, a fifty-strong monitoring team to observe general elections in an independent country, Nicaragua. This was seen as a way to overcome US hostility to the Sandinista regime, facilitate the voluntary demobilization of the Nicaraguan "Contras," and bring about the end of the armed conflict. Aware that the US government might refuse to accept the outcome of UN monitored elections were they to be won by the Sandinistas, Perez de Cuellar entrusted the leadership of the mission (ONUVEN) to former US Attorney General Elliot Richardson, a moderate Republican whose findings, the secretary-general rightly felt, the then-administration of George Bush senior would find unimpeachable. As it happened, the June 1990 elections resulted in a Sandinista defeat and the peaceful transfer of power to Violeta Chamorro, the opposition candidate. Later that year a joint UN-OAS commission (CIAV) succeeded in demobilizing and disarming the US backed Contras.

That same year, the UN also agreed to observe the elections in Haiti, which were seen as having the potential of being a turning point in that country's political life after the long years of the Duvalier family dictatorship. The elections proved to be the freest elections ever held in Haiti, with massive popular participation, and were won by Jean-Bertrand Aristide, who, appropriately, was fond of saying that though the majority of Haitians were illiterate they were "analphabètes mais pas bêtes." Aristide was overthrown several months later in a military coup.

It was fortunate that the General Assembly of the Organization of

American States had adopted that very year a "democracy charter" under which its members pledged not to recognize a regime issued from a military coup. I say fortunate, because the fall of Aristide was actually welcomed by many in the US administration and Congress, who saw in the Catholic liberation theologian the potential for another Castro whom, in years gone by, the US would have sought to overthrow as they had left-leaning figures like Jacobo Árbenz in Guatemala in 1954 and Salvador Allende in Chile in 1973. In 1991, however, the US administration had little option but to recall its ambassador from Haiti, though it soon attempted without success, in UN-brokered negotiations in which I was a participant, to look for a variety of formulas to restore Aristide as a ceremonial president with executive power vested in a US-approved prime minister.

Eventually, in late 1994, the Clinton administration, which for a while had pursued a policy not unlike that of his Republican predecessor, found itself in the ironic situation of having to seek Security Council authorization to intervene militarily in Haiti as the only way to force the Haitian military junta to accept Aristide's return to power. I have mentioned the cases of Nicaragua and Haiti as illustration that governments in some democratic countries at times not only choose to turn a blind eye to blatant fraud but also prefer to disregard the outcome of free elections when it happens not to suit their taste.

Then came Cambodia, where, in elections conducted by the UN in early 1993 in pursuit of the Paris Agreements, 90 per cent of voters turned up at the polls in a country that had never experienced free and fair elections, disregarding Khmer Rouge threats of disruption. Or take the case of East Timor when, following Soeharto's fall, lengthy negotiations, in which I was deeply involved, led to an agreement between Indonesia and Portugal for the UN to conduct a self-determination referendum in August 1999 (officially termed a "popular consultation" to save face for the Indonesian government, which had for years opposed the holding of a referendum to determine the wishes of its inhabitants). There again an astonishing 98.5 per cent of voters turned up to decide the territory's future, despite large-scale intimidation in the run-up to the vote by pro-Indonesian militias supported and paid for by the Indonesian army. Today East Timor has become a country where periodic, fair elections have become the rule, as indeed has also been the case with Indonesia.

I have described the above to explain why, when appointed at the beginning of 2000 as the personal representative of the secretary-general (PRSG) for Afghanistan and head of the UN Special Mission for Afghanistan (UNSMA), I was surprised to discover that, whereas earlier General Assembly resolutions on Afghanistan called for the holding of elections as part of an overall settlement of the conflict, that provision had disappeared from the text of more recent resolutions. Of course the idea of free elections in Afghanistan seemed quite a way off at the time, but nevertheless in my discussions with the Taliban leadership, with Ahmad Shah Massoud and the Northern Alliance, and with former King Mohammed Zahir Shah and the Rome Group I raised the question of whether elections were something they might envisage as part of an eventual, overall settlement. The Taliban rejected the idea, while not excluding the possibility of an elected advisory Shura, or council. To them, in an Islamic emirate, once Mullah Mohammed Omar had been acclaimed by the Ulema Shura in Kandahar in 1994, the Amir al-Mu'minin (leader of the faithful) could not be subject to future election. On the other hand, both Massoud and Zahir Shah agreed that elections should be held in Afghanistan at the culmination of a peace process, as they had been during the ten years of constitutional monarchy between 1963 and 1973 when three consecutive parliaments were elected by universal suffrage. (Later, elections of the non-free variety were held under Mohammed Daoud Khan and the Communist People's Democratic Party of Afghanistan regime.)

After September 11th, my office quickly put forward a plan, partly inspired by the Rome Group's proposal for an emergency Loya Jirga, or grand assembly, which was largely integrated in what became the Bonn Agreement signed in December of 2001. Although, following heated disagreement between a senior UN colleague and myself, the draft presented to the participants in Bonn failed to make any reference to elections, they were nonetheless included in the final Agreement, at the request of the two main participants at the Conference, the Northern Alliance and the former king's delegation.

In January 2004, the Constitutional Loya Jirga approved a constitutional draft elaborated by the Afghan Constitutional Commission, appointed under heavy jihadist influence by President Karzai, providing for an Islamic Republic and a presidential, highly centralized system of government. It had been the original intention to hold both presidential and parliamentary elections at the same time. However, since the technical preparations were more complex for the latter than for the former, the US envoy, keen to have Karzai elected ahead of the November elections in his own country as proof of the successful introduction of democracy in Afghanistan, insisted that presidential elections be held in September 2004. This demand had two unfortunate consequences: first, it conveyed the message that elections for president were more important than those for parliament and, second, it ensured that in future presidential and parliamentary elections would be held in consecutive years, thus imposing an additional financial, security, and logistical burden on the country, a situation which can now only be remedied by constitutional amendment.

The presidential elections were thus held in late September 2004 with the UN playing a major role in their organization and conduct. They were widely seen as fair and credible while at the same time producing the result desired by the West with Hamid Karzai emerging as the winner in the first round with 54 per cent of the votes.

Elections, even when free, will not bring about democracy unless they are accompanied by the establishment of rule-of-law institutions, by a series of reforms conducive to the creation of a level playing field and an environment free of intimidation, and by the growth of political parties and a fair electoral system. Sadly these elements remain largely absent in Afghanistan and the UN's role, never as strong as some of us would have liked, has progressively declined, partly because it was caught in a net of its own creation when, in Bonn, it coined the seductive but misleading slogan that the process would be "Afghan-led" (ignoring the fact that there were no legitimate representatives of the Afghan people to lead it), ensuring that the UN footprint in it would be light. This approach, which tallied with opposition to the very notion of nation building by Defense Secretary Rumsfeld and other senior Bush administration officials, deprived the UN of the means to play an essential role in the building of the country's institutions, police, and judicial system in particular.

At the same time, neither the US nor other NATO members showed much inclination to ensure that the Afghan government had the monopoly on the means of violence. On the contrary, the US continued to subsidize and collaborate with Northern Alliance warlords and commanders, who, in the wake of the Taliban defeat, installed themselves as ministers or deputy ministers, provincial governors, district administrators, and police chiefs, ensuring that from the very beginning a culture of bad governance, corruption, and impunity established itself in the country. It seemed as if the international community had forgotten that it was their corrupt and criminal acts during the period 1992–96 that had facilitated the Taliban conquest of most of the country.

It was against this background that parliamentary elections were held in September 2005 under the single non-transferable vote system, an unusual electoral system reportedly in use only in Jordan and Vanuatu, whereby voters elect their representatives to parliament in multi-member constituencies, currently corresponding to the country's provinces, with those scoring the highest number of votes declared elected. (This meant that in a province returning, for example, five members of parliament, the fifth winner might have collected just one per cent of the vote while the first had garnered 60 per cent.) Those, including President Karzai, who favoured this system, which discourages the formation of political parties, claimed that Afghanistan's bad experience with the "Tanzim" (the seven Jihadist parties who fought the USSR in the 1980s and later turned against each other) had led Afghans to dislike political parties. They also claimed that under a system of proportional representation the continued presence of armed groups would only strengthen the power of the warlords by enabling other candidates from their faction to ride on the top candidate's coat-tails.

The likelihood that warlords and other persons linked to illegal armed groups would successfully use intimidation to get themselves elected was a source of real concern, whatever the electoral system chosen. In an effort to prevent this, a vetting system composed of senior Afghan officials with international participation, including the United Nations Assistance Mission in Afghanistan (UNAMA), the EU, Canada, and Japan, was put in place. Before a candidate was excluded, proof of association with illegal armed groups was, naturally, required. Such evidence was to be supplied jointly by the Afghan National Army, the Afghan National Police, and the National Directorate for Security. Unfortunately, since all these institutions included within their senior ranks personnel connected to or drawn from the illegal armed groups, it was never likely that the vetting system would be successful and indeed it was not. In addition, the US Embassy, the US-led coalition, and the International Security Assistance Force (ISAF) evidenced their lack of interest in the process by either failing to attend or actively participate in the vetting group's sessions – the international military forces making it clear that they would not involve themselves in supporting the Afghan military or police in the event that an excluded candidate created a security problem.

The 2005 election was conducted by an electoral commission appointed by the president, pending the establishment of a legislature, under transitional article 159 of the Constitution. The commission's secretariat, however, was headed by an international electoral expert appointed by UNAMA, though across the country voting stations were manned by Afghan officials under UNAMA's provincial supervision. Voter participation in these elections, estimated at around 50 per cent, was considerably lower than the 70 per cent for the presidential election. The vote was marred in several of the more remote provinces by serious irregularities, including ballot stuffing and unverified counting procedures, facilitated by the fact that Afghan electoral officials served in the localities they came from and, not infrequently, had ties to one or another of the candidates.

Though international observers (most of whom rarely ventured out of the regional capitals for security or logistical reasons) such as the EU Election Observation Mission (EOM) gave a qualified imprimatur to the electoral process, it marked the beginning of growing Afghan apathy and disillusionment in the system, coupled with cynicism about the real objectives of the international community. Nevertheless, a parliament was now in place with a number of dedicated members and 26 per cent of the seats reserved for women. Yunus Qanuni, a Tajik politician who had led the Northern Alliance delegation to the Bonn talks, was elected speaker of the lower house.

Fast forward to early 2009. The security situation had dramatically deteriorated, with approximately half the Pashtun districts and one quarter of the country's total area considered by the UN to be so insecure as to be virtually inaccessible to government officials, an Afghan government that was widely unpopular and perceived as incompetent, corrupt, barely functioning rule-of-law institutions, and a Supreme Court regarded as subservient to the Executive and with an ill-defined role as the interpreter of the constitution. At the same time, a new administration was in office in Washington, which, far from regarding Karzai as its indispensable man, now saw in him a problematic ally. New presidential elections loomed in August 2009. The Independent Electoral Commission (IEC) had been again appointed exclusively by the president in disregard of transitional article 159 of the Constitution, which granted this right to him only pending the establishment of a parliament, now duly constituted. Moreover, virtually all the recommendations made by international observers to the 2005 elections (including the 2006 report of the EU EOM) on how to improve the electoral process had been ignored, while the failure to create a permanent voter registration system created opportunities for people to obtain more than one voter card.

As early as mid-2008 I had been raising the alarm, first with EU member states but also with the UN and others as well, warning of the likelihood of large-scale fraud unless the membership of the IEC was either truly independent or politically balanced and special measures taken to prevent large-scale fraud, particularly in those (largely Pashtun) areas where security conditions would prevent either the opening of the voting stations or independent monitoring of the electoral process. Equally worrying were the reduction of UNAMA's role to the provision of technical support to the IEC and the decision, despite the negative lessons that should have been drawn from the 2005 elections, to continue the practice of hiring electoral officers drawn from the very areas where the voting was to take place rather than switching them to other areas where there would be less chance of their being linked to local power holders.

A window of opportunity, however, existed for the international community to seize if it was truly interested in a fair electoral process. Karzai's presidential mandate expired on 22 May 2009, thus creating a void that could have been filled with the establishment of an interim government that would manage the country until the inauguration of a new president. You would have thought this would have been the moment for the US in particular – but also for UNAMA, the EU, and others – to demand such a body, which might have been composed of the country's leading figures, which would have decided whether credible elections were feasible in the existing security climate and, if so, how they should be organized and conducted. Not only was this opportunity missed, but there was never a serious attempt by donor countries to link their financial assistance to meaningful improvement in the administration of the electoral process. And so it was that the composition of the IEC was never seriously challenged and, when the Afghan Supreme Court unsurprisingly decided that Karzai could stay on as president until his successor's inauguration, the US and its Western allies meekly went along with the Court's opinion.

In these circumstances it should have come as no surprise that the presidential elections, where only an estimated 35 per cent of voters were reported to have turned up, were largely an exercise in fraud. The Western powers, however, rushed to proclaim the electoral process a "victory for the Afghan people," when it was precisely the reverse. The only hope of redressing the fraud, at least to some extent, lay with the Electoral Complaints Commission (ECC), a five-member body composed of three foreigners appointed by the UN, one selected by the Afghan Supreme Court, and a fifth designated by the Afghan Independent Human Rights Commission (AIHRC), a truly autonomous organization and one major achievement of the Bonn process. Though the ECC lacked many of the tools required to investigate the numerous allegations of fraud, it found sufficient evidence to decree by the end of October that over one million ballots be cast aside; as a result Karzai's vote percentage dropped to below 49 per cent, thus necessitating a second round against his nearest rival, former foreign minister Abdullah Abdullah.

With the EU EOM declaring the election flawed and the international media loudly criticizing its conduct, it was left to the US, the UN, and the EU to finally prevail on Karzai to accept the need for a second round. When he eventually did accept, it was perhaps to be expected that he was greeted by a chorus of international approval, with the US and NATO hailing his "statesmanship." With no one in the international community calling for a revision in the composition of the IEC or for improvements to the process to prevent the repetition of fraud, it was hardly surprising for Abdullah to announce his decision not to participate in the second round.

None of these chicaneries have been lost on the Afghan people who, "analphabètes mais pas bêtes," have drawn their own conclusions about Western commitment to representative democracy, while our own credibility when scrutinizing electoral processes in countries from Zimbabwe to Iran has been seriously eroded.

Having in practice given up on the need for credible elections, the international community, now looking desperately for an exit from Afghanistan, made almost no attempt to ensure that parliamentary elections scheduled for the second half of September 2010 would not become a repeat of those in the preceding year. Indeed, the president, not content with maintaining control of the "independent" electoral commission (now under a new chairman) and bizarrely accusing the

US, the UN, and the EU of being responsible for the fraud in the presidential elections, has managed to effortlessly undermine the independence of the ECC, whose members are all now appointed by him. The international members have been reduced from three to two, selected in consultation with UNAMA, and three Afghans, none designated by the AIHRC.

The communiqué issued at the conclusion of the International Conference on Afghanistan held in Kabul in July 2010, while declaring "the paramount importance of holding transparent, inclusive, and credible elections in the fall" and that "the Afghan Government in particular is fully committed to ensuring this objective," failed to indicate how this was to be achieved in practice.[1] Nor did donors link their financial support for the elections to any meaningful reforms being undertaken to ensure their credibility. The elections were run again under a single non-transferable vote system, no effort having been made by Western countries to encourage the development of political parties with reformist and pluralistic agendas. As was the case in 2005, the number of candidates in large provinces (some 440 were listed in Kabul that year on a ballot the size of a newspaper) was such that voters continued to find it difficult, without the use of unavailable magnifying glasses, to identify on the ballot the candidate for whom they wished to vote, a situation providing further opportunities for fraud.

The September 2010 elections were marked by decreased popular participation and profound irregularities, including far more electoral cards than the number of registered voters, intimidation and ballot stuffing, and fraud in vote counts, leading the IEC to reject some 25 percent of the voting cards. The combination of insecurity in many Pashtun provinces and the clever manipulation of the SNTV system by well-organized minorities led to the Pashtun losing some 20 seats in the lower house of parliament, further decreasing the president's hold on parliament and leading him to encourage the Supreme Court to set up a special tribunal to adjudicate election complaints, despite its broadly acknowledged lack of jurisdiction in this area. While parliament was eventually convened on 25 January 2011 with its membership intact, the Special Tribunal remains in place as a kind of Damocles' sword over the lower house, presumably to encourage its members to be more accommodating towards the president's wishes. What is clear is that the 2010 parliamentary elections have brought the three main organs of the state into even greater disrepute, bringing their legitimacy into question.

Over the past couple of years Western politicians and diplomats have become increasingly addicted to the refrain that "Afghanistan was not Switzerland," that elections could not be expected to be run as if the country was "Sweden," and that it had been a mistake to try to "impose" a Western system of government on a "tribal" society with a different set of historical and cultural values, as if that was what some of us had been trying to accomplish since 2001. This deeply patronizing, when not insulting, view of the Afghans barely hides the intentions of those who, in search for an early exit, have given up trying to rebuild Afghanistan's civilian institutions to a level comparable to, say, Bangladesh, Nepal, or Pakistan. It paves the way to a redefinition of "success" in Afghanistan by claiming, as Vice-President Biden sadly does in an unfortunate echo of Donald Rumsfeld, that the US is simply in Afghanistan on a purely anti-terrorist mission to defeat al-Qaeda and not to nation build or turn the country "into a Jeffersonian democracy."[2] In turn this approach fails to take into account that Afghanistan fell prey to Islamic extremism when the West, having succeeded in securing the withdrawal of the Soviet army, turned its back on Afghanistan, leaving the country prey to anarchy and civil war.

Afghans, even when they prioritize the need for peace, will continue to feel that they are entitled, like everyone else on this planet, to decide periodically and freely who should be their rulers. The failure of the international community to ensure the establishment of central and provincial institutions that are representative and accountable, and which Afghans would feel ready to fight for, further undermines the already faltering attempts at carrying out a counter-insurgency strategy. If the only reason for the West to remain militarily engaged in Afghanistan is to kill or capture "terrorists," there are many other cheaper and more efficient ways to achieve this goal. Neither the Western public nor the Afghan people are convinced that this is motivation enough to remain militarily engaged in Afghanistan at the cost of people's lives and billions of dollars. The demand for an early withdrawal continues to increase and when it comes, probably in 2015, it is likely to leave the Afghan people to their fate and no amount of spin will be able to disguise our failure in Afghanistan and our betrayal of its people.

3

Iraq's Conflicted Transition to Democracy: Analyzing Elections in a Violent Society

MARC A. LEMIEUX

Since January 2005, Iraqis have experienced three national elections, one constitutional referendum, two provincial elections, and two regional elections. Have peaceful and legitimate elections that meet international standards been possible under occupation? Were Iraqis rushed into elections? How much violence was there during these polls? How was voter participation affected by this violence? Have ethnic and sectarian divides been overcome or exacerbated by elections? Has institutional design mitigated political conflict in Iraqi society? What trends are evident in analysing voting behaviour since 2005?

This chapter will briefly examine Iraqi elections between January 2005 and March 2010 at national, regional, and local levels, including electoral frameworks, political and electoral violence, the role of occupying forces and local party militias, technical assistance, voting behaviour, and party coalitions in Iraq's transition.

The international community played a key role in supporting all Iraqi polls. The legitimacy of external expertise was reinforced by international support for Iraqi capacity to monitor and observe elections.

In turn, parties have learned how to build coalitions and shelve their militia tactics. Formerly violent anti-democracy groups have either been militarily routed or co-opted into Iraqi politics. This chapter will argue that Iraqi democracy, while in its infancy, has shown durable progress, promoting a pre-Baathist culture of coexistence and concession-making politics that has progressively mitigated some of the root causes of electoral violence since 2005. It is not electoral violence per se but rather political violence and the weakness of the state that have compromised Iraq's democratic experience. However, over time, inclusive political accommodation is prevailing over violence.

EARLY DEMOCRACY AND COALITION MAKING

Three characteristics have guided Iraqi politics since independence in 1932 – coercion, co-optation, and concession-making. Governments have changed by bloody coup several times. Political party members have been killed, banned, or co-opted into coalitions throughout Iraq's history.[1] Politically driven mob violence has been shocking. During the 1958 revolution, long-time Prime Minister Nuri al-Said was dismembered publicly. Less than a month after the US invasion, having just returned to Najaf from exile, Abdul Majid al-Khoei, son of Grand Ayatollah Abul-Qasim al-Khoei and scion of a revered Shia dynasty, was hacked to death by fellow Shia.[2]

The three Cs have been especially present in the exercise of Iraqi electoral democracy since 2005. There is no doubt that the rushed national and provincial elections of January 2005, which took place under a cloud of occupation, lost statehood, and inter communal frustrations, increased political and electoral violence, resulting in polarized local identities and unprecedented incidents of sectarian cleansing reminiscent of Bosnia, Lebanon, and Northern Ireland. Changes to the electoral framework for national polls in December 2005, however, resulted in increased party coalition-building and voter participation, which in turn enabled a significant reduction in violence.

Elections are not foreign to Iraqi history. While the British cartographer of Mesopotamia, Gertrude Bell, wrote in 1916 that the Arabs could not govern themselves except through British tutelage,[3] elected municipal councils had been established since the Ottoman period and were later abolished by the British.[4] Between 1924 and 1958, Iraqi society took part in sixteen indirect parliamentary elections, only two of which survived their full four-year term.[5] When two opposition parties threatened British interests during negotiations of the 1922 Anglo-Iraqi treaty, they were banned by the British high commissioner.[6] Since the creation of the post-Ottoman state in 1921, Iraq has experienced various forms of government (occupation, monarchy, elitist-democracy, republican dictatorship) that have had to deal with different kinds of groups (tribal, class, ethnic, professional, religious) and with the state. A number of the parties in the political arena today can trace their origins to the years before the Baath Party monopoly, which was assured by a 1964 ban on political parties. These include communists, Islamists, and Kurdish parties. As well, in 1992, many Shia and Kurdish party leaders in exile in London and Washington united in foreign-funded opposition to Baathism. Leaders of these parties joined the 2003 American-supported political process.

Three other groups joined the electoral process in late 2005: the Sadrists and two major Sunni-Arab coalitions, Hiwar or the Iraqi Front for National Dialogue and Tawafuq or the Iraqi Accord Front (including the Iraqi Islamic Party (IIP). The Sadrists joined the pan-Shia United Iraqi Alliance (UIA) that included Dawa and SCIRI leaders and was inspired by Grand Ayatollah Ali al-Sistani. The two Kurdish parties united, at the national and regional levels only, as the Kurdistan Alliance (KA). During 2004, the secular Iraqi National Accord attempted to convert itself into a multi-ethnic and cross-sectarian national coalition, which in 2004 was called al-Iraqiya or the Iraqi National Movement and included Communists, moderates, Iraqi nationalists, and former Shia and Sunni Baathists such as Adnan Pachachi's Assembly of Independent Democrats.

In preparation for the 2009 provincial polls, Prime Minister Nouri al-Maliki formed a new coalition called the State of Law. In preparation for the 2010 polls, Allawi took this inclusiveness further with support from influential Sunni and the successful 2009 Arab-led al-Hadba coalition[7] of Ninawa Province. In 2009, ISCI, the Sadrists, and several other Shia parties formed the National Iraqi Alliance (NIA).

THE ROOTS OF ELECTORAL VIOLENCE: FOREIGN AND DOMESTIC

Violence has featured regularly in recent Iraqi politics. For example, in April 2007 there was a suicide bomb attack on a national parliament in session that killed one legislator and seven other people. Rewind further to 17 May 2004, when the then-holder of the rotating presidency of the Iraqi Governing Council, Ezzedine Salim of the Dawa Party, was killed by a Baghdad car bomb while driving to work.

While, since the US invasion, electoral violence has always been present, the levels of electoral violence seen in the first hurried national and provincial polls of January 2005 has not been repeated, the result of several electoral design factors put in place for the December 2005 polls. These include a provincial rather than national proportional representation (PR) electoral system; the creation of forty-five national compensatory seats to reward national parties that obtain cross-provincial voter support; and, especially, the efforts of party coalition builders both before and after election day, which (1) avoided a second Sunni Arab boycott and (2) included Sadrists within the huge Shia tent of the Sistani-inspired UIA, later (2009) renamed the National Iraqi Alliance. The UN and Coalition Provisional Authority (CPA) decision to use a national PR system in early 2005 resulted in seat allocations that exaggerated the results of the Sunni Arab boycott and kept their representation in the Baghdad parliament to under 8 per cent of seats[8] instead of the 18 to 20 per cent reality. Provincial PR, which fixes the number of seats filled by the provinces in a national assembly, had been used by the UN in Cambodia's first democratic polls of 1993[9] and had earlier been suggested by CPA governance adviser Larry Diamond.[10]

Although numerous observers blamed the 2006 spike in the insurgency – arguably a civil war without Kurds – on the failure of the December 2005 elections to produce a clear winner, it is crucially important to distinguish election violence from wider political violence, as exemplified by the al-Qaeda attack on the Shia al-Askari shrine in Samarra on 22 February 2006, the most violent post-invasion incident to spark inter-Muslim conflict in Iraq.[11] In this sense, the January 2005 election was contributory to but not decisive for the escalation of political violence in Iraq.

The vote was also affected when American officials crudely prioritized the November 2004 Bush presidential re-election above the security environment in Anbar Province, where Marines waited until after the American election to storm Fallujah (a second time), subsequently driving insurgents north, with the result that, two months later, voters in Ninawa found access to polling stations next to impossible.

To expect high general voter participation in the 2005 election in either Anbar or Ninawa was highly unrealistic. Mosul saw very limited polling activity because of the conflict that had killed some Independent Electoral Commission of Iraq (IECI) staff and caused others to quit.[12] UN logistics officers stated that all IECI staff in Anbar and Ninawa had been imported from other governorates. As well, Sadrist and Sunni Arab distrust of polls under occupation caused hundreds of incidents of violence and intimidation in most provinces.[13]

Terrorist goals were aimed at accentuating violence between Iraqi sects, overturning decades of coexistence, in order to discredit the occupation, establish an Islamic Sunni state, and evict the previously exiled "returning Persian hordes." During each election, US troops and Iraqi security forces shut down borders and inter-provincial and urban traffic to prevent vehicular attacks on the process. By July of 2009, US troops had exited urban centres (except Mosul), leaving electoral security in the hands of Iraqi commanders.

Unlike Lebanon, Afghanistan, or Northern Ireland, Iraqi society is not deeply divided by decades of inter-communal civil war, poverty, foreign occupation, or regional interference. Saddam Hussein's Baathist legacy is notorious for its cruelty and aggression: the invasion of two neighbouring states, the deportation of tens of thousands of Fayli Kurds (Shia) to Iran, the Anfal campaign, a genocidal assault on Kurds, which included the gassing of Halabja in March 1988, and mass graves resulting from failed Shia revolts. But social divisions and neighbourhood ethnic cleansing campaigns by sectarian groups are recent post-invasion phenomena within previously coexisting mixed communities.

Political violence in Iraq since the fall of Baathism has principally been a reactive expression of communal protection and political self-preservation given the vacuum of state authority. Such violence resulted from the significant miscalculations and pure ignorance of foreign forces and their civilian administrators, as evident in CPA decrees disbanding the entire Iraqi Army and the banning of the top four (instead of top two) levels of Baathists from employment. The biggest recruiting poster for the insurgents came in the form of the March 2004 revelations of American torture techniques used on Iraqi detainees in Abu Ghraib prison.[14]

Anti-democracy groups in Iraq existed principally because of their exclusion from the political process, which encouraged their morphing into anti-establishment groups, elements that attracted insurgent infiltration. Had transitional powers been more inclusive of all factions (as with the 1991 Cambodian peace process that included the genocidal Khmer Rouge), violence could have been limited. Although unheeded, CPA governance adviser Larry Diamond had suggested a role for the Baath Party.[15]

At the time of Saddam Hussein's ouster in 2003, there were at least four sources of political violence and inspiration for anti-occupation and anti-democracy elements. These were: (1) Sunni-Arab Baath diehards who had lost decades of privilege previously enjoyed under the rule of Sunni-dominated elites in Baghdad; (2) a pro-resistance class of pseudo-imams and genuine clerics from both Muslim sects, divided into Shia-Arab Sadrists – aligned with a new militia called the Mahdi Army created by the young firebrand Muqtada al-Sadr – and the pro-violence Sunni-Arab Association of Muslim Scholars with its pro-Arab stance; (3) foreign-led Islamist fundamentalist groups and insurgents such as al-Qaeda in Mesopotamia; and (4) decentralized criminal gang elements recruited by the previous three groups.

Thousands of militants, wishing only to protect their homes and families, joined one of the above groups until they realized that, especially during the 2006 al-Askari surge in insurgent activity, they were being duped into turning against their identification as tribesmen, Iraqi nationals, or moderate Muslims by Islamist extremists, foreigners, criminals, and money. Islam forbids suicide: while about 10 per cent of all insurgents in 2005 were foreigners,[16] foreigners comprised 90 per cent of suicide bombers.[17]

The CPA was partly to blame for the formation of the Mahdi Army when it concurred with plotting Shia leaders, led by rival former exile Abdul Aziz al-Hakim (SCIRI), in denying al-Sadr a seat at the table of the July 2003 Iraqi Governing Council (IGC), an insult to the sole survivor of a decades-old religious and political dynasty. Both SCIRI and Dawa parties did not want al-Sadr as a rival on the Council.[18] Al-Sadr's exclusion led directly to the formation of the Mahdi Army one month later. The Mahdi militia led two failed insurrections in Baghdad and in numerous southern provinces against coalition forces and the IGC in April and August of 2004.[19] When the CPA decreed that Iraq's armed forces must be free of self-serving local militias, it deliberately ignored the Kurdish Peshmerga and SCIRI's Badr Brigades[20] in order to target Mahdi elements. Muqtada al-Sadr's rejection of elections as long as the country remained occupied was ignored by the new pro-CPA Iraqi elite who would handily dominate the January 2005 campaign.

When the CPA and unpopular IGC members tried to avoid holding direct elections under the concocted 15 November 2003 Agreement on Political Process, it was Grand Ayatollah Sistani who led the Shia call to elections by fatwa (religious decree), arguing the undeniable global principle that no legitimate constitution could be written by unelected citizens. Shia exiles and Kurdish elites on the IGC had desperately encouraged the White House to re-engineer Iraqi governance so that their new post-invasion gains could be directly transferred into parliamentary seats, thus vengefully relegating Sunni Arab politicians to minority status.

Shia exiles and Kurdish nationalists, like foreign and local insurgents, took full advantage of a Sunni-Arab lack of unity and cohesion, as Sunni-Arabs had never associated themselves with any identity beyond rural tribalism. Political naiveté also led to a Sunni-Arab boycott of the January national polls. The rushed electoral timetable, which suited already prepared Shia and Kurdish groups, did not allow the amateur Sunni-Arab players sufficient time to develop new post-Baathist political leadership, coalitions, and campaign strategies. While many argued that Sunni-Arabs were not interested in the 2005 elections, even if there were suggested delays to allow improvements in security and the strengthening of new political parties, others cried that obstructionists were feeding the insurgency.

Astute Sunni-Arab leaders would later come to realize their loss of access to Baghdad power brokers. Sunni clerics began to call on people to vote, some even decreeing it (as had Sistani earlier) and a few insurgent groups called on their elements to avoid violence at polling stations.[21] Nevertheless, the Iraqi Islamic Party had several of its candidates murdered in late 2005.

The eighteen-month 2007–08 surge of 30,000 US troops provided the means to counter insurgency activity in Sunni-Arab quarters. US General David Petraeus's policy of protecting the population, while briefly raising casualty figures, succeeded in separating genuine neighbourhood protection squads from criminal gangs, anti-government groups, and pro-Islamist forces. Tribal leaders, an under-rated but crucial element in Mesopotamian society, reasserted their influence among peoples who had long benefitted from the autonomy of tribal authority during Ottoman and British rule. After the CPA sidelined the tribes in 2003,[22] tribal institutions failed to mobilize into a viable force during 2005 elections.[23]

The surge allowed a political window of opportunity for tribal leaders, pro-Iraq loyalists, and pro-democracy forces to emerge, form coalitions, and prepare their eventually successful participation in 2009 and 2010 polls. The influence of tribal politics has now regained favour in Sunni Arab provinces at the expense of violent religious factions. The second highest percentage of support during 2009 provincial polls in Anbar predictably went to the US-sponsored Sahwa, or Awakening, councils, a coalition of tribes. According to a former British CPA official who advised US generals on relations with Iraqi society in 2007, the surge had a huge psychological impact, enabling significant bottom-up momentum on the Shia and Sunni street.[24] Control of Sahwa militia units passed to Iraqi government authority in October 2008, with fewer than half integrated into existing security institutions at a fraction of prior US pay.

MILITIAS AND THE RESUMPTION OF STATE POWER

While Iraq's old parties operated largely as family dynasties or tribal federations without leadership contests, many were backed by paid party militias. By June 2004, CPA head Paul Bremer had created by decree several electoral regulations, including Order 97, which prohibited the registration of any political party in possession of its own militia or financed by one. The 2009 election law also banned the registration of parties that maintained militias. While several coalitions of parties had formed during national polls, individual parties competed fiercely during local elections in January 2005, using their militias to advance political goals and safeguard their voters. Kurdish and Shia factional militias were also blamed for blocking voter access during the 2005 elections.[25]

Iraq's oldest still-active militia force is the Kurdish Peshmerga, which was instituted in the 1940s and later divided into tribal-based politicized units loyal to the two main Kurdish parties. A 1992 Kurdish strategic agreement failed to resolve historic tribal differences and prevent a mid-90s Kurdish civil war whose end was brokered by Americans in 1998. The agreement had also left intact the party-controlled Peshmerga militia forces,[26] which were not united under one regional minister until 2009.[27]

The Sadrist movement, which has the biggest militia, is also the second biggest Shia political component today. It was the kingmaker in 2006 power-broking and the source of much violence before finally joining the political process in late 2005. The Sadr family owes its decades-old religious success to Grand Ayatollah Mohammed Baqir al-Sadr, who was killed by Saddam Baathists in 1980 because of his views on clerical rule. Grand Ayatollah Mohammed Sadeq al-Sadr later took up Sadrist leadership, organizing spiritual and charitable campaigns for all Shia, especially in poor urban Baghdad areas (Sadr city). He was also killed by Baathists, in a Najaf attack in 1999. The family mantle fell to the young renegade Muqtada al-Sadr.

The biggest cause of a national reduction in intra-sectarian violence resulted from the integration of Badr forces into Iraqi security services, police, and army. SCIRI and its military wing, the Badr Brigades, were born in 1982 when Iraqi Shia exiles in Iran united to fight against Saddam Hussein's largely Shia army during the eight-year Iran-Iraq War (1980-88). After spending two decades in exile as head of the SCIRI, Ayatollah Muhammad Baqir al-Hakim returned to Iraq in May of 2003; he had been Najaf's leading ayatollah in the 1960s. Three months later, on 29 August, an enormous truck bomb exploded moments after prayers, killing him and some 125 others at the shrine of Imam Ali in Najaf, an act credited to the Jordanian leader of al-Qaeda in Mesopotamia, Abu Musab al-Zarqawi.[28]

While SCIRI leaders have been seen by most as puppets of Iran, an unofficial rule existed whereby Badr forces, unlike renegade Mahdi elements, would not engage US troops, most of which were not even based in southern Iraq. In August 2007, Badr units operating as Iraqi security forces routed Mahdi militiamen in Karbala during a two-day fight that resulted in over fifty deaths, with 270 wounded and thousands of fleeing pilgrims.[29] The Shia-on-Shia violence caused Muqtada al-Sadr to call for a six-month ceasefire, which was renewed indefinitely in 2008. American officers and White House neocons have persistently blamed anti-American Shia militia activities on Iranian-based training, equipment, and funding but with very little evidence.

Prime Minister Maliki's rise to national leadership in May 2006 was the product of a typical Iraqi compromise, resting on his militia-free, non-threatening posture which was sufficiently compatible with the polarities of religious ISCI and secular Kurds that one final Sadrist vote pushed him into the premiership. Maliki, a weak Dawa exile, adroitly balanced a teetering government of national unity. He gradually grew in strength and confidence until March 2008, when, to the surprise of US and British troops, his political advisers and military commanders convinced him to rein in Basra's anarchy and attack its criminal gangs, insurgents, Iranian profiteers, and Mahdi militiamen, a military gamble that, with a little help from several embedded American advisers, won him national praise as a strongman.[30] Coercion by Iraq's army, a reconstituted[31] and modernizing national institution,[32] prevailed where previous co-optation and concession-making had failed. This political triumph led to his forming the State of Law coalition in 2008 and subsequent 2009 and 2010 electoral gains. Because of this newfound popularity, Maliki refused to join the 2009 pan-Shia successor to the UIA, the National Iraqi Alliance (NIA).

THE INTERNATIONAL COMMUNITY AND IRAQ'S ELECTORAL FOUNDATIONS

Because of anti-foreign violence by insurgents, members of the international community paid dearly for efforts to strengthen governance institutions in Iraq. On 19 August 2003, twenty-two UN employees were killed in the bombing of UN Baghdad headquarters at the Canal Hotel. In January 2007, the convoy of a National Democratic Institute (NDI) party trainer was ambushed after leaving the IIP office in Baghdad; insurgents killed the American trainer and her three guards. During 2004–05, three local staff of the NDI were assassinated and more than fifteen staff resigned because of death threats.[33]

Democrats in the US Congress demanded that President Bush include the UN in the governance process.[34] However Bremer and myopic White House aides failed to seek counsel from people in Baghdad like UN Special Representative Sérgio de Mello. When in late 2003 the CPA finally realized the face-saving role the UN could play in managing Iraq's governance challenges, UN envoy Lakhdar Brahimi travelled the country to promote compromise. His 23 February 2004 report to the Security Council confirmed an eight-month electoral calendar once a legal framework was in place, which would include an electoral law and election commission, as outlined by CPA Orders 92 and 96.[35]

The UN, CPA, and IGC, along with the International Foundation for Electoral Systems (IFES),[36] established an election commission nominating process that ignored applicant's ethnic and religious identities. After UN vetting of those on the short list and international panel recommendations, commissioners of the Independent Election Commission of Iraq (IECI) were confirmed by the IGC in June. The IECI was comprised of seven voting and two non-voting members, including one woman and the UN's own Carlos Valenzuela, a graduate of sixteen UN electoral missions, who laboured tirelessly to meet training, procurement, logistics, and other deadlines.

Throughout 2005 polling, Iraqis voted under a closed-list, proportional representation system, partly because it afforded candidates the protection of anonymity within registered party lists. Unlike elections in January, where national PR meant that voters received the same national ballot in all provinces, December polls offered voters different national ballots in each province, depending on provincial registration. In March of 2010, the provincial PR system used a more visibly democratic open-list, advocated by several party leaders and Sistani but not the Kurds and ISCI, in which voters could also support a specific person on a party list, which is how thirty-nine of the seventy INA coalition seats were won by Sadrist candidates.

Teams of UN/IECI staff were embedded in logistical operations. Wherever possible, the IECI and UN were able to depend on US military logistics to meet election operation deadlines for delivery of materials, security of election locations and warehoused materials, transport of IECI staff, and election-day security. A team of IECI lawyers collected and reviewed complaints for consideration by a Transitional Electoral Panel of three judges who had been appointed by the Higher Judicial Council. A 2005 IECI investigation into some 100 suspicious ballot boxes from Kurdistan resulted in their being voided. While complaints against the process existed, they originated largely from parties unhappy with results or wishing to dispel the credibility of the process. The credibility of the vote survived throughout 2005, defended by the UN officials involved in investigating complaints.

In January 2007, the Independent High Election Commission (IHEC) was established by law with eight permanent voting members and one non-voting chief electoral officer selected by the Council of Representatives.

Election laws in 2004, 2008, and 2009 guaranteed one-quarter female representation on national and provincial councils. Additionally, a lesson learned from religious-inspired election violence in 2005, the election law of 2009 banned the use of religious symbols in campaign materials, a reaction to the 2005 campaigns by SCIRI and Sadrists, who used poster images of Ayatollahs Sistani and Hakim, and Muqtada al-Sadr's martyred father and uncle.

COMPARING VOTER PARTICIPATION, RESULTS, VIOLENCE, AND OBSERVATION

Following a six-week campaign, voter participation on 30 January 2005 reached 58.9 per cent (including diaspora Iraqis). Three parties dominated the results. The pan-Shia UIA ticket, which united SCIRI, Dawa, Fadhila, and other Shia Islamists and independents, won 140 national seats. The Kurdistan Alliance (KDP, PUK, Kurdish Communists, Turkmen, Kurdistan Islamic Union) took 75 seats and the al-Iraqiya list (Allawi) won 40 seats.[37]

At the provincial level, SCIRI polled highest in five of the nine southern Shia-dominated provinces and appointed six of the nine governors, including Baghdad.[38] Despite a Sunni Arab boycott, the IIP Dayala office chose to ignore the party's official national position and took fourteen seats in Dayala and thirty-four of forty-one seats in Anbar.[39] The boycott meant that Sunni Arabs failed to secure adequate representation on the governorate councils of multicultural provinces like Ninawa, Kirkuk, Dayala, and Baghdad, the first two of which were disproportionately run by Kurds. In 2007, as a means of reconciliation, eight seats were added to the Anbar council to recognize the Sahwa.[40]

The IFES Election Violence Education and Resolution (EVER) project to monitor political and election violence recorded 141 confirmed cases of election-related violence in Iraq between 12 December 2004 and 15 February 2005, corroborated by two independent sources. There were 38 incidents on election day, 59 per cent of which occurred in the Baghdad region. The number of election-related victims included 84 killed and 167 wounded, over 80 per cent of whom were in the Baghdad region. Targets or victims of violence included 93 election offices, 13 election workers, 26 election security agents, 8 election monitors, 36 voters, and 30 party members or candidates. Insurgents were blamed for over 90 per cent of casualties. Only 14 incidents were the result of party-on-party violence.

In the 15 December 2005 national polls, there were nineteen party coalitions and voter participation increased to 76.4 per cent, with the highest rates of voter participation still in Kurdish and Shia areas. The 275 seats were filled as follows: UIA (including Sadrists), 128; KA, 53; Tawafuq coalition (including IIP), 44; Allawi's al-Iraqiya list, 25; Saleh al-Mutlaq's Hiwar, 11; KIU, 5. Others accounted for the remaining 9 seats.

There were no international observers in Iraq during any 2005 polls, despite the efforts of the International Mission for Iraqi Elections (IMIE) which was based in Jordan and funded by Canada. The European Union refused to deploy observers. The Election Information Network (EIN), an Iraqi non-partisan non-governmental organization formed in 2004 that united over 150 Iraqi civic groups and was funded and trained by the NDI in Washington,[41] deployed almost 10,000 accredited local monitors, who covered 80 per cent of all polling centres.

The EVER project revealed that insurgent-related election violence decreased significantly after January, and had little impact on voting. Victims of election-related violence included 86 killed and 166 wounded. Targets included 6 kidnapped individuals, 48 polling stations, 33 party members, 30 election security agents, 28 party supporters, 21 voters, and 19 party offices. Among corroborated perpetrators of violence were 43 cases attributed to Iraq state agents and 30 to party supporters. The most violent provinces were Baghdad, Anbar, Sulaimaniya, Karbala, Erbil, Ninawa, and Dayala.

While voter participation in the January 2009 provincial polls averaged just over 50 per cent, all communities fielded independent candidates, parties, and coalitions, thus acknowledging the importance that a majority of citizens attribute to the democratic process. Voter participation would have been higher had voting procedures for internally displaced persons been better organized. In the fourteen voting provinces in January 2009, none of the incumbents from the 2005 provincial elections maintained their popular support, a clear indication of public dissatisfaction with failed levels of community service and disgust at corrupt, self-serving local party leaders elected in 2005. The biggest winner overall was Prime Minister Maliki's State of Law (SOL) coalition, which gained the largest number of votes in nine of the fourteen provinces, including 38 per cent in Baghdad and 37 per cent in Basra.[42] Al-Iraqiya came in second in Shia-majority Salahdin Province, home to Saddam's Tikriti tribe.

Overall, while the electoral period saw the killing of nine candidates[43] and intimidation of electoral commission staff, the exercise was applauded by the special representative of the UN secretary-general as "marked with very low levels of violence especially on the actual day of the elections when hardly any incidents of violence were reported, compared with over eighty serious security incidents on the election day in January 2005."[44]

Following over three months of post-election backroom negotiations typical of Iraqi political behaviour, talks concluded with Maliki's SOL coalition seating seven governors (Baghdad, Basra, Qadisiya, Karbala, Wasit, Dhi Qar, and Maysan) and four provincial chairs (Baghdad, Basra, Qadisiya, and Najaf).

By January 2009, the IHEC had accredited 83,000 observers, 43,000 of whom had been trained by the United Nations Assistance Mission in Iraq (UNAMI).[45] The IHEC received some 2,000 complaints, all satisfactorily investigated by a committee of jurists and specialists.[46] According to IHEC figures,[47] provinces with the highest percentages of valid votes were all in northern and central areas, indicating Shia community apathy and a significantly re-energized Sunni Arab vote since 2005, a dividend of the surge.

INTRA- NOT ANTI-ARAB KURDISH VIOLENCE

In Kurdistan, the January 2005 regional elections saw the KDP and PUK dominate the vote with 37 seats each. In both 2005 and 2009, regional elections to the Kurdish National Assembly (KNA) were marred by rural thuggery and by Kurdistan Alliance threats to state employees, who risked job losses or transfers.

In the December 2005 national polls, in the strongest display of inter-party violence, the KIU paid a price for not joining the KA. On 6 December, KDP agents killed four KIU party members, including a candidate, during coordinated attacks on nine KIU party offices, Zakho and Dahuk included. The investigation by IFES and NDI officials in Erbil showed that the KIU was attacked because it had decided, in contrast to the previous January, not to join the KA (The KIU later won five Baghdad parliament seats.) The attacks on the KIU were publicly denounced in press releases by the US, UK, and UN and reached the front page of the *Washington Post*.[48]

During the July 2009 regional elections, twenty-five Kurdish parties presented lists and had candidates who actively campaigned. The two incumbent parties abused their access to public resources such as media, security, and public places. The Kurdish (KDP and PUK) list and the newly created Goran (Change) list attracted the most campaigners, followed by the Service and Reform list of two Islamic and two leftist parties, also called the KIU coalition. Some fighting was witnessed between Kurdish and Goran list members, including both sides tearing up each other's banners. As in December 2005, the Erbil offices of the KIU were attacked by hundreds of Kurdish supporters, an incident pacified by the governor himself.[49]

By July, 321 international supervisors from Arab and foreign countries were accredited. The IHEC received 450 complaints and conducted investigations into 90 per cent of them.[50] With voter participation reaching 79 per cent, Massoud Barzani predictably won the presidency with 69.8 per cent support. The Kurdish list, however, dropped from its 2005 85 per cent to 57.3 per cent and fifty-nine seats, followed by the Goran list of former PUK deputy and media baron Nawshirwan Mustafa, which won 23.75 per cent and twenty-five seats, and the Service and Reform list, which garnered 12.8 per cent and fourteen seats.[51]

Kurdistan's regional political colours had blossomed in 2009. Compared to December 2005 when all Kurdish parties, except the KIU, united under one ticket, no such alliance materialized in 2009. Five political parties publicly disagreed with KA policies and practices. Because Kurds now enjoyed constitutional power in a federal Iraq, Goran's popular campaign focused not on the usual Arab-bashing of the past but on the delivery of local services, eliminating corruption, and the economy, issues that attracted a growing educated middle class.[52]

THE 2010 NATIONAL CAMPAIGN

From the moment the 2009 provincial election results were announced, the campaign to recruit coalition partners for the national elections began among over 295 registered political parties and independent candidates. After two failed attempts, parliamentarians passed an election law on 6 December that saw all votes by diaspora Iraqis (in sixteen countries) counted with regard to provincial seat allocations instead of through the assigning of extra-national compensatory seats. Only 5 per cent of 325 COR seats (15 seats) were not assigned to provinces: 8 reserved for minorities and 7 compensatory seats for parties with a national support base. The serious reduction in compensatory seats – 45 seats in late 2005 – disadvantaged parties with national cross-cultural reach, such as that previously enjoyed by Allawi's coalition, and benefitted provincial concentration. More importantly, the politically motivated banning of over 500 candidates by the NIA-dominated De-Baathification Commission marred polls.

The 7 March election witnessed 62.4 per cent voter participation, producing the following results: Allawi's nationalist secular al-Iraqiya list, 91 seats (including 12 in Southern Shia provinces) and 28 per cent of total votes cast; Maliki's nationalist Shia State of Law coalition, 89 seats and 27.4 percent; the Iraqi National Alliance of Hakim, al-Sadr, Ibrahim al-Jaafari, and Ahmed Chalabi, 70 seats (of which Sadrists took 39 thanks to the new open list system) and 21.5 per cent; the Kurdistan Alliance, 43 seats and 13.2 percent; Goran (based in Kurdistan and running in ten provinces), 8 seats; the Tawafuq coalition, 6 seats; the KIU coalition, 4 seats. The formation of a government requires support from a total of representatives elected in 163 seats.

On 3 June 2010, the UN Security Council issued a press statement commending the work of Iraq's IHEC and the support given it by UNAMI, and condemning terrorist attacks. The 1 June certification of results by Iraq's Supreme Court was delayed at the request of incumbent Prime Minister Maliki, who demanded a Baghdad city recount and ordered a court challenge of suspected Baathist candidates, a recount whose credibility was witnessed by UNAMI officials.

None of Maliki's verified complaints changed the fact that Allawi's faction had taken ninety-one seats and thus deserved the first chance to seek out coalition partners. Allawi himself was later rebuked by Grand Ayatollah Ali al-Sistani for having warned of civil war if his bloc was denied power. By June, four al-Iraqiya list members belonging to the winning coalition of former Prime Minister Ayad Allawi had been killed, three in the Mosul area.[53] Never appearing in public for safety concerns, Allawi has had to turn to the Americans to provide increased security measures around his home.[54]

In elections that the Islamic State of Iraq, an insurgent group, vowed to disrupt, at least two candidates were killed, while bombs struck four political party headquarters in Baghdad as well as a candidate's home in Ramadi.[55] The Goran list recorded at least seven attacks on its members, including one fatality and the torching of a Goran parliamentarian's office.[56] Prior to the campaign period, in coordinated attacks on 26 January, three major Baghdad hotels were struck, although no party or election officials were directly targeted. It was the fourth similar al-Qaeda-style mass bombing attack since August, all directly targeting government facilities and ministries. Christian minorities and their churches in Mosul were particularly targeted, forcing hundreds of families to flee.

The 2010 poll was a major logistical exercise under conditions of insecurity. According to UNAMI, 657 international observers were accredited, 115,000 Iraqi observers, 476,000 Iraqi political party agents, and some 2,000 foreign and local journalists.[57] Over 300,000 Iraqis worked for the IHEC. In Kirkuk alone, 141 members of the press watched the polls, while embassy staff from the US and Turkey joined a British NGO and some 2,000 observers in covering 230 polling stations.[58] The 2005 Declaration of Principles for International Election Observation acknowledges the limits of observation by international experts: "Election observation is a civilian activity, and its utility is questionable in circumstances that present severe security risks, limit safe deployments of observers, or otherwise would negate employing credible election observation methods."[59]

THE PROSPECTS OF CONTINUED VIOLENCE

Given the results of the 2009 and 2010 elections, and the still-awaited provincial polls of Kirkuk, heightened tensions between Kurds, non-Kurds, and a hesitant Baghdad government remain. Four years of disproportionate Kurdistan Alliance seats in two out of three northern provincial councils now publicly reflect demographic realities. The IHEC increased COR seat numbers in Baghdad and Ninawa. The Kirkuk situation remains unresolved with twenty-six of forty-one seats under Kurdish control.[60] While voters in Ninawa and Dayala dealt a serious blow to KA support in 2009 and 2010, this was much more a predicted normalization, a "natural redressing of the imbalance" created by the Sunni boycott of 2005.[61] Maliki had only once visited Kurdistan as prime minister, in August 2009 to meet and congratulate newly elected Kurdish President Massoud Barzani (elected unopposed in 2006 by the Kurdistan parliament).

In addition to shifting more troops to the US base in Kirkuk, US Army General Raymond Odierno had also received support from both Maliki and Barzani to move troops into Ninawa and disputed territories as a confidence-building measure. American-coordinated joint patrols of Kurdish and Iraqi troops at twenty-three checkpoints, twelve in Ninawa alone, along the unofficial "trigger line" between mixed Kurdish and Arab districts have continued since early 2010.[62] Iraqi army officers in Kirkuk continue to integrate four brigades of Kurdish forces into a national security framework, as agreed to by

Baghdad and Erbil leaders under US support.⁶³ UNAMI has also sponsored confidence-building talks between al-Hadba and the Kurdistan Alliance in Ninawa since the March elections.⁶⁴

Kurdish-Arab tensions since 2009 have dissipated in 2010, due not only to American and UN actions but also to the new mosaic of local politics in particular, framed by a Goran-led opposition and a new Baghdad-experienced Kurdish prime minister, Barhim Saleh, the former Iraqi deputy prime minister. Goran has rejected Jalal Talabani's renewal as Iraqi president in favour of a more conflict-mitigating measure that proposes a rotating presidency⁶⁵ as found in the 2003 IGC, the European Union, the UN General Assembly, and Bosnia and Herzegovina.

CONFLICT MITIGATION BY INSTITUTIONAL DESIGN

Iraq's new institutional framework, an asymmetrical parliamentary federation (as in Canada, Spain, and Sudan) elected by proportional representation and guaranteeing seats to women and minorities, embodies the principles of power sharing, concession-making, and coalition building. It encourages factions to participate in elections and policy debate through a system of checks and balances that mandates against exclusion. The most preferred electoral system in new post-Cold War democracies is the proportional representation (PR) system. In divided societies, PR is the optimal choice for ensuring broad representation.⁶⁶ The open list provincial PR option responds to the old argument by first-past-the-post (majoritarian) proponents that PR removes the relationship between voter and lawmaker, and thus reduces voters' ability to keep their own representative accountable and accessible. (Sadrists proved the irrelevance of that argument.) While PR systems are more likely to result in coalition governments, states using the list PR system have been rated as being twice as democratic as those using majoritarian systems.⁶⁷

One conflict-mitigating feature lost to Iraqis after the 2010 polls but tailored to societies seeking minority guarantees and ways to avoid the tyranny of the majority was a transitional, veto-wielding, tripartite Iraqi presidency,⁶⁸ whereby, unofficially but customarily, each of the three presidency council members – the president and two deputies – represented one of the three main Iraqi communities⁶⁹ and each had veto powers to reject parliamentary bills. Under the present system, the presidency council loses veto powers.[70] Accommodations must now depend upon inclusive parliamentary behaviour[71] and a balance of ministerial appointments.

On 12 November, Iraq's top three political positions were confirmed simultaneously, with Maliki again prime minister, Talabani again president, and Osama al-Nujaifi[72] (whose brother was elected governor of Ninawa under the al-Hadba banner) as Speaker of the COR. Allawi has been appeased by a new post as head of a National Council on Strategic Policies pending COR approval. Finally, on 21 December, a large thirty-four-seat cabinet not unlike that assigned by the CPA in 2004 was approved by parliament.[73]

As affirmed by the new Iraq, scholars have argued that parliamentary systems are more stable than presidential systems with their exaggerated winner-take-all concentration of executive powers. A constitutional vesting of powers in legislatures also spurs the development of political parties and concession-making.[74] Federal systems, the majority of which provide for upper chambers,[75] provide autonomy to geographic minorities while facilitating multiple national and other identities. Federalism is the oldest governance model for managing conflicts between ethnic and other groups.[76] For the above institutional reasons, the Iraqi state shows democratic promise.

CONCLUSION

While analyzing Iraq's electoral conduct since 2005, this chapter has challenged the position of some critics that Iraq's democratic progress remains unconsolidated, violence-plagued, foreign-directed, and temporary. Elections in Iraq have been possible because most Iraqis wanted them and have accepted their results as legitimate, a position supported by impartial UN efforts and by an Iraqi Supreme Court decision that confirmed the 2010 results.

No voter should ever be required to participate in elections during conflict. But calls to boycott fall on deaf ears when a multi-ethnic majority desires elections and only certain armed and politicized players prefer further delays, conveniently claiming they are necessary because of an apparently obstructionist occupation and an insurgency partially of their own creation. The international community and all other Iraqi coalitions prepared for elections, as determined by an UN-led consultative process. The 2005 election timeline stood firm, not only due to a strict US political agenda but especially because Grand Ayatollah al-Sistani had issued two fatwas to preserve Iraqi interests from anti-democratic American designs.

Throughout all Iraqi elections since early 2005, voters belonging to updated registries benefited from numerous choices of accredited candidates and political entities listed on foreign-printed tamper-proof ballots created based on credible and debated election laws managed by professional and impartial election commissions supported by international expertise and observed by trained domestic election observers striving for global standards of democratic practice. Unlike Afghanistan and Kenya, Iraq's elections have been neither flawed nor illegitimate, nor a stimulus to violence.

Given the formation of coalitions even at the provincial level, leaders are forced to use pragmatism and flexibility in the design of party platforms and policymaking in order to attract larger pools of voters and pass legislation. National and provincial polls in 2009 and 2010 with open list PR systems have encouraged greater political choice, transparency, and electoral legitimacy when compared to both 2005 polls. Four new parties and coalitions have joined the contest since 2005, including State of Law (nationally) and three local parties with significant regional and national impact: Goran (Kurdistan), al-Hadba (Ninawa), and Sahwa (Anbar). Unlike earlier Tehran-influenced pronouncements by SCIRI and Islamic Dawa that elections are contrary to sharia law, or only a Western ideal, Islamic parties have fully embraced the democratic process.

As recommended in the chapter by Reilly, holding local elections in 2009 was a serious advantage for the preparation and coordination of political and social forces in 2010. Iraq's new political culture and framework as a federal parliamentary system has given voters greater proximity to representation, access to local government services, and a way to accommodate ethnic and religious identities parallel to a common national framework. Iraq has, however, failed miserably at Reilly's second function of democracy, the rapid forming of a government, which in 2010 took nine and one-half months.

Compared with 2005 voting exercises, which were dominated by religious coalitions and regional identities, the polls of 2009 and 2010 reawakened Iraqi tendencies for more national, moderate, and even secular ideals, particular hallmarks of Iraq before the war with Iran. Coalition building and backroom inter-factional deal-making are practices that are far from new to Iraqi politics. The Iraqi experience with democracy during five years of public policy debate has, although slowly and with moments of violence, channelled political tensions into the formation of coalitions while mitigating concerns about the long-term viability of the state, one whose political maturity does not depend on foreign troops. While complaints and irregularities existed for all polls, the polls all met international standards of conduct with the general will of the people being reflected.

Although party campaigns during all elections remained limited in terms of use of the media, Internet, text messaging, and so on because of security factors, an increasingly informed and media-savvy Iraqi society commensurate with its educational standards nevertheless permitted informed voting to take place. Intimidation existed, not only given security fears but because incumbents, advantaged by their access to state bodyguards, remained reluctant to share the mantle of power. This was evident even in the safety of Kurdistan where credible observers continued to witness the use of intimidation by entrenched Kurdish parties frustrated by democratic newcomers.

Both Maliki and Allawi have portrayed themselves as strongmen deploying state and American military resources to kill anti-democracy forces. While Allawi transferred power willingly in early 2005, his Dawa Party successors, Jaafari in 2006 and Maliki in 2010, have failed to respect their leadership responsibilities and concede defeat, following the practice of leaders in violent societies. For some, conceding defeat honourably on camera portrays weakness.

Iraq's strongman culture remains very popular. Post-invasion polls have revealed a simultaneous desire for strong leadership and democratic practices. In moments of violence, the call for strength has taken precedence. Many Iraqis hold to this strongman culture while expecting more accountable and accessible representation, without corruption and violence, in the long term. Both are possible.

4

Democracy in Africa: Rumours of Its Demise Have Been Greatly Exaggerated

CHRISTIAN R. HENNEMEYER

Inordinate attention is paid to elections in Africa because, to paraphrase Samuel Johnson, they concentrate the mind wonderfully. Politicians, donors, and the media tend to focus unduly on the simple act of casting ballots, and in the most contentious races international electoral observers often enjoy star status for a brief period. But the event of an election cannot be considered in isolation. It is merely one piece in the democratic puzzle, albeit an important one. Studying polls without considering the environment in which they are held is meaningless. Media freedom, literacy rates, security, political opposition, the state of the judiciary, and the role of women and minorities are just a few of the many elements that influence the conduct and outcome of elections. As one American political operative used to put it, "only amateurs steal elections on election day."[1]

FIRST THE GOOD NEWS

While there is certainly much room for improvement in the conduct of African elections, some historical perspective is useful. For, as unsatisfactory as the majority of African electoral processes remain, they are in nearly all cases superior to the coup d'état, one of the more popular means of political change on the continent since independence. Coups, while invariably elaborately justified by their leaders as necessary for the health of democracy, are usually a front for self-enrichment by the junta, and often a means of settling ethnic or regional scores. While there are a handful of examples of coups resulting in political progress and economic growth – Jerry Rawlings in Ghana and Amadou Touré in Mali come to mind – most were at best corrupt and at worst disastrous. According to Monty Marshall, from 1959 to 2005 there were some 293 successful or attempted coups d'état in sub-Saharan Africa. While they have affected all regions of the continent, and include Anglophone, Francophone, and Lusophone countries, coups and *coups manqués* have been most common in West Africa.

Recent coups in Mauritania, the Republic of Guinea, Madagascar, and Niger, as well as reported attempts in Guinea Bissau and the Central African Republic, have raised fears of a resurgence of armed takeovers. Indeed, the UN Security Council noted in April of 2009 that "a pattern of unconstitutional changes in government has been re-emerging in Africa over the last several months."[2]

While this recent uptick merits serious attention, the reality is that most African nations now hold regular, scrutinized elections as a matter of course, in large part because of strong international and African condemnation of coups. During the Cold War, both the West and the Organization of African Unity (OAU) were notably discreet when it came to speaking out against undemocratic change. In 1989, then-President George H.W. Bush described Zairian dictator Mobutu Sese Seko, who had taken power by force in 1965 and remained there by electoral fraud, as "one of our most valued friends [on the] entire continent of Africa."[3] Contrast this warmth with the blunt reaction of the head of the AU (African Union, successor to the OAU) to the recent military takeover in Niger, a coup that many observers viewed as having some legitimacy: "The Chairperson of the Commission stresses that the relevant AU instruments systematically condemn any unconstitutional change and, accordingly, he condemns the seizure of power by force that took place in Niger."[4]

The Economic Community of West African States (ECOWAS) used similarly uncompromising language, declaring that "in accordance with its Protocol on Democracy and Good Governance [it] rejects any change of power through unconstitutional means and violence."[5]

Parenthetically, one by-product of the African coup is "big man syndrome," in which the leader becomes the personification of the state, and the citizenry is expected to obey without question. Historically, examples of this are legion and range from the good (Nelson Mandela) to the awful (Mobutu Sese Seko). Fortunately, this trend, like the coups that spawned it, seems to be weakening.

GREAT EXPECTATIONS

Difficult in even the oldest democracies, elections in Africa pose even greater challenges. First, it should go without saying that Africa's colonial era, which lasted longer than on any other continent, did nothing to sow the seeds of democratic practice. On the contrary, to varying degrees, British, French, Belgian, Portuguese, and Spanish rule stifled or pre-empted political parties, trade unions, ethnic and professional associations, and the press until the eleventh hour, leaving most newly independent countries ill suited to self-government. A stunning example of European blindness was the 1955 release of the quasi-official "Van Bilsen Plan," which posited a period of thirty years for the "political emancipation" of the Belgian Congo. Less than five years later, the Congo gained its independence and predictable turmoil ensued. A more recent example was Margaret Thatcher's characterization in 1987 of the African National Congress as "a typical terrorist organization,"[6] just three years before future President Nelson Mandela was released from prison.

Furthermore, the hypocrisy of Western nations trumpeting their democratic credentials while embracing some of Africa's least democratic leaders was obvious to educated Africans and generated a certain cynicism toward "democracy promotion" efforts. The United States' support of President Samuel Doe, who came to power in a bloody coup, is an example remembered by many middle-aged Africans. As the *New York Times* reported in Doe's obituary: "Amid the charges of human rights abuses and corruption, Mr Doe maintained a good relationship with the Reagan Administration, which maintained that he was steering Liberia toward democracy. Liberia was the largest per capita recipient of United States aid in the sub-Sahara from 1980 to 1985."[7]

With the fall of the Berlin Wall, there was great pressure from both inside and outside Africa for more political openness and inclusivity, and a wave of "national conferences," designed to discuss a country's political future, hit many traditionally undemocratic francophone states, including Benin, Cameroon, both Congos, Togo, and so on. Similar, somewhat less ambitious gatherings were held in Ethiopia, Somalia, and Namibia. Embraced as the panacea for all the ills that preceded it, electoral democracy now faced another serious challenge:

that of wildly exaggerated and unrealistic expectations. Understandably, given the simplistic emphasis placed on them by the international community, for many Africans elections and democracy have become synonymous. Thus the failure of the former implies a failure of the latter. A 2007 Afrobarometer working paper puts it thus: "Election is a means for realising some of the core values of democracy, especially the participation of the citizen in governance and the accountability of leaders. The quality of election therefore provides [an] indicator of the extent to which democratic governance has been consolidated in society. Given the intricate relationship between election and democracy, measurement of democracy is often conflated with the measurement of election quality."[8]

Nevertheless, recent surveys by Afrobarometer show that the majority of Africans throughout the continent reject military rule and in growing numbers continue to demand democracy, though many remain unsatisfied with its results. As the great Nigerian writer and activist Wole Soyinka has said of his people, "they're beginning to recognize the fact that there's nothing more secure than a democratic, accountable, and participatory form of government. But it's sunk in only theoretically; it has not yet sunk in completely in practical terms."[9]

THE CONFLICTUAL CONTINENT?

Africa is routinely viewed as the continent of conflict and chaos. In one sense, this is unfair; certainly Europe and Asia have far bloodier modern histories. World Wars I and II and the predations of Stalin and Mao have no parallels in Africa. Nonetheless, many of the world's recent conflicts have occurred in Africa, and in all of them civilians have been the primary victims. In the 1970s and 1980s, superpower rivalries, apartheid, and ethnic rivalry were some of the midwives to vicious wars in Angola, Ethiopia/Eritrea, Mozambique, Namibia, and Rhodesia. The 1990s saw the Rwandan genocide and two Congolese wars, as well as deadly civil conflicts in Liberia, Sierra Leone, Côte d'Ivoire, and Burundi. In this decade, we've been treated to Darfur, Somalia, and the eastern Congo's continued meltdowns, and many lesser conflicts in places like Guinea-Bissau, Uganda, Kenya, Nigeria, Congo-Brazzaville, and Chad. An exhaustive list would include several other places, but much of Africa remains remarkably prone to unrest and bloodshed.

Although their relative importance is debated, the roots of African conflict are widely accepted: imperialism, decolonization, tribalism, regionalism, religion, extractive assets, and so on. And what of elections? Are they catalysts for conflict or consolidators of peace? The answer is, it depends.

ELECTIONS AS CONSOLIDATORS OF PEACE

While there are worthy competitors such as Angola, Burundi, and Sierra Leone, without a doubt the most lauded recent African election was that of Liberia in 2005. There are many reasons for the pride taken by both Liberians and external agents in this poll. For one thing, it marked the end of a truly terrible sixteen years for the country, a period rife with war, terror, corruption, and decline. In addition, both contestants were apparent paragons of virtue: one was a wise female technocrat, the other a world-renowned footballer. In the end, the victor was former banker and World Bank official Ellen Johnson-Sirleaf, the continent's first-ever woman president. The elections were peaceful and largely honest and the unanimous conclusion was that Liberians had learned to settle political disputes by ballot rather than by bullet.

However, it is worth pointing out that similar pride was taken in the 1997 elections, in which Johnson-Sirleaf placed a distant second to strongman (and now indicted war criminal) Charles Taylor. The highly reputed Carter Center's electoral observation report read: "To fully understand them, Liberia's 1997 elections must be placed in the context of the country's long civil war and recent peace process. Although the elections had some serious problems, including overwhelming advantage enjoyed by Charles Taylor in terms of resources, access to media, and organization, they still marked a critical step forward in consolidating peace."[10]

The European Union report was even less nuanced in its comprehension, blithely stating that "the 8 November presidential run-off election has so far been peaceful and generally well administered, consolidating the achievements of the 11 October elections and advancing the process of returning Liberia to a normal functioning state. Voters were provided with a choice between two candidates in a genuinely competitive election process."[11]

This was, of course, the election in which Taylor supporters' slogan was "He killed my ma. He killed my pa. I'm going to vote for him!"

Less than two years after the votes were cast, the second Liberian civil war had begun and didn't end until Taylor's resignation and flight into exile in August 2003.

The hopes of 1997 for a new Liberia rising from the ashes of the destruction and despotism were misplaced for one basic reason: the man who started the war in 1989 was still in power. In a larger sense, fundamental questions of political life, the redress of grievances, and human rights had been neither discussed nor resolved. The belated conclusion for Liberia and her friends was that while elections can indeed consolidate peace, they cannot make peace. Making peace requires doing difficult things for which elections are completely inadequate: addressing sources of conflict, negotiating treaties, demobilizing combatants, promoting peace and reconciliation efforts, undertaking reconstruction and rehabilitation, investing in long-term economic and social development, and so on. Fortunately, the Liberian government and the international community had generally learned these lessons by the 2005 election. Nonetheless, there is little doubt that without massive external aid – from the UN, US, EU, ECOWAS, and others – Liberia would have been financially and logistically unable to conduct a credible election or take steps to manage the postwar period. Pointing to the 2005 polls as a Liberian triumph overlooks this reality. The mechanics were essentially an international affair in which most Liberians were secondary players (similar to the 2002 postwar elections in Sierra Leone).

However, even with such robust external assistance, Liberia's elections could have quickly turned to farce or tragedy had critical local ingredients been missing: in particular, an honest and competent electoral commission, candidates who respected the rules of the game, and a determination on the part of ordinary Liberians to avoid the missteps of the past. An Afrobarometer survey on Liberia released in late 2009 reveals some encouraging findings, including that while "only half of respondents are satisfied with the performance of democracy so far … large majorities are satisfied with election quality and report that basic freedoms are being effectively protected."[12] In a very real sense, this mixed scorecard reveals an attitude toward electoral democracy – far from perfect, but better than the alternatives – that is encouragingly comparable to that of many in established democracies.

"SELECTIONS"

Unlike Liberia, most African countries, of course, are not emerging from civil war. Nonetheless, other forms of tacit and active conflict profoundly influence the way elections are conducted and the way their outcomes are perceived. There is no better example of this than Nigeria, where politically minded citizens have coined political neologisms found nowhere else in the world, including words like "demoncrazy" for democracy, and "selections" for elections. This cynicism has deep roots in the country's post-independence history, which has seen fifteen attempted or successful coups, a number topped only by Sudan. Of Nigeria's first seven heads of state from 1960 to 1985, six were either overthrown in coups d'état or assassinated.

The divisions in Nigerian society are so numerous and so deep that its dissolution as a state has been predicted for decades. As recently as March 2010, Muammar Gaddafi, the chairman of the African Union just months before, proposed that the country be split into northern Muslim and southern Christian halves to stop the constant bloodshed and sectarian strife. Tension between Islam and Christianity is but one source of violence, one that some argue is manufactured or at least manipulated. Other problems include ethnic affiliation (the CIA's World Fact Book reports that Nigeria has 250 ethnic groups[13]), persistent and widespread poverty despite enormous oil wealth, the encroachment of armed jihadists, and governmental corruption and incompetence.

The magnitude of this last problem – corruption and incompetence – is tellingly illustrated by the appalling management and conduct of Nigerian elections. Traditionally dominated by the president's office, the Nigerian electoral body, known as the Independent National Electoral Commission or INEC, has rarely acted with real autonomy. Financially dependent on State House, subject to political interference, often poorly led and staffed, INEC has consistently failed to deliver credible elections. Consider the words of the European Parliament on the 2007 elections, affirming that "the Nigerian people are entitled to new credible elections, to be held under a truly independent and efficient Independent National Electoral Commission" and that "currently the INEC is not able to meet the organisational and logistical challenges it faces."[14]

Even the United States government, which has generally been quite tolerant of the electoral shenanigans of its strategic partner and major source of oil, recently felt compelled to denounce the ongoing charade. Speaking before Congress in February of 2010, US Assistant Secretary of State for African Affairs Johnnie Carson did not mince words: "I urged Nigeria's leaders to make electoral reform one of Nigeria's highest priorities. Nigeria's Independent National Electoral Commission (INEC) has performed poorly over the past decade and has not served the country well."[15]

It appears that the Nigerian leadership was listening, for in April of 2010, acting President Goodluck Jonathan finally sacked the unpopular head of the electoral commission, Maurice Iwu. Whether this alone will create a sea change is unclear.

The theory was that each election that followed the end of military rule in 1999 was supposed to be better than the one before. The election of 2003 was supposed to have been a vast improvement on that of 1999, and that of 2007 was intended to be the best yet, demonstrating Nigeria's dramatic political evolution. In reality, no such progress occurred; indeed, there are grounds for asserting the contrary, that elections have actually become less competitive and less legitimate.

The techniques used by Nigeria are common in developing (and some developed) nations. Many are listed in a 2008 article called "How to Steal an Election without Breaking a Sweat": control the process, manipulate the media, keep the observers out, misreport results, and foster incompetence and chaos.[16]

Yet was it ever realistic to expect honest elections in a country infamous for its political and financial chicanery? West Africa's greatest novelist, Chinua Achebe, put it succinctly: "Nigeria is what it is because its leaders are not what they should be." Year after year, Nigeria ranks in the lowest 25 percentile in Transparency International's Corruption Perceptions Index.[17] From traffic police to cabinet ministers, government employees are simply assumed to be on the take. Two senior officials viewed by many as honest, the former head of the anti-corruption unit and the minister of the state capital territory, were sacked from their positions and hounded out of the country. Following a 2009 visit, US Secretary of State Hillary Clinton described graft in Nigeria with one word: "unbelievable." Expecting INEC to swim in this toxic sea without being poisoned is naive.

Horrifyingly to honest Nigerians, General Ibrahim Babangida, one of the country's former military rulers, whose eight years in office were infamous for waste and corruption, has announced that he will be running for the presidency in 2011. Nevertheless, the situation is far from hopeless. There are several ways of improving, if not reforming, electoral politics in places like Nigeria.

First, political allies, trading partners, and donors must not be shy about using their influence. As politically incorrect as it may sound, democratic progress in Africa would not have advanced as swiftly as it has over the past two decades without robust external assistance. This support has usually taken the form of financial and technical assistance, but in the Nigerias of this world, some governmental arm-twisting may also be called for. The Obama administration, for example, has been slow to distinguish itself from its predecessor on African issues: one way to do so would be to put democracy promotion and human rights high on the list of policy priorities.

Second, there are technical interventions that can enhance electoral performance around the margins. Working with local advocacy groups to lobby for political finance reform can provide the legal basis for challenging the corrupting power of money in politics. Training political party members and civil society representatives in conflict mitigation techniques can reduce the potential for violence during the run-up to elections. Organizing parallel vote counts by civil society groups using text messaging can help keep the election officials and candidates honest, or at least constrain fraud. And encouraging institutional mentoring with other electoral management bodies within the region can be as productive as and notably less sensitive than partnering with organizations from Western nations.

Third, African regional bodies such as the AU, ECOWAS, the Southern African Development Community (SADC), and the SADC Parliamentary Forum can play key roles. Even the less politically active East African Community (EAC) and Communauté Économique des Pays des Grands Lacs (CEPGL) could be useful in holding member states to higher standards of electoral conduct, governance, and human rights.

As noted earlier, it is indisputable that elections alone do not make democracy. Particularly in sub-Saharan Africa, without activist citizens' groups militating and monitoring, national paths will be carved by governments alone, with predictably dismal results. Therefore, the recent, rapid growth of vibrant civil society organizations and bold human rights groups throughout Africa is not only impressive but also imperative. Even more phenomenal has been the proliferation of media and information technology. Huge numbers of Africans today can listen to private radio broadcasts, watch satellite television, communicate by cellphone with faraway friends, and surf the web. Contrast this with twenty years ago when most people had but one source for information – their government-sponsored radio or television station.

Stanford University's Larry Diamond puts it this way: "In the half-century since decolonization began, there have never been so many democracies and so much public pressure on democracy's behalf. Civil society has never been stronger, mass publics have never been so questioning and vigilant, and the natural impulse toward the reassertion of predatory personal rule has never faced so many constraints."[18]

In a more general sense, there have also been encouraging signs of independence from certain legislatures in several African countries. For example, in Kenya, Malawi, and Nigeria, parliaments have stymied presidential attempts to lift term limits. Although unsuccessful, opposition elements in the South African parliament recently attempted a vote of no confidence in President Jacob Zuma, significant in that this was the first such motion since the start of black majority rule. While progress on the judicial front has been notably less impressive, high courts do at times rule against the status quo, mainly in the former British colonies. Although Robert Mugabe has done his best to intimidate and emasculate his judiciary, Zimbabwean high court judges have had a history of acting autonomously.

OTHER ELECTORAL FARCES

The year 2010 was a busy one for African electoral officials, with sixteen countries holding presidential or legislative elections, or running referenda. Some were foregone conclusions, like Rwanda where the ruling Rwandan Patriotic Front gave President Paul Kagame another term in office with 95 per cent of the vote. Kagame is an icon to no small number of Rwandans who remember the genocide, but his victory also owes something to an ugly campaign of violence and intimation against the opposition, which included, among other things, the assassination of an investigative journalist and the decapitation of the vice-chairman of the Democratic Green Party.

Other predictable outcomes on the horizon are the probable re-elections of Blaise Campaoré in Burkina Faso (in office since 1987) and Côte d'Ivoire's Laurent Gbagbo, although one should recall that Gbagbo has postponed elections in his country every year since 2005.

Some elections, like Guinea's, were supposed to have signalled real democratic progress. With no history of free elections, the country held peaceful presidential polls in June, and the runoff between the two finalists was scheduled for September. Less than a week before election day, the polling was postponed after an astonishing series of events that included the death in hospital of the head of the electoral commission, shortly after he had been convicted of fraud.

Another country that was to have consolidated its short democratic tradition with free and fair national elections in 2010 was Burundi, but when all opposition candidates pulled out of the race, following a spate of grenade attacks and allegations of fraud, the incumbent Pierre Nkurunziza naturally won.

There will, of course, be some credible elections on the continent, such as those of Tanzania and São Tomé and Principe, but these will be in the minority. Most African elections in 2010 fall short of true democratic standards.

BACKSLIDING

As noted, there are still enormous swaths of the continent where democratic evolution is actively thwarted by the state. Some nations flirt with democratization but are ultimately unwilling to seize the brass ring: Nigeria since the return of civilian rule and Côte d'Ivoire in its current chaos fall into this category. Others are more open about their disdain for the messy, complicated process of democracy. Three of sub-Saharan Africa's largest countries – Ethiopia, Sudan, and the Democratic Republic of the Congo, comprising almost 25 per cent of the region's population – fall squarely into the non-democratic camp, although in somewhat different ways. Political thinker Thomas Carothers of the Carnegie Endowment underscores the challenges posed by these countries when he notes: "The remaining authoritarian or totalitarian governments are the survivors – the adaptable, clever ones, the economically successful ones, the resistant ones – who learned how to avoid being swept away by the third wave of democracy. They present a much deeper challenge to democracy promoters than did many of the authoritarian or totalitarian governments of twenty or thirty years ago, which were often brittle regimes."[19]

The first, Ethiopia, is a classic example of a heavy-handed autocracy that sees even the most timid attempts at civic activism as potentially treasonous threats to order and stability that must be quickly quashed. The official position is that, given the country's tragic modern history and fractious ethnic makeup, a firm hand is needed on the levers of power. Furthermore, the argument goes, Western-style democracy is a foolish distraction for a poor country that must focus on economic growth and social cohesion. Indeed, at the writing of this chapter, the Ethiopian government was jamming Amharic broadcasts from the Voice of America, despite being one of Washington's closest allies in the region.

An unmistakable sign of how the authorities view political liberalization was the expulsion from the country six weeks prior to the 2005 parliamentary elections of three US-based democracy promotion groups providing electoral technical assistance: the International Foundation for Electoral Systems (IFES), the National Democratic Institute, and the International Republic Institute. As for the elections themselves, the European Union's observation report noted that "while the pre-election period saw a number of positive developments and voting on 15 May was conducted in a peaceful and largely orderly manner, the counting and aggregation processes were marred by irregular practices, confusion, and a lack of transparency. Subsequent complaints and appeals mechanisms did not provide an effective remedy. The human rights situation rapidly deteriorated in the post-election day period when dozens of citizens were killed by the police and thousands were arrested."[20]

Ethiopia's President Meles Zenawi described the protests that followed the elections as an "insurrection."

In 2001, the state cleverly introduced a system of tiny administrative sub-divisions (*kebeles* and *woredas*), which serves the dual purpose of allowing government penetration to the lowest local level, while also created a cadre of over three million elected officials, most of whom owe their positions to the ruling Ethiopian People's Revolutionary Democratic Front (EPRDF) coalition.

Electoral manipulation and exploitation is but one way the EPRDF has maintained its long hold on power. It has also passed tough legislation controlling non-governmental and civil society organizations. A 2010 report by the *International Journal of Non-Profit Law* calls it "one of the most controversial NGO laws in Africa, and indeed in the world," and goes on to explain that "the Proclamation, among other things, restricts NGOs that receive more than 10% of their financing from foreign sources from engaging in essentially all human rights and advocacy activities."[21] In addition, strong new laws governing the media and anti-terrorism have been enacted. The latter is described by Human Rights Watch as "a potent instrument to crack down on political dissent, including peaceful political demonstrations and public criticisms of government policy that are deemed supportive of armed opposition activity."[22]

Ethiopia's May 2010 legislative elections consolidated the ruling party's grip on power by giving the EPRDF 499 of the parliament's 536 seats and nearly all of the regional council seats. The only credible external observation mission, that of the European Union, observed that while the voting was well organized, it "fell short of certain international commitments, notably regarding the transparency of the process and the lack of a level playing field for all contesting parties."[23]

Sudan shares with Ethiopia a similar fear of ethnic and regional fragmentation, as well as a phobia about Western influences, and has been equally zealous in protecting the status quo. The well-respected UK publication *Africa Confidential* says that the strategists of President Omar al-Bashir's ruling National Congress Party/National Islamic Front "appear to have digested both Communist and Nazi handbooks, achieving the kind of tight vertical hierarchy with horizontal decentralisation of power favoured by many totalitarian organisations (including, later, Al Qaida). Parallel systems keep key secrets intact and everyone in line. The party rules through its security apparatus."[24]

With a successful referendum on Southern autonomy (read, independence) in January of 2011, Sudan is at a critical stage. There had been enormous international pressure on Sudan to move forward with the referendum, especially from the United States, but it was not certain that it would happen. There was every chance that hostilities with the north could resume. Both sides were reported to be rearming, and the US's special envoy General Scott Gration has described the pre-referendum situation as "make or break." National elections in April 2010 were a mess, with serious disputes between north and south on census figures, voter registration, the composition of the electoral commission, access to the media, and so on. Although the outcome gave Sudanese President (and indicted war criminal) Omar al-Bashir a 68 per cent victory, this was undercut by the last minute boycott of several political parties, including the Sudan People's Liberation Movement, which governs the south. Furthermore, the continuing turbulence in Darfur, as well as violence in parts of the south and east of the country, demonstrated just how fragile the country's peace remains.

Finally, the Democratic Republic of the Congo (DRC) presents different and in some ways more challenging obstacles to democratization. While Ethiopia and Sudan are relatively organized and efficient states, the DRC has been a country in name only for the past two decades. Rarely does the current Congolese government strategically constrain routine political life through coercion and control, although probably not from lack of desire but rather insufficient capacity. The most formidable obstacles to civic activism, advocacy, and human rights are not a dedicated and efficient security service but rather the grinding poverty, violence, corruption, and chaos that have characterized recent Congolese history.

Since the early 1990s, various parts of the country have been embroiled in civil conflict, and during most of the period from late 1996 to mid-2003, the country was wracked by two large-scale wars, involving many of its neighbours. Nonetheless, in 2006, forty-six years after independence, the DRC, with a half billion dollars' worth of financial, technical, and security support from the international community, held national elections that were declared generally free and competitive by observer groups. A joint statement by many of these organizations, including the African Union, Carter Center, and European Union, declared that the elections were largely peaceful, that poll workers and political party agents had performed well, and that measures taken by the electoral commission "resulted in a remarkable improvement to the election operations."[25] Unfortunately, in an obvious sign that the DRC's political elites remained as undemocratic as ever, disputes over polling results led to violent armed clashes between forces loyal to the two main presidential candidates, Joseph Kabila and Jean-Pierre Bemba. As gunfire and mortars exploded in the streets of downtown Kinshasa, it appeared that the DRC's brief flirtation with electoral democracy was to be short-lived. Fortunately, heavy international pressure, combined with the presence of European armed forces, helped end the conflict.

Nonetheless, some real progress was made during these elections. Twenty-five million voters were registered, although there is merit to the belief that this was more a manifestation of interest in having a legitimate form of identification than a burning desire to vote. However, turnout was also high, with 80 per cent of eligible voters going to the polls. One bright spot was that Congolese voters clearly expressed their opinion as to who they did not want to rule them. As Herbert Weiss points out: "They voted against the people and authorities who had ruled them during the years from 1998–2003, when the DRC was divided between areas controlled by the Kinshasa authorities and areas run by various rebel groups."[26]

Ultimately, the DRC's 2006 elections were a necessary step after years of war and decline, but faith in democracy will not survive the lack of delivery of social and economic dividends. In 2009, the country ranked 162nd out of 180 countries in Transparency International's Corruption Perceptions Index.[27] Despite the continuing conflict and criminality in the east, with civilians comprising most of the casualties, the massive UN peacekeeping mission (MONUC) is preparing to draw down its forces. The DRC is far from out of the woods.

HOMEGROWN SUCCESSES

Despite Africa's many democratic failures, happily there are more than a handful of examples of real success as well. Although, like the backsliders described above, these felicitous examples are often quite distinct.

In its 2010 *Freedom in the World* report, Washington-based Freedom House lists nine African countries in its "Free" category: Benin, Botswana, Cape Verde, Ghana, Mali, Mauritius, Namibia, São Tomé and Principe, and South Africa.[28] Essentially, this distinction is bestowed on nations that assure their citizens basic political rights and civil liberties. If one excludes from this pantheon the small island states of Mauritius and Cape Verde, which have little in common with the rest of Africa, culturally, politically, or ethnically, only seven countries make the grade. Several are worth a second look.

Benin, Ghana, and Mali were all historically plagued by military coups but have been well-functioning democracies since the early 1990s, in part because of the "big man syndrome" working in a counter-intuitively positive fashion. In these places at least, the transformation of political culture seems to be linked to the exceptional actions of exceptional individuals. For example, Benin's Mathieu Kérékou was the first black African president to step down after losing an election, setting a critical precedent for his country. As mentioned earlier, Mali was profoundly influenced by the actions of

Amadou Toumani Touré, the people's hero who overthrew a military dictatorship and within a year handed power back to civilian authorities. Ghana's Jerry Rawlings can claim similar credit in rescuing his country from the ravages of successive military dictatorships.

However, the influence of historical figures is not the only factor in play. Nearly all of the countries on the Freedom House list have strong civil society actors and many have robust parliaments, all providing much needed counterweights to the political establishment.

Without question, the most significant democracy on the African continent is South Africa. For a number of reasons, including the symbolism of having broken the shackles of apartheid, its great economic power and promise, and the influence it wields over many parts of the region, it is crucial that South Africa succeed. However, the country's size and diversity make democratic governance decidedly more challenging than in, for example, its neighbour Botswana, which has the benefits of a large resource base (diamonds), small population (two million), and predominant ethnic majority (Tswana). Although vastly more complex, South Africa, blessed with a potent civil society, a scrappy although sometimes harassed press, a powerful private business sector, and influential trade unions and religious leaders, is unlikely to allow itself to become undemocratic. Nevertheless, a few areas warrant vigilance.

To begin with, several of the country's top political leaders, including President Jacob Zuma and African National Congress Youth League leader Julius Malema, seem chronically prone to displays of "big man" behaviour – often arrogant and foolish, and at times skirting legality – that are unsuited to a self-professed democracy. Second, the apparently overwhelming power of the ruling ANC, and the relative weakness of the various opposition parties, is worrying. Finally, the failure of successive governments to tackle the country's toughest social and economic problems could result in a dramatic loss of faith in democratic government. High rates of unemployment, criminality, migration, and HIV/AIDS are far greater threats to democracy in South Africa than coups d'état.

Fortunately, the mere fact that there are several large and relatively well-off African countries governing themselves democratically puts the lie to the dangerous notion that the continent is infertile ground for republicanism. Acknowledging that the political aspirations of Africans are essentially no different from those of any other people in the world is the first step to understanding Africa. No longer should it be seen, as Chinua Achebe put it, as "a place of strange, bizarre, and illogical things, where people don't do what common sense demands."

EXTERNAL ASSISTANCE

Helping to strengthen African democracy is a worthy goal – providing it is done correctly and the limits of this help are understood. Unfortunately, the handful of nations (all Western) that actually fund this kind of work often provide short-sighted and short-term funding. For example, while there is usually money available for election day observation in key countries, there is rarely support for vastly more useful long-term electoral missions to identify and potentially solve problems well before voters go to the polls. The United States government, despite being one of the largest contributors to democracy promotion programs, invests vastly more money in virtually every other facet of international development. To cite one example, in 2009 USAID spent more than twice as much on food aid for Chad than it provided globally to its main international elections partner, the IFES. While money alone will not make Africa more democratic, this imbalance highlights the skewed priorities of all major donor countries. Furthermore, democratic investments need to be made when there is still time to nurture positive outcomes: too often donors wake up to the need to support electoral work only months prior to election day, at which point the die is often cast.

Nonetheless, there are many useful and inexpensive ways to nurture electoral democracy:

- Help African Union members adhere to the laudably high standards of their own Charter on Democracy, Elections and Governance.
- Support local initiatives like the AU's Democracy and Electoral Assistance Unit, ECOWAS' Network of Electoral Commissions, and similar embryonic bodies.
- Encourage the many courageous civil society and human rights leaders throughout the continent as they press for electoral reform, better governance, and respect for human rights.
- Push for the creation of electoral commissions comprised of true professionals drawn from throughout the continent, to replace the many partisan and corrupt bodies. There is a precedent for this in some of Anglophone Africa's high courts.

- Back African regional and sub-regional blocs when they correctly criticize democratic backsliding, and pressure them when they do not.

Somewhat more ambitiously, one might envision a campaign to make electoral fraud an international crime. Certainly hijacking the democratic process can have life and death implications for citizens. When corrupt individuals gain public office through undemocratic means and use their positions to steal funds designated for health programs (Zambia), the lives of pregnant mothers and unborn children are put at direct risk. When venal politicians provoke ethnic violence (Kenya), real people are killed or displaced from their homes.

THE FUTURE

A snapshot in time is just that: a passing moment captured. Judging Africa's political future by the events of today is misleading. In the past two centuries, the continent has undergone the predations of slavery, the despoilment of imperialism, and the rivalry of the Cold War. Given this grim history, the fact that many countries now hold regular elections, allow the growth of civil society, and permit a variety of political tendencies should be cause for celebration.

Certainly there continue to be warning signs, ranging from tribal politics to endemic corruption to high-level nepotism. Despite these concerns, my sense is that the demographic and social trends in Africa promise more, not less, democracy in most of the continent. Rapid urbanization, the world's youngest population, access to independent news sources, spreading internet and cellular connectivity, bold civil society organizations, an engaged diaspora, rising literacy rates, and changes in attitudes toward women are just some of the important factors that are contributing to a growing demand by people for a greater voice in their own governance.

Certainly dictatorial regimes will try to cling to power and some of them will continue to use violence and fraud to prolong their tenures. Ultimately, however, Africa will likely outgrow its youthful flirtation with autocracy and join the growing ranks of the democratic.

Having begun with a Samuel Johnson reference, it makes some symmetrical sense to conclude with a quote by the man: "No government power can be abused long. Mankind will not bear it ... There is remedy in human nature against tyranny, that will keep us safe under every form of government."

5

Elections, Governance, and Secession in Sudan

KHALID MUSTAFA MEDANI

In January 2011, the people of the southern provinces of Sudan voted overwhelmingly to declare the independence of Southern Sudan from the North. The referendum was the culmination of an armistice in the longest-running civil conflict in Africa, between the central government seated in Khartoum and the Sudan People's Liberation Movement (SPLM) of Southern Sudan. The Sudanese civil war killed over two million people, mostly southerners, and displaced upwards of four million more. The conflict formally ended following the conclusion of the Comprehensive Peace Agreement (CPA) signed by the ruling National Congress Party (NCP) and the SPLM in Naivasha, Kenya, on 9 January 2005.

Chapter 1 of the CPA, the Machakos Protocol of 2002, affirmed the "right to self-determination" for southerners and provided for extensive southern autonomy pending the referendum to be held in 2011. The vision underpinning the CPA was to foster respect for the remarkable ethnic, religious, and cultural diversity of Sudan's various regions. An important component of the subsequent implementation of the CPA signed in Naivasha was to make a southern vote for unity with the North "an attractive option" in the referendum. However, the interim period that followed the CPA failed to accomplish this objective for three important reasons. First, because the CPA included only the South and not the other outlying regions of Sudan, including insurgent forces that have battled Khartoum in Darfur and eastern Sudan, it failed to foster a genuine vision of pluralism. Second, since the peace accord was brokered by two non-democratic parties – namely, the NCP and the SPLM – it was never intended to include the participation of Sudanese civil society or the country's sub-national communities.

Finally, and perhaps most importantly, while the CPA stipulated that "free and fair" elections be held prior to the referendum in order to induce southerners to vote for unity and promote greater democracy for the entire country, this did not occur. Indeed, as Ben Reilly has pointed out in his contribution to this volume, elections held in societies prone to civil conflict are instruments used "not only to promote democracy but also frequently to attempt to consolidate a fragile peace." In this regard, what made the result of the January 2011 plebiscite a foregone conclusion was the failure on the part of the Khartoum regime to uphold its commitment to convene genuinely democratic elections in the run-up to the vote for self-determination in 2009. The fact that the regime in Khartoum was chiefly responsible for administrating the elections, determining voter enrolment, and even demarcating the electoral boundaries meant that the outcome of the government-controlled elections would invariably maintain the political status quo in both North and South. In this respect, the elections of April 2009 served primarily as an instrument for forging a minimal level of peace between former warring parties rather than as an institutional mechanism to promote a new democratic order.

The question at hand is, then, having failed to build unity out of diversity, will the emergence of two new nation-states in the Horn of Africa result in a more durable peace or plunge the region into a new round of civil conflict? Drawing on the literature on secession and conflict resolution, this chapter addresses this question by focusing on the probability of renewed conflict following the 2011 referendum in which over ninety per cent of Southern Sudanese voted in favour of self-determination. Given the now inevitable emergence of "two Sudans," I outline a framework for identifying the potential for future conflict and offer a historically grounded analysis of potential scenarios following the referendum vote of 2011. More specifically, I focus on key contentious issues that could determine whether Sudan's partition will pave the road to peace or conflict in the future: the existing arrangements to divide oil export revenues, the persistence of conflict over ethnic and religious identities, the status of the oil-rich Abyei region across the new common border, the domestic and regional consequences of the Darfur conflict, and the important question of political reform in North and South Sudan.

LEARNING FROM THE PAST: SECESSION AND CONFLICT

The most important question in the case of the Sudan has been posed in other secession-based conflicts: Will partition prevent the recurrence of ethnic civil conflict? There are two general views on this subject in the scholarly literature. On the one hand, proponents of partition (the formation of one or more states out of the lands of an existing state) maintain that secession can prevent future conflict if it manages to separate warring factions and create homogeneous units where ethnic groups' security fears are reduced.[1] On the other hand, other scholars insist that partition often leads to future conflict primarily because identifying new borders does not prevent the recurrence of war or low levels of violence.[2] As Nicholas Sambanis has argued, this is primarily because secession requires population transfers and a level of ethnic homogeneity that is nearly impossible to achieve.[3] Moreover, the potential for continued violent inter-ethnic antagonism and a recurrence of civil conflict between the secession state and the rump (i.e., original) state is more likely within the context of continued disputes over territory and natural resources.[4]

Indeed, not only does the presence of natural resources increase the prospects of war and prolong conflict by providing funds to rebels and state actors alike, it may create a new political community organized around ethnic lines.[5] For Sudan what is at stake in this debate is whether, at this juncture in the country's history, secession will lead to peace or conflict, and what aspect of the dispute will prove more difficult to resolve: the dispute over the demarcation of new borders, or economically based territorial disputes over oil resources located along the north-south border.

Answering these crucial questions requires an examination of the record of secessions and violence. While there is no scholarly consensus on either the potential benefits or pitfalls of division within the context of secession-based conflicts,[6] the literature on the subject of the aftermath of secessions provides some important lessons for Sudan. In particular, there is broad agreement on some of the factors that may determine whether secessions are followed by peace or conflict. Most notably, these include whether separation produces ethnically homogeneous states, the extent to which the process is managed peacefully to limit the leaders' ability to use force "to revisit the secession-created boundaries,"[7] and whether the two parties agree on political and economic divisions prior to the secession.[8] Moreover, while the historical record demonstrates that secessions are no better or worse in ending civil wars than other political solutions,[9] lessons from other countries have shown that ethnically based territorial disputes are more likely to lead to armed conflict while democracies are less prone to a recurrence of violence in the aftermath of separation.[10]

In the case of Sudan, determining the likelihood of future conflict necessitates posing four interlinked questions: What role have state elites played in shaping the conflict between the North and South? To what extent will the persistence of ethnic-based grievances, particularly along the disputed regions, represent a challenge to the prospects for sustainable peace? What is the role of external actors in overseeing a peaceful process of secession? And what are the prospects of further political divisions within the North and the South following secession? More specifically, to what extent will the continued concentration of power in the hands of the NCP and the SPLM play out in further fragmentation in the outlying regions of the country, including Darfur?

One of the most important lessons that can be drawn from past secessions is that partition is most effective where populations are already separated in ethnic terms at the time of secession and where the international community is willing to separate groups, using mass population transfers if necessary.[11] In this respect, in the case of Sudan, the probability of conflict recurring is quite strong for a number of reasons that have not obtained in those cases of more peaceful partition. First, Sudan is not divided into homogeneous regions, despite conventional depictions of the conflict as being essentially that between an "Arab" North and an "African" South. The ethnic, religious, and linguistic heterogeneity of both parts of the country make the demarcation of homogeneous entities difficult to determine in political terms. Second, there are multi-ethnic regions in the centre of the country. In particular, there are an estimated 1.5 million Southern Sudanese residing in the greater metropolitan area of Khartoum. Finally, and most importantly, oil resources are located in the south and along disputed North-South borders. In this context, the likelihood of economically (i.e., oil revenue) based territorial disputes is quite high and promises to be far more difficult to resolve than the dispute over ethnically demarcated borders. This is particularly true in the context of the disputed Abyei region. Abyei is not only rich in oil;

it is also inhabited by Arab and African ethnic groups linked politically to their benefactors in the North and South respectively.

BACKGROUND TO CONFLICT: ETHNIC AND ECONOMICALLY BASED TERRITORIALIZED DISPUTES

The civil war in Sudan is routinely depicted as rooted in a conflict of national identities between "Arabs" and "Africans," a religious quarrel between Muslims and Christians, or a combination of both.[12] In reality, the North-South conflict is best understood as one of several violent disputes between the central state in Khartoum and the periphery, whether in the South, the Nuba Mountains, the eastern provinces, or the western Darfur region. The Khartoum regime has reacted to the various rebellious regional forces with increasing violence, in great part to discourage the discontented peripheral regions from rising up in a united front against what Francis Deng has termed the "Arab-dominated" centre.[13] One of the problems associated with resolving the conflict in Darfur, as well as ensuring that the southern secession proceeds peacefully, has much to do with this understanding of the conflict, and the fact that the Bashir regime in Khartoum has been successful in propagating the notion that the various insurgencies harbour fundamentally different political agendas and represent different cultural groups.

The eruption of the north-south conflict began shortly after independence in 1956. Following a brief experiment in parliamentary democracy (1956-58), Sudan witnessed the first of three authoritarian-military regimes. Sporadic warfare between the army and southern guerrillas began in earnest under the military regime of General Ibrahim Abboud and has outlasted several central governments, military and civilian. To be sure, the government bureaucracy and the army office corps have always been dominated by Muslim northerners whose native language is Arabic and who claim Arab lineage, whereas the South is populated by tribes who profess Christianity or animist religions. That is, cultural and religious differences have contributed to the fighting, particularly since Khartoum tried to impose "Islamic" penal codes and sharia law in 1983. For its part, the SPLM has also increasingly defined its identity as "African" and has looked to Sudan's African neighbours for support and patronage during the four-decade-long civil war. What is noteworthy, however, is that having asserted their "African" identity by effectively resisting what they perceive as Arab domination, the South has set an example for other regions, such as Darfur and the eastern provinces, which have similarly demanded equality and a more equitable distribution of power and resources.[14] Nevertheless, the core grievances of the South are not related to issues of cultural identity as such, but rather the inequitable distribution of state investment and political power that has been centred in the north.

"Greed" and oil in particular were certainly driving forces behind the escalation of the conflict between the regime and the South.[15] That is, while the primary cause of Sudan's civil war cannot be attributed to natural resources (i.e., oil) alone, Sudan's increasing natural resource dependence has determined the conduct of both the civil war and the negotiations that ended military confrontation between the warring parties. Following the discovery of oil in 1983, successive regimes in Khartoum have been keen to ensure that there would be no opposition to their designs to develop the oil economy. In a strategy used later in Darfur to devastating effect, the Sudan Armed Forces, along with its armed militias, conducted devastating aerial bombardments against civilians in the oil-rich areas of the south. In addition, since the Khartoum regime was unable to find willing recruits to join in what it termed a "jihad" in the south, it encouraged ethnic tensions using local communities in its proxy war. It did this essentially by arming Misiriya and Baggara nomadic tribes, and allowing them to pillage and destroy the communities of the African Dinka and Nuer pastoralists of the south. By the early 1990s, the Bashir regime had expanded its military campaigns against civilian populations in the south and the Nuba Mountains, a campaign that become more deadly as Khartoum began to profit from increasing oil revenues.[16] Indeed, while Sudan's civil war is rooted in the historical marginalization of the South by successive northern governments since independence, the fact that oil development laid the spark for the Sudanese civil war and eventually exacerbated the severity of the war itself is beyond dispute.[17]

ISLAMISM AND THE FAILURE OF DEMOCRACY: THE DILEMMA OF UNITY WITH PEACE

If the discovery and development of oil resources exacerbated the territorial and economic dispute between Khartoum and the South, by the late 1980s another new pattern of Islamist politics emerged that sharpened the cultural and religious conflict between the two regions in ways that have been difficult to resolve. Political Islam emerged as a strong force in Sudanese civil society as early as the 1970s, but in recent decades its chief legacy in terms of Sudan's civil conflict has been in obstructing the forces of democracy in ways that have undermined national unity. This is clearly evidenced if one examines the origins of the Islamist-backed military coup of 1989 that overturned Sudan's last democratic experiment. Indeed, contrary to recent scholarship arguing that democracy does not promote internal peace because electoral competition in poor countries is rarely able to produce accountable and legitimate government, the short-lived experience of democratization in Sudan points to its "peace-promoting" possibilities.[18]

To be sure, democratic consolidation has a poor record in Sudan. No multiparty election has produced an enduring democratic transition and elected governments in Sudan have been overthrown three times by military coups. As in many African countries, successive multiparty elections in Sudan have faced shortcomings of leadership, a divisive legacy of colonial rule, and ethnic, sectarian, and regional instability. Moreover, a range of corrupt practices – ranging from ballot stuffing, intimidation, and the use of government resources and state-controlled media – has long characterized Sudan's three failed experiments in parliamentary democracy (1956-58, 1964-69, and 1985-89).[19] What is noteworthy, however, is that in terms of resolving the North-South conflict, democratic contestation has had the potential of brokering peace within a national unity framework – that is, forging peace with unity rather than peace with secession.

While Sudan's third, and last, multiparty period (1985-89) did not represent the wide spectrum of Sudanese allegiances (the southern parties, for example, boycotted the elections due the war in the south), multiparty competition opened avenues for a resurgent civil society that placed pressure on the civilian government to resolve the civil war. In December 1988, widespread strikes and demonstrations erupted in Khartoum, led by a newly revitalized coalition of workers, farmers, professional syndicates, civil servants, and artisans.[20]

The possibility of democracy resulting in a peace dividend in Sudan seemed likely. In mid-June 1989, Prime Minster Sadiq al-Mahdi's government announced that a cabinet meeting on 1 July would formally repeal the September Laws, contingent upon the review of a legal committee comprising representatives from all political parties. On 4 July, a government delegation and the Sudan People's Liberation

Army (SPLA) were to meet to propose a permanent resolution to the civil war.[21] Twenty-four hours before the 1 July meeting, a group of mid-ranking officers took over the Republican Palace, the parliament, and the national broadcasting station, rounded up top party and civil society leaders throughout the north, and announced the Revolutionary Command Council under the leadership of Lt. Gen. Omar al-Bashir. It quickly became evident that the Islamists had mounted the 30 June coup.[22]

The Islamists had been marginalized by widespread popular support for a swift resolution to the country's economic problems by ending the civil war. Their twofold aim was to pre-empt any peace agreement that would repeal the imposition of Islamic law and to reverse the influence of pro-democracy forces, many of which had been incorporated into the government following growing protests. Bashir and the leaders of the National Islamic Front (NIF) immediately cancelled the North-South ceasefire, imposed a stricter "Islamic" legal system, and outlawed all political parties and other "non-religious institutions."[23] Consequently, the war in the south took an abrupt turn for the worse. The Army bombed camps of southern war refugees and paramilitary militia expelled southerners from displaced camps around the capital. In the mid-1990s, the Bashir regime called for jihad and armed proxy militias in the Nuba Mountains and South Kurdufan in order to execute scorched earth tactics that included attacking refugee camps as far afield as the Sudan-Uganda border.

By the time of the ceasefire brokered in 2003, upwards of two million southerners, most of them civilians, had been killed. The sheer magnitude of human suffering led to stronger calls for self-determination in the south and increasing support for an orderly "separation" of the two regions by the international community – two factors that have historically determined whether secessionist attempts fail or succeed.[24] It was because of the war and instability in the south that Chevron and later Talisman Energy sold their interests in the oilfields to Khartoum.[25] By the late 1990s the US and Canada had barred their oil companies from doing business with Khartoum due to the Islamist-backed regime's war against southern rebels, leaving the door open for China, Malaysia, and India to expand their oil operations in the country. They now dominate the oil sector in Sudan, with the Sudanese government owning only 5 per cent of the Greater Nile Petroleum Company consortium.[26] Beijing presently derives 6 per cent of its oil from

Sudan and Chinese officials have countered accusations that their policies toward Sudan have undermined security and fuelled civil conflict in Darfur by arguing that those concerns are internal to Sudanese affairs and Beijing is "not in a position to impose upon them."[27]

A 'COMPREHENSIVE' PEACE OR NEGOTIATING A PEACEFUL DIVORCE?

By the late 1990s, the two warring sides were at a stalemate, both believing victory was at hand and neither willing to concede the other's demands. Talks led by the East-African Intergovernmental Authority for Drought and Development initiative achieved agreements in principle that collapsed as the prospect of implementation loomed. The Bashir regime, by this point, had divested itself of the National Islamic Front's radical ideologues because of increasing infighting between Islamist leader Hassan Turabi and the more politically pragmatic-minded Bashir.

At this juncture, external actors played an important role in brokering the Comprehensive Peace Agreement. The Bush Administration's Sudan envoy, former Senator John Danforth, in particular played a key role. One of the reasons for the initial success of the peace talks is that the US did not insist that hostilities cease before mediating talks between the two combatants. Danforth, for instance, developed a key confidence-building step by brokering an agreement on the protection of civilians that did not explicitly require Khartoum to cease its military campaign in the south. But the key US contribution to the negotiations, which SPLM leader John Garang eventually accepted, was that self-determination would be limited to the South and would not extend to other marginalized regions, including Darfur. In so doing, Khartoum was able to block any moves toward genuine democratization by Sudanese civil society while simultaneously pursuing a separate "peace" with South Sudan. After the extended stalemate, external actors composed of the US, Britain, and Norway stepped in to broker a peace agreement focused on resolving the issues of the separation of state and religion, and self-determination for the South. The door was now open for the signing of the CPA.

As with post-conflict peace accords in Africa, Sudan's CPA represents what Donald Rothchild has termed a "minimalist route to implementation" between two formerly warring parties, neither of whom has been able to achieve a military victory against its rival.[28] It is, in other words, a negotiated agreement among ethnic and military elites who accept a minimal form of elite participation designed to achieve political stability while avoiding opposition from other forces in society. While these elite-power sharing systems are not as participatory as democratic regimes of the type addressed in other contributions to this volume, they do share a resemblance to democracies in that they are characterized by an ongoing process of bargaining among elites with the objective of achieving a transition to stable social relations.[29] This is what the CPA was designed to accomplish. It consists of a series of protocols on power sharing, wealth sharing, border territories, the status of Khartoum, self-determination, state and religion, and security arrangements.[30] Notably, in addition to recreating an autonomous region of South Sudan, the CPA brought southerners into the central government in coalition with the Bashir regime. John Garang was made president of South Sudan and first vice-president of Sudan. Perhaps more importantly, oil revenues were to be divided evenly between the central and southern governments. There was, among many Sudanese, an atmosphere of hope that the CPA could usher in a new era for a united Sudan, whose political factions would no longer exploit ethnic and religious differences in accordance with zero-sum power calculations. This optimism, however, was dependent on two aspirations that have not been realized. The first was that the CPA would eventually extend to incorporate the legitimate grievances of other outlying regions, including Darfur and the East, and that the international community would implement one of the CPA's most important stipulations: the convening of free and fair elections prior to holding the referendum.

The first harbinger of Sudanese pessimism with regard to the unity option was, of course, the Darfur conflict that erupted in 2003. The conflict itself was sparked by the ongoing peace talks between the North and South. When the forces of Darfur's Sudan Liberation Army (SLA) took up arms against Khartoum, it was in the hope of acquiring similar concessions along the lines of the resource- and power-sharing formula granted to the South. Instead, Khartoum ordered the brutal bombing of Darfur and utilized the now notorious paramilitary forces of the Janjaweed against the rebels. Five years later, the International Criminal Court in The Hague indicted Bashir for "crimes against humanity and war crimes" in Darfur, the first time in history that a sitting president has been so charged. In July 2010, the ICC issued a second arrest warrant for Bashir, this time for charges of genocide.

The conflict in Darfur has highlighted the deep-seated structural flaws of the CPA in ways that could determine the probability of future conflict in a number of respects. First, it signalled the problematic associated with viewing the crisis in Sudan as one between North and South, irrespective of the fact that long-term peace in the country requires a more comprehensive solution to the problem of an authoritarian regime at the centre and disaffected populations in other outlying regions beyond the south. Second, by assuming that a North-South peace is the primary component to resolving the civil conflict, the CPA discounted the fact that neither northern nor southern Sudan is homogeneous in population. There are millions of African southerners residing in the north and thousands of Arabs in the south. This was made apparent by the riots that broke out in the Sudanese capital and in the southern capital of Juba in 2005, when Garang was killed in a helicopter crash. Millions of southerners were angered by the "lack of respect" accorded by the state to their leader. The ensuing riots took on an ethnic dimension, as the shops of Arabs were attacked while those of "Africans" were spared. Rioters from Khartoum's internally displaced person camps directed their rage against police stations, government offices, and other symbols of the state. Millions of people from the Nuba Mountains, Darfur, as well as the south inhabit the camps around Khartoum, and the discontent there is rooted in the state's failure to integrate the displaced into the local economy as well as the state's counter-insurgency campaigns against their ethnic kin in other parts of the country.

In an alarming statement, in September 2010 Bashir's minister of Information, Kamal Obeid, announced that the Southern Sudanese will not be granted rights of citizenship in the north "if they vote to secede." Moreover, he threatened to expel southern residents, stating that they would not enjoy the right to employment or being treated in hospitals in the north. On 3 October 2010, presidential adviser Mustafa Osman Ismail went further, calling on the country's youth and students to prepare for war to defend the country against the challenges it would face in the event of Southern Sudan's secession.[31] While Bashir later criticized these statements, claiming that they did not reflect official government policy, it is clear that influential members of the NCP support the expulsion of southerners in the north, and even war, if the South votes for an independent country.[32] The fact that there is no indication that southern secession will produce two ethnically homogeneous states of the type that would engender a sustainable peace following Sudan's partition suggests that ethnic conflict in both the south and the north is a real probability unless cooperation on key outstanding issues is achieved. There are estimated to be more than 1.5 million southerners settled in the north and it is unclear whether they will be afforded the right to work, reside, and move freely between the two countries after separation.[33] Moreover, while the SPLA currently holds the greatest political influence in the South, the organization continues to be dominated by the Dinka tribe. Less known is the fact that the Equatorian ethnic groups of the far South have long experienced economic and political oppression and land dispossession at the hands of the SPLA.[34]

The fact that Sudan's last experiment with electoral democracy (1986-89) placed pressure on the country's political parties to bridge the divide between North and South Sudan meant that the hopes of many supporters of a united Sudan rested on the CPA's stipulation that elections be held prior to the southern plebiscite for independence. However, the combined effects of international pressure over Darfur, the indictment of Bashir by the ICC for "war crimes," and increasing domestic unrest, not only in Darfur but also in the eastern provinces along the borders with Eritrea,[35] convinced many previously hopeful Sudanese supporting unity that the vision of a pluralistic new Sudan was a chimera.

Ultimately, however, the lack of credibility associated with the elections of 20 April undermined any hopes of peaceful, democratic reforms that would not only usher in the possibility of greater political participation in the north but also help to make, in the words of the CPA, "unity more attractive" to the Southern Sudanese prior to the plebiscite for self-determination. The ruling NCP's manipulation of the elections and vote rigging were clear from the start. In 2008, the SPLM leadership rejected the census figures reported by the central government, which were to determine the number of eligible registered voters in the run-up to the elections of April 2010. The Bashir regime announced that their figures showed that there are 8.26 million people in the southern provinces, or 22 per cent of the total population. SPLM leaders claim that the south has a third of Sudan's population, and they viewed the census figures as an attempt to backtrack on the fifty-fifty oil revenue sharing agreement brokered by the CPA.

Ultimately, the NCP and SPLM forged a strategic alliance to ensure that both parties remained in power, albeit for different objectives. The NCP wanted to ensure the status quo in the north and the continued exclusion of other political parties from decision-making at the centre. For its part the SPLM's primary objective, especially following the death of the pro-unity Garang, was to preside over a successful referendum that culminated in independence for the South. Consequently, the elections of April 2010 were not only unrepresentative of Sudanese society, their ultimate purpose was to pave the way for the referendum the following year. This is not to say that dissent from the regime does not remain endemic; dissent was clearly in evidence in the 2010 April elections, when all the major opposition parties (including SPLM candidates running in the north) boycotted the national elections amid widespread allegations of fraud. Nevertheless, both parties achieved their primary political objectives: the SPLM won re-election to office in the autonomous South with 93 per cent of the vote, while the NCP, running in a largely uncontested field in northern Sudan, held onto power by "winning" 68 per cent of the vote. The results were not remarkable given the fact that the main opposition parties boycotted the elections. Far more significant, however, was the fact that SPLM northern candidate Yasir Arman, who withdrew his candidacy just prior to the vote, garnered 22 per cent of the vote. This signalled a "protest" vote on the part of many in Sudanese civil society. Moreover, the fact that Arman, an influential northerner who served as the deputy secretary of the SPLM in the north, received such a large margin of the vote reflected the desire for democratic reform and unity between North and South among a large segment of Sudanese civil society.[36]

In retrospect, the shortcomings associated with the compromise agreement between two essentially elite factions in northern and southern Sudan played an important role in preventing the reorganization of a unified Sudanese state. These shortcomings may also set the stage for the current obstacles toward a peaceful secession process. Indeed, it is a historical irony that the negotiated settlement of the CPA was essentially the brainchild of an internally negotiated framework agreed upon by the full range of Sudanese democratic forces and civil society in 1995 under the umbrella of the National Democratic Alliance (NDA). The "brittleness" of the elite pact that was created with the help of external actors (namely, the US, Britain, and Norway) is thus primarily a result of the motivations of two non-representative factions who benefited from the promotion of a minimal form of elite participation.

The record of peace agreements in Africa shows that externally induced pacts have proven far less durable and effective in forging sustainable peace than internally negotiated power-sharing agreements. In this regard, it is hardly surprising that the CPA has suffered from three important weaknesses: the reluctance of the central government and the SPLM/A to incorporate new political parties and regional opposition movements into negotiations, the concentration of power in the hands of two belligerents to the exclusion of other groups' political aspirations and human rights concerns, and the prioritization of narrowly defined security concerns rather than a commitment to national reconciliation and democratic transformation in Sudan. Taken together, these flaws associated with the nature and implementation of the CPA have not only aggravated the dilemma of ethnic security in the disputed north-south border regions, they have also stood in the way of resolving the biggest threat to peace and stability in Sudan: the conflict in Darfur. Indeed, it is now widely acknowledged that the SLA, which initiated the insurgency in Darfur, timed its insurrection in response to their exclusion from the power and sharing agreements brokered at the Naivasha peace talks. In other words, the potential for resolution to the conflict in Darfur, as well as other marginalized regions in the east and far north, continues to be dependent on their inclusion in the peace process. The continued absence of other forces participating in negotiations on power and wealth sharing in particular has undermined democratization and the resolution of the Darfur conflict. Doubtless, it will also prove to be the biggest challenge to a sustained peace between Khartoum and the South over an extended period following the southern vote for self-determination and the secession of the Southern Sudan.

SECESSION AND CONFLICT RECURRENCE: THE DILEMMA OF DEMARCATING NEW BORDERS

As in other cases of secession, in Sudan the debate over the most legitimate demarcation of new borders within the context of multi-ethnic residential populations is the most explosive issue determining whether a recurrence of conflict will occur. Territorial disputes become harder to resolve over time because partition, redefinition, and compensation become more difficult to implement as disputes mature.[37] Moreover, territorial disputes are further prolonged when local ethnic groups harbour an emotional identity-based attachment to the land. In the Sudanese case, the status of Abyei remains the most explosive issue in this regard. Indeed, presently, while key issues such as national debt, citizenship, and wealth sharing remain outstanding, the biggest risk of a recurrence of conflict is the fact that the referendum scheduled to be held in Abyei has been delayed indefinitely. By the terms of the CPA, Abyei, which lies on the north-south border, is entitled to a separate referendum on whether to join South Sudan or remain part of the North. By all accounts, there is significant popular sentiment behind the former choice. In 2008, for example, some 60,000 people fled Abyei to the south after government-backed militia attacked the main city. Moreover, Khartoum moved to grab a larger share of the country's oil and gas wealth by effectively annexing the Abyei region in South Kurdufan, site of the rich Heglig oilfields. The next year, a ruling by a special tribunal in The Hague altered the borders of the Abyei region, effectively awarding the central government control of the oilfields and the all-important Greater Nile Oil Pipeline to Port Sudan on the Red Sea.

The Permanent Court of Arbitration (PCA), based in The Hague, not only ceded key oilfields to North Sudan but gave the South most of the land, including the town of Abyei, which has large fertile lands that have economic as well as cultural value to both the Arab Dinka and Misiriya tribes of the region. Little wonder that this territory has emerged as a key flashpoint of potential conflict and is proving a major obstacle to a peaceful "divorce" between North and South Sudan.[38] For its part, the SPLM interpreted the PCA's ruling as meaning that the cattle-herding Misiriya tribe have no right to vote in areas assigned by the PCA to the Dinka. But the Misiriya declared that they would disrupt voting in Abyei by resorting to force if they are not allowed to participate. The Misiriya, backed by the ruling NCP party, fear that when the South secedes they will lose their traditional grazing rights, their primary source of livelihood. How important Abyei is to future peace and cooperation following the South's secession was made clear by US Department of State spokesperson Phillip J. Crowley: "To reach a genuine agreement on Abyei that paves the way for referendum, you have to have a buy-in by all of the major players, and that includes not only North and South, but also the tribal areas in and around Abyei. They have to be part of the solution."[39]

DEMOCRATIZATION AS CONFLICT RESOLUTION: POST-REFERENDUM SCENARIOS FOR SUDAN

While it is difficult to ascertain with certainty whether Sudan will experience widespread recurrence of civil war or low-level violence, there is little question that tension between northern and southern Sudan will continue unabated. The question that remains has to do with the probability of a recurrence of conflict. That is, whether the South will secede through force or whether the two new independent states will emerge because of an agreed-upon, peaceful process of separation. These two scenarios are, in turn, dependent on whether negotiations over post-referendum arrangements involving disputes over water, debt, wealth sharing, citizenship, and, most importantly, the North-South border, including the oil-rich region of Abyei, will be concluded peacefully. At present, however, the likelihood of a credible popular consultation process in South Kurdufan and Blue Nile states is remote. Failure to generate popular legitimacy among the Arab and African ethnic groups in these disputed territories will most likely result in a cycle of border clashes with the central government and the SPLM/A supporting local militias. This would no doubt serve as a "tinderbox," sparking a new round of civil war. Consequently, the probability of a peaceful secession process in the short term hinges largely on an agreement over who is eligible to vote in the referendum and on the crucial issue of the demarcation of boundaries.

However, in the longer term, the state of governance in the north beyond 2011 is the single most important criterion that will determine whether Sudan moves toward long-term peace and stability or increased conflict. There is a commonly shared grievance on the part of Sudanese in the south, the east, and Darfur that political and economic power is concentrated in Khartoum and its immediate environs. This is the root cause of Sudan's multiple regional conflicts. Consequently, while the vast majority of southerners have voted for independence, the state of Sudan's governance will be a crucial issue in any future attempts to resolve the Darfur crisis and maintain peace and stability along the border regions of South Kurdufan and Blue Nile. How these issues are resolved and whether this will be pursued within a national or narrowly focused reform agenda will determine whether Sudan moves toward a sustainable peace or plunges further into conflict.

The main issue for both South and North Sudan has to do with what Paul Collier famously outlined as a problem of "bad governance" that is often compounded by "bad neighbours," and the ways in which natural resources such as oil can often subvert democracy, undermine development, and engender civil conflict.[40] This problem is clearly evidenced by the Bashir regime's unwillingness to implement a national reform agenda, as stipulated by the CPA, that includes decentralization of power and resources, a more inclusive and representative national civil service, and the reform of national laws culminating in free and fair national elections. More specifically, the failure to make progress on the question of political reform will mean that insurgents in Darfur and the East will continue to resort to violence in order to gain rights from the centre similar to those granted to the Southern Sudanese. This could threaten regional stability. Moreover, as other cases of secession have demonstrated, under a more open, democratic, and transparent government at the centre, there is a greater likelihood of a sustainable and durable peace. In the case of Sudan, democratization remains the best option for peaceful North-South coexistence and for the resolution of regional conflicts, such as the one in Darfur. Moreover, the reform of political institutions in both Khartoum and Juba will help increase the possibility of cross-border cooperation between the two independent states and encourage peaceful coexistence based on a durable commitment over post-referendum arrangements.

Finally, of the many implications of southern secession, oil revenue sharing is the most contentious, with a high risk of a return to war if mutually beneficial arrangements are not brokered peacefully prior to southern independence. The significance of oil production in Sudan became prominent immediately following the signing of the CPA in 2005. Over the last decade Sudan's rapid economic growth, averaging 7 per cent annually in aggregate terms, has been due to the development of the oil industry. As late as 2008, oil revenue accounted for 15 per cent of GDP (US$10 billion in oil exports and $60 billion in GDP) and upwards of 75 per cent of the government budget.[41] But while Sudan is predicated to continue producing increasing levels of oil over the next decade, the oil boom has been concentrated narrowly in the service sector and has not improved the deteriorating livelihoods of the majority of Sudanese. Not surprisingly, the regime in Khartoum has been reluctant to give up oil revenues, and while

Southern Sudan has received 50 per cent of its share from oil revenues so far, tensions between Khartoum and the SPLM/A have risen sharply over the lack of transparency associated with these transfers. More ominously, there remains the absence of an agreement ensuring transparency in the sharing of oil revenue after July 2011. Moreover, with no agreement on border demarcation and the fact that the bulk of Sudan's oil is in the south but the pipeline runs through the north, the recurrence of armed conflict over this coveted resource remains a grave threat in the aftermath of secession. The potential for resolving this contentious issue will depend on the involvement of foreign stakeholders in Sudan's oil industry, and on the fact that both parties understand that cooperation is the only way to secure a stable flow of oil revenue to both sides.

CONCLUSION

The imminent emergence of "two Sudans" in what is Africa's largest country raises new challenges for the continent and the global community. The spillover effect of renewed large-scale conflict would threaten peace and security for the rest of the Horn of Africa, Kenya, Uganda, and the eastern DRC. These neighbouring countries risk being affected by forced migration, displacement, humanitarian crises, and cross-border armed groups and militias. In addition, a recurrence of conflict in Sudan would undermine international agreements on the use of the Nile waters (two-thirds of which are within the Sudan's borders) and, in so doing, embroil Egypt and Ethiopia in protracted involvement in any potential conflict between Khartoum and the newly independent South Sudan. Moreover, failure to resolve the conflict in Darfur peacefully would continue to impact the domestic stability of Chad and the Central African Republic. Sudan's stability is also a matter of concern for emerging powers, such as India and China, which have invested substantially in the country's oil sector.

Consequently, what remains to be examined, and what is of important significance worldwide, is how post-secessionist arrangements will be managed to help promote stability rather than exacerbate the country's multiple conflicts. In Sudan, this will depend on how deals are negotiated on wealth transfers (oil revenues, debts, Nile water management) and on power and sovereignty transfers (citizenship, border security, and more inclusive and transparent southern governing institutions). In light of the regional and international implications of the partition of Sudan into two new nation-states, resolving these issues peacefully is of vital importance. Moreover, this will require a concerted and genuinely comprehensive solution that can only be accomplished through sustained cooperation among the wide range of Sudan's sub-national political forces and the international community.

6

Election-Related Conflict Resolution Mechanisms: The 2006 Elections in the Democratic Republic of the Congo

EUGENIA ZORBAS AND VINCENT TOHBI

The Democratic Republic of the Congo (DRC) is known by many epithets. The term "kleptocracy" was used to describe President Mobutu's thirty-two-year rule combining authoritarianism, corruption, and state decay. The DRC was the site of "Africa's World War" (1998–2003), which drew in six neighbouring armies and spawned three major rebellions and countless smaller ones – remnants of which still persist to this day.[1] UN officials tell us it is the "rape capital of the world."[2] Though casualty figures are heavily disputed, the conflict is generally recognized as being the "deadliest since World War II."[3] The DRC is also the quintessential "resource cursed" country: it holds the world's most important cobalt reserves (used for such things as batteries), 70 per cent of the world's coltan (used in cell phones), an estimated 30 per cent of all diamonds, and important deposits of gold, copper, and other minerals. Yet the country's per capita GDP was estimated at US$182 in 2008 and the UN Human Development Index ranked the DRC 176th of 182 countries in 2009.[4]

The 2006 presidential, parliamentary, and provincial elections were meant to signal a break from such labels. The DRC was officially moving from a conflict to a post-conflict phase, and from a failed state to one reclaiming its sovereign rights and responsibilities and embarking on the road to reconstruction and development. These twin goals – promoting peaceful democratic processes over armed conflict and signalling the return of legitimate domestic authority – are characteristic of many post-conflict elections. As Reilly notes in his chapter in this book, they are usually unrealistic to begin with. In the DRC, political violence occurred during and immediately after the elections and large-scale hostilities have occurred every year since the election.[5] Moreover, the state's authority continues to be absent in large parts of the country, particularly in the east, where parallel administrations continue to tax citizens and trade illegally in natural resources.[6]

We will return to the doubts the case of the DRC raises with respect to the centrality of elections in post-conflict peacebuilding in the conclusion to this chapter. But, in line with this volume's objective to derive lessons from elections in conflict-prone contexts, it is nevertheless useful to distinguish the attainment of intended electoral outcomes from the management of electoral processes – in which the DRC may yet have some lessons to offer.

Accordingly, this chapter will examine the international financial, military, and diplomatic support to the DRC election process and argue that unprecedented sustained and coordinated support, particularly in the diplomatic realm, helped prevent its derailment. The South Africa-based Electoral Institute for the Sustainability of Democracy in Africa's lower-profile but novel Conflict Management Panels, which operated across the country throughout the election lifecycle, will also be examined. The chapter closes by reminding readers that, though the electoral process in the DRC was successfully managed, the DRC cannot be cited as an example of a post-conflict context where elections were effective in encouraging state- or peacebuilding, reconstruction or development.

A COLOSSAL TASK AND A REAL CONTEST

The challenges posed by holding elections in the DRC involved not only politics and security (we will return to how pivotal these were), but also geography, demography, and infrastructure. By a number of measures, these were the biggest elections the UN had ever supported. By size, the DRC (2,344,885 sq. km) is not only the third largest country in Africa but also a "Western Europe without roads," twice the size of Afghanistan, Côte d'Ivoire, Haiti, Liberia, and Sierra Leone (all countries in which the UN has assisted elections) combined. Further, the DRC has a large electorate (28 million), all of whom had to be registered by its Independent Electoral Commission (Commission Électorale Indépendante, CEI) at over 9,000 centres. The last census had been organized in 1984 and many voters had no identity papers of any kind.

Over 50,000 polling stations were established, and 40,000 registration officers, as well as 200,000 polling officers, recruited and trained. Thirty-three candidates competed for the presidency alone, 9,587 candidates for 500 seats in the National Assembly, and 218 parties or coalitions presented candidates nationwide. One hundred and seventy different ballots had to be printed and delivered to fourteen logistical hubs, from which the UN peacekeeping mission, the United Nations Organization Mission in Democratic Republic of the Congo (MONUC), transported the material to 210 sites where they were handed over to the CEI, which ensured transport onward. The secure and orderly payment of police officers and election officials had to be organized – not a simple task when no countrywide banks exist and with officials located in hundreds of often remote locations.

The elections involved multiple rounds of voting. The first was a December 2005 referendum for a new constitution; national parliamentary and first round presidential elections were held in July 2006; and provincial parliamentary and second round presidential elections were held in October. Senators and provincial governors were elected indirectly, by provincial deputies, in January 2007.

Last, but pivotally, an interlocking legal framework had to be put in place in a short timeframe to allow the elections to proceed. Essential legislation included the electoral law itself but also the laws on voter registration and on political parties, laws to establish the five bodies known as democracy support institutions,[7] a pivotal law on nationality, an amnesty law, the budget, and others. The constitution, approved by 84 per cent of voters in a referendum with an estimated 62 per cent turnout, was promulgated in February 2006 and was another integral part of the required legislative architecture. Judges and staff at the Supreme Court and appellate courts had to be trained in these new laws and supported materially and logistically so they could do their job. Their security also had to be protected: the Supreme Court building in Kinshasa was attacked and burned on 21 November 2006 as judges were considering a complaint against the provisional results of the presidential runoff which showed that the main challenger to incumbent President Joseph Kabila, Vice-President Jean Pierre Bemba, had lost.[8]

Ultimately, Joseph Kabila won the second round and was inaugurated in December 2006. His main challenger, Jean-Pierre Bemba, won 42 per cent to Kabila's 58 per cent of the vote. Kabila carried the eastern provinces (with over 90 per cent of the vote in South Kivu) and Bemba

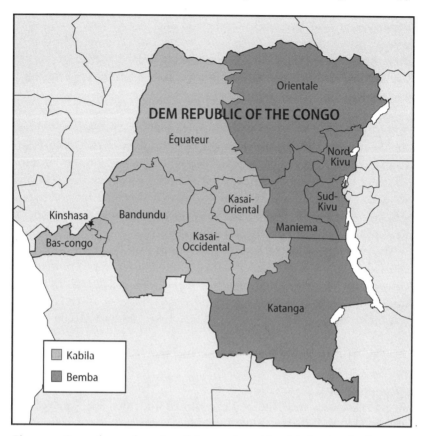

Figure 1. Second round results of the 2006 presidential election in the Democratic Republic of the Congo. Adapted from ElectoralGeography.Com (http://www.electoralgeography.com/new/en/wp-content/gallery/congo2006p/2006-congo-presidential-second.gif).

polled strongly in the west (especially Équateur and Kinshasa itself but also Bas-Congo and Western Kasai); this revealed a marked east-west divide roughly equivalent to the Swahili and Lingala-speaking parts of the country (see figure 1). Bemba initially contested the results, sparking the attack on the Supreme Court mentioned above, but ultimately conceded defeat in a statement crafted with important behind-the-scenes international involvement – as detailed below. The coalition backing Kabila, the Alliance for the Presidential Majority, won absolute majorities in both the National Assembly and Senate and, in the most blatant evidence of electoral fraud and lack of party discipline, won all provincial gubernatorial races except one (Équateur Province), even though the opposition alliance backing Bemba, the Union for the Congolese Nation, had won majorities in five of eleven provincial assemblies.[9]

Despite these "isolated cases," the collective verdict of the election observation missions sent by the European Union, the African Union, the Southern African Development Community (SADC), the Francophonie, the Carter Centre, the Electoral Institute for the Sustainability of Democracy in Africa (EISA) and others was that the elections were on the whole free and fair – and that the incidents of fraud, which in the presidential race had favoured both major contenders, were not of a scale to change the final results.[10]

The elections were "relatively" peaceful as well. That the Kinshasa-centred violence in particular was contained, given the very inauspicious security context heading into the elections, is a testament to the international community's successful deployment of all the conflict resolution tools at its disposal – military, financial, and diplomatic.

A HEAVILY INVESTED INTERNATIONAL COMMUNITY

After protracted negotiations under South African and international auspices, a peace deal, dubbed the Global and Inclusive Agreement, was signed by all parties to the Congolese conflict in Pretoria in 2002. The Agreement paved the way for a transition period (2003–06) culminating in elections. A key security component of the Agreement was that pro- and anti-government military forces be integrated into one national army, the Armed Forces of the Democratic Republic of Congo (Forces Armées de la République Démocratique du Congo, FARDC). Yet by 2006 (and to this day) the FARDC remained a grouping of various armed factions with no unified chain of command, poor training, little equipment, low morale, and an ongoing practice of commanders embezzling funds destined for salaries and operations. The extensive mafia-like business dealings of criminal networks operating within the highest ranks of the FARDC have been documented by a UN-mandated group of experts reporting to the Security Council Sanctions Committee.[11] Some analysts considered the new integrated army to be the worst human rights abuser in the country.[12] The Congolese National Police is only marginally better.

Though ultimately none disrupted the elections, several militias remained outside the peace process and added to security concerns. Foreign-armed groups such as the Democratic Forces for the Liberation of Rwanda remained in the bush, for example. Numerous Congolese rebellions in Ituri, Katanga, and the Kivus also remained in the bush, including what would soon become the "post-conflict" DRC's most prominent rebellion and biggest thorn in Kinshasa's side, the National Congress for the Defence of the People led by dissident General Laurent Nkunda and established in July 2006 – in the middle of the election period.

The more immediate threats to the process, however, were the private armies of the two lead presidential contenders. Kabila reportedly had roughly 12,000 Presidential Guard troops under his control and Bemba, a personal protection guard of between 800 and 900 men. Both candidates refused to send their troops for integration into the FARDC, fearing for their personal security. The situation reached a breaking point when it became clear that a runoff was required, as no presidential candidate had won over 50 per cent during the first round in July. On the same day that first-round presidential results were to be announced (45 per cent for Kabila, 20 per cent for Bemba), both men's forces exchanged heavy fire in Kinshasa. Fighting lasted over three days, from 20 to 23 August, and at one point Kabila's forces surrounded Bemba's residence, trapping diplomats from over half a dozen Western and African countries, members of the International Committee in Support of the Transition (discussed below), who were with Bemba at the time attempting to mediate.[13]

The international community was already deeply invested in the peace process by the time the elections were being planned, and was therefore eager to safeguard this financial and diplomatic capital, as well as find a palatable exit strategy and potentially even reap some rewards from their aid dollars via bilateral business deals. The clearest sign of the international financial, diplomatic, and military investment in the Congolese peace process was the US$1 billion key donors were spending annually at the time on the UN peacekeeping force, MONUC, known since July 2010 as the United Nations Organization Stabilization Mission in the Democratic Republic of the Congo (MONUSCO).[14] Indeed MONUC/MONUSCO was, and remains at the time of writing, the largest and most expensive UN peacekeeping force in the world.

In a push to see the transition through, the international community collectively became even more deeply involved: the direct cost of the DRC elections ultimately came to an estimated US$450 million, on top of which came the peacekeeping costs, plus costs associated with a special EU military backup force (EUFOR-DRC, cost €100 million) and of course donor humanitarian and development aid that continued to be disbursed alongside support to elections. About 1,000 international experts from the UN, international institutions, and NGOs were involved in some aspect of the elections. One hundred and six UN aircraft (the equivalent of Africa's second largest air fleet) and hundreds of vehicles and even boats were put at the disposal of the CEI for the transport of staff and materials.

Given the state of the national security forces, securing the elections was in large measure going to be up to MONUC and its approximately 18,000 uniformed personnel. The EU had agreed to send EUFOR-DRC to backup MONUC for a four-month period; with operational headquarters in Germany, the EU force had 1,300 "over-the-horizon" reserve forces in Gabon, a light presence (1,100 troops) in Kinshasa, as well as a strategic reserve in Europe (about 1,600 troops) and air support based in Chad if required.[15]

HIGH-LEVEL MEDIATION

The sums mentioned above are important, but when compared to per capita/per election round spending on other internationally supported elections, the DRC was, relatively speaking, a very good deal. The international community spent US$1.40 dollars per capita on elections in DRC, but $5.80 in the 2005 general election in Liberia and $5.70 in the 2004 election in Afghanistan.[16] In terms of uniformed personnel, MONUC's 18,000 and EUFOR-DRC's cumulative 4,000 troops both inside and outside the country were not negligible, but paled in comparison to the size of the country and the task at hand. Analysts criticized the troop numbers, mandate, and geographical restriction (Kinshasa) of the EU force as "cosmetic."[17] And comparisons to other cases underscored the disconnect between needs and means: 40,000 NATO troops were sent to tiny Kosovo, for example.[18]

Perhaps a more convincing sign of a sincere, serious involvement by the international community was the high-level mediation efforts led by a group of ambassadors operating in the International Committee in Support of the Transition (Comité international d'accompagnement de la transition, CIAT) on the one hand, and the prominent international personalities of the Comité International des Sages (international committee of the wise or CIS), on the other.

At the height of the election tensions, the fourteen African and Western diplomats of the CIAT – including the representatives of the EU, AU, and UN, as well as ambassadors from Angola, Belgium, Canada, China, France, Gabon, Russia, South Africa, the UK, US, and Zambia – worked together, at times daily, and in a highly coordinated manner not seen before or since. The pressure they were able to bring to bear on all actors was considerable: the fourteen represented the DRC's major donors who collectively funded approximately half of the DRC government annual budget.[19] And, through the special representative of the secretary-general, who also acts as the head of the peacekeeping mission, a certain amount of military power was at their disposal as well. On top of the institutions and resources each of the CIAT members represented, CIAT also benefited from a legal status as a formal body of the transitional government – it had been established and mandated by the Global and Inclusive Agreement to mediate between signatories and help implement the transition.[20]

Like CIAT, the CIS worked to resolve election-related conflicts, but its mandate, size, source of influence, and style of work were different. The CIS was agreed to in an April 2006 joint declaration of the five Congolese democracy support institutions, with the double endorsement of then UN Secretary-General Kofi Annan and AU President Denis Sassou Nguesso. Led by former President of Mozambique Joaquim Chissano, Senegalese Prime Minister Mame Madior Boye, and Tanzanian Judge and former Electoral Commission Chairman Lewis Makame, their influence was based entirely on the rapport they were able to build with key electoral actors and the personal moral authority they derived from their status as eminent African politicians and officials.[21] Most influential was Chissano, because of his status as a former head of state. Their role resembled more that of special envoys than official mediators and, as such, there was no formal decision-making process or binding agreements between the Sages and their Congolese interlocutors.

The CIS held eight sessions of consultations over a six-month period starting shortly before the first round of elections on 30 July. They met all thirty-three presidential candidates and listened to lengthy allegations of electoral fraud without challenging them. Instead, the CIS encouraged candidates to begin collecting evidence of such fraud immediately so they could present it to the courts after the preliminary results were announced, as prescribed by the constitution. The CIS also met with the leaders of the most important political parties in the National Assembly to discuss forming coalitions and the role of a political opposition. They met with key political figures such as the presidents of the National Assembly and Senate, and repeatedly with the four former vice-presidents of the transitional government – two of whom were former rebel leaders who, along with President Kabila, could potentially revert to violence if they made the calculation that elections results were too unfavourable. The CIS further met with representatives of the CEI and the Higher Media Authority (Haute Autorité des Médias, HAM) as well as various civil society representatives and religious leaders, considered public opinion leaders. The fact that the CIS was solicited by many of these key actors, including particularly Vice-President Bemba, was encouraging.

Whereas CIAT apparently suffered from the sheer size of its membership and from lack of cohesion between some of its members toward the end of the transition,[22] there were no such problems within the three-person CIS, with Chissano clearly in a leadership role. Moreover, whereas some of the Western ambassadors and the UN itself were perceived as pro-Kabila, the CIS seemed to be perceived by candidates in the various electoral races as impartial. This, and the fact that they were African politicians, and in the case of Chissano a former rebel who had successfully navigated through a post-conflict election, made the advice they could proffer more credible and much more relevant. Presidential candidate and vice-president in the transition, Azarias Ruberwa, solicited Chissano's advice on bodyguards and personal security, for example. Ruberwa was perhaps the biggest loser of the electoral process and was considered a high-risk spoiler. Having led the Congolese Rally for Democracy, at one time the largest rebel group with a third of the national territory under its control, Ruberwa, who was closely associated with Rwanda, won 1.7 per cent of the vote in the presidential election.[23] Chissano took Ruberwa's security concerns seriously and a lengthy conversation during which Chissano shared his personal experience on vetting bodyguards, including the importance of national ethnic representation, ensued. Chissano also explained the regulations that safeguarded the role of opponents in the Mozambican parliament to the newly elected opposition members of the National Assembly, worried about their potential marginalization under a Kabila regime.

However the single most important role the CIS probably played was in the wake of the November 2006 attack on the Supreme Court as it considered Bemba's challenge to second-round results. Though the intervention was not publicized due to its sensitivity, Bemba had reached out to Chissano for advice and, during a lengthy discussion, Chissano was apparently able to convince Bemba to concede defeat, appeal for calm, and vow to take up a role within the democratic opposition. Chissano walked Bemba through what elements should be included in his concession statement and at times suggested specific phrasing that ultimately found its way into Bemba's statement, released the following day. An assessment by the CIS secretariat concluded: "Even though it is difficult to attribute Vice-President Bemba's public statement to accept the results to the mediation efforts of the [CIS], it was certainly made in the conciliatory spirit of the advice given by the Committee and not in the usual language used by Candidate Bemba ... [M]any key stakeholders attributed the ... surprisingly peaceful end of the electoral process to the work of the Committee."[24]

But the CIS and CIAT's interventions were not necessarily welcomed by all, especially those within the *espace présidentiel*, Kabila's influential palace clique of unelected advisers, who chafed under the sustained international pressure for restraint. They had already been unpleasantly surprised at not winning outright at the first round and began more or less openly resenting the "informal international tutelage" they deemed themselves to have been put under.[25]

As a result, since 2006 government authorities have gone to some lengths to assert themselves, immediately discounting proposals to have the CIAT, CIS, or other iterations (such as the African Forum)[26] continue their work post-elections. Even during the period of the elections, access to Kabila was not easy and he even refused to see Chissano and others after the preliminary announcement of the results of the second round – when tensions were at their absolute highest.

PUTTING OUT FIRES: EISA AND LOCAL CONFLICTS

EISA, the Electoral Institute for the Sustainability of Democracy in Africa, is an NGO established in Johannesburg in 1996. From monitoring elections in southern Africa, it has expanded to broader democracy and good governance promotion covering the African continent as a whole. In 1999, EISA first introduced Conflict Management Panels in South Africa, in partnership with the South African Independent Electoral Commission. The panel model consists of training community leaders tasked with identifying the nature and origin of real or imagined local conflicts, working with local electoral commission staff to promote transparent and free elections, encouraging voter turnout, and, where possible, actively getting involved in resolving conflicts around elections and election results via mediation, facilitation, and arbitration. The panel model has been adapted and used by EISA in more than fifteen African countries, including the DRC.

Indeed from 2005–06, 3,200 panel members were recruited, trained, and deployed into all territories and constituencies across the DRC.[27] They were chosen to represent particular communities and select groups within these communities – customary (traditional) chiefs, religious leaders, youth, women, civil society or labour union representatives, public administration officials, and so on. Panel members did not have an affiliation with a particular candidate or political party and were chosen after popular consultations to identify credible people who had shown wisdom, leadership, and impartiality in their daily lives. If circumstances warranted, members of specific ethnic groups were deliberately sought out for the panels: Hutu, Tutsi, and Nande in North Kivu, Hema and Lendu in Ituri.

Relying on training tools EISA had developed and fine-tuned since 1999, training sessions were organized and adapted to the DRC setting. The training tools cover psychosocial aspects of conflict: the phenomenon of rumours is discussed, as are human emotions such as anger. Distinctions between intra-communal, interpersonal, and inter-communal conflictual relations are made and notions of groupthink and the influence of opinion leaders on groups are discussed. The training encourages participants to find local examples and anecdotes to illustrate each kind of conflict. Electoral principles and the specific texts of DRC's relevant laws were also covered extensively as election-related disputes can often be linked to a misunderstanding of these principles and laws. Training materials are made accessible to even those mediators who might be illiterate through the inclusion of audio-visual materials.

Once trained, the panels are deployed to their respective home regions. EISA encourages mediators to identify streets, markets, public places, or areas adjacent to voting centres where they can approach fellow citizens. Training and deployment are usually timed to precede voter registration – that is, the beginning of the electoral exercise – and finish after the announcement of results so that the panels can function over the entire election lifecycle. In the DRC, mediators were also given work kits that included T-shirts, jackets, caps, and badges so they could be identified but also distinguished from CEI staff and others.

During the course of the election, the panels are meant to act as mobile social intervention units, early warning systems for the CEI, and as a type of mapping unit compiling monthly reports that include statistics for a database that details types of conflicts, conflict-provoking agents, and zones of recurring conflict. EISA's approach to election-related conflict resolution places independent electoral commissions in a central position – in part, because in many post-conflict contexts the judiciary is perceived as partial, inaccessible, or without the necessary means. In the DRC, the panels were granted legal status vis-à-vis the IEC.[28] Each panel was, therefore, under the direct responsibility of each local division of the CEI. The panels' reports were sent to the CEI, which coordinated mediation activity at a national level with EISA technical assistance. The CEI actually used some of its own funds to help finance the project, further evidence of CEI buy-in and the regard in which the CEI held the work of the panels and EISA. Indeed, the early warning and conflict mapping functions of the panels helped the CEI fulfill one of its core mandates, to prevent and mitigate election-related conflicts.

The panels are not security forces, do not interpose themselves forcefully, and are obviously not armed. But within the limits and liberties conferred by national laws and the parameters set out by the CEI, panels nonetheless were able to intervene quite successfully in numerous contexts in all parts of the country to mediate conflicts surrounding misinterpretations of electoral legislation, political intimidation, hindrances to the secrecy of the vote, and free political campaigning. For instance, in July 2006 a panel member explained to a National Assembly candidate in Bandundu Province that he could not use a local government vehicle to conduct his campaign and convinced him to return the vehicle.[29] The same month, a panel was able to intervene to allow a candidate from a small local party in Équateur Province to campaign in a market area as she had planned; she had been blocked by members of a major national party who claimed the area was their stronghold and that there was, therefore, no campaigning by other parties allowed. In Bas-Congo Province on election day, a panel was able to calm an angry crowd of voters who had been turned away from a voting office.[30] The voters were travelling on 30 July and had not been aware that they could only vote in the offices where they had registered; they were ultimately convinced to leave peacefully. In Maniema and Katanga Provinces, panel members intervened and stopped illegal, ongoing campaigning by several candidates to the National Assembly in voting centres on election day.

As illustrated by these examples and the many more that EISA has documented, the mediators used the mediation skills and knowledge of the electoral laws and procedures they were taught, combining this with Congolese traditions of storytelling and negotiation, to help diffuse conflictual situations. The authority of each mediator within his or her group of origin also helped them intervene with credibility.

The continuing violence in the DRC, despite significant peacebuilding efforts, represents a real failure of international policy. One explanation for this is that the international community sees its role and realm of intervention through a peacebuilding "frame" in which continued violence is a normal condition in Congo, and national and regional leaders the only legitimate interlocutors.[31] This belief system – and the focus on national and regional actors in particular – persists even though violence and institutional dysfunctionality are known to be interlinked with, sometimes even driven and organized by, local actors and agendas. EISA's efforts were aimed at engaging with some of these local actors and agendas, to complement the work of the international community, led by the CIAT and the CIS, which focused entirely on national-level conflict and Kinshasa-based actors.

The end of elections doesn't mean the end of social and political conflicts. With Swedish funding, EISA-trained mediators have been able to reorganize themselves to concentrate on other social conflicts, such as tensions between ethnic communities, land disputes, disputes between customary or traditional authorities (such as *Mwamis*), and so on. Since 2008, some of the mediators have received further training and have been operating in ten of the DRC's eleven provinces, where they continue to monitor and report monthly on social and other conflicts and work to draw the attention of local authorities to these conflicts with a view toward their resolution. But the work of

EISA seems to be unique – not only in its methods but also in its persistent focus on local conflict management – suggesting that international peacebuilding efforts remain overly focused on the international and national actors, neglecting all important linkages between international, national, and local actors and local dynamics and incentive structures. EISA's work is also limited by insufficient resources and funding constraints, as well as weak state institutions; panels are a cost-effective and more accessible form of alternative dispute resolution, but they are not substitutes for a functioning legal apparatus.

CONCLUSION: WHAT'S PAST IS FUTURE

One year after the end of the elections, the UN SRSG for DRC wrote:

> A major global challenge to us all in the global community is to remain engaged following successful elections in countries emerging from conflict. ... Ironically, the exponential increase in popular post-electoral expectations too often confronts a countervailing donor tendency to reduce support after successful elections ...
>
> In most post-election situations, therefore, a "sustainment strategy" is more urgent than an "exit strategy." For this to happen, there must be a change in our own thinking.[32]

Official Development Assistance (ODA) figures show that, for most donors, aid levels tapered off precipitously after 2006, reinforcing the idea that, despite such calls to stay engaged, the elections were indeed little more than an exit strategy. The international community nonetheless remains present in the DRC, most visibly through MONUSCO. Yet it is unclear whether general elections planned for 2011 will be peaceful, much less free and fair (even with the lowered bar of 2006). What funding levels donors will be willing to provide for these oft-overlooked yet key "second" elections remains to be seen.

The holding of the 2006 elections was in itself a significant achievement that offers some lessons applicable to other conflict settings: the military, diplomatic, and financial support of the international community helped bring the elections and the transition process back from the brink of collapse in August and November 2006. The CIAT allowed for unprecedented daily coordination of all major international actors. However it is the work of the CIS that seems to hold particular promise – with important caveats, including first and foremost finding skilled, well-suited and willing eminent persons. In the DRC, the CIS had access and influence unparalleled by other members of the international community, based almost entirely on its chief's past personal experience as a rebel turned respected politician, the esteem accorded to the high offices each member had held, and the fact that they were African brothers and sisters. The CIS further benefited from being mandated not only by international organizations (the UN and AU) but also by Congolese (democracy support) institutions.

All these efforts and resources were heavily focused on Kinshasa and national-level actors. EISA's Conflict Management Panels helped diffuse numerous local conflicts across the country, many of which arose out of an ignorance or a (wilful?) misinterpretation of electoral laws. Though international actors assume these to be lower profile and therefore less important, it is precisely these kinds of conflicts that fuel popular distrust and help legitimate the rhetoric of those who would use violence to confront the state.

The achievements above were marred by instances of violent repression of political opponents during the polls, a clear drift toward authoritarianism in Kinshasa since the polls, and continuing impunity and state failure. What's more, violence in both the east and west resurfaced almost immediately after the elections and, strategically, the 2006 electoral results further emphasized the degree to which the country remained divided (see figure 1).

In this way, the 2006 elections can be qualified as a success only in terms of the execution of the process. In terms of the intended outcomes, disappointing on all fronts, the DRC speaks more to the argument of delaying elections in war-to-peace transitional contexts and engaging in more "institutionalization" before "liberalization."[33] For these reasons, the DRC case compellingly reinforces Reilly's conclusion that it is increasingly difficult to argue that elections are a central component to a successful post-conflict peacebuilding strategy.

7

Dying to Win: Elections, Political Violence, and Institutional Decay in Kenya*

SUSANNE D. MUELLER

They must be taught to accept defeat and look forward to other good things for if no one was a loser then what would happen?

Kimani Njogu[1]

This paper examines the lessons learned from Kenya's 2007 post-election violence and what has happened since then. It notes that the root causes of the violence still persist, have not been addressed, and easily could be reignited. Faced with a situation where institutions and the rule of law have been weakened deliberately and where diffused violence is widespread, both Kenya's transition to democracy and the fate of the nation remain vulnerable. The argument here is that the problems faced in holding and managing elections in conflict situations often are not simply technical. Instead, in Kenya and elsewhere, many difficulties are symptomatic of larger political and institutional questions related to democratic change that are more difficult to analyze in causal terms or to address.

Democratic theorists, including Robert Dahl and others,[2] have long understood that democracy consists of considerably more than multiparty elections. At the heart of the democratic experiment are two underlying caveats bordering on truisms. First, there must be a willingness to lose elections and not to win them by any means and at all costs, including killing one's opponents. In established democracies, both politicians and the public generally accept that tomorrow is another day to get their person elected. Second, and central to democracy and the democratic process, is a belief in the integrity of the rule of law and institutions that must be matched by the way in which laws and institutions operate in practice. Where this does not occur, democracy is vulnerable. However, there is little by way of agreement about the underlying causes or events that give rise to these two factors or trigger the incentives for elite consensus necessary for their emergence.

Clearly, the acceptance of loss and institutions bound by the rule of law do not emerge as a result of altruism but are instead the product of other factors.[3] Nevertheless, in their absence, a vicious circle ensues. As Acemoglu and Robinson note, where political elites are not constrained by checks and balances and are not forced to be accountable,[4] they will use their de facto power to undermine de jure changes and "avoid democratic institutions which are more costly for them" in terms of power and rents.[5] One such cost is an undesirable shorter time in office. To avoid this outcome, Collier and Hoeffler find that incumbents in new democracies more than doubled their time in office, from 6.4 to 15.8 years, by using "dirty [electoral] tactics" such as rigging.[6] This suggests that politicians have powerful incentives to subvert laws and institutions that keep them from gaining or retaining power. Politicians don't want to lose and will do whatever is necessary to stay in power. When they are successful, this creates dangerous incentives and possibilities for even further deinstitutionalization and even greater dissipation of the rule of law. A vicious circle then ensues, with institutional decay and lawlessness begetting more of the same as well as inviting further recourse to violence once institutional constraints are removed.

Boone's research finds that the less constrained elites are in terms of laws and institutions, the greater the likelihood is that they also will resort to other means to gain or retain power, including using violence. In her discussion of electoral populism in Côte d'Ivoire, Boone shows how land was expropriated and rules concerning citizenship were changed as both were mobilized as forms of electoral patronage. This meant that existing institutions, laws, and rules were all irrelevant and up for grabs with the introduction of multipartyism. The only thing that mattered was "who was in control of the central government," not what was on the books. In short, once sacrosanct rights concerning land and citizenship suddenly became malleable, nothing was "fixed" or "neutral." This paved the way for the possibility of expropriation, violence and "politics in which losers h[ad] few incentives to abide by outcomes generated through elections."[7]

In situations comparable to those in Kenya, institutional checks and balances and rules concerning accountability may exist on paper. Often, however, they are overridden personally by politicians, civil servants, and others operating under an entirely different set of informal incentives, sanctions, and enforcement mechanisms. Public trust in institutions and the rule of law then dissipates. This increases the propensity for electoral and other contests to be resolved in the streets through violence rather than around tables or in courts. This may induce a vicious circle-like syndrome with violence rather than the law or institutions becoming the likely arbiter. Violence undermines democracy. Furthermore, in circumstances where violence is a cost-effective way of competing for power and there is no consequence for using it, it is difficult both to ensure non-violent political competition and for it to be about much more than "who will protect me from harm from the other side." Also, violence tends then to beget more violence. Politicians are dying to win and, freed of institutional and legal constraints, are able and willing to use violence to achieve their ends.

In these circumstances, there is every reason for both local and international organizations to try to improve institutions involved in the electoral process. However, in the absence of incentives to adhere to the rule of law and a well founded practical belief in the integrity and legitimacy of institutions, institutional reforms may be bypassed, undermined, and not accepted by the political elite or the public. In situations like these, particularly where violence has previously been used as an arbiter and where the incentives of the political class have not changed, more violence and a further breakdown of order is increasingly likely.

In Kenya, many local and external organizations have been engaged in attempts to improve the electoral process. For the most part, existing efforts to consolidate democracy have focused on changing formal laws and institutions without considering the incentives and enforcement mechanisms that are necessary to support them. This has involved a variety of technical initiatives: trying to institutionalize a more equitable playing field surrounding the conduct of elections; improving the nomination process and how political parties function before, during, and after elections; creating a better, improved, and more independent electoral commission, electoral rolls, vote tallying, and monitoring procedures; and addressing other issues that surround the electoral process, including constituency delimitation and access to the media. However, these efforts are not self-enforcing as they do not necessarily affect the incentives or ability of actors to arbitrarily change rules or to resort to extra-institutional and violent modes of behaviour. Hence, the question arises whether, given the intensified political and ethnic divisions and the continued diffusion of violence in Kenya since the 2007 election, the consensus exists to improve institutions in these areas and, even if they are changed on paper, whether these improvements will be subverted or undermined in practice in an electoral crunch or for other reasons. In short, formal institutional changes may not inhibit more rounds of violence in the future. An election might or might not be the precipitating factor. Also, as the diffusion of various types of violence proliferates, the catalyst next time could be something else entirely.

These issues and observations feed into broader questions that have been raised but have been far from answered fully by political scientists, policy makers, and practitioners: whether observers were too quick to put the democratic label on what are mostly "virtual democracies" or exercises in "competitive authoritarianism";[8] whether certain underlying structural conditions (e.g., levels of economic development, institutionalization of the rule of law, sequencing, etc.) are essential prerequisites for genuine multiparty democracy;[9] whether as others argue, the evidence supports the view that engaging in multiparty democracy is in itself a positive practice that facilitates democratic behaviour; or whether, even if this is sometimes true, the effects of electoral participation may still be heavily diluted by some of the broader political economy factors discussed above.[10]

While discussing these issues fully in the context of Kenya is outside the scope of this paper, much of what has happened there raises similar questions. Kenya's rising and entrepreneurial middle class and the belief that it would embrace the rule of law and strong institutions to protect its interests intellectually underlay the positive but incorrect spin on Kenya's transition to democracy.[11] Many thought that with its peaceful 2002 election, Kenya had made it, ignoring the fact that the two main contestants for president not only were members of the same ethnic group but that many underlying generic factors had not changed. The results of the 2002 presidential election, in turn, seemed to buttress the notion of voluntarism: the idea that elections themselves, and later the 2005 referendum on the constitution where Kibaki government did not contest its loss, were positive signs of good practices that promoted democracy. In fact, as elections in Kenya and the theorizing about them continued, so did the proliferation of non-state violence, the emergence of possible "shadow states,"[12] the personalization of power, a zero-sum view of winning infused by ethnicity, and the persistence of unreformed institutions. This was coupled with the hollowing out of institutions and a hardening of the notion of winning at all costs, with ethnic polarization increasing and the nation becoming more violent and fragile.

The discussion here indirectly grapples with some of the above issues. It is divided into three parts. The first part discusses the roots of Kenya's 2007 post-election violence, drawing on a previous article.[13] The second part examines these same factors one by one. It argues that they still are very much in place and, if anything, have increased in their intensity. This increases the likelihood of more and possibly greater violence in the future, something reinforced by the failure of the political class to deal with impunity and to establish a Special Tribunal recommended by the Commission of Inquiry into Post-Election Violence (CIPEV), often referred to as the Waki Commission.[14] The third part of the paper outlines the challenges of peacefully managing political and electoral conflict in situations like Kenya and suggests possible approaches for the future. Principal among these is the necessity to understand that, given the persistence of existing incentives and enforcement mechanisms, formal changes to improve democracy, whether by strengthening electoral institutions and practices or by adopting a new constitution, as Kenya recently has done, continue to run the risk of being undermined in practice.

THE ROOTS OF VIOLENCE AND CONFLICT IN KENYA'S 2007 ELECTION CRISIS

In an earlier article[15] I discussed three underlying factors that predisposed Kenya to violence and were ignited by a too close to call contested election. I am reiterating them here because they still shape Kenya's landscape and still predispose it to more violence, whether electoral or non-electoral, something discussed in the next section.

The three factors at the root of the 2007 implosion were a gradual decline in the state's monopoly of legitimate force and a consequent generalized level of violence not always within its control; deliberately weak institutions, mostly overridden by a highly personalized and centralized presidency that could but did not exercise the autonomy or checks and balances normally associated with democracies; and political parties that were not programmatic, were driven by ethnic clientism, and had a winner-take-all view of political power and its associated economic rewards. The central point here is that violence was diffused, could be ignited easily but not controlled, and was not; that institutions outside the presidency normally associated with vetting a contested election were not viewed as being sufficiently neutral to do so and did not; and that the nature of Kenya party politics predisposed both leaders and followers to see politics as a do or die zero sum game, which is what the 2007 election became. Had the election not been so close, these same factors might have been held in check for a while. Nevertheless, they were and are dangerous and looming problems that put Kenya on a precipice and led to it descending into a spiral of death and destruction along ethnic lines, thereby fracturing the already fragile idea of state and nation.

Diffused violence

In the case of diffused violence, gang violence, increasingly out of the state's control, had become a larger and larger feature of Kenya's landscape, starting with the collapse of the Soviet Union and the decision to allow multiparty elections in 1991. Responding to international financial and local pressure, former president Daniel arap Moi agreed to accept multiparty elections in Kenya by rescinding the controversial section 2(a) of the constitution that had institutionalized a one party state. However, in practice, he detested the idea of multiparty democracy and was prepared to win at all costs, including using violence. Moi and his supporters used so-called "Kalenjin warriors" in the Rift Valley and elsewhere to kill and displace opposition voters from other ethnic groups, most of whom were Kikuyu, Luo, and Luhya, while civil servants working for the state turned a blind eye or aided and abetted this process. This happened before and during the 1992 and 1997 elections. This violence and these militias spawned other gangs and other militias, including the now famous Mungiki, Sungu Sungu, the Sabaot Land Defence Force, and a host of still others with menacing names commensurate with their activities, including the Taliban, the Baghdad Boys, and others. Moi's decision to hire extra state militia and to engage in what Katumanga has aptly called the "privatization of public violence"[16] had short and long-term consequences.

In the short run, Moi won both the 1992 and 1997 elections by undermining any notion of free and fair elections. The gangs used on his behalf killed and displaced his opponents, who themselves were divided. Before and during elections in the 1990s, politicians hired gangs: some to intimidate members of anti-government parties, others to protect themselves against pro-government gangs, and still others to do whatever was necessary to keep their opponents from voting and to win at any cost.

Over the longer run, whether between the two elections in the 1990s or before, during, and after the 2002 and 2007 elections, these extra-state militias and gangs took on a life of their own in many parts of the country. Gangs moved into the slums of Nairobi, the rural areas of Central Province, and into other parts of the country. Gangs such as Mungiki and others acted as well organized shakedown gangs, offering various types of "you can't say no" protection and services for fees. They moved into areas neglected by government or where officials and police turned a blind eye in exchange for kickbacks for themselves. During this process, extra-state violence became institutionalized with gangs like Mungiki infiltrating many businesses, much like the mafia. In addition, the state increasingly began to lose its "monopoly of legitimate force,"[17] with gangs increasingly taking over much of the geographic space and functions of government. Hence, what began as an electoral exercise to win the presidency and the majority in parliament at all cost gradually dissipated government control over its territory, threatening the integrity of state and nation. This meant that, by the time of the 2007 election, diffused gang violence was lying in wait and could be tapped, which is exactly what happened. One of the legacies of all these years was that using violence to win was acceptable, including in the case of a disputed election.

Deliberately weak institutions

A second factor predisposing Kenya to violence following the 2007 election was that institutions outside the presidency had been deliberately weakened over time through a series of constitutional amendments under both President Kenyatta and President Moi. They increased the power of the presidency and reduced that of other arms of government, including the judiciary, parliament, and various parts of the civil service. Furthermore, many of the checks and balances normally characteristic of democracies were abandoned both formally and informally. Civil servants and various arms of government understood how their bread was buttered and tended to defer to the president. Political and economic statism ensured that opposition was costly and would be punished.[18] This weakening of autonomous institutions paved the way for gross repression and torture under Moi and the pervasive corruption of the 1980s and 1990s. The latter included setting up nominally private banks that were no more than officially sanctioned money-laundering operations and paving the way for huge scandals under President Moi, such as the notorious Goldenberg and Anglo Leasing scandals (with the latter continuing under President Kibaki), as well as many dubious land grabbing exercises. During all these periods, the courts were seen as partisan and under the thumb of the executive: no one was ever prosecuted for torture, for the electoral violence of the 1990s,[19] or for corruption. Over time the state outside the president developed the seemingly contradictory characteristics of being deliberately weak and simultaneously predatory. While state predation lessened after the 2002 election of President Kibaki, it re-emerged after 2005, albeit initially in a more attenuated form.[20] This further decreased the legitimacy of state institutions.

Before the 2007 election, the Electoral Commission of Kenya (ECK) was also deliberately weakened. In 2007, President Kibaki bypassed an agreement to consult with the opposition before appointing new commissioners to the ECK and replaced them all before the election, including making his former lawyer the vice-chair of the Commission. He also created a number of new judicial vacancies, including appeals judges, before the election.

Because of the above practices, institutions that had already been seriously weakened totally lost their autonomy, independence, integrity, and legitimacy over time. Furthermore, even as late as 2007 there was no agreed upon an independent institutional arbiter to deal with allegations of rigging and that the election had been stolen. Hence, the dispute over the election took to the streets, even though much of the violence appears to have been organized in anticipation of possible loss.

In short, the combination of diffused violence that could be tapped, the willingness to win at all costs, and the graduation dissipation of the rule of law and strong institutions, all predisposed Kenya to implode.

Non-programmatic Clientist Political Parties and Zero Sum Ethnic Politics

Kenyan political parties are barely distinguishable in terms of ideology, programs, platforms, or organization. Many are no more than changing sets of ethnic coalitions. Even today's main leaders, including President Kibaki and Prime Minister Odinga, have moved opportunistically from one party to another as necessity has dictated.

Politics is viewed primarily as a winner-takes-all zero-sum ethnic game. The national economic cake is the prize, with various ethnic groups arguing that it is their turn to eat. The means to this end is controlling the state and having a fellow co-ethnic become president. As parties are not programmatic and institutions are weak, politicians are seen primarily as personal distributors of private rather than public goods. Even though alliances and cross-ethnic coalitions are necessary to win the presidency, the winner is seen by others as the chief ethnic in charge. Herein lies the importance of winning and not losing, particularly as political losses have meant being excluded from access to state resources.

Given the non-programmatic nature of Kenyan political parties, the lack of institutional checks on the president, his consequent personal power, and the expectations of benefits from clients, ethnicity is seen as critical in determining the distribution of national resources. In part, this explains the length to which leaders and followers are willing to go to get their person in power and the means they are willing to use to achieve their ends. Thus, politically inspired violence has accompanied successive multiparty elections from 1992 until 2007.

Even though many co-ethnics do not appear to gain materially from one of their own being in power, voting in Kenya generally falls along ethnic lines. One reason for this is what one might call the fear factor, or what I have called elsewhere "exclusionary ethnicity." In short, voters sometimes vote defensively against non-co-ethnics or coalitions of non-co-ethnics as the least bad alternative. Following the electoral violence since the 1990s when politically organized gangs killed, maimed, or destroyed the property of specific ethnic groups supporting the opposition, this fear increased along with defensive voting. While individual voters might like to gain materially as a client voter of a co-ethnic, even if that is not possible, they also vote out of fear that worse things might happen to them if a non-co-ethnic comes to power. This fear is enhanced because of the potential of the state to be arbitrary, predatory, and unpredictable, with laws being adjusted or bypassed to suit those who are in power.

President Kibaki's abnegation of his 2002 election promise to make Raila Odinga his prime minister and the 2005 watering down of a referendum to do so increased distrust between the Kikuyu and the Luo and other marginalized groups. The nature of non-programmatic winner-take-all clientist political parties fed into the polarization of ethnicity for political ends, which could be violently ignited after the contested 2007 election and was. Underlying this was a deep, long-seeded distrust about what would happen if another ethnic group or coalition of ethnic groups took over, as well as a willingness by the political elite and its opponents to win at all costs to hold on to or to obtain political power and all the material rewards that come with it.

Because of the factors just discussed above, two tenets fundamental to democracy were not accepted: political loss and the rule of law, which was perceived as arbitrary and subject to personal influence rather than legitimate and neutral. This in part is why violence prevailed and could do so again. Everyone was dying to win and willing to let others die on their behalf so they could.

THE CONTINUED SALIENCE OF DIFFUSED VIOLENCE, WEAK INSTITUTIONS AND ZERO-SUM POLITICS[21]

Since the 2007 elections the salience of the above factors not only has continued but has intensified. The demonstration effect of successful gangs has spawned new gangs, which have taken on a life of their own in the face of deliberately weakened institutions. Community vigilante groups initially organized to protect themselves from militia now have come to resemble them and ordinary citizens increasingly are being extorted on multiple fronts.[22]

Violence

In terms of violence, neither gang nor state-sponsored violence has been checked. Gangs have continued to proliferate, have increased their shakedown operations, and, in some areas, such as in Nyeri,

Murang'a, Meru, and the slums of Nairobi, have become virtual shadow states. Increasingly, the state has lost or abrogated its monopoly on legitimate force and finds it difficult to maintain peace or order. In part this is because politicians, having used gangs to gain or maintain power, now are themselves beholden to them or afraid of them. This bodes ill, not just for any future elections but also for the future of Kenya.

There are many different types of gangs: gangs engaged in extortion; freelance gangs that come and go; highly organized ethnic militia such as the Kikuyu Mungiki and, to a lesser extent, the Luo Taliban, among others; gangs connected to politicians and the police; gangs that over time have become independent of the forces that initially supported them; and new vigilante groups.

A May 2009 report by South Consulting Group[23] noted there has been "no systematic attempt to disband these groups." As a result, although these gangs are not trying to take over the state or to foment civil war,[24] their existence and activities have led to a dangerous erosion of the state's authority and its monopoly of legitimate force. In some areas, such as Nairobi's slums and parts of Central Province, including in the president's home area of Nyeri, gangs have effectively begun to displace government. They shakedown citizens and politicians, tax them, and demand protection fees to engage in ordinary activities such as building houses and even stopping at intersections. They also ominously mete out justice in informal courts, known in one area as "The Hague." Citizens are frightened. They dare not make reports to the police, who sometimes demand kickbacks from gang members, and have no place to turn. In some areas, individuals in parts of Nyeri have formed retaliatory vigilante groups to attack Mungiki groups themselves, leading to a further breakdown of law and order, increased extortion, and proliferating crime.

Elsewhere in the Rift Valley, where most of the deaths from the 2007 elections occurred, there are reports of increasing fear, polarization, hostility, and rearmament[25] and comments such as "never again" by the Kikuyu and "next time we will finish the project" by the Kalenjin.[26] Increasingly, the choice of weaponry now is an AK-47 rather than bows and arrows.

There has been no political leadership on how to address this proliferating violence, whether from the political elite or ordinary politicians who either are afraid of the gangs themselves or have supported them in the past. Human rights groups and the UN's Special Rapporteur on extrajudicial, summary, or arbitrary executions have castigated the police for killing innocent youth in their attempts to wipe out Mungiki.[27] In urban slums such as Kibera, chiefs and other officials are afraid to go after gang members and other thugs, as they fear they might be connected to high-level politicians.[28]

The combined effect of this is that gangs hold sway in many parts of the country, with the state having become impotent, indifferent, or having colluded with gangs to gain power to begin with, thereby making them untouchable. Increasingly, there is a powder keg–like quality to the situation. New gangs have formed in the past year and there is a growing lack of trust between ethnic groups and classes.[29] More and more individuals report having experienced violence in their lives and feeling unsafe,[30] something that bodes ill not just for Kenya's political, but for its economic, future. One result of the 2007 post-election violence was that two of Kenya's key sources of revenue, tourism and horticulture exports, declined by approximately 35 per cent and 40 per cent, respectively.[31] Even now, in many areas, gangs effectively have become government, perversely having taken over much of its physical space and functions, leaving citizens trapped.

A recent survey by Synovate reports that in areas affected by the 2007 election, 40 per cent of its respondents predict more violence in 2012.[32] In another survey, commissioned for the *Fourth Review Report* of the Kenya National Dialogue and Reconciliation Monitoring Project, 77 per cent of those surveyed blame politicians for inciting violence between different groups. This finding dovetails with surveys done in February 2008 by a group from Oxford.[33]

Institutions and Zero Sum Politics

Since the February 2008 agreement to form a "grand coalition," government has adhered to parts of the Annan agenda. It has set up commissions to investigate the election and the post-election violence, disbanded the former Electoral Commission of Kenya and established the new Interim Independent Electoral Commission as well as a constituency delimitation commission, the Truth, Justice and Reconciliation Commission, and other entities. In April 2010, after contentious discussions and negotiations, parliament also passed a new draft constitution prepared by a special Committee of Experts that was ratified by 67 per cent of the public in a referendum held on 4 August 2010.[34]

Just as in 2005, the referendum was peaceful and the passage of the constitution was heralded as evidence of Kenya having discarded violence and embraced a new era of peace. However, a peaceful referendum may not be a portent of peaceful elections in the future. The most important point is that the 2010 referendum was not an election; it was not about who gained and lost power or wealth. Also, it was not close and the state deployed 18,000 security forces in the Rift Valley alone.

Furthermore, behind these new recent formal entities and legal changes, the incentives that guide political life are much the same. Politicians are still mostly concerned with positioning themselves and their ethnically rooted parties for the 2012 election, are amassing wealth, are reluctant to pay taxes, and seem more intent on building expensive mansions for the vice-president and the prime minister and refurbishing various rural state houses than dealing with famine and hunger in the countryside. There also has been much political wrangling between President Kenyatta's largely Kikuyu-dominated Party of National Unity and Prime Minister Raila Odinga's Orange Democratic Movement, supported by but increasingly fractured between the prime minister and its Rift Valley supporters, led by Member of Parliament William Ruto, who campaigned against the new constitution and increasingly has been sidelined by both Kibaki and Odinga, who united in favour of its passage in what may be no more than a temporary[35] display of Kikuyu Luo unity harking back to the 1960s pre-independence Kenya African National Union alliance against Kenya African Democratic Union. Furthermore, nothing has changed in terms of the idea that it is necessary and important for particular ethnic groups and coalitions to control the state, at the very least to keep other groups from doing so. This underlying trajectory has led to continued standoffs between various factions in parliament and between the executive and the prime minister.[36]

As this continues, it is not clear that the political elite and their supporters are any more prepared to lose elections than they were before, or that there is much interest in establishing viable neutral institutions that will uphold the rule of law. Instead, every appointment or construction of a new institution is perceived to be part of someone's political agenda, which it often is, and is fought. This occurs because every political act has the potential to tilt the balance of power permanently away from one's own ethnic group. In a winner-take-all setting, this is a fearful event.

This continuation of politics as usual has been most apparent than in the failed attempt to establish a special tribunal, recommended by the Waki Commission, to investigate and prosecute high-level perpetrators of the 2007 post-election violence.[37] Initially, parliament, which was supposed to pass laws anchoring the tribunal in the constitution and insulating it from the local courts, failed to muster the majority to do so. It missed its deadlines. For both good and bad reasons, different MPs voted for and against the bill in February 2009. Some voted against having a special tribunal because they felt it could not operate on Kenyan soil without being subverted, even if there was an international presence. Other MPs felt it was important for the country for justice to take place locally and that it was possible. Still other MPs wanted the case to go to the International Criminal Court (ICC) in The Hague. Some MPs preferred the ICC alternative because they thought this was the only way to avoid political interference and seek justice. Others opted for The Hague because they thought it would take longer to pursue perpetrators and the ICC would go after fewer of them than a special tribunal. (Under the rules of complementarity in the Rome Statute, cases can be taken up by the ICC only if a country itself is unable or unwilling to prosecute high level perpetrators for genocide, crimes against humanity, or war crimes.)

When it concluded its work, the Waki Commission passed over an envelope with a list of high-level organizers and financiers of the 2007 violence to the former secretary-general of the United Nations, Kofi Annan. Once Kenya's parliament voted down the bill to establish a special tribunal in February 2009, Annan then gave the Kenyans a number of additional extensions that were missed. Later, he met a government delegation in July 2009 when it came to Geneva and The Hague to discuss the situation and to plead for more time. At that point, Annan finally had had enough of Kenyan attempts at procrastination and passed on the envelope to the ICC's chief prosecutor, Luis Moreno-Ocampo. Thereafter, the Kenyan delegation signed minutes with Moreno-Ocampo agreeing to take steps to establish a special tribunal or an "alternative judicial mechanism," after which it would report back to Moreno-Ocampo on their progress at the end of September 2009.

As of August 2009, Kenya's cabinet had failed to agree on the proposed law to establish a special tribunal, splitting, among other matters, over clauses that would deny the president immunity and would keep the attorney general from interfering in cases so as to make the law consistent with the Rome Statute. Instead, Kenya's cabinet decided it would like to try all cases in its own courts, having promised to reform the judiciary or expand the Truth, Justice and Reconciliation Commission for this purpose. These proposals were roundly criticized by the Kenyan public and human rights groups. Afterwards, some MPs, led by Gitobu Imanyara, put together a new private member's bill to establish a special tribunal. At the time, it was not expected to garner enough votes to pass. However, even before this point was reached, the bill failed to obtain a quorum in parliament and thus could not even be debated. In their earlier agreed upon minutes with Moreno-Ocampo, the Kenyan delegation had promised to "self refer" to the ICC if it failed to implement its agreement, something that never happened. In November 2009, Moreno-Ocampo requested permission from the ICC's pre-trial chamber of three judges to begin a formal investigation of those most responsible for Kenya's post-election violence. On 31 March 2010, he received authorization to do so in a two to one majority opinion.[38] Since then, the ICC has been investigating the Kenya case. In mid-December 2010, the ICC's chief prosecutor submitted evidence to the Court's Pre-Trial Chamber to seek its approval to prosecute six publicly named high-level perpetrators of Kenya's 2007–08 post-election violence. The list includes top level political figures: three cabinet ministers, Kenya's most senior civil servant, the former chief of police, and one radio broadcaster.[39] Following the announcement, parts of the political elite have gone on a rampage against the ICC while the majority of citizens surveyed in opinion polls continue to support it. The counterattack has included embracing accused co-ethnics and passing a motion in parliament to pull Kenya out of the Rome Statute by repealing the International Crimes Act of 2009.[40] Some argue the motion flies in the face of Kenya's new constitution, which incorporates all international treaties signed before its passage. From the standpoint of this article, it is simply one more example of the ongoing malleability of the rule of law in Kenya and continued political attempts to subvert it, notwithstanding its recent new constitution.

Part of the reason for the Waki Commission's recommendations for a special tribunal was to pursue justice for the victims of the 2007 post-election violence and to deal with the issue of impunity. No high-level figures in Kenya have ever been prosecuted for the increasingly deadly violence surrounding elections since the early 1990s, much of which stems from the continued refusal to lose elections and the willingness to use violence to win. The failure of the Waki Commission's recommendations to set up a special tribunal and the stasis that followed showed that there continues to be no political stomach for high-level political figures to shed some of their own and to pursue justice. More recently, the sudden about-face by Kenyan parliamentarians to swiftly reform the judiciary and to set up a tribunal to try perpetrators of the post-election violence is not indicative of any newfound commitment to the rule of law. Instead, it is a cynical and unlikely attempt to wrest the cases currently before the ICC away from it and back to Kenya to ensure that business as usual rather than justice prevails.

The incentives guiding the above decisions to date indicate there is still no desire among the political class for strong autonomous independent institutions, applying the rule of law, or accepting political loss. Given the continued diffusion of violence, its escalation, and the lack of countervailing institutional forces, the next presidential election in 2012 could be as, if not more, challenging as the last one, notwithstanding provisions in the new constitution to hedge against that possibility. Violence may once again be the arbiter, before, during, or after the next election, if Kenya does not reignite before then. Politicians still are dying to win and violence or the threat of violence continues to be the order of the day.[41]

Following the submission of the Waki Report to the government of Kenya in October 2008, potential witnesses who might be called upon either by a special tribunal or by the ICC have increasingly been hunted down, intimidated, run out of the country, and even killed. They include ordinary citizens, possible witnesses, human rights workers attempting to protect witnesses, MPs, priests, civil servants, and others.[42] Various forms of harassment have escalated further since the ICC referred the Kenya case to its pre-trial chamber. The message being sent to victims of the post-election violence, witnesses, and their human rights defenders who want justice and would like to see the rule of law prevail is clear: keep quiet or watch out and suffer. The disincentives for action are very costly. This reinforces the existing status quo, further weakens institutions, and increases the propensity for violence still further.

LESSONS LEARNED AND CHALLENGES IN MANAGING ELECTORAL CONFLICT

The report of Kenya's Independent Review Commission (IREC) in September 2008 recommended a number of technical and institutional changes that needed to be implemented to improve the quality of elections in Kenya. Among them were a new electoral commission, a new voter register, changes in a number of electoral procedures, including tallying, demarcating more equally sized constituencies, and developing sound dispute settlement mechanisms, and others.

To date some of these suggested changes have taken place or are being considered. However, Justice Kriegler also noted in his report that in assessing the 2007 election it was important distinguish between "anomalies, failures, and malpractices traceable to gaps or provisions in the constitution and laws of Kenya from those that can be attributed to a bad culture encompassing impunity, disrespect for the rule of law and institutional incompetence." He went on to argue that in Kenya in 2007, "nominally democratic elections" took place "within [the] old practices of a one party state." He noted that relevant laws were on the books but were not adhered to.[43] Kriegler also maintained that the incentives to apply relevant laws were non-existent, and insisted "nobody would have dreamt of seriously acting against people in high places or even highish places."[44]

This correct observation by Kriegler supports numerous other commission reports. This includes the Akiwumi report on the so called "ethnic clashes" of the 1990s, which noted that civil servants, lawyers, and others who tried to follow the law and report infringements were punished, whereas those who turned a blind eye or undermined the law were rewarded.[45]

These observations also were reiterated and confirmed throughout the Waki Commission's report into the post-election violence in its discussion of the role of civil servants, the police, politicians, and the public and in its chapter on impunity.[46] The Waki Report argued that "impunity is especially common in countries that lack traditions of the rule of law, suffer from corruption, or that have entrenched systems of patronage, or where the judiciary is weak or members of the security forces are protected by special jurisdictional immunities."[47]

Furthermore, the report also noted "there is of course, a symbiotic relationship between the politicians and their supporters which continues to fuel impunity. Politicians rely on their supporters to enforce impunity while their supporters, who are the handmaidens of the violence, get protection from their political godfathers. This interference normally comes in the form of "orders from above."[48] In short, laws and institutions in these situations are mostly extensions of personal power; they are not autonomous from each other or guided by checks and balances.

In a recent article, Gyimah-Boadi has argued that "elections are now widely accepted as central to the project of democratization, and … are invested with unrealistic expectations and powers to resolve all sorts of problems."[49] This is particularly so where one of the main problems is that elections are taking place, but in situations that are not democratic. For those interested in "promoting good practice in electoral conflict management,"[50] the first challenge is to admit, diagnose, and understand the situation on the ground, differentiating between what can and cannot be accomplished in different circumstances. Burnell notes there is little discussion in the literature about why countries that seem to share some of the same predisposing characteristics do not all have the same outcomes, whether in terms of civil strife or electoral violence.[51] This is an avenue of research worth pursuing.

Clearly, it is worthwhile for practitioners to develop early warning systems and to understand the possible triggers of electoral violence in specific places; to put in place mechanisms to protect vulnerable groups; to improve institutions involved in the electoral process; to engage in efforts to educate those involved in elections, monitors, and the public; and to develop acceptable electoral dispute mechanisms.

However, in political systems where political power is highly centralized and personalized, designed to skirt the law, and to undermine the integrity of institutions, the above changes, while necessary, are not sufficient, may not work, and may not even be used. Ultimately, one needs to change the norms and incentives of both politicians and the public. As Justice Kriegler noted with respect to Kenya, "The solution is not merely in constitutional and legislative changes." It is tempting to concur with Justice Kriegler that "the culture of impunity needs a fix too."[52] However, this is easier said than done as the absence of enforcement is symptomatic of, not the cause of, underlying political disincentives to change. Clearly, not all places are amenable to change nor do they necessarily have the incentives to make the difficult choices necessary to embrace the rule of law and the move away from violence.

One difficulty in Kenya is that political power has continued to be very attractive even in the post-Moi era. This increases the likelihood that, in an increasingly ethnically polarized situation already imbued with violence and underwritten by clientism, where the state is losing both its legitimacy and its monopoly of legitimate force and diffused violence is the order of the day and where institutions are deliberately kept weak, contenders are increasingly likely to resort to violence again to win elections or for other reasons. Furthermore, the financial incentives to become an MP are huge (Kenyan MPs earn some of the highest salaries in the world, around Ksh 13.25 million (US$189,000) per annum, mostly untaxed) and hard to change.[53] Parliament itself decides on its salaries and all attempts to reduce them or to tax them have been shot down.

When it comes to the general public, many of those who participated in the post election violence in Kenya were also those who suffered and died. However, we know little about the ordinary perpetrators and the specific incentives that led them to use machetes against citizens from other ethnic groups. This clearly is an area in need of more investigation by practitioners and scholars. To manage electoral conflict, it is also necessary to understand the motives of those who engage in violence as well as how much of the gang labour that kills is impressed into service by politicians and others rather than voluntarily performing such acts.

In the end, much that results in electoral violence or an inability to contain it stems from factors and incentives outside the electoral process itself, something obvious to many but in need of further thought in terms of its practical implications for managing conflict. This is certainly the case in Kenya, as noted in the earlier parts of this paper. The failure to appreciate the gravity of these factors, the incentives exogenous to elections and the technical factors related to them, as well as the implications of the mounting severity and diffusion of past violence are some of the reasons policy makers, practitioners, and most scholars did not anticipate the 2007 post-election violence in Kenya.

Much of the literature on managing elections in conflict-prone situations is devoted to questions of whether new electoral institutions, different administrative arrangements (centralization versus decentralization or federalism, more or fewer checks and balances among institutions), or different types of electoral systems (various genres of proportional representation) can be used to change incentive systems so as to diffuse the potential for violence, particularly in developing countries.[54] Apart from the lack of consensus among analysts, it is worth reiterating here that the history of institutional change in Kenya has been the hollowing out of formal changes to preserve the status quo and the hegemony of the political elite.[55] This would suggest examining Keefer's finding that different types of formal political and electoral systems are not significant predictors of political conflict[56] before assuming that implementing similar changes in Kenya would work. Also, as Andrew Reynolds has noted, "like medications, institutional remedies themselves are seldom if ever sufficient" and "constitutional therapists often get it wrong."[57] Even scholars, like Roger Southall, who believe that proportional representation deserves more consideration in Kenya admit there "is a marked circularity about Kenyan politics" that has "negated reform and left politicians unaccountable."[58]

Furthermore, the answers to two great unknowns continue to haunt policy-makers and others: first, under what conditions do political competitors abjure violence and how can outsiders accelerate this process, if at all? Even if it is an inherent good, it is not clear how much promoting the usual types of electoral assistance provided by donors actually helps, in situations such as those in Kenya, even though it is far better than doing nothing, nor is it obvious what would help.

What one does know is that countries that have experienced conflict are at a higher risk of more conflict.[59]

CONCLUSIONS

The above discussion raises a number of issues and questions that pertain to Kenya but go beyond it. They deserve to be explored, even if not fully, in this article.

The mask of elections amid the deliberate weakening of institutions in order to personalize and maintain power and the simultaneous diffusion of violence to win power is dangerous. In contrast to the past, in Kenya the integrity of the state itself still may be threatened increasingly by simultaneous but different violent pressures from militia and other groups controlled by competing ethnic factions in a nominal coalition government as the fabric of nationhood disintegrates. The question arises not only if it is possible to hold democratic elections in this environment but if diffused violence can be contained when a state has not only lost its monopoly of legitimate force but also its legitimacy. The increasing groundswell of disgust from below could turn ugly, including the possibility of inciting a reversion to authoritarianism or worse. Furthermore, the use of coalitions may be the beginning of a retreat away from a multiparty situation and back to a one-party state in another form.

The broader question of the causes and consequences of the above syndrome is of interest to both policy-makers and scholars concerned with democratic transitions. Moi's aim in using extra-state militia to eliminate his electoral opposition in the 1990s had the unintended side effect of chipping away at the state's monopoly of legitimate force. This was not its goal. Almost twenty years later, violence is diffused and out of the state's control. Pandora's Box is open. A collective action question arises here: under what circumstances do political elites, who themselves theoretically need peace and order to further many of their own political and economic interests, not have the incentives, power, or ability to take back the state's monopoly, instead of participating in destroying it, and why?

The further question of why the increasingly prominent private sector has not acted as a bulwark against institutional decay and rising violence rather than being a part of it, a point raised in the introduction, is another important question. What factors prevent it from assuming its historic role, why is it still so wrapped up with the state rather than autonomous from it, and what are the implications, if any, of this situation for the transition to democracy?

The discussion of the causes and legacies of Kenya's 2007 post-election violence and the more general observations above suggest that those engaged in electoral conflict management face genuine difficulties about how to proceed. One major problem is that well known good electoral management practices, which certainly should not be abandoned, are often undermined deliberately by forces exogenous to elections themselves and may not be subject to quick fixes. In Kenya, the political class continues to revert to stasis. Their response to the ICC's evidence against high-level perpetrators makes it clear they are still prepared to dismantle laws and institutions in pursuit of political power, even if it entails embracing impunity and undermining their own much-heralded new constitution.

8

Lessons Learned and Forgotten: The International Community and Electoral Conflict Management in Kenya*

STEPHEN BROWN

The link between elections and violence in Kenya is quite different from most other countries examined in this book. In most cases, from Afghanistan to the Democratic Republic of the Congo to Sudan, post-conflict elections are an integral part of a peace process that is meant to end conflict and usher in an era of stability. Ben Reilly's chapter in this volume, among others, lays out the logic of this sequencing, including some of the pitfalls of this "democratic peace" paradigm: ideally, violent conflict is replaced by non-violent electoral competition in a process that enjoys sufficient legitimacy and "buy-in" that the losing side will not return to arms but rather assume the role of "loyal" opposition and try once again to win the vote in the next elections.

In Kenya, the phenomenon of election violence erupted onto the political scene in the early 1990s. In this case, however, the causal arrow is practically reversed: rather than channelling violence through peaceful means, electoral competition actually seems to foment violence, before elections and immediately afterwards. The cycles of violence occur so closely in line with the election cycle that one is well justified in calling it electoral violence. There has, in fact, been no large-scale conflict in Kenya that has not been directly related to elections, nor has conflict even constituted an actual civil war, unlike the events in most of its neighbours and further afield in Africa and elsewhere. As a result, Kenya cannot usefully be labelled a post-conflict country or follow the peace-and-democracy paradigm.

This chapter seeks to analyze the role of external actors in preventing violence from erupting in Kenya and seeking a peaceful solution to end it. It argues that Western countries and their representatives in Kenya have a very poor record of conflict management, with the exception of their contributions to the crafting of the National Accord of February 2008, which ended the most recent and most serious bout of election-related violence. This is in stark contrast to their paltry efforts to end the violence in 1991–92 and 1997–98, or even to acknowledge that it consisted overwhelmingly of state-induced attacks on presumed opposition supporters. International actors were much more willing to intervene when, as was the case in early 2008, the government was not alone in committing massive abuses and the conflict paralyzed the country. Had Western donors acted more effectively when faced with the violence of the 1990s, learned from it, and kept the lessons in mind, and had they better understood and thus not grown complacent after the relative peace of the electoral competition in 2002 and 2005, they would have been in a much better position to prevent the violence of 2007–08 and, failing that, to help negotiate a better long-term solution than the current power-sharing agreement.

This chapter examines in turn the international community's involvement in violence mitigation and lessons learned (or not) during four periods: (1) the two violent elections of the 1990s; (2) the two peaceful polls of the 2000s; (3) the 2007 elections and ensuing crisis; and (4) the period that began in 2008 with the formation of a Government of National Unity. It concludes with the prospects for renewed violence in Kenya and the significance for electoral management more generally, in order to identify and try to replicate good practices while understanding and trying to avoid bad ones, to the extent possible.

THE TWO VIOLENT ELECTIONS OF THE 1990S

The Return to Multipartyism and the 1992 Elections

The general elections held in December 1992 and December 1997 were both preceded and followed by a significant number of violent attacks. Kenya's post-independence political violence began in October 1991 in Rift Valley Province while the country was still a one-party state, ruled since independence by the Kenya African National Union (KANU). Violence started in Nandi District and spread to others across the southern Rift Valley and neighbouring districts in Western and Nyanza provinces. Members of the Kalenjin ethnic grouping, some Masai, and others considered "indigenous" to the area, who generally supported KANU, killed or violently drove away from their homes and land members of "non-indigenous" ethnic groups, especially the Kikuyu, often destroying their dwellings, livestock, and other possessions in the process. By early 1993, the violence had killed more than 1,500 people and displaced at least 300,000 more.[1]

Superficially, these could appear to be "ethnic clashes" or "land clashes," as they were usually known. However, the timing and manner of the attacks suggest that they were cases of systematic state-induced violence to resist democratization and ensure continued KANU rule. Senior KANU and government officials incited, financed, and planned the attacks, including providing training, logistical support, and financial incentives, while state security officials made no effort to stop the attacks or arrest the perpetrators – in fact, some police officers actually participated in them.[2] Though the attacks expressed a certain degree of underlying ethnic resentment rooted in historic inequalities, no such large-scale conflict had ever taken place before in Kenya. Because the ethnic loyalties overlapped quite closely with support or opposition to continued KANU rule, the violence had the effect of ridding KANU-dominated zones of presumed political opponents (who became effectively disenfranchised), intimidating and punishing those that remained, and freeing up resources (mainly abandoned land) to reward supporters.

During this period, domestic groups were increasingly pressuring the government for an end to single-party rule. In December 1991, soon after Western donor countries suspended foreign aid, President Daniel arap Moi reluctantly announced that the constitution would be amended to restore multipartyism. Perversely, this concession caused the level of violence to rise, as KANU would have to compete electorally, using violence and other illegal measures to ensure that it remained in power.

The December 1992 elections were held in this context of violence and massive displacement of presumed opposition supporters. KANU used an array of measures to ensure that Moi was returned to the presidency and that KANU retained a majority in parliament, including voter registration irregularities, gerrymandering, preventing opposition candidates from filing their papers, vote buying, ballot-box stuffing, and fraud in the tallying of results.[3] One Kenya scholar called it a "C-minus" election, clearly deficient albeit sufficient to pass.[4] A fragmented opposition made Moi and KANU's victory easier. It also deflected from criticisms that Moi had stolen the elections. Still, there is reason to believe that that KANU would have taken more extreme measures had a united opposition been more of a threat, as Moi was unprepared to hand over power.[5] In any case, donors accepted the results, resumed development assistance, and rescheduled Kenya's debt.[6]

The international community reacted with horror to the atrocities, but interpreted it through the lens of ethnic rather than political conflict. Donor officials in Kenya and abroad publicly deplored the atrocities and called on all sides to cease immediately – ignoring the fact that not only was the violence entirely one-sided, barring a few small revenge attacks, but the state and the ruling party officials were behind it. Privately, many were fully aware of its political nature. In fact, some public documents reflected this knowledge. For instance, the US Department of State's report on Kenya's human rights practices for 1993 cites "credible allegations of the involvement of government officials in instigating the clashes" and recognizes that "substantial evidence exists of the complicity of high ranking government officials in financing, arming, and then shielding the attackers from prosecution" and that independent reports strongly suggest "the Government bears primary responsibility for the destruction and loss of lives."[7]

Nevertheless, donors did not want to act accordingly and risk antagonizing the government by getting directly involved. Instead of setting up their own programs, at least eight bilateral donors pooled their funds through the United Nations Development Programme (UNDP), which worked closely with the government. As a result, assistance for the displaced was channelled through the same government that continued to abuse their rights and displace more Kenyans. While supposedly providing care for the displaced, resettling them, and promoting reconciliation, the government restricted access to the areas in order to prevent opposition politicians, local and international NGOs, and donor officials from being able to report on the nature and extent of the violence and the identity of the instigators and perpetrators. In 1995, when the situation became too intolerable to continue, the UNDP terminated the project.[9] It was left to NGOs, especially church groups, to assist the victims, often with donor funding, which soon ran dry. Once the displaced were resettled elsewhere, their "ethnic cleansing" from their former place of residence became permanent.

The 1997 Elections

The level of violence surrounding the 1997 elections did not reach the same level as five years earlier but was still significant. The repression of peaceful pre-election demonstrations in July–August 1997 by state security forces caused some sixty or more civilian deaths. Other pre-election violence occurred mainly in Coast Province, primarily in the Likoni-Kwale area, a KANU-dominated zone. As in the Rift Valley five years earlier, armed bands of men attacked "non-indigenous" ethnicities, in this case from "upcountry." Some 70 to 100 people were killed and a further 100,000 to 200,000 were displaced.[9] After the elections, members of opposition-supporting ethnicities were once again targeted in the Rift Valley as punishment for supporting the "wrong" side.

Having presumably learned from the poor quality of the 1992 elections and now foreseeing the risk of large-scale violence re-erupting, donors were much better organized and coordinated in 1997 than they were in 1992. More than a year before the December 1997 elections, they expanded their Democratic Development Group consortium, which had a half-dozen members, to include twenty-six foreign missions, including non-donors such as Brazil, the Czech Republic, and Hungary. In the run-up to the elections, the group issued joint communiqués. Though some private notes to the government were more strongly worded, the publicly released ones were watered down to the members' lowest common denominator and thus did not clearly identify the government as the main source of political violence.[10]

In December 1997, President Moi was re-elected on a grossly unlevel playing field and polls marred by irregularities. Donors again expressed concern over some electoral practices, but – despite the greater coordination of donor observation missions – accepted the overall result. They deliberately suppressed evidence presented by their own joint Election Observation Centre that KANU had not legitimately obtained a majority in parliament.[11] Within weeks, donors rescheduled US$560 million of loans to Kenya,[12] signalling that it was back to business as usual between the Moi regime and donor countries. Domestic observer reports were more critical, but released weeks later and widely ignored.[13]

The Election Observation Centre's report made no mention of the election violence on the coast and probable disenfranchisement of more than 100,000 presumed opposition supporters.[14] The election observation report funded by the United States Agency for International Development (USAID) fared only a little better – it mentioned the violence against "immigrant [sic] communities" that may have changed the outcome of the election in Mombasa's Likoni constituency, but blamed both KANU and the opposition for the violence.[15] The subsequent State Department report to Congress was more willing to identify perpetrators, acknowledging "indications that the violence had political roots, with local KANU political leaders reportedly involved in the planning."[16]

Lessons to Be Learned

In sum, donor responses to electoral abuses in 1992 and 1997 were very weak. Though their internal reports recognized the great extent to which the elections were neither free nor fair, they were deemed good enough. In 1997, the greater coordination efforts of the donor observer missions suggest some learning about the importance of working together and producing consolidated reports. However, with the "diplomatic massaging" of the publicly released reports mentioned above, donors showed a lack of commitment to revealing the true extent of the abuses they had identified. As a result, they provided extra legitimacy to an authoritarian regime that had failed to hold free and fair democratic elections.

Equally if not more egregious was the donors' refusal to address, let alone publicly acknowledge, the role high-level government and KANU officials played in organizing and financing the large-scale political violence that marred both polls. Though the identities of the officials were widely known, these officials – and the regime – enjoyed complete impunity for the atrocities they caused. Donors signalled that they were "watching closely" and many expected that the additional scrutiny would prevent future misdeeds.[17] Unfortunately, they fatally overestimated the influence of international attention. The lack of action against high-level perpetrators in the early 1990s created no disincentive for them to deploy similar tactics in 1997–98 and, more dramatically, in 2007–08. Here, the learning process was on the perpetrators' side: their sense that they would not be punished in any way was confirmed. Donors, however, did adopt some additional measures to decrease the probability of mass violence recurring around the 2002 elections. That the violence did not in fact recur is a phenomenon that warrants examination.

TWO PEACEFUL POLLS IN 2002 AND 2005

After the significant violence accompanying the 1992 and 1997 elections, the lack of any similar degree of violence associated with the 2002 elections and the 2005 constitutional referendum is a phenomenon that requires explanation.

The 2002 Elections

Kenya's December 2002 elections were momentous in many ways, most significantly for the fact that, for the first time in Kenyan history, KANU was voted out of office. Moi was constitutionally barred from running again and had chosen as his party's candidate Uhuru Kenyatta, the son of Kenya's first post-independence ruler but a political novice. Numerous KANU stalwarts, many of whom expected to succeed Moi at the head of KANU, defected in frustration to the opposition alliance, the National Rainbow Coalition (NARC), and backed its leader, Mwai Kibaki, as presidential candidate.

Though the elections fell short of being free and fair, NARC's lead was far too large to be easily erased, in part because donors had once again mounted a strong joint electoral observation team. Opposition leader Kibaki was elected with over 62 per cent of the popular vote, compared to only 31 per cent for Kenyatta.[18] Once Kibaki assumed office, Kenya completed its transition to democracy, at least according to formal definitions, a monumental milestone.

To the great relief of Kenyans and international observers, comparatively little political violence accompanied the 2002 elections. The donor community was happy to claim credit, not only for the dissuasive effect of its conflict monitoring network but also for the support it had provided for civic education over the previous decade. Kenyan NGOs and church groups, who had carried out nationwide civic education campaigns, were also quick to cite their own efforts as the main causal factor in conflict prevention.

Such interpretations, however, were naive, self-serving, or a combination of the two. If Kenyans did not attack each other this time because they had been sensitized to the fact that such violence is wrong, that would imply that they did not know that the mass atrocities in the 1990s were egregious behaviour. This line of reasoning also ignores the fact that political leaders formed militias and gangs in the 1990s with the express purpose of carrying out attacks and that financial incentives, rather than voter immaturity or ethnic enmity, also played a convincing explanatory role in 1997.

Instead, the lack of widespread violence in 2002 can be explained by a combination of numerous factors. First, due to last-minute, high-level defections from KANU to NARC, much of the machinery of past violence also passed to the opposition. Second, the political configuration did not follow clear ethnic lines, especially as the two main presidential contenders were both Kikuyu. Unlike the two previous elections, there was no clear political logic as to who would attack whom and where: ethnoregional groups that had generally been on opposite sides in 1997 became allies in 2002. Third, NARC's two-to-one lead in the polls was too decisive for organized violence to have an impact.[19] Realizing this, and knowing that a Kibaki presidency would not be much of a threat to KANU politicians' interests, KANU officials' efforts to rig the poll and intimidate voters were only "spasmodic [and] half-hearted."[20] Fourth, political leaders from various ethnoregional groups had committed to sharing power within a NARC government, thereby eliminating the winner-takes-all scenario that encourages a no-holds-barred battle for power.[21]

The 2005 Referendum

The referendum held in 2005 on a proposed new constitution could also have been a flashpoint for ethnicized political violence. The plebiscite, however, was not accompanied by any significant conflict. Though this is not the place to explain the intricacies of the constitutional reform process, one very important fact overshadows all others when considering the relative absence of violence: the low stakes in the referendum. The government, which presented the new draft constitution for popular approval, had unilaterally amended the version to be voted on to make it more favourable to the incumbents. (Those opposed to it felt that it did not go far enough in reducing the power of the president.) When the proposal was defeated (58 per cent to 42 per cent), the status quo actually favoured the government more than the new constitution would have. The "no" campaign thus won a political and moral victory, but the status quo prevailed.[22]

Unlike the 2002 elections, one could identify ethnoregional blocks that generally supported one or the other position in the referendum. The Luo and Kalenjin, for instance, mainly voted no, while the Kikuyu overwhelmingly voted yes. Had the stakes been higher, this could have translated into inter-ethnic violence. The power barons on both sides who could have mobilized their fighters did not feel the need to do so, for the reasons explained above.

Drawing the Wrong Lessons

The 2002 and 2005 polls were surprisingly peaceful and lulled Kenyans and donor officials into a false sense of security. Rather than identify the real reasons that there had been no large-scale attacks like those that took place in the 1990s, which presaged re-escalation in the future,[23] they prematurely concluded that political violence was no longer a problem in Kenya, even though those responsible for past violence remained in power and had not been held accountable, and the logic of election violence could easily return under a different ethnopolitical configuration. Besides drawing the wrong conclusions, they forgot some key lessons from 1992 and 1997, which prescribed close donor coordination and vigilance as a, admittedly imperfect, method of preventing violent conflict from re-emerging in conjunction with future elections. As a result, not only did they fail to take measures that might have prevented or at least mitigated the violence that emerged immediately after the December 2007 elections, they were also completely unprepared to deal with it.

THE 2007 ELECTIONS AND ENSUING CRISIS

The causes, both proximate and underlying, of the latest bout of electoral violence, as well as the forms it took, have been amply examined elsewhere.[24] This chapter seeks instead to analyze the international community's failure to predict the violence and its actual response to it.[25]

The Failure to Predict

As mentioned above, there were good reasons to expect that electoral violence would recur in Kenya. The structural factors that buttressed inter-ethnic hostility had in no way been reduced since the 1990s. The authoritarian state apparatus and mode of governance remained essentially unchanged, despite democratization, and the legacy of Moi's rule aggravated the root causes of conflict.[26] Numerous instigators of past violence were still active politically. The ethnically based militias that the latter had used in the 1990s were still at their disposal. The winner-take-all nature of the profoundly neopatrimonial system promoted intense rivalry over very high stakes.[27]

Because of the rotation of Western diplomatic and aid staff, donor officials in post in Nairobi in 2007 had no direct knowledge of the violence of the 1990s. Few, if any, had even witnessed the 2002 elections. International staff members thus had no personal memory of the lessons of past conflagrations. Even those who had been there the longest would have experienced only the relatively peaceful 2002 elections and 2005 referendum. With jobs focusing on the present, they had few professional incentives to study the events of the previous decade.

Nonetheless, there were warning signs during the 2007 campaign that serious violence could emerge. Donors ignored the 600 or so deaths that occurred in the final months leading to the vote, most of which were the result of the police's extrajudicial killing of suspected members of Mungiki, a Kikuyu religious group *cum* protection racket *cum* political militia.[28] They also missed the rise of hate speech on Kikuyu- and Kalenjin-language radio stations, each of which attracted listeners almost exclusively from its specific linguistic and thus ethnic group.[29] In addition, the campaign atmosphere was very tense and the polls suggested a close presidential race between Raila Odinga of the Orange Democratic Movement (ODM) and the incumbent Mwai Kibaki of the Party of National Unity (PNU), both of whom drew largely on specific ethnoregional groups. No matter who was declared the winner, there would be extreme discontent and a high risk of violence, both spontaneous and planned.

The most significant warning sign of electoral malfeasance occurred a few months before the election, when Kibaki replaced of nineteen of the twenty-two members of the officially independent Electoral Commission of Kenya without consulting the opposition, whereas according to a 1997 agreement (never actually enshrined in law) he was supposed to let the opposition name a proportional number of commissioners.[30] Donors did not make any significant protests over this politicization of the electoral commission in favour of the incumbent. Instead, they continued to fund the commission through the UNDP and to repeat that it would be the final arbiter of the results, which – if credible – would discourage and delegitimize violence, even if they could not prevent it. This made it harder for donors to reject the results announced under duress by the chair of the electoral commission, even after their observers had not been allowed to monitor the final count and donor officials had tried unsuccessfully to convince him not to announce the results before they could be verified.

Donors' Reactions

Most international observer teams, including those from the European Union, the East African Community, and the International Republican Institute (an organization funded by the US Congress), did not endorse Kibaki's re-election.[32] The US State Department did send congratulations to Kibaki at a press conference in Washington DC, the only Western officials to endorse his victory, though they soon disavowed it. Donors as a whole agreed that urgent measures needed to be taken to end the violence, which escalated as soon as Kibaki was announced the winner. In the face of spreading violence, Western officials called for all sides to show restraint and for the political leaders to come to a compromise that would involve some form of power sharing.

Donors thus rejected any scenario involving a recount, a forensic analysis of the results, or any other form of action that would have helped determine the legitimate winner according to the democratic rules in place. No Western government called on Kibaki to step down from the presidency, or at least step aside until results were verified, thus legitimizing his position. Instead, donors abandoned the principles of rule of law and the will of the people in favour of a politically expedient ad hoc compromise that eventually ended the political crisis and violent conflict.

Various Western ambassadors and officials on mission from African and Western countries endeavoured to bring the two sides to the negotiating table, but Kibaki and Odinga both felt that they were the legitimate winner and initially refused to consider relinquishing their competing claims to the presidency. The African Union appointed a Panel of Eminent African Personalities, headed by former UN Secretary-General Kofi Annan, to take the lead in mediation, a move strongly supported by Western countries. The negotiations were difficult and protracted, and required multiple interventions by donors to move them forward, including the threat of reduced levels of foreign aid, visa bans for top officials, and targeted sanctions. Finally, at the end of February 2008, two months after the contested elections, Annan convinced Kibaki and Odinga to sign a National Accord based on power-sharing principles and the formation of a Government of National Unity, including the creation of the post of prime minister for Odinga.[32] The violence ceased almost instantly, even if it took another six weeks and more donor cajoling for the politicians to agree on the composition of the cabinet.

Lessons to Be Learned

Various lessons should be drawn from the experiences of 2007–08. First, donors should be very careful not to prematurely discard the possibility of election violence. To avoid this trap, donor officials need to be better versed in the recent political history of the countries where they are posted and not focused merely on the short-term. They need more time to study the country and so should be kept in their posts longer to take advantage of their knowledge. Second, institutional support and capacity building is of fundamental import but cannot be carried out in a technocratic way only. Donors' continued uncritical support of an increasingly partisan electoral commission proved to be one of the gravest mistakes of the election, as the commission's breakdown was a central event in the political crisis. Third, if conflict does break out, close cooperation among donors and with other involved organizations is essential for mediation and conflict resolution. Kenya's National Accord would not have been possible if the various international actors had worked at cross-purposes. Fourth, continued donor involvement can be crucial. In Kenya, repeated pressure, including the use of threats, was key to getting both sides, especially the incumbent, not only to come to an agreement but also to implement it.

More effective than conflict resolution is conflict prevention. As Susanne Mueller argues elsewhere in this volume, there are no guarantees that international pressure could have changed or can change domestic political actors' behaviour and attitudes and prevent election violence. Donors' efforts may not be sufficient, but they might be necessary. At a minimum, they can play some positive part. Donors placed very little emphasis on encouraging meaningful institutional change during Kibaki's first mandate or addressing the fundamental underpinnings of ethnic tensions, which reduced the government's need to take action in these areas. The Kenyan executive is extremely powerful vis-à-vis other branches of government and civil society, which makes aid donors an important provider of checks and balances and gives them a crucial role to play in holding the government accountable. It is difficult for the international community to act alone and force the government to undertake actions it does not wish to take, but it can be quite influential when it joins forces with domestic political actors for a well-defined goal.[33]

THE "GOVERNMENT OF NATIONAL IMPUNITY"

In the years that followed the signature of the National Accord, tensions between the members of the Government of National Unity frequently emerged. Some were more symbolic, such as who had precedence according to protocol, the prime minister or the vice-president. Others were far more practical, including the prime minister's power to suspend a minister, notably one that he had appointed himself. NARC and ODM coexisted uneasily, but they shared a common interest in preventing any form of accountability for the post-election violence. Cabinet ministers and members of parliament from both sides were implicated in grave human rights abuses, potentially including crimes against humanity.[34]

As a result, while paying lip service to the establishment of a special tribunal with significant international membership to try the suspects, on multiple occasions parliamentarians blocked attempts to pass enabling legislation. Likewise, though the government promised to cooperate with the International Criminal Court (ICC), should the latter decide to pursue some of those who bear the greatest responsibility for the violence, it refused to refer the matter to The Hague – despite being demonstrably unable or unwilling to try them domestically. When in December 2010 the ICC issued summons to appear to six high-level Kenyan officials – including Deputy Prime Minister and Finance Minister Uhuru Kenyatta, two other ministers, and the former police commissioner – on charges of crimes against humanity, many senior Kenyan politicians sought ways of escaping the court's jurisdiction – notably by reviving the idea of a local tribunal under the aegis of the new constitution, mobilizing African Union-support, or withdrawing from the court, none of which could actually halt The Hague's prosecutions.

Currently, international actors are the only ones who could hold perpetrators to account, even if only a handful of the worst offenders. In fact, were it not for the Commission of Inquiry into Post-Election Violence (known as the Waki Commission after its chairman, Justice Philip Waki), created as a result of the National Accord, threatening to hand over evidence to the ICC (which it eventually did), it seems unlikely that the government would have taken any steps at all to implement its recommendation of setting up a special tribunal. The latest proposal to do so seems unlikely to be in place before the 2012 elections. Thus, unless the ICC obtains convictions, no accountability will be achieved for the electoral violence of 2008, just as there has been complete impunity for the "ethnic clashes" of the 1990s.

In December 2008, interviews in Nairobi revealed many donors' strong commitment to the establishment of the special tribunal, which they believe would prevent violence from erupting anew in conjunction with the next general elections, due to be held in 2012; in fact, some donors threatened to withhold aid if the recommendations of the Waki Commission were not implemented, which has not happened.[35] Further interviews in January 2010, however, revealed that donors no longer consider implementation essential.[36] This could be interpreted as pragmatism, since the international community cannot force the Kenyan government to pass legislation. (MPs boycotted en masse attempts in 2009–10 to debate the legislation to create the special tribunal, which could not be discussed for lack of quorum.)

However, it could also be that donors have moved the goalposts and focused instead on constitutional reform (approved in an August 2010 referendum) and the establishment of a new electoral commission in time for the 2012 elections rather than issues of accountability and violence, or that they believe that institutional reform will be sufficient to prevent future conflict. The MP who introduced the special tribunal legislation as a private member's bill (after the government failed to re-introduce it after its first failed attempt) has complained about the lack of donor support for his efforts.[37] Now that the ICC is moving toward prosecution, it remains to be seen how effective donors will be in compelling the government to cooperate, potentially including handing over non-cooperative suspects to The Hague.

Lessons to Be Learned

Both the broad coalition that constituted NARC and supported Kibaki during his first mandate and the current Government of National Unity, created by the 2008 power-sharing agreement, depend on cross-ethnic elite cooperation. In their desire to achieve maximum support, both governments welcomed into their fold politicians of all stripes, including several responsible for the violence of the 1990s and 2008. Such conditions favour the status quo and, given their dependence on regional powerbrokers who played a role in the violence, such governments are unlikely to muster the political will to prosecute alleged perpetrators. Though the post-2008 coalition government is deeply fractured, the political elites on both sides share a common interest in shielding their key members from accountability. Given the number of officials from KANU's single-party days who served in Kibaki's government, which defeated KANU in the 2002 elections, and who remain in government today, one can trace a strong continuity between not only the Moi's authoritarian state and today's formally democratic one but also many of the main political players then and now. Though a formal democratic transition has taken place, it is in many ways not a significant one. Given the partial nature of the transition, domestic transitional justice mechanisms, such as the proposed special tribunal and the Truth, Justice and Reconciliation Commission created in 2008, are unlikely to hold high-level officials accountable – or prevent future political violence.

CONCLUSION

Western donors have done little to manage and even less to prevent the political violence that has plagued Kenya to varying degrees since 1991, with the notable exception of their concerted effort to end the political crisis that followed the hotly contested 2007 elections. Their main shortcoming in the 1990s was the lack of political will to confront and hold accountable the government for its deliberate use of political violence as part of a strategy to resist democratization and prevent electoral defeat. Though donors learned the importance of coordinated electoral observation, this did not prevent them from legitimizing elections that were patently short of being free and fair, notably in 1997, including the suppression of politically sensitive evidence of KANU's blatantly unfair practices. Because of the relative peacefulness of the 2002 elections and 2005 constitutional referendum, donors forgot the dangers of election violence and were caught unprepared when it made a dramatic re-entry into the political scene after the 2007 elections. Given that the violence was no longer one-sided and only state-induced, donors joined forces and sustained pressure on both sides to reach an agreement and restore peace, working with domestic and regional actors, most notably the African Union's mediation team. Though it took two months, this eventually ended the violence through a power-sharing agreement. This political compromise, however, came at a price: with those responsible for the worst crimes sitting in parliament and in cabinet, the newly created Government of National Unity would take no effective measures to hold its own important members accountable. Since the government has failed to create a special tribunal to try suspects and donors have shifted their focus to institutional reform, the issue of accountability is left to a distant international actor, the ICC.

None of these actions has yet made political violence any less likely to re-emerge in the future. As argued by Susanne Mueller in this volume, reforming the procedural aspects of elections (redefining boundaries, appointing a truly independent electoral commission) and promulgating a new constitution will only be effective in the presence of the rule of law and strong disincentives against using violence as a political tool, both of which Kenya sorely lacks. In this regard, continued impunity constitutes a "worst practice." The international community risks becoming complacent, just as it was prior to the 2007 elections. Meanwhile, political militias continue to operate freely, tensions remain high, and local communities arm themselves in preparation for renewed violence in 2012, if not sooner.

Though the Kenyan case does not fit the standard scenario for post-conflict democratization, since democratization and elections were the proximate cause of violent conflict rather than the posited solution, certain generalizations hold for electoral conflict management elsewhere. To conclude that the international community should not encourage democratization in order to save lives is an overly simplistic and rather dangerous interpretation, which also plays into the hands of authoritarian leaders who want to retain their autocratic power. Rather, it points to the need to understand why and how various actors will deploy violent tactics to resist political liberalization and avoid losing elections – and what incentives, disincentives, and other means can be put into place to try to mitigate, if not completely prevent, political violence. This involves using a conflict-sensitive lens when fielding observation missions and designing electoral systems and reforming political institutions more generally. Equally if not more important is the need to acquire a nuanced understanding of local political dynamics and informal political institutions, which often follow a neopatrimonial logic rather than a rational-legal one. Kenya's experiences warn against donor complacency and naivete, as well as the dangers of continued impunity for grave violent crimes. If international actors want to fight election violence more effectively, they will need to be both smarter and bolder – which is especially challenging in such volatile electoral processes.

PART THREE

Policy and Practice in Electoral Conflict Management

9

Merging Conflict Management with Electoral Practice: The IFES Experience

LISA KAMMERUD

For election assistance practitioners, elections, conflict, violence, and security issues merge in every program. As Ben Reilly notes in this volume, elections in post-conflict scenarios are expected to do more than provide choices between government leaders and structures as well as a peaceful transition of power. They may also be expected to reconcile groups, cement alliances, or lessen the influence of undesired militant groups.

Though elections without the burden of post-conflict trappings do not have the same level of expectation, those elections may also be troubled by conflict.[1] Many elections in transitional democracies, such as Kenya, India, Guyana, and Kyrgyzstan, have socio-economic, ethnic, political, or religious cleavages that may potentially be aggravated by elections. There may be insurgent groups that threaten the integrity of the electoral process (Bangladesh). There may be a dominant party or state actor(s) that routinely intimidate participants in the electoral process (Azerbaijan, Zimbabwe). There are a variety of conflict dynamics in most elections where technical assistance organizations, like the International Foundation of Electoral Systems (IFES),[2] operate.

Viewed from an election assistance perspective, a conflict-response perspective, a security perspective, or the perspective of any particular sector, the solutions to conflict around elections will tend to involve the actions that each sector generally pursues. Indeed, from a donor perspective the objective of addressing conflict potential around elections often differs from the objective of holding a technically correct election.

With the aforementioned issues at play, the main hurdles in achieving better results have been sector-driven solutions (tunnel-vision) and searches for "silver bullet" solutions (the one solution, framework, or partner that would best address the problem). The former leads to disconnected development objectives that leave programs too narrow. The latter leads to programs that fail to address country contexts. In both cases, a perceived solution, rather than the existing problem, leads the analysis.

Field experience shows that there is no substitute for careful country analysis or cross-sector cooperation. Yet these are often afterthoughts in the rush to deploy and implement short-term programs used to address wider goals. If country analysis and cross-sector cooperation are to be more consistent and more effective, a conflict perspective must be joined with election programming. This integrated conflict and elections programming approach, or ICEP, provides a holistic perspective that addresses the country context and conflict dynamics while increasing cross-sector cooperation.[3]

This chapter takes advantage of lessons learned from more than two decades of democracy and governance work by IFES. It shows that integrating a conflict lens into electoral programming, increasing cross-sector cooperation, and supporting programs with long-term impact potential yields the best payoff in reducing conflict throughout the electoral process.[4]

BACKGROUND

There has been a recent surge of interest in the problem of elections and conflict and what to do about it.[5] One of the recurring themes is that some part of election assistance should better incorporate conflict prevention or mitigation. Indeed, recent research by academics and practitioners shows that the causes of election violence in many countries are rooted in existing cleavages that may be escalated by procedural or political triggers.[6] Despite these insights, in practice, the divide between conflict-related programming and election-related programming remains wide.[7]

IFES was one of the first practitioners to begin examining election violence as a discrete form of conflict. The Election Violence Education and Resolution (EVER) project, launched in 2003, involved research, assessment, and fieldwork.[8] EVER was designed to increase the capabilities of civil society organizations working to reduce election violence around the world. In the field, the program showed that community-based monitoring of electoral violence makes a difference in the behaviour and awareness of stakeholders and the public in many country contexts.

Lessons learned from EVER were incorporated into wider IFES programs: assessing conflict triggers outside electoral procedures, reviewing electoral law for conflict risks, underscoring the importance of information sharing between sectors, and providing a defined approach with an increased understanding of patterns in election violence.

The approach used by EVER defined election violence as "any harm, or threat of harm, to any persons or property involved in the election process, or the election process itself, during the election period."[9] EVER monitors gathered information on the perpetrators, victims, types, impact, and timeline of election violence by documenting incidents over a set period of time (generally the beginning of a campaign period to a few weeks after the official announcement of results).

This type of incident-level data is not often systematically collected and EVER data remains a valuable and unique dataset. For instance, the EVER team supplied the United Nations Special Rapporteur on extrajudicial, summary, or arbitrary executions with extensive data, research, and contextual information for his recent report on election-related killings.[10] The EVER program has also helped IFES understand the range of patterns of election violence. Though every country dynamic is different, six types of driving forces behind electoral conflict were distilled after testing the original EVER typology in the field: (1) political party rivalries (other non-state actors), (2) politicization of existing conflicts and escalation of ongoing conflict(s)/violence, (3) post-conflict belligerents and socio-economic cleavages still in play (internal and external to election processes), (4) ongoing armed conflict (internal and external to election processes), (5) state-sponsored violence, and (6) anti-state violence. Accounting for these forces can help determine program response.[11]

Some countries experience one or more of these dynamics. They may be aggravated by weak rule of law, corruption, and triggers within or outside the electoral process.

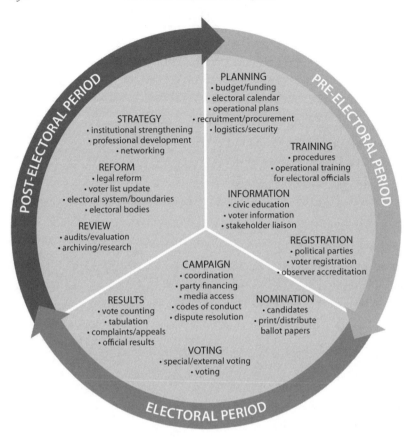

Figure 1. The electoral cycle. Adapted from *Electoral Management Design: The International IDEA Handbook* (Stockholm: International IDEA, 2006), 16, fig. 2.

Designed to bridge the gaps between conflict programming and electoral programming, EVER grew into a niche service line for IFES. At the same time, it was clear that a broader programming approach that could be applied to all the variety of ways in which election conflict manifests and could facilitate improvements across the board in electoral programming was necessary.

Given the divisions between conflict and elections programming described earlier, we needed an approach that would tie together all electoral work that addresses conflict, explicitly or implicitly. From these two elements, the approach to ICEP was constructed.

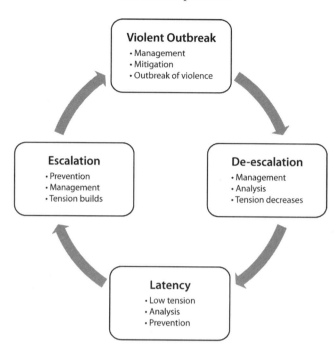

Figure 2. The conflict cycle

INTEGRATED CONFLICT AND ELECTIONS PROGRAMMING

Integrated Conflict and Elections Programming (ICEP) is a holistic framework that explicitly incorporates insights from the conflict management/resolution field to provide broader themes for collaboration between actors. By overlaying the conflict cycle and election cycle and its program responses, a guide to conflict-sensitive programming emerges.

Recognizing that elections are part of a cycle, the interaction of social and political dynamics between elections should be taken into account in election assistance activities (see figure 1). The conflict cycle similarly implies that conflict programming should address the range of issues before, during, and after the outbreak of violent conflict. In the same way that the electoral cycle presents phases of the election process, the conflict cycle presents phases of conflict. A simplified conflict cycle (see figure 2) begins with a build-up of tension.

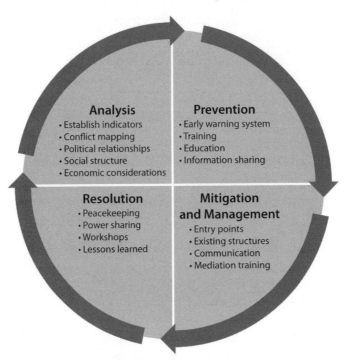

Figure 3. The conflict-response cycle

Unresolved tension allows conflict to emerge, escalate, de-escalate, and return to a latent stage (tension) if root causes remain unresolved.

The conflict cycle underscores the unending recurrence of conflict if causes are not resolved. This helps identify links between causes, tensions, outbursts, and solutions that help determine effective responses. These conflict-responses, or conflict programming objectives, can be placed in four categories – analysis, prevention, mitigation, and resolution – which address different phases of the conflict cycle (see figure 3).

Using this lens to understand conflict in the election cycle helps election practitioners expand their menu of programming responses beyond sector-specific solutions (such as discrete security or justice sector actions). It encourages a thematic, cross-sector approach that addresses the full range of stakeholders' roles over the entire conflict cycle.[12]

What does it look like?

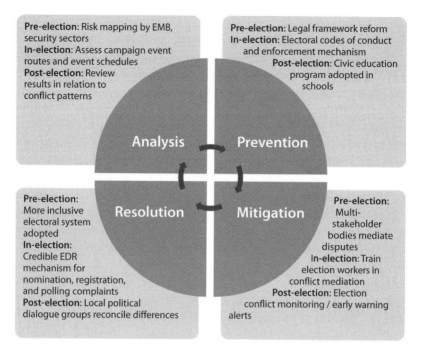

Figure 4. Integrated Conflict and Elections Programming (ICEP): Responses to conflict mapped to each stage of the electoral cycle.

As seen in figure 4, if one maps election assistance activities onto conflict-cycle program objectives, every stage of the electoral cycle has a matching conflict response (analysis, prevention, mitigation, and resolution) that can be achieved through elections programming.

For example, as Ben Reilly describes in this volume, some decision points that occur between elections, such as when to hold elections, can be crucial in determining whether the electoral process increases or decreases the potential for conflict. The process Reilly describes is an incorporation of conflict analysis and preventive thinking into electoral design. The same could be said of ensuring a good public communication strategy for an election management body (EMB), as noted by Johann Kriegler in this volume. The EMB can play a positive role in mitigating conflicts that arise, and is even more effective if mitigation is explicitly incorporated in assistance and planning.

In the post-election period, looking at the dispute resolution process, as done adeptly by Sarah Staino and Johann Kriegler in this volume, the potential for conflict prevention, mitigation, and resolution is apparent. The link between what Reilly, Staino, and Kriegler discuss is that in every phase of the electoral cycle, every assistance activity, can be matched with a corresponding similar conflict response. However, the conflict perspective cannot be applied ad hoc but must be fully integrated. The way forward in electoral assistance and electoral programming is to explicitly link electoral programming and conflict programming strategies. This creates more effective conflict responses in electoral programming.

Stakeholders in different sectors, such as EMBs, security institutions, civil society, government, media, and political parties, have different roles during electoral preparation and in conflict analysis, prevention, management, and resolution in the election cycle. Taking a holistic approach to conflict, rather than a sector-based approach, encourages *cross-sector programming and coordination;* it also emphasizes the need for *long-term investment and vision* in programming.

The ICEP framework differs from most others in that it is useful regardless of specific conflict dynamics or patterns of election violence because it does not impose a set of priorities or programs. It also does not require a separately funded initiative or team but can be integrated within existing programs to leverage present resources and generate innovative new programs or increased investments.

In presenting this approach, I seek to address the lack of conflict perspective, cross-sector cooperation, and long-term vision that hampers obtaining better results in dealing with elections and conflict. Do note that I will not map out all electoral programming options related to each conflict response, nor will I cover in detail what each sector should do to improve its work in preventing or managing electoral conflict. I will highlight how the holistic approach can support innovative ways of connecting existing program themes, describe what innovative trends and programs it has inspired, and show how it can fill gaps in existing programming. For the purposes of this chapter, I will also highlight the role of the EMB in all conflict response phases.

IMPLEMENTATION OF ICEP

Conflict Analysis

The need for conflict analysis in development assistance is generally well-understood; however, it is not as widely accepted or implemented in relation to electoral assistance. Good conflict analysis related to elections (which here includes assessments, conflict mapping, conflict tracking, or other tools that help identify patterns, causes, and/or future directions of conflict/violence) would help identify the main drivers of conflict.

There are new initiatives aimed at improving conflict analysis. Recently, the United States Agency for International Development (USAID) has begun using the term "election conflict trigger assessment" and has published an *Election Security Framework*; a working group hosted by the International Institute for Democracy and Electoral Assistance (IDEA) is studying harmonization of tools for election violence assessment; and mash-ups of social media and mapping technologies like the Ushahidi platform are demonstrating conflict tracking and analysis in near real-time.[13] Implicit and informal conflict assessments already occur in electoral assistance. For example, IFES's Pre-Election Technical Assessments (PETAS) and legal review processes are frequent activities that are beginning to incorporate conflict risk assessment more explicitly. Thus the best solution may be to create a standard for ensuring that conflict analysis in some form is included in the design of electoral assistance programs. This standard should demand that electoral assessments such as PETAS and legal and procedural reform explicitly include conflict assessment and that conflict analysis and risk assessment capacities are integrated into security planning and strategic planning exercises.

In Lebanon, for example, a methodology was designed by IFES and local partners to support the capacity for risk assessment in the lead-up to the 2009. This increased cooperation and information-sharing between election officials, security agencies, and local government. Each electoral constituency was evaluated along standard indicators and assigned a high, medium, or low risk for electoral violence. The results were shared with a key group of stakeholders, including political parties and civil society organizations (CSOs). This process was done repeatedly throughout the electoral cycle and was immediately used to benefit security planning and responses. Though this model involved extensive resources, it can be easily replicated with fewer resources by scaling up the geographic level of analysis, simplifying the map and graphics, and/or leveraging the resources of local actors who are already gathering information. At a minimum, indicators could be developed and shared among local actors, such as security agencies and election officials, to provide a standard information-gathering process.

A poor example of integration of conflict analysis and electoral system design is seen in Afghanistan, as noted in this volume by Ben Reilly, Francesc Vendrell, and Gerald Schmitz. Afghanistan's process was not conducive to reducing the influence of warlords or reconciling ethnic cleavages or interest groups. Analysis, however, showed this only after the fact and the political will to change the system is no longer present. In contrast, the electoral system chosen hastily in the 2005 Iraqi elections, which was seen to fuel divisions and violence, was later modified to better serve the public, as Marc Lemieux points out in this volume.

The future of conflict analysis in elections may include increased technology. Ushahidi and other platforms able to visualize multi-faceted datasets on maps offer a new level of immediacy and collaboration to conflict and crisis information-sharing. Information on conflict developments that was gathered manually via media and security reports in Lebanon may be gathered in part by automated systems in the future; the ability to update the system remotely by text messaging or email means that no report, no emergency, is out of reach as long as the reporter can reach a mobile signal.

Many challenges exist to putting good conflict analysis into practice. For domestic actors like EMBs and other stakeholders, it can be difficult to integrate analysis, per se, into their work because of competing priorities and pressures, not to mention a perpetual lack of human resources. For international assistance providers and donors, obstacles also include competing priorities and limited financial resources to support such efforts. Practical solutions to these challenges include demonstrating immediate benefits, incorporating conflict risk analysis into other electoral assessments, and making the process collaborative to improve relationships.

By seeking opportunities to capitalize on security planning initiatives that are underway, or sharing conflict assessments funded under a different development area with the electoral sector, electoral assistance could create ways to make conflict analysis a standard part of electoral assistance without added cost. Rather than design elaborate frameworks, it may simply be helpful for election assistance to incorporate analysis into existing programs.

Conflict Prevention

Many common electoral programming activities already incorporate conflict prevention strategies. The challenge has been how to pursue these efforts and increase cooperation among actors more effectively. Note that if one uses a holistic approach, actors would be engaged in conflict analysis that helps inform prevention activities and thus helps identify priority actions for a particular country.

Much has been written about conflict prevention and electoral processes in general. Currently, there are many efforts underway to improve conflict prevention in electoral processes. The United Nations Development Programme's (UNDP) *Guide to Elections and Conflict* and International IDEA's *Electoral Justice* handbook both serve to illustrate best practices and lessons learned in conflict prevention.[14] Yet these efforts do not explain how to fully incorporate a conflict lens into electoral practice. Therefore, this section highlights ways that ICEP bolsters innovative or less obvious prevention practices. There are several areas where better cooperation, country context, and long-term vision could be improved through an integrated approach to conflict prevention. These include EMBs' capacity and credibility, training, coordination, monitoring, and education.

1. EMB CAPACITY AND CREDIBILITY

The role of the EMB is crucial in conflict prevention. From the long period of planning and electoral reform that characterizes the interim between elections, to pre-election planning, to election day, to results management, the EMB is on the front-line and should take the lead in the electoral process. It bears great responsibility for the processes and the perception of the processes it oversees.

While it is essential for an EMB to be as competent and knowledgeable as possible, as Johann Kriegler points out, a technically problematic electoral process (such as in South Africa in 1994) can be outweighed by public perception of the EMB as credible and trustworthy.

The ability of an EMB to contribute to conflict prevention depends on its credibility and competence in ensuring the integrity of the electoral process.[15] Most EMBs have some credibility challenges in relation to one segment or another of the social and/or political sphere. Some may be reluctant to take the initiative to make strong statements or activate sanction mechanisms. Others may be willing, but lack the legislative mandate for action. Some EMBs may act independently but lack true budgetary independence. Others may have appointment processes that are seen as biased by the opposition. The strengths of a particular EMB must be leveraged. How can election assistance best support the development of a proactive EMB that responds to misinformation, political disputes, and media inquiries with equal swiftness and transparency?

Conflict analysis can help assess an EMB's areas of weak credibility, competence, and potential impact on conflicts. Certain factors affect credibility and often alter perceptions. These include the EMB appointment process, degree of budgetary independence, extent of mandate and enforcement powers, internal professionalization, staff integrity, public outreach, transparency, and inclusiveness. The first three factors can only be changed through procedural reforms between elections, but the latter characteristics can be improved upon at any point in the electoral cycle.

For example, in Uganda, the election authority is appointed by the president, who is also the leader of the ruling National Resistance Movement (NRM). This creates a problem of credibility. The opposition will not support the EMB because of mistrust, even if efforts at improvement are made. The Ugandan police force is seeking a budget that is equal to almost the entire elections budget to be ready for potential violence.

In late 2010, assistance to the Ugandan EMB was directed at transparency and accountability measures. The EMB initiated hotlines for phone calls and SMS-based question and answer lines. It enabled web access to voter registration information and polling stations lists. Nearly 150,000 downloads of polling stations lists were recorded and over 2,700 voter searches were conducted in August and September 2010.¹⁶ The increased transparency and increased public participation could improve EMB credibility in the lead-up to the 2011 elections.

This is a good example of the level of public impact that must be made with any effort to increase EMB credibility. To adequately fulfill its role in conflict prevention, the EMB must plan for frequent and active public information and media outreach, develop transparent and open processes, and serve as a driving force for stakeholder cooperation. In high-risk security situations, limitations on public events and freedom of movement must be taken into account in considering recommendations for meetings, training, and outreach.

2. EMB TRAINING STRATEGIES

Training within the EMB can be improved by incorporating the conflict perspective, internally. This would bolster the long-term professionalism of the EMB as well. Implementing conflict resolution and/or mediation training for key members of EMB staff and poll workers as standard practice could make a large difference in voter experiences – from voter registration, to polling, to counting, election officials encounter a variety of conflicts with or between voters. On a higher level, such training facilitates inclusiveness in relationships with stakeholders. Participants could be selected based on their roles within the EMB (those who interact with the public, such as poll workers, or those with responsibilities to liaise with other stakeholders). For the latter recommendation, the well-established Building Resources in Democracy, Governance and Elections (BRIDGE) methodology could be used.¹⁷

New training methods should also extend to the security sector and joint approaches should be developed to bolster understanding and relationships between the electoral and security bodies. There is general acceptance of the need for inclusive security planning and intensive cooperation between the security sector and other sectors to address election violence. However, security sector assistance is still quite separately funded and implemented, while the level of coordination in the field varies greatly and almost always begins at the last minute.

> SOUTH SUDAN: Navigating Conflict within Security Agencies
> Since the Comprehensive Peace Agreement (CPA) was signed in Sudan in 2005, security reform in South Sudan has proceeded slowly. The Sudan People's Liberation Army (SPLA), one of the principle belligerents in the decades-long civil war, was required to move many of its ranks into the new South Sudan Police Service (SPSS) and cede general authority for law and order to the nascent police force. Yet in the lead-up to the April 2010 elections, there were many examples of the SPLA and the public disregarding SPSS authority.[18]
>
> Security coordination and training for the April 2010 elections began only about six months before the elections. The priorities were joint meetings and workshops to acknowledge the role of the SPLA as a reserve force and promote the SSPS as the first line of security for election officials on polling day. Joint Operations Centres (JOCs) led by electoral authorities were set up at the state and county levels. Though these arrangements were not perfectly implemented, the mere existence of the JOCs and facilitated training and workshops all contributed to an unprecedented level of collaboration between electoral officials, the SSPS, and SPLA.[19]

In many transitional democracies, the security sector and culture with regard to the rule of law are in need of consolidation and improvement. Unless one is facing a post-conflict or ongoing conflict situation, the responsibility for election security falls largely on domestic police forces – whose capacity building is usually low on the list of international development objectives. Yet it is expected that, despite its problems, the security sector will come through during elections. These issues could be better addressed if more attention was put toward the intersection of security sector reform and electoral assistance. In particular, training for security agencies is rarely overseen by election officials and may not start in time to train all needed personnel, nor does it usually have the input of conflict-sensitive experts or other stakeholders.

The EMB should have input in the training process or hold joint sessions. Security actors and electoral officials need to be fully informed about the rules of engagement on election day. Security actors should discuss the treatment of political rally disruptions and other "minor" violence such as property damage, in addition to crowd control/management. Training must go beyond simply who is in charge when at the polling station. A between-elections initiative to design modules on election integration into existing security sector training academies is recommended.

3. MULTI-STAKEHOLDER COORDINATION

Convening regular, multi-stakeholder consultative meetings in the lead-up to the elections is another way EMBs can improve conflict prevention and mitigation, and build relationships with stakeholders. This works best when local-level groups complement a national body, providing opportunities for parties, security agencies, civil society, and election officials to share information, correct misinformation, and develop coordinated strategies to reduce violence and improve the electoral process.

> GHANA: Prevent Rumours, Prevent Violence
>
> In Ghana, during the lead-up to the December 2004 elections, two types of multi-stakeholder bodies met regularly. One was the Inter-Party Dialogue Committee (IPDC) established by the Election Commission. The IPDC included a variety of stakeholders and was particularly instrumental in preventing violence on at least one occasion. The driver of an election candidate hit someone on a bicycle and killed him. Immediately, rumours spread that the driver purposefully ran over a rival party supporter. Left unchecked, this could have spurred retaliation. After a quick investigation by the police, the IPDC met and swiftly issued public statements noting the police had concluded that the incident was an accident. According to IFES EVER monitors, this cooled tensions and put the rumours to rest.

4. MONITORING AND WATCHDOG INITIATIVES

Activities that provide accurate, continuous information on election violence or electoral violations can improve conflict prevention because they address impunity, secrecy, and rumours that often foster electoral conflict. In addition to improving the capacity and credibility of the EMB, bolstering monitoring mechanisms helps limit the opportunity for fraud and corruption, reducing the potential for conflict. Monitoring and reporting mechanisms can range from transparency measures the EMB introduces, to political finance regimes, to conflict monitoring and early warning systems, to election dispute resolution case monitoring, to election observation, among many others.

Though not usually characterized as a conflict prevention activity, political and campaign finance regimes create avenues through which the electoral, legal, and media sectors can better monitor, detect, and sanction violations to reduce the flow of money to conflict and violence. Civil society organizations can monitor corruption, campaign spending, election dispute cases, and other elements of the electoral process to contribute to increased information for stakeholder action and public accountability for wrongdoing.

Paradoxically, although conflict monitoring is touted by practitioners and donors alike, it is often the first to be cut from a tight electoral assistance budget. However, recently there has been increased interest in election conflict monitoring and reporting systems. Election conflict monitoring was recommended specifically as a successful strategy in the recent Special Rapporteur's report on election-related killings.[20] The rise of web-based, user-content-driven monitoring portals has brought unprecedented international media attention to conflict monitoring.[21] Practitioners and partners have a responsibility to better understand when monitoring mechanisms can be effective and to advocate more strongly for funding support.

The most effective monitoring and reporting initiatives tie into intervention mechanisms or include advocacy components, as the IFES EVER program does. They also incorporate web-based and/or new media technologies to improve outreach. For example, in Burundi, as part of the Amatora mu Mahoro (Elections in Peace) early warning network, IFES used the EVER methodology with text-message-based reporting and online mapping via Ushahidi to facilitate information exchange between partners, stakeholders, and the public. International and local stakeholders followed the reports on an online portal where incidents of violence were mapped geographically and by type of incident (intimidation, physical harm, murder, and so on).

> **BANGLADESH: No One Wants to Get Caught**
> In 2006-2007, IFES partnered with Odhikar, a well-known human rights network in Bangladesh, to conduct an EVER program. Approximately sixty monitors and division coordinators participated in training and were deployed to forty-five constituencies around the country (including some in Dhaka). Odhikar held press conferences to detail the findings of each biweekly report. Monitors reported that, in some areas, local political leaders were concerned about being "watched." Monitors reported that local leaders from different sectors increased joint meetings on security in several areas, and political leaders in constituencies where IFES did *not* have monitors also warned their supporters to avoid violence because they were being monitored![22] Although the January 2007 elections were postponed due to increasing violent conflict in certain areas of Dhaka, overall, the total number of incidents decreased from month to month in most constituencies where EVER monitors were present. This suggests that efforts had impact locally, where the national political dynamics and party leadership perhaps had less influence.

Education

Public and stakeholder education is essential for conflict prevention and mitigation. Specific approaches include voter education, civic education, training on election dispute mechanisms for parties, political finance monitoring, reporting procedures, and security sector training, among others.

Although civic education is widely acknowledged as key for building a strong democratic culture, it is not often directly linked to conflict prevention in the electoral context. Yet in fact citizens who understand their rights and responsibilities also understand the appropriate limits of political competition and government influence. They are less vulnerable to legal manipulations by political actors and more aware of legitimate means of resolving grievances.

Civic education also provides a forum for discussing tolerance, conflict management, and the need to resolve conflicts peacefully. This helps to create long-term change in the way that people view citizenship, violence, and electoral politics in relation to the institutions of their particular democracy.[23] Ideally, EMBs, CSOs, Ministries of Education and Youth, among others, should collaborate to support and advocate civic education for youth and adults that extends beyond the election period and remains continuous and consistent in its message.

Overall, the international community could increase successful election conflict prevention efforts by investing more in the basic building blocks of EMB capacity and credibility, security and election sector training, and civic education. Support to monitoring and reporting mechanisms would complement these efforts by offering independent sources of information.

Despite the adoption of the electoral cycle approach in theory and awareness of the need for capacity building and planning between elections, in practice the EMB is not given the same type of continuous attention and capacity building as other state institutions. As Johann Kriegler points out in this volume, weaknesses in the Kenya EMB were not evident on the surface of the 2002 election process. From our experience, increased attention to fundamentals and capacity building might have made a difference in its response to political pressure and allegations of wrongdoing in 2007.

Conflict Mitigation and Management

How can conflict mitigation improve electoral assistance programming? Intervening in conflicts is not only the responsibility of security forces. Public awareness and workshops are not the only tools of CSOs and non-security partners. Prosecution of perpetrators, rapid response mechanisms, mediation of disputes, and coordination of security responses all fall under conflict management and mitigation. They all require increased cooperation. Mechanisms for prevention, such as watchdog initiatives and multi-stakeholder coordination, often have a mitigation and mediation role as well. Where else do we see election assistance activities overlap with these activities, and where do activities need to be added within electoral assistance?

Effective, practical, and cost-effective strategies to bolster conflict mitigation benefits require adequate EMB authority for clearly defined integrity and enforcement mechanisms, cross-sector information sharing, and public advocacy for peace. These three areas will help frame the following discussion of tools and strategies for mitigation.

1. INTEGRITY AND ENFORCEMENT MECHANISMS

Electoral and/or political party codes of conduct must be drafted with realistic monitoring and enforcement authority to avoid becoming part of the pattern of impunity for electoral offences and violence.

This means the enforcement body should be able to identify and sanction offenders who fail to conform to the codes of conduct, convene multi-stakeholder dialogues, or trigger responses to conflict and violations. The enforcement regime must be objective, independent, and unbiased so the jurisdiction assigned and the substance of sanctions are proportional and reasonable. In some cases where the EMB or political party regulatory body may have the authority to sanction violations of a code of conduct, they often do too much or too little – either they can abuse their power, or they fear repercussions for using it. In other cases, the sanctions may involve disproportionate measures, which EMBs would be reluctant to invoke. In any of these scenarios, it is likely that either use of the enforcement system will be avoided or its use will increase, rather than reduce, tensions.

SIERRA LEONE: Enforcement and Rapid Response Bolster Codes of Conduct

In Sierra Leone in 2007, the Political Party Registration Commission (PPRC) set out early in the electoral cycle to pursue its mandate to monitor and enforce compliance with the Political Party Code of Conduct. However, the PPRC did not want to act merely as a national board to hear complaints. The institution set up District Monitoring Committees (DMCs) to respond to disputes, both formal and informal. IFES worked with the PPRC to develop and train the DMCs in conflict mediation to perform rapid response dispute resolution. When disputes or violence occurred, the DMCs sent teams to work with political actors to resolve conflicts, which contributed greatly to a credible and peaceful electoral process.

To overcome such challenges, identifying obstacles in implementing an effective code and sanctions should occur early in the process. The goal should be better system implementation. Increasing capacity for monitoring and enforcement should be built into EMB assistance.

Other regulatory mechanisms can also contribute to the credibility, integrity, and conflict-sensitivity of the electoral process. The presence of strong and transparent campaign finance regimes can discourage corruption that raises the costs of holding elected office. Lower reward lowers the stakes of the contest, and this may lower the attractiveness of violence as a campaign strategy. Decreasing corruption can also temper the flow of money to armed groups or other instigators of violence. In the same spirit, timely, fair, and accessible EDR mechanisms can reduce the potential for conflict by providing a legitimate alternative to violence. These initiatives are crucial and can be monitored for compliance, providing a check on the institutional will and ability to establish such mechanisms and a way to engage the public through this accountability exercise.

2. INFORMATION SHARING AND COORDINATION

The conflict monitoring, security training, and general cooperation issues discussed earlier could also benefit attempts to mitigate or manage conflict. A less-than-credible EMB will not be able to mobilize, calm, or reassure tense voters or party supporters while rumours of election fraud spread. Security agencies without proper training may intervene inappropriately to manage a conflict situation and escalate violence instead of quelling it. If conflict monitoring efforts do not share information with security and EMB actors swiftly and transparently (and vice versa) opportunities for mitigation can be lost.

Multi-stakeholder bodies created to improve information sharing and air disputes can also respond to escalating conflict through public statements, by mobilizing constituencies for peacebuilding activities, or otherwise using their influence to quell violence. An investment in media monitoring and capacity building for responsible reporting to prevent conflict can also contribute to de-escalating situations.

Coordination mechanisms are most important in difficult security environments. In high-security operations, where international and domestic agencies work together, Joint Operation Centres (JOCs) or Joint Election Operating Centres (JEOCs) are often created. Such centres gather election officials, security agencies, government officials, and, in some cases, community leaders to coordinate security planning, implementation, monitoring, and responses.

3. PUBLIC ADVOCACY FOR PEACE

Similarly, without a complementary public education and awareness campaign or advocacy efforts for peaceful elections, the dynamics of violence may be unlikely to change – particularly in societies where violence is perpetrated by those among the most vulnerable populations. In many countries, impunity and lack of political will have set patterns of election in place so firmly that many take the violence for granted; a public campaign against election violence reminds all that such violence is not acceptable.[24]

For example, Guyana had seen recurrent post-election violence since 1992, stemming from ethnic, political and socio-economic grievances. In 2006, support was bolstered in the areas of EMB support, media monitoring, conflict tracking through EVER and other public education efforts, and social cohesion. These efforts improved electoral administration, heightened awareness of election conflict, and increased local-to-national communication. Renewed public attention to election conflict helped pressure political parties to denounce post-election violence and call for acceptance of results. For the first time since 1992, there was no widespread post-election violence.[25]

Conflict Resolution

The meaning of "conflict resolution" depends a great deal on one's field of work. In the electoral cycle the concept of conflict resolution is both useful and challenging. As a concept, it suggests addressing root causes and potential for reconciliation of communities. The term is more straightforward if one refers to election-related conflicts that can be registered with dispute resolution bodies, law enforcement, the election commission, or other institutions. That is, EDR refers to formal complaints and dispute resolution bodies resolving specific differences or conflicts that occurred during the electoral period. Thus, resolution for some of these cases would mean the prosecution and punishment of perpetrators. However, resolution of the grievances that often drive election-related violence, such as resource, representational, political, socioeconomic, ethnic, or religious conflicts, requires a long-term approach related to conflict transformation and reconciliation processes. But both institutional and deeper-reaching mechanisms need to be supported for effective change to happen in electoral conflict dynamics.

For resolution of disputes around elections, procedural efficiency and procedural awareness are equally important in order to avoid aggravating conflict risks. Alternative dispute resolution mechanisms are also helpful tools to ensure justice after a dispute. They can focus on negotiated resolution, rather than punishment, of irregularities or wrongdoing. As mentioned previously, eliminating impunity for perpetrators of violence requires change in traditional law enforcement mechanisms, even if some cases can be dealt with by electoral tribunals. Judicial sector activities should be complemented by the ongoing work of government agencies and EMBs in engaging in lessons-learned processes to improve performance in the future.[26]

For example, in 2007 in East Timor, a thematic approach to conflict prevention and resolution fuelled an assistance strategy to support both conflict monitoring and the entire election dispute resolution process. The EDR system was revamped, from complaint forms, to case management, to outreach and education efforts. Civil society partners and IFES trainers met with citizens, political parties, journalists, and dispute adjudicators to ensure that all stakeholders understood their rights within the system, how and when to file complaints, or how to contribute to their resolution. Publically releasing lists of resolved cases as complaints were heard proved highly beneficial. This unprecedented effort dramatically increased the effectiveness, credibility, accessibility, and transparency of the system.

Unfortunately, there are many examples of long-term grievances that drive electoral conflicts. Electoral assistance is currently limited in its ability to address these. In Bangladesh, at the national level, the political will to reduce conflict, denounce violence, or address old grievances is low. In Nepal in 2007 and 2008, Terai communities were plagued by violence from armed separatist groups pursuing goals stemming from unresolved representation issues. Recurrent election violence in Jamaican garrisons is deeply rooted in the corrupt relationship between money, patronage, and politics that exists outside of the electoral process. In Zimbabwe, the ruling party has little interest or incentive to yield real power and enforces its will during electoral periods against opposition groups.

An election-focused intervention, even if inclusive, community-led, and effective, cannot resolve any of these long-term problems alone.

Looking for long-term solutions requires different tactics. For example, as noted earlier, monitors in the EVER program in Bangladesh in 2006 and 2007 reported that, as monitoring went on, monitors learned that local political leaders in some constituencies did not want to be "caught" using violence and encouraged their supporters to avoid it. It is possible that ongoing intervention at the local community level could capitalize on the gains of the EVER team. In other cases, CSOs that are active during elections can engage with the same stakeholders and push for resolution of long-term issues between elections. Seeking longer-term projects that emphasize dialogue, education, training, and electoral reform could go a long way toward conflict resolution.

CONCLUSIONS

Frameworks, theories, conferences, and technologies may offer ways forward in developing strategies for reducing conflict around elections. However, practitioners, domestic and international, will eventually take those theories and design and implement solutions applicable in the field.

A key problem in addressing elections and conflict is the lack of cross-sector cooperation and continued reliance on sector-specific programming with sector-specific goals. Conflict considerations and electoral considerations have been separated in part because of easier bureaucratic management and common funding practices. Although the two are distinct development sectors, the separation of programming is arbitrary. Donors and program design teams must create new ways of incorporating conflict responses in electoral programming. Elections themselves will not resolve conflicts, but conflict-sensitive election assistance can contribute to the analysis, prevention, mitigation, and resolution of conflicts. The backbone of a good, conflict sensitive approach is explicitly linking the conflict-response cycle and the election cycle.

Overall, the ICEP – integrating conflict analysis, prevention, management, and resolution throughout electoral cycle programming – allows for a systematic approach, rather than a sector-based approach.

Effective conflict analysis will stem from deepening current electoral assessment programming, integrating analysis into security and strategic electoral planning, and gathering insights from analysis done by other sectors.

Increased commitment to long-term institutional capacity of EMBs, improving security and electoral training practices, and supporting broad civic education programs will improve conflict prevention.

Election assistance that incorporates mitigation responses increases the capacity to develop integrity and use enforcement mechanisms in election processes, facilitates better information sharing, and supports public awareness and advocacy for peace.

Conflict resolution as it is currently used in electoral programming is geared toward the short-term resolution of disputes. Better conflict resolution efforts should include long-term investment in consensus-building efforts to resolve grievances.

Looking at the election cycle from the conflict cycle perspective and explicitly linking the programming responses in each cycle is an ideal road map for integrating conflict sensibilities with election assistance. This approach is all about learning from practice and grounding theories and observations in actionable recommendations and good practices. It is imperative to focus on the inter-related roles key stakeholders play through cross-sector coordination and by continuing to invest in the long-term for sustainable results. Through this holistic approach we will continue to improve the effectiveness of election assistance and reduce violence and conflict around elections.

10

Preventing and Mitigating Election-Related Conflict and Violence: The Role of Electoral Justice

SARA STAINO

By their very nature, elections are a vehicle for constructive conflict, designed to manage and channel diversity of opinion in productive directions. If an election is free and fair, perceived as just, and accepted by all stakeholders, it can offer legitimate and non-violent avenues of change.[1]

Democratic institutions such as, for example, electoral management bodies (EMBS), are established to represent social interests and respond to public needs.[2] While strong and well-functioning institutions are well placed to represent social interests, weak or dysfunctional institutions are often either unable or too inefficient to do so. Well-functioning institutions are effective means not only for responding to public needs but for mediating and uniting diverse interests within a given society and for preventing and mitigating conflict, violence, and social deprivation.[3]

In relation to elections, the two key institutions responsible for managing and channelling conflict in productive directions are the EMB and the electoral dispute resolution (EDR) body: the EMB in the way it sets electoral policies and implements electoral operations, and the EDR body in the way it ensures the legality of electoral practices and enforces the rule of law.

Although electoral justice and dispute resolution remains largely unmapped, with few comparative studies on the subject, electoral dispute resolution plays a decisive role in democracies by ensuring the stability of the political system and adherence to the legal framework.

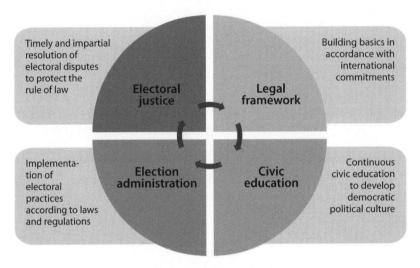

Figure 1. Conflict prevention stages of the electoral process

A robust electoral justice system with functioning and independent EDR mechanisms can mitigate and resolve disputes when they occur. While EDR mechanisms alone do not guarantee credible elections, their absence or malfunctioning can aggravate grievance and conflict.

The aim of this chapter is to explore the role EDR plays in the prevention of election-related conflict and violence. It provides a brief overview of fundamental conflict prevention stages of the electoral process, categorizes different systems for EDR based on the classification used in International IDEA's *Electoral Justice* handbook, and explores the role EDR plays in the mitigation and resolution of electoral disputes and thus, in the prevention of election related conflict and violence.[4]

CONFLICT PREVENTION STAGES OF THE ELECTORAL PROCESS

There are different means and mechanisms to prevent and mitigate electoral conflict. Figure 1 above illustrates four fundamental stages, or components, of the electoral process that offers effective opportunities for conflict prevention and mitigation. The four stages are (1) the legal framework of elections, (2) civic education and development of political culture, (3) implementation of electoral practices, and (4) resolution of electoral disputes and protection of the rule of law.

The different stages of the cycle are linked, essential, and complementary components for understanding, preventing, and resolving election-related conflicts.

A comprehensive legal framework committed to democratic principles and values can be created, civic education can be conducted and a political culture developed, professionalization of EMBs can take place and elections can be well administered and organized, but if there are no functioning electoral dispute resolution mechanisms in place to enforce electoral justice and ensure the legality of the electoral process, trust can be lost and credibility jeopardized. Instead of contributing to democracy and stability, unresolved irregularities and fraud can turn elections into catalysts for grievance and conflict, resulting in mistrust, the rejection of election results, and violence.

Building the Basics: The Legal Framework of Elections

A legal framework is an essential building block for democratic governance. It provides the foundation on which democratic institutions and processes are built and it is a fundamental instrument for the protection of the rights of citizens and political parties.[5]

To ensure democratic elections and build a solid foundation for the prevention of election-related conflict, the legal framework needs to endorse citizens' equal civil and political rights to elect their government representatives through periodic and genuine elections, as well as safeguard the rights of political contestants to stand for election and compete on a level playing field. In addition, the legal framework should ensure the basic rights of voters, political parties, and candidates to legal remedy before legitimate authorities, providing the effective opportunity to file appeals and challenge any violations. Finally, in order to address disputes and resolve conflicts effectively, the legal framework needs to empower the existing electoral justice mechanism to deal with disputes in an efficient, timely, and independent manner, providing it with the powers, tools, mandate, resources (both financial and human), and timeframe that these operations require.[6]

Without a legal framework that guarantees and protects basic democratic rights and meets international commitments, no effort to improve the other components of the cycle will produce the desired positive impact on the democratic development of a country.

Civic Education and Development of Political Culture

The second conflict prevention component of the cycle, as shown above, is continuous civic education to promote a political culture of awareness and the professionalization of electoral institutions and those working directly or indirectly with electoral processes.

Civic education, voter information, capacity development of EMB staff, and consensus building of electoral stakeholders (such as political parties, legislatures, the media, and civil society) are all key educational activities that promote the development of a political culture. These activities are mutually reinforcing for the increased understanding of the rule of law, public accountability, stakeholders' rights and responsibilities, and other broad concepts underpinning a democratic society. They are also key to promoting social cohesion, building consensus on common codes of conduct, and increasing citizen awareness and voter motivation. This is particularly the case in post-conflict countries, in societies where there have been major changes and challenges to the electoral system and/or procedures, and in cases where there is a newly established EMB or a large population of newly enfranchised voters.

Increased awareness, professionalism, and social cohesion are among the most effective safeguards against outbreaks of violence during a highly tense electoral process.[7] However, to achieve the desired level of political and social awareness requires a long-term commitment by government institutions, civil society organizations, and the general public. In addition, civic education and professional development are continuous processes required throughout the electoral process, including during the pre- and post-election periods.

Electoral Administration and Implementation of Electoral Practices

The third stage to avoid or mitigate possible causes for election-related conflict is to ensure the proper enforcement of the law.

Due to the size and complexity of electoral operations, and the tight deadlines and high political pressure during the election period, the implementation of electoral practices is one of the most politically sensitive and conflict-prone stages of the electoral process. Without proper enforcement of procedures, even the best legislation can be bypassed or ignored. In order to safeguard the integrity of the electoral process, protect civic and political rights, and prevent election-related violence, the timely implementation of electoral practices according to the law must be ensured. This is one of the core tasks of the EMB.

Efficient implementation of electoral activities is key, but in order to conduct credible elections and avoid potential conflict, an EMB must also enjoy the trust of the stakeholders and must be perceived as implementing electoral practices in a professional and non-partisan manner.

EMBs that are assured structural independence from the executive in the constitution or law are in a better position to enjoy public trust than those that are part of governmental structures. However, such formalized structures provide no guarantees of independence. To be truly independent, an EMB must enjoy a normative independence from the executive and other political influences in its decision making and actions, meaning that the EMB can be independent in its behaviour and carry out its work without fearing repercussions from government or other political forces. To obtain this form of independence, the EMB has to be professional enough to stand up to political pressure, have financial independence, and have its members appointed by means other than direct decision and influence of the executive.[8]

This fearless independence of decision and action can help build public trust in electoral practices, thus preventing mistrust, suspicion, and frustration, which lead to electoral conflict and violence. It is, however, important to note that even an independent EMB can be perceived as partisan. To build public trust among stakeholders, it is crucial for an EMB to demonstrate its independence by transparent, consultative, and inclusive decisions and actions throughout the electoral process.

Resolution of Electoral Disputes and Protection of the Rule of Law

The fourth and final stage to prevent conflict and outbreak of election-related violence is the timely and impartial resolution of disputes and the protection of the rule of law. Functioning electoral dispute resolution mechanisms are the ultimate guarantor of the principle of free and fair elections and help ensure peaceful elections.[9] The following sections focus on the role of EDR mechanisms and the importance of electoral justice for the prevention and mitigation of electoral-related conflict and violence.

ELECTORAL JUSTICE AND DISPUTE RESOLUTION

There are different ways to define the concept of "electoral justice." According to the International IDEA handbook on electoral justice, the term refers to the various means and mechanisms that, on the one hand, aim to ensure that electoral acts and procedures and their results conform to the law[10] and are not marred by irregularities and, on the other hand, aim to protect or restore the enjoyment of electoral and political rights.[11] As such, electoral justice is not only the ultimate guarantor of free and genuine elections and credible electoral processes but also a fundamental instrument for ensuring democratic legitimacy.

There is a wide array of means and mechanisms to ensure that electoral processes adhere to the law, are compliant with legal frameworks, and respect civic and political rights. As for all judicial proceedings, clear rules and mechanisms for the handling of complaints and disputes, with unambiguous and accessible appeal procedures, need to be put in place in order to ensure electoral justice and integrity.

Through a properly functioning electoral justice system, complaints can be addressed and potential mistakes and inaccuracies can be corrected, avoiding public grievance and mistrust toward the EMB and the electoral process itself. An inaccuracy or irregularity that is not adequately dealt with can create discontent and, in an already politically or socially tense situation, result in violence.

If the justice system can adequately protect the electoral rights of citizens and political parties and ensure that electoral procedures are not marred by irregularities and that procedures are timely and impartial, violent outbreaks related to the electoral process may be prevented. In this way, electoral justice plays a decisive role in the prevention and mitigation of election-related conflict and in the political stability of a country and, as such, should be seen as an important contributing factor for the consolidation of democratic governance and for peaceful transition in post-conflict situations.

Finally, a distinction should be made between the two forms of dispute resolution encompassed in the overarching term of "electoral justice": the *formal* mechanisms for electoral dispute, carried out through institutional means; and more *informal* (or alternative) ones that may or may not be included in legislation.

CATEGORIZATION OF ELECTORAL DISPUTE RESOLUTION SYSTEMS

In both legal-electoral and political science definitions, EDR systems are defined as institutional/formal systems of appeals through which electoral actions and/or procedures can be legally challenged.

EDR systems have a variety of legal challenge mechanisms and tend to involve a number of bodies responsible for resolving disputes at different levels (see table 1). These bodies can be administrative, jurisdictional, legislative, or even international. An example is the EMB, which in most cases is responsible for resolving disputes at the administrative level, while some other body may be in charge of issuing the final decision on challenges made to EMB decisions.

This categorization focuses on the legal nature of the formal institution responsible for dispute resolution at the highest instance, tasked with issuing the final decision on electoral challenges and disputes. Electoral actions and challenges can be entrusted to one of the following bodies/organs:

- legislative body or other political assembly
- jurisdictional organ
- electoral management body with jurisdictional powers
- international or national ad hoc body[12]

To protect the independence of the judicial branch and to keep the judiciary from dealing with highly political issues, the oldest EDR system (originating in the United Kingdom in the mid-nineteenth century) tasked political institutions with the responsibility of resolving electoral disputes. The final decision on disputes was vested in the legislature, in legislative committees, or in other political assemblies.[13]

Today, purely legislative/political dispute resolution systems are quite uncommon, and in order to avoid a situation where members of legislature judge and certify their own elections, legislative powers are often combined with judicial powers. In these so-called *mixed legislative-jurisdictional systems* (which are used, for example, in Argentina, Italy, Germany, and the United States), the judiciary most commonly plays a role in resolving lower-level electoral challenges, while the legislative organ is entrusted with the final decision of the validity of the results.

As a response to concerns of priority being given to political and party interests in mixed legislative-jurisdictional systems, some EDR systems entrust the final decision on electoral disputes to regular courts of the judicial branch, generally to the Supreme Court. This *judicial system* is seen to better guarantee free and fair elections, as electoral disputes are resolved by judges based on the constitution and other legal provisions. Judicial systems are quite common and can be found, for example, in Bosnia and Herzegovina, Ethiopia, Japan, Kenya, Lesotho, Moldova, Russia, Taiwan, and Uganda.

When putting the final decision to the judiciary, it is important to consider independence and credibility, especially in emerging or consolidating democracies. In countries where the judicial system does enjoy trust, its independence must be carefully safeguarded.

In order to protect the judiciary and prevent ordinary judges from getting involved in political disputes or being subject to political pressure, many countries have chosen to entrust the final resolution of electoral challenges to non-regular courts, such as constitutional courts (e.g., Armenia, Burkina Faso, Cambodia, France, Mozambique, Romania, and Portugal), administrative courts (e.g., Colombia, Finland, Latvia, and the Czech Republic), or specialized electoral courts (e.g., Mexico, Peru).[14]

Specialized electoral courts enjoy functional independence: they can be permanent or temporary and part of the judicial branch or autonomous from the three classic branches of government. The main advantage of these courts is that their specialization in electoral jurisdictional issues may translate into a more professional and timely resolution of disputes. A disadvantage, however, is the high costs that these permanent courts entail.

An additional system of EDR can be found in Costa Rica, Nicaragua, and Uruguay. This is the case of EMBs *with jurisdictional powers*. These EMBs are autonomous or independent bodies that, while issuing the final resolution on electoral challenges and deciding on the validity of the electoral process, also perform the function of organizing and administering electoral processes. The resolution of disputes by these bodies is final and not subject to further review by any jurisdictional, administrative, or legislative body. In addition, EMBs with jurisdictional powers tend to also have constitutional powers and thus they form a fourth branch of government. The benefit of this system is that it creates very strong and stable electoral institutions; however, it can be debated whether the "judge and the jury" function is best vested in the same body.

Finally, powers for resolving electoral disputes can be entrusted to an *ad hoc body* in a transitional and provisional arrangement. This might be an institutional solution sponsored by international organizations in order to guarantee credible and genuine elections to overcome serious conflict – such as in Cambodia in 1993 or Bosnia and Herzegovina in 1996.

TENDENCIES AND IDENTIFIED TRENDS

Just like electoral systems and electoral management bodies, EDR systems are often the result of legal tradition and evolution in each country, as well as of prevailing political forces. Traditionally, electoral dispute resolution systems have not been a focus of attention or reform, but comparative studies show that there have been considerable changes in the design and structure of EDR systems since World War I, particularly in the past two decades.

The main trend in comparative law is the "judicialization" of electoral procedures, where legislative bodies are being replaced by judicial bodies for the resolution of electoral disputes.[15] This trend is based on political expediency and the belief that the constitutionality and legality of elections is better ensured if disputes are resolved by judicial bodies. This is a positive trend as it professionalizes, de-politicizes, and strengthens the authority of the body in charge of resolving electoral disputes, thus increasing the legality of the process and public trust for the institution.

Following the First and Second World Wars, the trend was to entrust electoral dispute resolution to constitutional courts, whereas, since the third wave of democratization, the trend has been toward specialized electoral courts – a phenomenon clear not only in Latin America but also in Africa and Asia. In addition, there has been an increase in the responsibility of regular EMBs (who do not enjoy jurisdictional powers) for resolving electoral disputes at a lower/first instance and at the administrative level. An important indicator of these trends is that EMB members in an increasing number of countries come from the judicial branch (or are appointed in similar fashion) and are given guarantees equivalent to those of the highest-ranking judicial officers.

As is the case for electoral management bodies, any means that can strengthen the position of individual members of the EDR body helps ensure the independence and impartiality of the institution itself and helps increase its credibility.

CONFLICT PREVENTION THROUGH EFFECTIVE ELECTORAL DISPUTE RESOLUTION

Electoral practices marred by irregularities disrupt free and fair electoral processes, harm public trust, and lead to low voter turnout and to the possible rejection of election results. This in turn may lead to destructive conflict and the outbreak of election-related violence that could force candidates to resign, prevent or postpone elections, and influence the legitimacy of the elected government.[16] Thus, when elections take place in complex political contexts, such as in countries emerging from deep-rooted conflict, it is essential to prevent any triggers that could result in violence.

Due to the length, complexity, and scope of the electoral process and the high stakes of electoral competition, elections offer plenty of opportunities for shortfalls, misunderstandings, and misperception. The best guarantee against violence that an effective EDR system can provide is the ability to correct irregularities arising at any point throughout the electoral process in a timely fashion. From issues of candidate and voter registration, political party financing, and media coverage to voting day operations and tabulation of results, breaches of the legal framework and infringement of civil and political rights can be corrected to ensure a legitimate electoral process. Safeguarding the integrity of the electoral process and fully enforcing the civil and political rights of voters and electoral contestants are the two main aims of EDR mechanisms. In addition, electoral stakeholders should also be ensured the right to a fair trial and the right to independence of the judiciary (or any other body in charge of resolving electoral disputes).[17] To meet these aims effectively, a well-designed and comprehensive EDR system must provide some structural and procedural guarantees.

Structural guarantees are important for ensuring the autonomy, independence, and impartiality of the entity in charge of EDR. These guarantees include, among other things, a three-dimensional independence of the EDR body and its members (formal independence stated in the constitution and/or law, financial independence, and normative independence of EDR members decision and action); as well as its impartiality, accountability, integrity, and professionalism.

Procedural guarantees ensure the effectiveness and efficiency of electoral dispute resolution processes. These include the availability of effective electoral justice, either free of charge or at a reasonable cost; the ability to complain at the lowest level (at the polling station); the right to a defence or hearing; consistency in the interpretation and application of electoral laws; and full enforcement of judgments and rulings. Other key procedural principles are transparency, clarity, and simplicity of the provisions that regulate the electoral dispute resolution system, as well as proper information and easy access to the services they provide.

Finally, and considering that electoral processes operate under very specific and tight deadlines, the procedures governing electoral disputes require prompt decisions, dealing with issues in a timely manner, within the electoral timeframe established by the legal provisions.[18] Although sufficient timelines should be provided to allow EDR mechanisms (courts and electoral bodies) to properly investigate, review, prosecute, and make decisions upon the complaints and appeals submitted to them, it is important to note that the timeframes for resolving electoral disputes are generally significantly shorter than for civil disputes. In addition, most electoral activities and decisions are dependent on each other. Any delay in decision-making can have a series of negative consequences for the conduct of elections, ultimately affecting the outcome and legitimacy of the electoral process and/or leading to grievances, conflict, and violence. If realistic deadlines are set in the law for each phase of the electoral process (such as voter registration or the validity of candidatures), and if the deadlines, both of complainants and courts, are properly communicated the timeframe is more likely to be kept and many problems can be avoided.

HIERARCHICAL COMPLAINT AND APPEAL PROCEDURES

The opportunity to make a complaint about or appeal any electoral decision is an important safeguard of election integrity and lies at the core of this subject. The legal framework, therefore, needs to include effective mechanisms that allow electoral contestants and voters to lodge complaints and appeals arising from the electoral process. The electoral law should also set out clear hierarchical procedures for the handling of election-related complaints and appeals. In addition to respecting the electoral legal framework and the tight deadlines of electoral processes, these procedures also need to be established in accordance with the broader legal framework governing general judiciary and civil proceedings.[19] A system that tracks the type, status, and number of complaints can be a useful tool for the monitoring and speedy resolution of disputes and for making sure no complaints fall through the cracks.

Usually, the first step in the complaints process is an administrative review, where the EMB or policymaking body may have the authority to review complaints at a first instance. A review is part of the internal checks of most electoral administrations and may examine a complaint related to the registration process (either of voters or of political parties and candidates), to the proceedings on election day, or to the counting and tabulation process. Disputes that are not resolved at this first instance risk grievances building up and could, in volatile situations, grow into greater conflicts that turn violent. For this reason, it is important to emphasize the significant role played by an EMB in preventing electoral disputes and resolving them at the most basic levels of the electoral administration. EMBs at the sub-national level can be both trained and monitored to ensure consistency in dealing with complaints.

Although the majority of EMBs are entrusted with powers primarily of an executive nature (related to implementing electoral activities), it is not uncommon for EMBs to also enjoy other powers; for example, powers to investigate and prosecute violations of electoral laws and to resolve disputes of an administrative nature and/or disputes that do not necessarily fall within the jurisdiction of the courts.

To ensure integrity in the review process, the decisions made by the EMB (or any other body deciding on challenges at the first instance) are generally subject to appeal with an independent and impartial judicial authority. This enables the complainant to seek a review of the decision with a higher-level institution. The appeals process serves as a check on the decisions made in the initial review and may deter arbitrary or biased decision making. Appeals are part of the checks and balances on decisions made by a lower court or after administrative review of a complaint. Each system handles appeals differently according to its legal and institutional framework but, notwithstanding the system in place, it is important to have a clear and simple procedure that allows the review of lower-level decisions in a systematic and neutral manner without due delay.[20]

Regardless of where the jurisdiction for the final decision on electoral disputes lies (in a legislative, judicial, or ad hoc body), it is good practice for electoral justice systems to involve a number of bodies and a variety of challenge mechanisms for resolving complaints and disputes at different levels. The table below illustrates three cases where complaints go through different challenge mechanisms.

The more trust the EMB and the EDR mechanisms enjoy, the greater are the chances for complainants to turn to the formal mechanisms to solve their disputes and accept and abide by the outcome of the EDR process. In addition, the law should clearly state which institution has the final say and which decisions are final and binding, without leaving any room for misunderstandings.[21]

Finally, it is important to be aware that accusations of fraud and irregularities could also be used as a political strategy to overload EMBs and EDR bodies with complaints as an attempt to undermine the credibility of the elections and the legitimacy of the outcome. This could overburden the system, affect the ability to meet crucial deadlines, and have serious consequences for the electoral process. If serious enough, it could create conflict rather than resolve it.

In order to ensure free and fair elections, an electoral justice system also needs to ensure that *all* electoral acts and regulations are in harmony with each other and in accordance with the law. This relies on the existence of an adequate legal framework and efficient institutional arrangements that provide the authorities in charge of electoral dispute resolution with a comprehensive mandate and sufficient powers, resources, and tools to carry out their functions in a timely and effective manner throughout all stages of the electoral process (including the post-election period). Examples of EDR systems

Table 1
Challenge Mechanisms for Resolving Complaints and Disputes at Different Levels

Country/ Case	Complaint			Challenge instance		
	Issue	Target	Issuer	First	Second	Third
A	Party registration	Civil registry office	Political party	EMB (high-level officer or organ)	Judicial body* for final resolution	—
B	Vote counting	Polling station	Political party or voter	EMB (high-level officer or organ)	Regular court	Constitutional court for final resolution
C	Vote tabulation	Tabulation centre/EMB	Political party or voter	EMB (high-level officer or organ)	Legislative body	—

Note: In the first case (A), the final decision on a complaint (in this case on party registration) is made by a judicial body, while in the third case (C) it is made by a legislative body. The second case (B) illustrates a complaint in which there are provisions in the law for two successive judicial challenges of EMB decisions: the first is before a regular court (or an electoral court), while the second, and in this case final challenge (third instance), is before a constitutional court, for example.

* The judicial body could be a regular, constitutional, administrative, or electoral court.

designed to properly cover all stages of the electoral process are the specialized and permanent electoral courts found in Mexico and Peru.

DIVISION OF RESPONSIBILITIES AND INTERACTION WITH EMBS

A key issue to be established in the legal framework, in addition to the appellate procedures and the authority of the EDR body, is the clear division of responsibilities among the different institutions involved in dispute resolution at different levels.

It is common to find that many components of the judicial system interact and overlap in different ways with EMB activities and that the division of responsibility is sometimes unclear. In order to avoid both gaps in the legislation and overlap of responsibilities between different institutions, it is crucial that the electoral law make a clear demarcation of the respective jurisdictions of the courts and administrative electoral bodies and that it eliminate arbitrary interpretation through the use of clear and consistent language.[22] Whichever arrangement for resolving electoral disputes is adopted, it should be clear which competent authority has jurisdiction for resolving conflicts and disputes, both at the different stages of the electoral process and at different hierarchical levels of the process.

The conflict prevention role of EMBs is an essential contribution to processes of democratic transition and consolidation. This has been particularly clear in young democracies in cases where the electoral justice system in place is not yet adequately developed to resolve disputes and in cases where the system in place does not enjoy the trust of the public. The fundamental role played by EMBs in resolving electoral disputes (even when they do not make the final decision in the hierarchical structure of electoral challenges) is especially evident in cases where the EMB is independent and autonomous from the executive, such as in India, Canada, Mexico, and South Africa.[23]

However, the relationship between the dispute resolution and electoral management bodies is a sensitive matter that needs to be carefully considered. It is sensitive not only because of the lack of clear divisions of responsibilities and possible overlaps and misunderstandings but also because EDR mechanisms in most cases deal with issues such as challenges to EMB decisions (as shown in table 1), disputes between the EMB and other stakeholders, and the legality of EMB regulations, administrative procedures, and practices. In addition, EMB members and staff may be subject to judicial investigation or civil litigation. The very nature of the relationship between these two bodies is delicate as the decisions taken by one can greatly affect the activities, effects, and public perception of the other. In cases where the EMB has the final say on complaints (as in Costa Rica and Uruguay), the relationship between the higher and the lower instance is of course a different one, as they lie within the same body. However, other issues, such as conflicts of interest, might be problematic in these cases.

Maintaining a good and professional relationship between the two bodies, while keeping the appropriate distance so as not to impinge, or appear to impinge, on the independence of either, is essential. However, this tends to require that the EMB be cooperative in investigations or the dealings of electoral justice. It will be difficult to maintain a good relationship between the two bodies if the EMB obstructs a dispute resolution body's access to relevant electoral materials or sites, if its presentation of evidence on disputes is not professional, or if it in any way attempts to limit the powers of the body in charge of resolving electoral disputes.[24]

PROSECUTION AND ENFORCEMENT OF ELECTORAL INTEGRITY

Impunity breeds fraud and corruption and fosters an atmosphere of unethical behaviour and practices. Failure to enforce legislation – by correcting irregularities, prosecuting and punishing offenders, and holding them accountable for their actions – will weaken the rule of law and the integrity of the electoral justice system. In the short term, this may lead to grievances, augmented political tension, and mistrust of electoral institutions, as well as increased probability of electoral conflicts and violent outbreaks. In the long term, it may foster a culture of impunity that could be extremely difficult to break. In particular, in countries that are in transition or emerging from a history of violent conflict, such a culture can become a serious threat to the consolidation of democratic governance.[25]

Unfortunately, some countries undergoing transition do not necessarily have the legal and judicial infrastructure required to support an investigation and sanction the perpetrators. There may be legislative gaps in the system and they may not have the appropriate means and measures to investigate and resolve disputes due to lack of personnel, resources, or institutional experience. As a result, investigators or prosecutors may not be able to prove that the law has been broken, even though it is evident that an offence has been committed, and thus may not be able to hold anyone accountable. A culture of impunity takes root, particularly where the law enforcement system is inoperative or virtually non-existent. In these cases, it could be advisable to strengthen the EMB and entrust it with EDR responsibilities. As an example, in the late 1990s, the legal system of Cambodia had proven to be very weak and unable to solve human rights cases effectively. Despite this, no law enforcement powers were given to the National Elections Committee for the 1998 elections and all electoral violations were referred to government authorities. Due to its restricted mandate, the National Elections Committee was unsuccessful in its efforts to deal with election law violations and prevent violence. No one was ever prosecuted.[26]

Prosecution serves as a deterrent for those who might consider illegal acts and is a key element in safeguarding the rule of law and deterring a culture of impunity.[27] However, building a national judicial system and the necessary infrastructure is a long-term process. In some countries where there is no history of an independent judiciary, the only way to compensate for gaps in the legal system may be by establishing an electoral commission with wide-ranging powers of the type normally exercised by judicial institutions.

ALTERNATIVE DISPUTE RESOLUTION MECHANISMS

Some electoral disputes cannot be solved by formal resolution mechanisms and must be diverted to alternative mechanisms. To accommodate this need, there is a longstanding tradition, particularly in Africa, of more informal means of managing electoral disputes. These are normally referred to as alternative or traditional dispute resolution mechanisms.

There are two sets of alternative EDR mechanisms: the mechanisms that play an important complementary and/or supportive role, especially when the formal mechanisms do not enjoy the necessary independence and credibility or the proper financial means to solve electoral disputes in a efficient, timely and professional manner; and the more ad hoc alternative mechanisms that are needed in extraordinary cases of political crisis or institutional failure, where high-level interventions such as power-sharing agreements, for example, are required.

Examples of alternative mechanisms of a complementary nature include the establishment of multiparty liaison committees at the national, provincial, or local level that can enable the EMB and political parties to consult regularly and address issues that arise,[28] and the creation of mediation committees at the local level composed of prominent and respectable members of society who have leverage in the community. Such mechanisms can help in the rapid resolution of electoral disputes, which in the hands of an inadequate or partial EDR system might never be properly solved. However, decisions made by community leaders through alternative mechanisms at the local level are likely to be influenced by moral and cultural customs rather than by law and may not protect the electoral rights as well as a formal mechanism established within the legal framework.

Very difficult and politically sensitive issues, such as disputes over election results (which tend to be among the most difficult to resolve), may require high-level intervention and political solutions. This was, for example, the case in Kenya, where the National Dialogue and Reconciliation Process was initiated by the Panel of Eminent African Personalities led by Kofi Annan, former secretary-general of the United Nations, to mediate dialogue and reconciliation after violent outbreaks following the presidential elections in 2007. Although these political deals are made to reach a peaceful resolution after violent conflict, they can undermine electoral dispute resolution mechanisms and the democratic vote itself. As the case of Kenya proves, investigations into fraud become less important when a fragile peace is sought. In addition, in some cases political parties or candidates who stand to lose an election can instead gain political leverage from a conflict that leads to a political deal.

CONCLUSION

Well-functioning and effective EDR mechanisms are the ultimate guarantor of peaceful, free, and fair elections. Still, the conflict prevention and mitigation role played by EDR mechanisms has received surprisingly little attention. Not only is the field under-researched and largely unexplored, it often does not receive proper attention in electoral assistance programs. This can partly be explained by a long tradition of event-driven electoral support that has heavily focused on specific electoral events and where, consequently, the post-election period (often starting after the announcement of results and having to deal with contentious disputes over these) has been much neglected. In addition, there is a tradition in the field of electoral assistance to support and work closely with EMBs. As electoral dispute resolution in many cases is entrusted to the judiciary or other jurisdictional organs, these institutions and processes have not received the level of attention and support they both deserve and need.

A more integrated and comprehensive approach should be taken to the understanding of electoral administration and dispute resolution and in the design and implementation of electoral assistance programs. This is only possible if one considers the entirety of the electoral process and recognizes the importance of both the post-election period and the electoral linkages with institutions other than the EMB. It may very well be the judiciary that possesses one of the most important tools for the prevention and mitigation of election related conflict and violence.

Finally, it should be stressed that, in the longer term, the ultimate aim should not be increased assistance to EDR bodies and mechanisms but the existence of well-functioning and efficient autonomous EDR institutions that enjoy public trust and can guarantee legitimate electoral processes. In addition, and preferably, electoral practices should be implemented in a correct and lawful manner and respect for the rule of law should be the norm. No electoral process can ever be perfect but, ideally, electoral processes should be good enough to make electoral disputes and their resolution the exception rather than the rule.

11

Electoral Dispute Resolution: A Personal Perspective

JOHANN KRIEGLER

Although I have been involved in one way or another with various messy elections over the last sixteen years, I am by profession a lawyer who has spent most of his professional life in the courts in and around South Africa. Of elections I knew little, of their management nothing at all.

My introduction to electoral administration was belated, accidental, and traumatic. Shortly before Christmas 1993, owing to a bad phone connection, I thought I was agreeing to serve on an electoral court for South Africa's first democratic elections, due to take place some months later. I was a judge of our appellate court at the time and the job would be a sinecure, so I agreed without a moment's reflection. Two days later, to my profound shock, I learned that, far from accepting a fairly run-of-the-mill judicial task, I had agreed to lead mission impossible: I was to head the Independent Electoral Commission (IEC), a makeshift and motley outfit tacked together hastily by politicians and tasked with delivering the country's first-ever inclusive elections just four months down the line.

Had our rag-tag band of enthusiastic amateurs known that proper elections could not be mounted in less than eighteen months to two years, we would have given up in despair. As it was, we came home on a wing and a prayer, thanks largely to inspired national leaders, the infinite forbearance of our compatriots, and more than our fair share of good luck. In true cliffhanger fashion, we collected the last of the results literally as we drove to their formal announcement. One of our international commissioners, Professor Jørgen Elklit, was feverishly double-checking the seat-allocation arithmetic even as I was making appropriate introductory remarks. President Mandela was duly inaugurated on a brilliant autumn morning, his country united in its celebration, and the world stunned at the peaceful transition that South Africa had managed to pull off.

The point of this anecdotal introduction is to contextualize my idiosyncratic electoral philosophy as it has evolved over years of electoral work in far-off and inhospitable places. I am an election junkie, hooked since the roller-coaster ride of 1994, addicted to the unique adrenalin rush that only a close or tricky election brings. I am deeply moved by every aspect of this unique manifestation of democracy in action.

Not by all elections, though: the sophistication of first-world political campaigns – the genius of the strategists, the analysts and speech-writers; the Barnum & Bailey hoopla of an American party convention; the seamless expertise of the media and the mounting checkerboard of red and blue states – these are all endlessly entertaining, but for me are only an intellectual and professional interest. Generally, old democracies with their routine, predictable balloting and ever-shrinking turnouts are a bore. Even the 2000 US presidential election, with its butterfly ballots, hanging chads, and other arcane features, although a technical and legal whodunit, had little of the human drama I look for. For me the finest hour of that election was in its aftermath when the losing candidate, as vice-president, presided with infinite dignity at a Senate hearing where petitioner after petitioner who wished to support him had to be non-suited. That was democracy. That was the rule of law.

My preference is for "new" elections: they produce real human drama; they reveal the indomitable spirit of simple women and men. How can anyone ever forget the picture of my black compatriots lined up in their tens of thousands across the land, standing for uncomplaining hours in serpentine queues, chatting the time away with their fellow South Africans? After generations of discrimination and humiliation, they were waiting to endorse their human dignity. The simple act of marking a ballot-paper had become a symbol of liberation. Remember the old lady who, when asked if she wasn't tired of standing in the hot sun so long, replied quietly that she didn't mind: she'd waited forty years for that day.

Five years later, East Timor's independence referendum was equally gripping. In the predawn gloom one could sense rather than see the people, hundreds upon hundreds of them bunched together for safety in numbers, heading for the polls in silent defiance of the Kopassus thugs of the Indonesian Army and the Aitarak militia, its bullyboy surrogates. I have the same sensation when I cast my mind back to interviewing aspirant Iraqi electoral commissioners for their country's first free elections. I asked one of them whether she didn't fear for her life if selected. I can never forget her withering look and reply: How could she shrink from doing her duty toward her children? To this day, her quiet, resolute courage gives me a shiver down the spine.

I make no apologies for using emotive language in describing these events. Elections are important, or should be important, and first and last they are about human beings, flesh-and-blood men and women, and their emotions. Elections are about people, not prescripts and procedures. Of course statutes and regulations are fundamentally important, but never to the extent that they obscure the underlying rationale of elections. Ideally, elections are periodic national milestones, symbolic events demonstrating the polity's unity in diversity. A national election should be a demonstration, if possible a celebration, of a momentous event in the life of the nation – and, as with human birthdays, the younger the nation, the more momentous the election.

That is not to say that an electoral administrator, in starry-eyed wonderment, should forget that elections are about realpolitik, about political power. Human beings are capable of great wickedness and all manner of fraudulent schemes, especially where temptation and opportunity overlap. Elections, being about the allocation of state power and with it state resources, are therefore pre-eminent occasions where the temptation to take a short cut, to steal a march (maybe even the election), may prove irresistible. Ironically, while elections serve to promote participatory democracy best where the contests are close, such close-run races are all the more seductive. Electoral one-horse races are comparatively easy to administer but are relatively undemocratic; where the competition is keen and voters are given a real choice, the political temperature rises, as does the potential for things to go awry.

A comparison of Kenya's national elections of 2002 and 2007 presents a textbook example of this irony. In 2002 it became obvious well before polling day that a coalition of opposition forces was sufficiently powerful to be more than a match for the battle-weary incumbent KANU party of lame-duck President Daniel arap Moi. Campaigning, especially in the presidential race, was accordingly quite uneventful. Nobody was surprised when everything went smoothly enough on polling day and the KANU presidential candidate conceded defeat long before the final result was announced. The Electoral Commission of Kenya's handling of the election was admired all round and its chair basked in the adulation of a grateful electorate. The nasty truth, however, known to the commission and plain to those who bothered to look more closely, was that the elections were flawed in a number of critical respects, extending from grossly disparate constituency sizes and an unreliable voters' roll through shambolic nomination processes all the way to outdated and unreliable procedures for data collation and transmission. Had the electoral administration been subjected to strain of any consequence, something would have had to give. But because all's well that ends well, nobody gave this unpalatable truth much thought, not even the commission.

In 2007 the selfsame chair was at the helm, leading essentially the same electoral team; the legislation remained much the same, there was an improved voters' roll, and substantially more polling stations. The central tallying exercise was to be done electronically and the announcement of results was to be a spectacular media event. Some weeks before polling day, the chair confidently predicted a peaceful election. On the surface, all might have looked propitious but there were ominous portents of trouble. Of these, the most important was that the political and regional alliances were so evenly matched that predicting the winner was speculative in the extreme. It was clear, though, that whoever might eventually win, it was going to be a neck-and-neck presidential race down to the wire. As polling day drew near, party agents, pollsters, and other prognosticators were perplexed. Expectations rose, as did tensions. The ethnic composition of the main opposition party gave rise to overt xenophobia, reflected in increasingly strident campaigning. Sporadic violence erupted but little was done to bring the culprits to book. Meanwhile the administrative shortcomings of 2002 festered under the surface while contact between the commission and the political parties remained remote.

In the event, it was indeed a photo finish and the counting dragged on for days, both sides claiming victory. Rumours of a stolen election emerged and rapidly gained momentum. Ultimately, strong-arm security tactics and a news blackout fanned the tension into outbreaks of public violence around the country. Over the ensuing weeks well over 1,200 men, women, and children were slaughtered and some 300,000 were forced to flee for their lives in waves of ethnic violence. When, many months later, a commission of inquiry toured the country, we were told repeatedly that the root cause of the violence was the devious machinations of the electoral commission. The national hero of 2002 had become public enemy number one. Had he dared to show his face in the Rift Valley or Kisumu, he would surely have been lynched. Yet the only real difference between the two elections was the closeness of the contest.

The immediate and obvious lesson to be learned from this startling reversal of public opinion is that close contests increase the risk of violent contestation – not that any seasoned electoral administrator really needs to learn such an obvious lesson. There are two less obvious but much more important lessons, however, that do warrant discussion.

First, elections are made or marred by the broad electorate and society. They are exercises in public perception and confidence. Perception comes to be taken for truth. If the public accepts the integrity and veracity of the election results as announced by the election administration, the election will have succeeded. Conversely, general scepticism about the integrity of the process may cause an election to fail in one of its primary purposes, that of regulating the peaceful transfer of political power within a body politic. Public opinion is therefore crucial to the success of an electoral undertaking. It follows that in tight contests it is infinitely more important to monitor and moderate public perceptions than, for instance, spending limited time and resources on recruiting, briefing, and deploying droves of voter-education volunteers or domestic observers. The ultimate obligation of an electoral administrator is to deliver a credible election, an election that is accepted by the electorate at large.

The second lesson, related to the first, is that elections are political exercises driven by political forces and therefore require that the election administration establish, maintain, and even nurture close rapport with political parties.

The importance of public confidence is illustrated by comparing two starkly different sets of elections that took place during 1994 – in South Africa and in Mexico. The South African vote was a first-time effort, seriously deficient in a number of technical respects, starting with the absence of a voters' roll (or even a trusted national census). Even at the end, it was badly flawed, winding up with mandatory reconciliation procedures at the count being dispensed with at the last minute. Hundreds of polling stations were identified, proclaimed, staffed, and equipped only days before polling. Many didn't open on time or at all, so extra polling days had to be tacked on; stickers were added to ballot papers to accommodate a last-minute party registration. Unscheduled write-ins had to be allowed, counting clerks went on strike, and monitors picketed for higher wages: in all, it was a right royal mess excoriated and derided by international observers.

The Mexican elections were incomparably better. Everything was technically immaculate, from timely and comprehensive voter registration, voters' smart cards, and a conveniently low ratio of voters to polling station, through slick balloting procedures and magnificent ballot boxes, down to speedy and graphic results-announcement. The electoral administration was determined to show the electorate and the world – and in fact showed clearly – that, notwithstanding generations of one-party rule and a history of election rigging, these elections were manifestly free, fair, and extremely competently administered. The international community applauded what was clearly a technical tour de force.

Yet South Africans chose to overlook the manifest deficiencies in their elections and enthusiastically accepted the results – and this was a society that had, until shortly before, been deeply divided and headed for a racial conflagration. Not a life was lost to violence, not a polling station had to be closed, even temporarily, for reasons of security. The major political parties abandoned any thought of court challenges, boycotters of the transition quietly joined the reconstituted nation, and on Nelson Mandela's presidential inauguration day joined in singing the new national anthem and saluting the new national flag. In Mexico, however, where the process had been exemplary, there was widespread suspicion and cynicism, the integrity of the process was seriously challenged, and the political stability of the country was in jeopardy for months thereafter.

While I cannot speak with inside knowledge of this ostensibly undeserved turn of events in Mexico, I can, I believe, explain the South African success. At the time it was called a miracle and I suppose in a sense it was, but it was achieved by human agency, not magic. At out very first get-together we in the IEC realized that our only hope of pulling off the elections in the time available would be to draw as much as possible on the human and material resources of the non-governmental sector, government agencies being suspect in the eyes of the liberation movements. Indeed, there was a general lack of trust of any agencies on either side of the main political divide and the IEC had to establish its own independence, impartiality, legitimacy, and competence. At the same time we also realized that, even if we could manage to deliver the elections on time, they would be far from perfect.

We therefore concentrated on establishing the IEC's brand and image. We needed every ounce of goodwill we could generate and made it our business to work as closely as possible with the political parties and establish open and frank lines of communication with the media. Party liaison committees were organized at all relevant levels, down to the polling station, and fulfilled a vital function not only in familiarizing the parties with the progress of the voting process and its problems, but in drawing them into a working relationship with one another. We got to know and understand them, and they us – and one another. So we stumbled onto the safest safety net for a difficult election, the old Roman imperial solution: co-opt the potential troublemakers. For an electoral administrator this means, quite simply, that from the outset you ensure that you get to know the political role-players and consult them on all questions that might prove contentious. Obtain buy-in and sign-off by the political contestants at all potential points of dispute: acknowledge their crucial importance in the electoral exercise and manifestly take their views seriously. This is crucial. Not only is it sound in principle but it serves to avoid or, at least minimize, last-minute disputes.

Purely administratively, elections are infinitely complex, detailed and consequently unpredictable undertakings, and anywhere along the line something can go wrong (and invariably does). Therefore, the electoral management must be exemplary in its strict adherence to clear and well-publicized rules for the whole process – and their manifestly fair and consistent enforcement. But while these things are essential for legitimacy, they are all merely means to an end. Order, discipline, planning, regulation, these necessary attributes of electoral management unfortunately tend to become an end in themselves, the object of the whole exercise, to which all else must yield. In young democracies, inexperienced administrators, uncertain of themselves and their ability to hold the whole contraption together as things start heating up, become martinets. Political parties become a nuisance, to be tolerated with ill-concealed impatience. Politicians become adversaries instead of partners. The media are increasingly regarded as hostile, at best negative and faultfinding, untruthful and mischievous.

Tragically, what ought to be a vigorous competition for public office becomes a sterile display of administrative hubris, often at considerable risk to the entire electoral enterprise. The administrators forget that their primary function is to deliver elections that are accepted by the electorate as manifestly free and fair. And, of course, once the referee assumes a predominant role in the contest, not only is the game marred but the authority and credibility of the referee is put in jeopardy. It is common in elections, especially in close contests, for losers to nurse a grievance, an inarticulate sense of having been done wrong, somehow, somewhere. Where the electoral management has been conducted high-handedly, aloofly, opaquely, it is all but impossible to prevent or dispel such an impression after the event.

More importantly in the present context, this kind of confidence building really comes into its own in the context of electoral dispute resolution (EDR). Consulting the political parties, heeding their views, and co-opting them into the planning not only makes them aware of the challenges faced by the electoral administration but develops a sense of shared responsibility for the success of the undertaking and for cooperative problem-solving. This has particular relevance for EDR. Where political parties are individually and collectively in ongoing liaison with the electoral administration, complaints can and should be aired and attended to as they arise, there and then, usually at the work-face; but if not, they can still be dealt with promptly at the appropriate higher level(s). Modern techniques of alternative dispute resolution and/or mediation can be employed, especially when the dispute is between parties whose representatives have served on a standing liaison committee together and have built up a relationship of give and take.

Additionally, this approach serves as an early electoral dispute detection and resolution device. One of the seemingly intractable conundrums of EDR arises from the conflicting demands of politics and law. Every electoral administrator knows how important it is to avoid delays, or perceived delays, in the process of counting, collation, tallying, and publication of election results. Once the public drama of the polling phase has played out, a distinct impatience seems to grow in the electorate, to a significant degree fed by the media. The Kenyan elections of 2007 demonstrate what can happen when unexplained delay gives rise to the perception that the time is being used to doctor the results.

It requires little thought to appreciate that there is a news vacuum in the aftermath of the story-laden polling drama. Suddenly there is nothing to report, no good copy to fill the pages and airwaves. During this lull, it is incumbent on the electoral administration, in its own interest, to provide copy – in the language of my media mentor, you must feed the beast. If you don't provide good copy for the media, they'll find their own. As if by magic, rumour, speculation, supposition, and suspicion start popping up. Over time, tensions rise and accusations start flying. In an unstable society, violence may well erupt. Time is therefore inherently of the essence in getting the results out there in the public domain.

At the same time, however, the manifest integrity of the electoral process is no less important. Adjudication should never seem superficial, slapdash, or hurried. The litigants, especially the ultimate losers, should go away feeling that their complaints were taken seriously and entertained with due deliberation. Every significant electoral dispute, one that, individually or together with others, could have a bearing on the result, has to be resolved; and the resolution must be seen to be procedurally fair and substantively sound in law. This takes time, especially where factual disputes, relating to events in diverse and remote parts of the country, have to be resolved according to the time-honoured and trusted adversarial procedure so beloved of the common law and required by public opinion.

To the best of my knowledge, no one has yet come up with a truly satisfactory comprehensive solution to this conflict between the political demand for expedition and the law's need to deliberate. Ordinarily dispute resolution, being a form of adjudication, would tend to favour deliberation, but EDR requires a special kind of adjudication. It has its own peculiar needs. Elections are, as I have tried to emphasize above, political events, relating to political contestation between political competitors for political power. The disputes to which they give rise are accordingly irretrievably political, requiring peculiarly adapted political approaches for which most judges are ill equipped. Huffy silence is the usual response I get from my fellow judges when I utter this heretical statement. But it is true.

Electoral disputes are seldom, if ever, of a private-law nature, no matter that they may appear to relate to a dispute between individuals. They are therefore less amenable to the ordinary adversarial dispute resolution mechanisms known to judges in the English-speaking world where two parties are in quasi-combat and the judge acts as referee. Judges steeped in common-law tradition and practice are uncomfortable with the more amorphous, messy, and shifting atmosphere of an electoral dispute. Whoever deals with such a case should be mindful of this special feature. It plays a role in determining, right at the outset, who has and who has not got standing, who is entitled to notice of the challenge, and who is entitled to be heard. It plays a role when the adjudicator is called upon to determine at a hearing in what order the parties are to present their cases, whether there should be oral evidence with cross-examination or merely written depositions, and how much time is to be allowed. And then, once the merits of the dispute have been determined, the adjudicator must be particularly mindful of the need for remedies that will meet the unique exigencies of the particular case.

Another feature of electoral disputes that requires special attention is the overlap between criminal and civil law that bedevils the monitoring and enforcement of electoral prescripts and their breaches. A particular act can, at the same time, constitute an ordinary crime dealt with by the police and the prosecuting authority; an actionable civil wrong, potentially founding a claim for damages and/or injunctive relief; and an electoral offence to be dealt with by the electoral administration. A simple example would be the violent invasion by a gang of thugs, hired by a candidate, to break up a public meeting organized by a competing candidate. The police and prosecutorial arm of state are, often understandably, reluctant to be seen to be intervening in a political dispute, the courts feel much the same, and the electoral administration is left with the obligation to deal with the matter in the midst of its more pressing administrative tasks. As a result the wrongdoers are often allowed to get away with their misconduct, the victims remain remediless, the authority of the election management is impaired, and, of course, the rule of law and the integrity of the election suffer.

In Kenya, for instance, nobody made a concerted effort at any stage after the restoration of multiparty elections in the early 1990s to come to terms with the special demands of EDR and the enforcement of electoral fair-play rules. Nobody bothered to establish who, if anyone, bore the final responsibility to ensure that the electoral Queensberry Rules were honoured. As a result, we were told during our subsequent inquiry that nobody could remember when anyone had last been prosecuted for the commission of an electoral offence. Though there were rules governing the conduct of individuals and political parties, they existed on paper, not in the real world. There it was a free-for-all where vote buying, intimidation, and corruption were rampant. Little wonder, then, that at many of our public meetings the electoral commission was described as a toothless bulldog.

However one might classify electoral disputes for the purposes of jurisprudential taxonomy, even a suit brought by loser A to unseat winner B concerns much more than their competing political aspirations. In principle, every voter who voted in the challenged election has an interest in the outcome; so does everybody within the jurisdiction of the legislature concerned. And it goes without saying that the case would be of material interest to political parties functioning in such an arena. Indeed, every citizen has an interest in the integrity of the electoral processes. This feature in itself establishes the unique nature of EDR.

Of course, there are compelling practical reasons why EDR demands its own peculiar approach, methods, and remedies. Here, pre-eminently, it is imperative to use quick and flexible means to resolve the dispute and craft an appropriate remedy in a dynamic and rapidly changing context. Here, pre-eminently, justice delayed may be justice denied. Often it serves little purpose, from the perspective of the complainant or the public, to make some carefully considered and legally well-founded finding long after the election. Moreover, and more importantly, pragmatic, politically sensitive EDR with timely and practical remedies not only serves to defuse disputes before they fester and grow but enables the electoral administrator to accommodate both political and legal imperatives.

This has recently been demonstrated by the impasse that arose in the tense Afghan presidential election in the latter half of 2009. The tension did not arise from the closeness of the contest (since the rest of the field lagged far behind the incumbent President Karzai) but because, in a contest beset by enormous security challenges and political instability, there was doubt whether, once the large number of electoral disputes was resolved, the president would reach the requisite majority of fifty per cent plus one, a majority which, if not attained, would trigger a run-off. At that stage, after the election and with the country holding its breath, the specially created EDR body was confronted with the Herculean task of resolving thousands of disputes from around the country, this while the political barometer was falling and national stability was at risk as long as the result remained in doubt. Politics and not law ultimately provided the solution.

Similarly, the Kenyan crisis that arose in December 2007 was in large measure ascribable to the absence of an effective EDR mechanism. Despite a badly flawed campaign, giving rise to numerous instances of undemocratic conduct, including widespread complaints of blatant abuse of incumbency advantage, intimidation, and corrupt practices, nothing of any consequence was done to stop the rot. And then at the eleventh hour, when vociferous and apparently substantiated complaints of fraud on the part of the electoral administration were raised, the chairman of the commission, backed by the minister of justice, blandly told the incensed objectors that the commission could do nothing: those who were dissatisfied with the result could go to court in the fullness of time. It was not that such advice was wrong in law, but the referral itself proved highly inflammatory. This is hardly surprising. The political impartiality of the Kenyan judges was suspect and, besides, everybody knew that in Kenya it could take years before the courts would finally determine an election petition. Indeed, while I was in Kenya in 2008, a Kenyan court, after more than two years of deliberation, dismissed an election petition, not on the merits of the complaint but on a preliminary and peripheral point relating to service of the initiating process.

The maxim justice delayed is justice denied has particular resonance in EDR. It is not only a basic tenet of the common-law system of jurisprudence, which forms the framework of most EDR systems with which I have worked, but it is of universal application in electoral law and administration. Even in a mature and exemplary democracy such as the United States, which wisely makes constitutional provision for an ample interlude between election day and inauguration, post-election dispute resolution can be politically and judicially awkward. In the Bush/Gore race, a significant part of the dispute related to the accuracy of the count and had to be determined after the completion of the various tallies and their public announcement, but this is certainly not necessarily the case with all electoral disputes. On the contrary, many electoral disputes can be, and in some jurisdictions are routinely, dealt with and even finally disposed of well before polling takes place. Thus, for instance, disputes relating to a person's right to be included in the register of voters, or the legality of a candidate's nomination, or the location of a polling station cannot be dealt with satisfactorily after the election, for it would be too late to afford the injured person or party adequate redress.

Besides this objection of principle, there are sound practical grounds for dealing with disputes as and when they arise. First, the exemplary, deterrent, and/or educative functions of an early EDR intervention can have a far-reaching impact on subsequent events. Dealing summarily and firmly with a campaign transgression can have a salutary effect far beyond the particular complainant and offender. Deterrence, personal and general, has long been recognized as one of the principal objectives of a legal penalty. Second, trial lawyers know that it is always better to deal with factual disputes as soon after the event as possible, before evidence goes stale, and it is desirable and cost-effective to deal with such disputes as close to their locus as possible. Such speedy and decentralized adjudication can comfortably be slotted in from time to time during the run-up to polling. Third, as observed earlier, ongoing EDR serves to prevent an embarrassing backlog being dealt with in haste at a time when other demands are being made on the electoral administration. This holds good for whichever of the various EDR mechanisms is employed, but is particularly important where the whole or a part of the adjudication is to be performed by the election management body or where such body has to play a significant part in EDR by investigating complaints, producing witnesses, preparing case dockets, and the like. One does not wish to have such obligations superimposed on the stressful and time-sensitive activities relating to the ascertainment and publication of the election results.

Now it is necessary to pause for a moment to look at the broader context. EDR is not a subject entire unto itself. Nor is it a topic to be reduced to casuistic dos and don'ts, often derived from cases governed by totally different statutory frameworks or occurring in societies and electoral situations that are really not usefully comparable. When one is dealing with a dispute resolution issue in, say, Sierra Leone or Southern Sudan, it seldom serves much purpose to cite a passage from an American textbook dealing with a judgment, however elegant, written by a judge in Ohio relating to the particular facts of the case and the applicable statutory framework. Elections are political enterprises that take their colour and content from the political atmosphere of the society in which they are held, and EDR must always be rooted in its specific context. Of course there are general principles of law that are applicable to EDR, but the problems I have encountered have not related to such principles. On the contrary, these problems have usually arisen because people became enmeshed in peripheral and procedural issues, in lawyers' jargon, losing sight of the fact that EDR is a process in aid of an election, not a lawsuit in its own right.

That said, I still blush when I recall how, unwittingly, I was all but summarily imprisoned for contempt of court in a country I'd rather not name. Speaking on invitation at a symposium convened and chaired by the local chief justice for the specific purpose of debating the role of the judiciary in the country's upcoming elections, I expressed myself rather robustly when decrying the dread (dead?) hand of the judiciary in EDR. While politicizing the judiciary was deplorable, I opined, "judgifying" politics was obscene. Ideally, judges did not belong in elections and elections did not belong in the courts. Warming to my topic, I suggested that seeking to apply ordinary legal procedures to electoral disputes was to put a saddle on a pig, and that the most damning fault of the judiciary was its penchant for frustrating and stultifying the political process by inordinately reserving judgment in electoral cases – for as long as six months or, heaven forbid, a year. I only discovered much later that, some days before the symposium, the chief justice had delivered himself of a long and learned judgment in a celebrated election case. He had laboured over it for years; I then realized why I had been unceremoniously ushered onto the airport bus.

But while I am thoroughly ashamed of having been so rude to my host and realize that my choice of language was boorish, I have not changed my opinion. Courts often fail to afford adequate relief in electoral disputes. That is not to say that I disagree with the judgment of the chief justice. To tell the truth, I have not read it, but I have read the majority finding of the supreme court of another country, delivered years after that country's presidential election. For all practical purposes, the majority held that, while the president had certainly been elected unconstitutionally, it was too late to do anything about the matter – so he had better remain in office. Readers will probably remember that in Zimbabwe some thirty-eight opposition cases challenging the outcome of the country's penultimate parliamentary elections never had the benefit of judicial consideration. For one reason and another, the judges of the Zimbabwe High Court never managed to get around to these cases.

Even where there can be no suggestion of judicial foot-dragging, electoral cases take time. These cases are often replete with factual disputes, the relevant electoral legislation is often sloppily drafted, and, to cap it all, judges and the parties' legal representatives are usually not familiar with this kind of case. Lawyers and judges are by training, professional attitude, and custom not suited to EDR. Elections need speedy, practical adjudication, not the careful, reasoned, researched, and finely milled products of the wheels of justice. This quick and appropriate electoral adjudication can only really succeed, however, if there is active cooperation by all concerned.

I would like to mention one or two other lessons I learned in my own country in 1994 that are relevant to EDR. Because we had to get started in such a great hurry (and, of course, because of our inexperience), we made many mistakes. This meant we had to adjust and adapt to exigencies as they arose – the elections simply could not be postponed. The peace process had assumed its own dynamic and it would have been disastrous to try to change pace, to be seen to be hanging back, as we headed down the main straight. We discovered, ironically, that being captive to the politically predetermined period was liberating. We could not agonize about the mandatory deadline and the limits it placed on the entire electoral timetable. We could not postpone decisions, could not allow others to procrastinate, and had to take action there and then, once and for all. It actually made things easier for us and, once they had gotten used to it, for those with whom we had to interact.

When, in the final stages of the process, while the results were trickling in and every one of the major political parties used the breathing space to raise objections to some or other aspect of the administration or a competitor's conduct, they could be dealt with at the gallop. At the national level, where these major issues were debated, we all knew and understood one another and, I believe, everybody trusted the IEC. Disputes could be resolved and complaints addressed quickly and relatively easily. This does not mean that our responses were always satisfactory: on the contrary, but in the context of the broader national interest most people were content with second best. What worked for us should work for any electoral administration tasked with delivering an election in a transitional or developing democracy.

A parting thought from 1994: failure was unthinkable. The country could not survive being thrown back to where it had been before. That would probably have precipitated the racial conflagration that informed commentators had been predicting for so long. This literally vital concern served to concentrate the minds of not only the electoral administrators but the political leadership and the electorate at large. Because we dared not fail, there was an increased willingness to cooperate, to tolerate, to give a helping hand, and to put aside selfish interests. The elections came to be perceived as a national project, one in which all South Africans had a stake and one which all South Africans wished to see succeed. That, you might say, is banal; it obviously applies to all national elections. But for us it wasn't true at the outset. There were boycotters, spoilers, old-time racists (white and black) who didn't want peace or the negotiated accord to be perfected by credible transitional elections.

As the electoral process got underway and gathered momentum, most of these disaffected groups were isolated by the concerted desire for success. At the same time, as I have mentioned before, the need for constant consultation with the political parties in order to facilitate the changes we had to make as quickly and smoothly as possible necessitated open lines of communication with the political parties. By working closely with us and with one another, the party agents came to recognize one another as something more than competitors, as colleagues, compatriots facing similar problems, possibly with shared complaints about the inefficiencies of the electoral administration, almost a camaraderie.

In the process, party-political disputes and personal animosities tended to fade. Considering South Africa's history of rigidly enforced racial segregation, the rising tide of violent resistance, and the increasingly draconian security counter-measures for the preservation of apartheid, this rapport between political party agencies was a remarkable bonus. It can, I believe, stand similarly challenged electoral administrators in good stead. I should add that we, more by luck than design, pitched the membership of the national party liaison committee at exactly the right level. We did not have the leaders or their main lieutenants playing politics and grandstanding but persons of sufficient authority to conclude binding agreements on behalf of their parties while at the same time functioning at the operational level and being concerned with day-to-day administrative problems. There was similar liaison at the local level to ensure buy-in by the parties in respect of the location of polling stations and the like. This, too, served the valuable secondary purpose of allowing opponents to become competitors, which in turn facilitated the resolution of campaigning, polling, and counting disputes.

In the result, we developed by serendipitous happenstance a form of continuing dispute resolution by negotiation, mediation, and consensus seeking that contributed materially to the South African electorate's ready acceptance of the results. An associated contributor to the success of the undertaking was a shared commitment to the process: the realization that failed elections would spell disaster was ever-present. What worked in South Africa can surely work in elections of reconciliation, reconstruction, or emancipation anywhere in the world.

PART FOUR

Canada's Role in International Democracy Promotion

12

Is Democracy Promotion "Globaloney" or a Categorical Imperative?*

THOMAS S. AXWORTHY

Election fraud in Afghanistan, monitored and confirmed by the international community, had the potential to force a runoff election in that war-torn land between the sitting president and his main contender. While the disputed election results of 20 August 2009 should not have been allowed to stand as they gravely impaired the legitimacy of a future Afghan government and its NATO defenders, the alternative – conducting a second election on 7 November, as ordered by Afghanistan's Independent Electoral Commission – would have been no minor undertaking, carrying with it the distinct possibility of significant loss of life due to the civil war. The latter option was only narrowly avoided when Hamid Karzai's opponent, Abdullah Abdullah, pulled out of the contest before the runoff, stating that he did not think that the election would be free and fair. The subject matter of this book is, indeed, the stuff of high politics, and even personal drama. Grant Kippen, a fellow of the Centre for the Study of Democracy at Queen's University and the leader of the UN-backed Electoral Complaints Commission that adjudicated and validated the many instances of Afghan fraud told the *Toronto Star:* "It was quite nerve-wracking, very tense for us, a lot of days into long nights."[1]

This study on elections in dangerous places, organized by the North-South Institute, is only the latest evidence of the Institute's continuing commitment to exploring the connection between democracy and development. One of the best studies of the objectives and pitfalls of democracy promotion is still the Institute's 1992 publication *The Challenge of Democratic Development* by Gerald Schmitz and David Gillies.[2] Both of the authors remain vitally engaged in issues related to international democracy promotion: Gerald having advised parliamentarians as the Library of Parliament's leading expert on the subject; David as the energetic editor of this book. I should add that, during 1991-93, Schmitz was seconded to the Institute as the founding director of a program then termed "human rights and democratic development," of which David is now the successor.

That 1992 work was published some twenty years after a burst of democratization in the 1970s, which Samuel Huntington described as a "third wave," and today we have had almost an additional twenty years to ponder the questions outlined so well by Schmitz and Gillies. The points I intend to raise have the benefit of fifty years of prior work and study. Democracy promotion is a hot and controversial topic in the field of democratic development, but it is not a new one. Yet the worth of an idea in public policy is not whether it is new or old, but whether it is right or wrong. My belief is that democratic promotion is very much an idea for our times and that Canada should join our allies in the international community by making this value central to our foreign policy.

The work of this volume has been largely devoted to the critical mechanics of election preparation and management – the role of independent electoral commissions, the impact of different types of systems to heighten or diminish ethnic conflict, the potential for elections to bestow legitimacy, or in the case of fraud, take it away. I will not comment on the details of these cases but will instead focus on the structural issue of the necessity for democratic frameworks and infrastructure, and the moral issue of whether Canada should play a role in helping societies and states create structures that give citizens a say in how they will be governed. Canada has had freely elected assemblies since 1758 in Nova Scotia, making us one of the oldest democracies in the world. We have benefited enormously from our success in making representative institutions work. The question I want to address is this: Do we have a moral obligation or a state interest in making democratic attainment for others as essential a priority as democratic engagement has been for us?

In answering this question, I will refer both to my personal experience in working abroad on democratic transitions and the lessons learned by the Centre for the Study of Democracy since its founding in the mid-1990s. Over the years, the Centre has had teams working on different aspects of the democratic puzzle in Afghanistan, Ukraine,

Mexico, China, Ghana, Liberia, Palestine, Costa Rica, and Bosnia. My conclusions reflect this accumulated experience.

THE FREEDOM IMPERATIVE

The nature of the regime has been a contentious topic in the study of international relations since Immanuel Kant's 1795 essay on perpetual peace. Kant argued that permanent peace could only be achieved by establishing international law in relations between states, not through the fluidity of traditional balance-of-power equations. To achieve this rule of law, there must be a vital precondition – only republics whose citizens have a voice in deciding peace or war can be relied upon to promote amity. "The civil constitution of every state," he writes, "should be republican." And once this is achieved, the second definitive article for perpetual peace is that "the law of nations shall be founded on a federation of free states."[3]

Kant's enlightenment ideals were almost immediately translated into a fully fledged foreign policy doctrine by English liberals like Charles James Fox, John Bright, William Gladstone, and Richard Cobden and American idealists like Woodrow Wilson. Kant's contemporary, Charles James Fox, the leader of the English Whigs, said about the enmity between Britain and France: "If our two countries have liberal governments at the same time, the cause of the human race is won."[5] Another contemporary of Kant, Prince Klemens von Metternich, took exactly the opposite view, forestalling democracy and liberal principles in the Austrian Empire and across Europe through a Concert of Europe devoted instead to order and balance-of-power politics. Metternich believed that disorder is worse than injustice and that the task of political leaders therefore is to prevent revolutions. This realpolitik tradition of Metternich and Otto von Bismarck contrasts with the idealist tradition of Fox and Wilson.

Today, the schools of idealism and realpolitik continue to contend in the debate over democracy promotion. Admirers of Metternich, such as Henry Kissinger, believe that "the most fundamental problem of politics ... is not the control of wickedness, but the limitation of righteousness."[5] If stability is the primary goal, the nature of the regime is less important to proponents of power politics than persuading an authoritarian elite to agree to common aims. Thus, Pakistan's Pervez Musharraf had to be supported because he promised stability, whatever damage he inflicted on democracy. And beyond the belief that it is difficult to base a foreign policy on morality, supporters of realpolitik believe that influencing the internal evolution of states is too difficult and requires undue expense and stamina from Western publics. A recent issue of *The Atlantic* magazine, for example, describes the transformative foreign policy goals of President Obama as "globaloney." The national editor of *The Atlantic* criticizes Obama for telling Americans that the United States "shouldn't shy away from pushing for more democracy." This, the editor believes, is "the antithesis of statecraft, which requires discriminating on the basis of power, interest, and circumstance."[6]

Yet, if Metternich continues to have a strong following in today's foreign policy debates, so too does Kant. Andrei Sakharov, the eminent Russian physicist and dissident, had a very different value system from his contemporary, Henry Kissinger. Sakharov believed that the international community should never trust a state that did not trust its own people. Trusting the people means getting them to choose their own rulers in free and fair elections. He wrote, in *Alarm and Hope*, that "as long as a country has no civil liberty, no freedom of information, and no independent press, then there exists no effective body of public opinion to control the conduct of the government and its functionaries. Such a situation is not just a misfortune for citizens unprotected against tyranny and lawlessness; it is a menace to international security."[7]

As Russia has made a sad return to semi-authoritarianism, Sakharov is not often mentioned today, but he is a twentieth-century hero of democracy. Having ascended to the summit of the Soviet Union's scientific establishment, in 1968, he wrote a book supporting human rights, which aroused animosity in the establishment that had once revered him. By the 1970s, he stood vigil outside Soviet courthouses, while political trials were underway; in 1980, he was exiled to Gorky, but at least he lived to see glasnost before dying of a heart attack in 1989, as a member of the Congress of People's Deputies, leading the fight to end the political monopoly of the Communist Party. "Peace, progress, human rights," he said in his 1975 Nobel lecture, "these three goals are insolubly linked to one another: it is impossible to achieve one of these goals if the other two are ignored."[8]

As well as making the Kantian connection between domestic democratic structures and international peace, Sakharov emphasized the importance of the international community in strengthening the morale of dissidents and freedom fighters. He scolded Western intellectuals for doing too little in publicizing the human rights abuses in his country and he rejected Kissinger's argument that stability was all-important. He wrote to President Carter: "It is very important to defend those who suffer because of their nonviolent struggle for an open society, for justice, for other people whose rights are violated. It is our duty and yours to fight for them."[9]

Years after Sakharov's death, I witnessed first hand the strength of his argument about the necessity of outside moral support. Working in Ukraine, I met a young woman active in the Orange Revolution, who told me about flying to Washington to pay her respects to Ronald Reagan after his death in 2004. She never forgot that Reagan had described the Soviet Union as an "evil empire." It was an empire, and it was evil. Reagan's honesty gave her and her family hope, despite the daily oppression of the Soviet state. She knew that she was not alone in her desire for freedom, and the hope kindled by a faraway American president sustained her through trying times.

Sakharov's defence of democracy, human rights, and the moral necessity to speak out is as relevant today as when he was a lone figure standing vigil. He knew that choosing democracy was a moral choice. He knew that a country that does not respect the rights of its own citizens would not respect the rights of its neighbours. The case for democracy is both moral and self-interested, because one of the few generally accepted laws in international relations is that consolidated democracies rarely go to war with one another. Morality and security should impel Canadians today, as they did the great Russian physicist, to make democracy a supreme value.

CANADIAN ASSETS

In July 2007, the House of Commons Standing Committee on Foreign Affairs and International Development (SCFAIT) released its report *Advancing Canada's Role in International Support for Democratic Development*, which recommended that Canada "commit to making support for democratic development a key priority of overall Canadian international policy."[10] The Centre for the Study of Democracy (CSD) at Queen's had already prepared a paper in 2005 for the Institute for Research on Public Policy on a blueprint for "the Democracy

Canada Institute," which concluded "that a country experienced in parliamentary democracy in a federal state with a multicultural society and a social democratic ethos might have things to say of interest to some parts of the world."[11] This paper formed the basis of the Centre's recommendation to SCFAIT.

The CSD's study promoted the idea of a new agency, but it also cautioned that modesty is of the essence in assessing the potential of democratic promotion. People change only gradually, and it is the norms of culture or society that determine behaviour most of the time. A country without a democratic culture will have tremendous difficulties in building one quickly enough to meet the demands of donors. Another contemporary of Kant, Edmund Burke, recognized this critical point when he wrote: "To love the little platoon we belong to in society, is the first principle (the germ as it were) of public affections."[12] Generations build on generations to determine the habits of the heart. Canada's habits of the heart cannot be easily transferred to Afghanistan, but by changing the incentive system, you can gradually change behaviour. Cultural traditions are critical, as Burke says, but Kant demonstrates that by changing the regime, you can, over time, change the culture. If Burke cautions us not to rush, Kant says not to give up hope.

The groundbreaking SCFAIT report defines democracy as "the participation of citizens in decision-making which affects their lives. The ultimate objective is to assist the population to develop the ability to intervene on its own behalf in the decision making process at the local, regional, and national level and to assist the public powers to create institutions to safeguard the rights and liberties of citizens."[13] In assisting the public powers to create institutions, the CSD report noted that "Canada's political parties have highly developed grassroots organizing models that are relevant in many developing countries. Unlike the large, publicly funded European parties, or the private money-reliant American parties, Canadian political parties are decentralized, volunteer driven, have modest budgets with both private and public funding and operate under strict political spending limits."

These characteristics of our party system have made individual Canadian party activists welcome contributors to the work of many international democracy promotion agencies: 300 Canadians, for example, have volunteered to be part of the missions of the National Democratic Institute in Washington, DC. Yet, as the SCFAIT report reveals, while individual Canadians have been active, political party development has never been a major feature of democratic development in Canadian aid policy. Parties are the critical conveyor belts between the opinions of citizens and the activities of government, but Canada has never invested in strengthening this vital function. Therefore, the CSD recommended that any new agency should concentrate "on political party assistance, including training in campaigns, electioneering, and media relations, which would introduce a tool largely absent from Canadian foreign policy. Programs would also include enhancing democratic transparency, election monitoring, promoting civic participation (especially among women), and assisting in the building of democratic institutions."

Observers of Ottawa's parliamentary cockpit may wonder about the utility of using Canadian party practice to inform the world, but I am optimistic that, however much our parties fight at home, they are united abroad in support of democratic institutions. The very subject of promoting democracy abroad, for example, has been a multiparty and cooperative exercise. Representatives of all parties worked diligently on the House of Commons study of the issue, and a majority of SCFAIT members supported its bold report, though both the New Democrats and the Bloc Québécois wrote dissenting opinions. Members of Parliament traditionally moan about their committee reports being ignored, but on democracy assistance the Conservative government has behaved in an exemplary way by explicitly endorsing recommendation 15 of the SCFAIT report on the necessity for a democracy promotion agency. The government's 2008 speech from the throne commitment to the creation of "a new, non-partisan democracy promotion agency ... to support the peaceful transition to democracy in repressive countries and help emerging democracies build strong institutions,"[14] cooperatively builds on the SCFAIT's months of work. Further, to answer many of the specific questions raised by parliamentarians, the government commissioned an independent panel of practitioners experienced in the details of promoting democratic practice abroad. With media attention focused almost entirely on partisan conflicts in Parliament, especially in Question Period, we should not forget that Parliament often does work, especially in committees. The new priority of democratic promotion is a case in point.

As well as emphasizing party development as the specific focus of any new Canadian democracy agency, the CSD also promoted a particular structural model. It recommended a multi-partisan institute, like the Netherlands Institute for Multiparty Democracy, where adherents of Canadian parties, across the spectrum, would work together in joint teams to display their expertise. My experience has been that there is a mutual camaraderie among politicians from all sides of the House. Those who have shared the delights and pains of knocking on doors (and having them slammed in one's face), asking for votes, dealing with intrusive journalists who demand, urgently, the most intimate details about your cousin's financial dealings, and, most of all, those who know what spouses and families go through when the siren song of public service sounds are an exclusive club. The bitter debates in Parliament turn into shared anecdotes, much laughter, and mutual learning when Canadian politicians work together abroad.

As well as being multi-partisan, a new Canadian democracy promotion agency must be an independent instrument that reports to Parliament, rather than to the Executive. Official departments of state, like the Department of Foreign Affairs and International Trade or the Canadian International Development Agency, must deal with all types of regimes, whatever their democratic legitimacy. As I described earlier, the dictates of realpolitik demand that the government take the world as it is and work with all sorts of regimes in the promotion of Canada's national interest. But an agency that reports to, and is funded by, Parliament has much more freedom to work with foreign opposition parties, dissidents, and even governments-in-exile. In the delicate and controversial work of assisting in the building of democratic party systems, risks must be taken. To do this, an agency requires the flexibility and independence of a parliamentary instrument, rather than the solid virtues of an aid bureaucracy.

LESSONS FROM THE FIELD

In advancing the concept of an independent, multiparty democracy promotion agency, the CSD recommended that such a body have an annual budget of at least CAN$50 million, which would place it in the mid-range, between the large German and American foundations, and the smaller Nordic entities. This figure was not pulled from a hat but was based on our evaluations of the type of organization necessary to make a serious impact on party democracy building. Such an enterprise requires a long-term investment in field offices, which can slowly, but steadily, build local partnerships, provide ongoing assistance, and be there for the long haul. Democratic parties are not built by consultants flying in for a day or two. Annual costs of field offices are in the three-to-four-million-dollar range, and in a high security zone like Afghanistan, the costs double.

In a major evaluation of several different kinds of democracy assistance programs (party assistance, human rights, gender equity, civil society, values education, and public administration reform) in several different countries (Mexico, Bosnia, Afghanistan, China, Ukraine, and Ghana), the CSD found that the key to successful programming is detailed in-country knowledge before programs begin and the absolute necessity for local ownership or authorship of democratic programming.[15] Democracy building is a people business. If we are serious about local ownership, we must be serious about funding. If the Canadian government is unable to commit to funding in the fifty-million-dollar range over a reasonable period, then it would be better not to go through the bother of creating a new agency. Committing to building parties is not like putting new slipcovers on old aid furniture. It requires building local showrooms in several different locations.

Even with a healthy budget of $50 million, difficult choices will have to be made and criteria set. Such a figure will only allow five to seven field operations as a core activity. In managing, evaluating, or exploring the feasibility of programs in many countries abroad, the CSD sets its own criteria on where it can or should work, and the following examples illustrate criteria that a new agency may want to consider.

The CSD's largest program over many years has been working in Ukraine on democratic values education. Ukraine has a democratic culture and institutions and it is always easier to work to improve institutions than to create them. The presence of democratic institutions, therefore, is a useful criterion. But Ukraine is also under stress, not least from a semi-authoritarian neighbour. So, democratic need is a second criterion. Canada also has a large and active Ukrainian community with strong cultural and historic ties; such ties are a third criterion. Canada does not have historic ties with Afghanistan, as we do with Ukraine, but we are fighting a war there, so Afghanistan ranks highly on the criteria of critical Canadian priorities. A democratic promotion agency could play a major role in Afghanistan after 2011, when Canada's military commitment will change.

We are part of the Americas and therefore have special responsibilities to our own hemisphere. Haiti is a long-time priority and certainly meets the criteria of democratic need, as well as hemispheric balance. The earthquake in January 2010 only made this more obvious. The CSD has worked to create a network of allies across the Americas and we have partnered with well-regarded local experts centred in Mexico. We are also members of the Commonwealth and Francophonie, so Haiti meets an additional criterion. Kenya, discussed at length in this volume, meets the criteria of Commonwealth ties, democratic assistance need, and the presence of democratic institutions, though they are under great stress. Lastly, there are certain places where Canada has advantages over others in the field. For many years, I organized an education program with the University of Havana, and I know that Cuba is strongly authoritarian. Nevertheless, Canada has special and long-standing ties there. The ability to play a significant role is another criterion that should guide a new Canadian agency, just as it does the CSD.

If a new agency were created, Canada would join many predecessors in the field. Our primary mission should be direct assistance for democratic transition through a dedicated field infrastructure. Canada could also contribute to the democratic assistance community as a whole. The CSD sponsored an international conference on democratic evaluation in February 2008 as part of its broader evaluation exercise.[16] It was a consensus of that conference that all the major democratic promotion institutions should cooperate in comparing and testing the best evaluation techniques. The need is great. Michael McFaul, an international expert, for example, describes the field thus: "Everyday, literally tens of thousands of people in the democracy promotion business go to work without training manuals or blueprints or simply well constructed case studies in hand. Published case studies of previous successes are hard to find in the public domain, which means that democracy assistance efforts are often reinventing the wheel or making it up as they go along. Even basic educational materials for students seeking to specialize in democratic promotion do not yet exist."[17]

The conference endorsed the CSD idea of a wiki of democracy promotion experiences, stories, evaluations, and techniques that practitioners from every agency in the world could access and contribute to. The Americans and Europeans have decades of practice in assessing what works and what does not in democracy promotion. A new Canadian democracy promotion agency could take the lead in bringing the field together to produce a cooperative international program in evaluation techniques and dissemination of information.

As individuals, Canadians have long been active in the field of democratic development. Organizationally, Canadian institutions like the North-South Institute, the Parliamentary Centre, the Forum of Federations, Rights & Democracy, CANADEM, and Elections Canada have impressive track records in their specific areas of expertise. These institutions should continue to be supported. However, more must be done. We need to build new capacity to take on the critical mission of democratic party development. Democracy is not a luxury. It is a categorical imperative. As Andrei Sakharov said about humanity's capability to determine its own fate, "the future can be wonderful, but it might not be at all. That depends on us."[18]

13

Ongoing Dilemmas of Democratization: Canada and Afghanistan

GERALD J. SCHMITZ

These have been trying times for democracy optimists even if the recent popular uprisings that deposed entrenched despots in Tunisia and Egypt have set in motion a wider challenge to autocracy in a region long deprived of democratic oxygen. According to Freedom House, there was a net decline in respect for civil and political rights worldwide in 2010 for the fifth consecutive year, the longest continuous period of decline in the nearly forty years since it has been making country assessments. The number of electoral democracies dropped to 115, compared to 123 in 2005, the lowest total since 1995.[1] The Economist Intelligence Unit also saw democracy as "in retreat," observing: "The dominant pattern in all regions over the past two years has been backsliding on previously attained progress in democratization." Add to that "the delegitimation of much of the democracy-promotion agenda" due to its association with "military intervention and unpopular wars in Afghanistan and Iraq."[2]

Canada therefore confronts a difficult environment as it considers increasing support for democracy internationally. Afghanistan, the major recipient of Canadian development and military assistance over the past decade, has arguably moved backwards in terms of democratic state building. Indeed the overall score Afghanistan received on the *Economist's* multi-dimensional democracy index in 2010 was 18 per cent lower than what it obtained in 2008, dropping its ranking from 138th to 150th among the 165 countries surveyed.[3] The fraud-plagued presidential and provincial council elections of August 2009 and the equally flawed parliamentary elections of September 2010 have undermined the Afghan government's legitimacy, raising questions about Canada's continuing role in democratization efforts.

Understanding the troubled state of democracy building in Afghanistan requires some historical context. It is also important to set out the scope of the democratization agenda and take stock of the conditions prevailing in Afghanistan. While the general case is being made for Canada to increase democracy assistance, far more debatable is what can realistically be done in Afghanistan. The challenge facing Canada and other external actors is to improve the chances for an eventual positive democratic outcome in Afghanistan, learning from the mistakes made during a decade of post-9/11 international intervention.

A HISTORICAL NOTE ON AFGHANISTAN AND DEMOCRACY BUILDING

Every time the mistakes of history are repeated, the price of the lesson goes up.
Anonymous[4]

Certain "realists" today contend that Afghanistan is not ready or suitable for modern liberal democracy, regarding it as an inherently violent and "backward" country.[5] The historical truth, as is so often the case, belies such simplistic negative notions. In fact, after World War I and the Third Anglo-Afghan War, Afghanistan was briefly blessed by enlightened progressive leadership under Amanullah Khan, inspired by the example of Ataturk in Turkey. As Fitzgerald and Gould observe: "Instituting Afghanistan's first constitution in 1923, [Amanullah] took the truly revolutionary steps of giving women the right to vote, guaranteeing civil rights to all minorities, and establishing a legislative assembly, courts, and penal, civil, and commercial codes, as well as prohibiting revenge killings and abolishing subsidies for tribal chieftains and the royal family."[6]

To put this in perspective, Canadian women outside Quebec first exercised a near-universal right of suffrage in the election of 1921 (though more limited franchises had been granted a few years before that in some provinces and federally). Women had to wait until 1940 to get the right to vote in Quebec and until 1951 in the Northwest Territories. Racial and religious exclusions persisted into the postwar period. Moreover, Canada's first peoples (all Afghans are "indigenous") were only granted national voting rights in 1960.[7]

Not surprisingly, Amanullah faced stiff opposition to his reforms from conservative Islamic circles. What should disturb our modern consciences is that the British Empire aligned itself with the reactionary Islamist forces in fomenting unrest against him. Yet the reforms proved to be popular. Amanullah was emboldened to introduce an even more secular liberal constitution in 1928 guaranteeing full equality rights to women whereupon the empire struck back, helping a violent rebellion that overthrew him and forced him to flee the country. His replacement as ruler was a Tajik bandit and murderer, Habibullah Kalakani. The reforms were undone.[8]

Fast-forward to the 1960s and the so-called "decade of democracy" under the 1964 constitution brought in during the reign of Mohammed Zahir Shah, which affirmed parliamentary institutions and women's rights, albeit in a more limited way than that of 1928. This was after the 1963 resignation of the Shah's cousin and brother-in-law Mohammed Daoud, appointed as prime minister in 1953, who proved to be a polarizing figure. Daoud was a strong nationalist but his overtures to the Soviet Union got him nicknamed the "Red Prince," paving the way for the further growth of rival radicalized Communist and Islamist movements (many of whose leaders were suspected of being clients of the CIA, the Kremlin, and/or Pakistani intelligence). The hopes of democratic advocates were briefly raised when a new Afghan parliament convened in 1965. Unfortunately, the seeds of chaos had also been sown, leading to a succession of coups, civil wars, and catastrophes. Daoud's return to the country and seizure of power in 1973 simply reinforced that path. He only lasted until the first Communist coup in 1978.[9]

The historical record plainly shows that Afghan efforts to build a modern liberal democracy were resisted and later fatally undermined by great power and then Cold War political "games," *not* that these efforts never took place or did so only in an intrinsically inhospitable societal environment. Of course, they were championed mostly by urban elites in the face of domestic opposition of a mainly religious and rural nature. But the key point is that for decades the principal external actors did more to hurt than to help secular democratic aspirations in Afghanistan. No wonder they never lasted. They were never given much of a chance. The price is still being paid, and it is going up.

DEMOCRATIZATION AS THEORY, PRACTICE, AND EXAMPLE

You can only learn democracy by doing it.

Michael Hardt[10]

The agenda of democratization is best conceived as both expansive and contested. A core principle is that government must rest on the consent of the governed. The consolidation of a process for periodic free and fair elections – as well as accountability measures between elections – is an important means to this end. But democratic aims should go beyond the establishment of procedural minimums. They should be liberal in the sense of adhering to internationally affirmed human rights precepts, and broadly developmental in terms of building capacities for the exercise of civil and political rights.

Writing eighteen years ago, David Gillies and I cautioned that "developing democracy, and sustaining it, is an immense continuing challenge even for 'developed' societies."[11] Without an engaged citizenry, democratic institutions can atrophy or become a hollow shell. Determining the best forms of liberal democracy in a particular society – for example, which type of electoral system should be used – ought to be the result of a democratic process supported by a democratic civic culture. Where this is absent, or, as in Afghanistan, swept away by decades of warfare, elections are not necessarily a good starting point for the work of democratization.

Among the main recommendations of the Democracy Dialogue symposium sponsored by Canada's Department of Foreign Affairs and International Trade (DFAIT) in November 2009 was that "national elections should not be rushed after violent conflict. The international community should help promote knowledge of institutional choices for democracy, as well as democratic principles and norms through grassroots engagement programming, while ensuring there is careful consideration of cultural sensitivities and historical contexts."[12]

The importance of participatory democratic learning is clear. In this regard, it is unfortunate that the so-called advanced democracies are not more exemplary. Falling voter turnouts and dismal voting numbers among the young are just one symptom of a common affliction – that is, declining trust in governments and in politicians and political parties, and, more generally, alienation from the political process.

Referring to recent global surveys of the state of democracy, notably the annual surveys conducted by Freedom House and the Economist Intelligence Unit, setbacks overshadow the few advances, to the point that some have spoken of a "democratic recession." A number of post–Cold War democratic transitions are in danger of failing. With over half of the world's population still living under authoritarian or illiberal rule, including backlash (as in Russia) and military coups (as in Thailand, Niger, and Honduras), a plausible question emerges: Has the high water mark of democracy already passed?

Circumstances demand thinking harder about the most effective ways and means to combat democratic malaise and improve prospects for democratization under challenging circumstances. For Canada, pursuing democratic goals has both a domestic and an international agenda. The more credible democratic commitments are at home, the more Canadian practices can serve as a positive example abroad. That is not to make the mistake of considering democracy as an "export," as if its promotion was akin to selling some sort of superior "model" to be emulated. What can be discussed is increasingly sharing Canadian democratic experiences and expertise that are valued by others: supporting and accompanying indigenous democratic actors – citizens and civic institutions, political parties, movements for democratic change, and so on – in their democratization efforts.

POSITIONING CANADA'S ROLE IN INTERNATIONAL DEMOCRACY ASSISTANCE

The issue of using aid to promote democracy was galvanized in the early 1980s by the US Congress's creation of a National Endowment for Democracy. Given the opposition to President Reagan's ideological "democracy crusade" – which included supporting the Contras in Nicaragua – Canadian proponents argued for a distinctively more moderate and modest approach. The multiparty Special Joint Committee of the Senate and of the House of Commons mandated by Prime Minister Mulroney in 1985 to review Canada's international relations was persuaded that Canada should have a role in democratic political development – political parties excluded – and its June 1986 final report, *Independence and Internationalism*, recommended the creation of an agency for human rights and democracy assistance. This was subsequently seconded in *For Whose Benefit?*, the landmark

May 1987 report of the Standing Committee on External Affairs and International Trade (since 2006, the Standing Committee on Foreign Affairs and International Development), which remains the only comprehensive parliamentary examination of the Canadian International Development Agency (CIDA) and official development assistance polices and programs.

It was fortunate that Joe Clark was foreign affairs minister at the time because he embraced these ideas against considerable NGO and bureaucratic resistance. Even the co-rapporteurs engaged by the government to examine setting up such an agency were so concerned that the word "democracy" would raise fears of following US policy that they recommended it be dropped in favour of the bland "institutional development." Thankfully, that advice was not taken and an act to set up the International Centre for Human Rights and Democratic Development was passed in 1988.

Over two decades later, the Centre – which now goes by the name Rights & Democracy – has numerous small projects to its credit, almost all in the area of human rights. However, with a tiny core annual budget in the CAN$5 million range for many years (raised to about CAN$11 million currently), it was eclipsed by a growing panoply of US and European democracy promotion agencies. Apart from the first years when it was headed by a former federal party leader Ed Broadbent, few Canadians were probably aware of its existence until controversy erupted in early 2010 over allegations of undue government interference in its board of directors.[13]

The limited and scattered nature of Canada's democracy assistance was comprehensively addressed by the Standing Committee on Foreign Affairs and International Development in their study of the subject during 2006–07. The Committee's July 2007 report, *Advancing Canada's Role in International Support for Democratic Development*, was ambitious, calling for several new arms-length agencies, a Canadian foundation for democracy support, and an emphasis on getting involved in assisting multiparty democracy. In light of the troubles at Rights & Democracy, the question of parliamentary oversight and autonomy from government direction will undoubtedly loom large in the creation of any new agency.

Notwithstanding a reprise of familiar concerns about association with discredited US ideological rhetoric on democracy promotion – a lot of which was driven by antipathy to the George W. Bush agenda –

the Committee went out of its way to acknowledge the complexities of the enterprise and to insist on a distinctively independent Canadian approach. Calling for significantly more funding devoted to democracy assistance, the Committee cited Canada's International Development Research Centre (IDRC) and the Netherlands Institute for Multiparty Democracy as examples of the scale and arms-length nature of what could be done.

The Canadian government's November 2007 response to the Committee's report seemed positive overall, promising a three-member expert panel to study the idea of creating a substantial new foundation and the release of a whole-of-government strategy within six months. While matters languished with ministerial shuffles, a fractious minority parliament, prorogation, and an election, the re-elected Conservative government's November 2008 speech from the throne surprised by skipping ahead to an outright promise of a new multiparty democracy promotion agency "to support the peaceful transition to democracy in repressive countries and help emerging democracies build strong institutions."[14]

Somewhat curiously, though, the responsibility for this file was moved from the minister of Foreign Affairs to that of the new minister of State for Democratic Reform, Steven Fletcher, appointed to this position on 30 October 2008. More months of uncertainty followed another prorogation and a second throne speech focused entirely on economic recovery from the global recession. Things were nonetheless slowly percolating behind the scenes. At his first appearance before the Committee in February 2009, Harper's fourth foreign affairs minister, Lawrence Cannon, indicated the government was still committed to a new democracy promotion agency and used the analogy to IDRC.[15] Fletcher affirmed that "we need to lay the foundations for an agency that will allow for a dynamic ability to help countries in a fast-changing world. ... It is absolutely critically important for our foreign policy going forward ... and I'm very much aware of the importance of getting this correct."[16]

The government subsequently appointed a four-person advisory panel chaired by one of this volume's authors, Thomas Axworthy, then head of Queen's University's Centre for the Study of Democracy (and a former principal secretary to Prime Minister Pierre Trudeau), which began deliberations in June 2009. Its summary report, made public in November 2009, focused on implementing the Standing

Committee's recommendation that the Canadian Parliament, following all-party consultations, "consider setting up a centre for multiparty and parliamentary democracy, with a parliamentary mandate."[17] In proposing a "Canadian Centre for Advancing Democracy," with an annual CAN$30–70 million budget based on a five-year cycle, the panel included a number of stipulations to ensure that its governance would be fully at arm's length from the government of the day. The centre should concentrate on carefully selected countries and operate a network of field offices, including some in "high priority, but high conflict states like Afghanistan and Haiti."[18]

The government's March 2010 throne speech was silent about the agency. Further evidence of democracy promotion being put on the back burner was the disbanding of CIDA's Office of Democratic Governance and the disappearance of a Democracy Unit within DFAIT. As of early 2011 it was unclear what, if anything, would come of the idea for a new agency. Axworthy publicly regretted the lack of action as a missed opportunity. Canada should not be sitting on the sidelines, he wrote in February 2011: "As a new democratic wave crashes into the autocracies of the Middle East, Prime Minister Harper should return to his original good idea and make democracy central to our foreign policy."[19]

AFGHANISTAN VIEWED FROM CANADA

Notwithstanding a decade and counting of heavy international intervention, landlocked Afghanistan remains one of the world's poorest, most corrupt, drug-dealing, war-ravaged, and insecure countries. But if that is the negative lens through which most outsiders see the country, it misses a great deal and does little to explain why this is the case.

Truth be told, Afghanistan was almost invisible to the average Canadian until the Soviet invasion of late December 1979. Even then, the main story was the subsequent Western boycott of the 1980 Olympics in Moscow. Not much thought was given to a land that has been a civilizational crossroads for millennia, an object of imperialist "great games" for centuries, an axis of Cold War scheming for decades (US policy covertly used Pakistan and Islamist fighters to make this the Soviet Union's Vietnam), and a post–Cold War catastrophe of civil war followed by extremist misrule and state collapse. Even now, after becoming the post-9/11 epicentre of the so-called "war on terror," Afghanistan comes across to many as an intractable mystery, a hopeless case. General knowledge of its history and culture is nearly non-existent.

Perhaps that did not seem to matter since Afghanistan would never have come on to the radar screen of Canadian foreign policy, much less have become its number one priority, were it not for al-Qaeda's haven there and the 9/11 attacks. The mission was sold as essential to curb security threats to ourselves from foreign terrorists. That, and not the much-vexed attempt to build a minimally stable, more or less functioning democratic Afghan state, remains the primary government rationale for staying there. In other words, the core rationale has always been more about us than what happens to the Afghans: their well-being is secondary to the safety of Canadians whatever the persuasiveness of the argument about linked security interests.

After a brief deployment of combat troops in 2002, Afghanistan receded from Canadian news headlines until 2006 when Canada sent a several-thousand strong force to the dangerous southern province of Kandahar and casualties rose sharply in fighting against a resurgent Taliban. Canada has lost over 150 soldiers, several aid workers, and one diplomat since 2001.[20] Many more Canadians have suffered injuries because of their service. Canada made a substantial contribution to the first post-Taliban elections of 2004–05, but it was those losses that commanded public attention and eroded support for the Canadian combat mission in Kandahar, which, according to the terms of a March 2008 parliamentary motion upheld by the government, must end by July 2011. Under pressure from allies, the Canadian government in November 2010 announced a post-combat contribution of up to 950 military trainers and support personnel until March 2014. Staying "inside the wire," they would not be involved in dangerous field operations.

Levels of violence have shown an escalating trend in recent years. The year 2010 was the worst since the war began in terms of foreign troop deaths and Afghan civilian casualties according to reports by the United Nations and independent sources.[21] The Taliban-led insurgency has a substantial presence in most of the country and, notwithstanding President Karzai's inauguration of a Peace Jirga, or council, in October 2010 as part of reconciliation and reintegration overtures, continues to demand the removal of foreign troops as a precondition for serious political negotiations. As well, electoral fraud and persistent corruption are eroding the Karzai government's already low standing both inside and outside the country.

Turning the overall security situation around is a many-sided challenge. The regional dimension is most apparent in the presence of Taliban sanctuaries in Pakistan across the disputed porous border. Moreover, as Carlotta Gall reported on the same day as the release of the new Obama administration's March 2009 white paper on Afghanistan and Pakistan, "Pakistan's military intelligence agency continued to offer money, supplies and guidance to the Taliban insurgency in Afghanistan as a proxy to help shape a friendly government there once American forces leave."[22] Several years later, the weakness of Pakistan's civilian authorities remains a large impediment to progress.

Within Afghanistan itself, coinciding with a major increase in US troops, much depends on the ultimate effectiveness of an uneven evolution in counter-insurgency strategy toward protection of the population and an increased concern with governance issues. Admiral Mike Mullen, chairman of the Joint Chiefs of Staff, meeting with his Canadian counterpart Walt Natynczyk, chief of the Defense Staff, prior to President Obama's February 2009 visit to Ottawa, talked about a "need to surge civilian capacity." He added: "If we don't get the governance piece right – and get it right pretty quickly – then the security pieces are going to struggle to make any kind of significant difference."[23]

Prime Minister Harper, interviewed a few days later by Fareed Zakaria (noted author of *The Post-American World* and *The Future of Freedom: Illiberal Democracy at Home and Abroad*) for the CNN program GPS, conceded that "we're not going to win this war just by staying ... we are never going to defeat the insurgency."[24] He was seen to suggest that the best that could be achieved was "to have an Afghan government that is capable of managing the insurgency." Afghanistan's then-ambassador to Canada, Omar Samad, worried about creating a perception of "defeatism" and retreat from democratic aims.[25]

Concerns about both security and governance objectives have grown rather than abated. Although an unclassified summary of the US *Annual Review of Afghanistan and Pakistan* released on 16 December 2010 claimed some progress on the former, it acknowledged that this was still "fragile and reversible."[26] Many experts are more critical. Just days before, a group of noted academics and independent observers had sent an open letter to President Obama, which underlined that "the situation on the ground is much worse than a year ago." Calling for an immediate direct US initiative in moving toward a broad-based negotiated political settlement with the Taliban, the letter argued that "the Taliban will likely be stronger next year."[27] Without mentioning democracy, the signatories lamented that "the highly centralized constitution goes against the grain of Afghan tradition, for example in specifying national elections in fourteen of the next twenty years."

The democratization agenda in Afghanistan has never been made clear to Canadians. Mixed signals abound and public perceptions have also suffered from serious doubts about democratic accountability in the making of policy toward Afghanistan and in the implementation of international commitments respecting democracy and human rights. A panel appointed by the government in 2007 to review future policy options stated in its January 2008 report: "The aim there is not to create some fanciful model of prosperous democracy. Canadian objectives are more realistic: to contribute, with others, to a better governed, stable and developing Afghanistan whose government can protect the security of the country and its people."[28] Unfortunately the Karzai government – widely viewed as tainted by fraud, corruption, and warlord alliances – has ceased to be credible on issues of better governance, still less basic electoral democracy. The next sections elaborate on what has led to this state of affairs and on the flawed nature of the electoral processes, but also indicate possible areas for advancing political reform with international support.

THE ROCKY ROAD TOWARD DEMOCRATIC GOVERNANCE IN AFGHANISTAN

What Afghanistan and its people desperately need is ... long-term strategies for sustainable democracy ... Despite the West's commitment to Afghanistan it still remains a country whose history and struggle for democracy is largely obscured by myth and propaganda.

Sima Wali[29]

The only way Afghanistan will become a truly sustainable democratic state in its own right is to make sure that Afghans develop the necessary skills to manage the basic building blocks.

Waillullah Rahmani[30]

Creating conditions for democratic governance took a backseat to "war on terror" motives in the wake of the Taliban's overthrow, with unfortunate consequences. The US ambassador to Afghanistan at the time, James Dobbins, and the UN's first special envoy, Ladkar Brahimi, regret what did not happen at the December 2001 Bonn conference, when it was in fact the Iranians who first raised the issue of democratic elections.[31]

The Taliban were defeated de facto but retreated to sanctuaries in Pakistan. No peace terms were signed and, excluded from the Bonn and subsequent processes, Taliban forces were treated as a terrorist enemy outside the "legitimate" Afghan political system. Ironically, many of the "new faces" in the post-Taliban regime had past Taliban associations, including President Karzai, himself an influential "Westernized Taliban supporter" in the mid-1990s.[32] One finds former civil-war era mujahedin warlords or sympathizers wearing new guises throughout Afghanistan's executive branch of government, courts, and legislative bodies. The youngest female member of the Afghan parliament, Malalai Joya, was ostracized in 2007 for denouncing the impunity enjoyed by these power brokers as well as the continuing collusion that keeps them in place.[33]

Notwithstanding elections, international actors are working with a compromised Afghan government beset by staggering corruption and administrative deficiencies. As Alexander Thier put it in his introduction to *The Future of Afghanistan*: "The foundations for the stable reasonably democratic state at peace with itself and its neighbors articulated in the Bonn Agreement, the 2004 Afghan Constitution, and the 2006 Afghanistan Compact have not proven sufficiently robust to counter Afghanistan's punishing poverty, the rampant narcotics trade, or a rising insurgency."[34]

The manifest failings of a highly centralized aid-dependent state have led many to insist on the need for long-term timeframes, honesty and realism in setting objectives, and, not least, accountability to Afghans who have been promised much more than is probably attainable. The lack of a deep knowledge of Afghan society and history inhibits clear thinking argues Rory Stewart, who lived in Kabul for several years before becoming director of the Carr Centre for Human Rights at Harvard University.[35]

If domestic "social engineering" raises the spectre of hubristic technocratic "fixes," how much more so "country engineering"? Indeed Stewart calls Afghanistan "the graveyard of predictions." As mentioned earlier, democratic development is not without antecedents in Afghanistan, most recently during the decade of relative stability following the 1964 constitution, from which the 2004 constitution drew heavily forty years later. However many of those who supported liberal reforms, mainly the urban educated classes, left the country after the pre-Communist government was overthrown. In the rural areas, multiple, diverse, and deeply entrenched tribal patriarchies prevail. Moreover, chapter 1, article 3, of Afghanistan's new 2004 constitution prohibits any laws contrary to "the holy religion of Islam."[36] As the country's ulema (council of Islamic clerics) remains extremely conservative, compliance with international human rights norms is an uphill struggle, notwithstanding elections and the creation of an independent human rights commission.

Helping Afghanistan become a viable democratic state is a matter of generational investments. Yet given the duration and escalation of conflict, Western publics are understandably wary of long-term involvements. Domestic debates within donor countries mainly revolve around troop deployments, mission extensions or renewals, temporary "surges" with withdrawal dates, and, increasingly, talk of "exit strategies." In Canadian policy terms, without significant measurable progress in 2011, it is doubtful that the credibility of long-term democratic governance and peace building goals can be maintained.

More generally, in an excellent recent article – "Can Outsiders Bring Democracy to Post-Conflict States?" – John Schmidt, currently a senior analyst in the US Department of State's Bureau of Intelligence and Research, usefully synthesizes a number of key points. He asks the right fundamental questions: "First, we should try to understand the factors that actually influence prospects for establishing democracy in a society. Secondly, we should evaluate to what extent outsiders can manipulate these factors to produce sustainable democracies."[37]

Schmidt lists seven critical factors: economic and development indicators; rule of law; ethnic and religious differences; secularism; previous experience with democracy, neighbours, and other outsiders; political culture; and post-conflict factors. Afghanistan does not make the grade on any of these, nor is it "post-conflict." Citing Afghanistan along with Iraq, Somalia, and the Congo, he observes that "outside intervention has failed even to end the violence, making it exceptionally difficult for democracy to take hold." He also notes that even well-resourced, post-conflict interventions may not produce sustainable democracies: "That scenario depends on whether the outsiders are prepared to settle questions of who should govern through free and fair elections *once the outsiders have left*." Although Schmidt calls

Afghanistan "a poor candidate for democratic change," he at least concludes on a note of possibility: "Since outsiders can bring democracy to post-conflict states *only sometimes* – when the political cultures of those societies are ready for it – it is critical to have the best possible understanding of just when those occasions might be."[38]

DILEMMAS CREATED BY THE 2009 AND 2010 ELECTIONS

Democracy cannot be established by the number of elections.

Ali Jalali[39]

Among peace consolidation specialists, the consensus is that the second and third elections are the decisive ones. In addition to the symbolic success of holding elections, patience is required in establishing structures and institutions that can support a political system that excludes violence as a means to an end.

Marc André Boivin[40]

Circumstances were far from optimal leading up to Afghanistan's second electoral cycle. The 2004 presidential and 2005 legislative elections, while reasonably successful, left many problems unaddressed. Indeed, in late 2008, Canadian Grant Kippen, who would become chair of Afghanistan's Electoral Complaints Commission (ECC) in 2009, observed that "the optimism surrounding the initial elections appears to have been replaced by disappointment, scepticism and frustration among the Afghan population. The deteriorating security situation, rising ethnic tensions, and the increasing influence of local warlords and commanders now threaten to undermine the upcoming electoral process."[41]

Matters were not helped in February 2009 when President Karzai, whose term was to expire on 21 May, abruptly called for early April elections[42] that would have been logistically and operationally impossible. While in the end his appointed Independent Electoral Commission (IEC) confirmed the 20 August date, with the Supreme Court of Afghanistan ruling he should continue in office until then, the disputed tactics increased domestic and international suspicions of his motives.

Although these were the first Afghan-led elections, they were supported by some US$500 million in international funding, including CAN$35 million from Canada, managed by the UNDP's Enhancing

Legal and Electoral Capacity for Tomorrow (ELECT) mechanism. A thorough pre-election review by the International Crisis Group (ICG) stated at the outset: "The expense of the current exercise is unsustainable and highlights the failure after the 2005 polls to build Afghan institutions and create a more realistic electoral framework." It went on to identify a host of deficiencies, inter alia: a biased IEC, unreformed electoral and political party laws, poor security and inadequate UN preparations, a much-abused voter-registry update process.[43]

With respect to the latter, Kippen, then ECC Chair, observed: "The major issues were multiple and under-age registrations. A lot of the men registered their 'women' with no proof being offered or in many cases demanded by the [voter registration] officials. The overall registration number is probably inflated by at least one million people, and that doesn't include the cards that are being printed up in Pakistan as we speak. You will probably see a lot of Pakistani Pashtuns crossing the border in the week or so before August 20th, so that they are in-country and able to vote on election day."[44]

In addition, the provincial council elections, as remained the case for the September 2010 parliamentary elections, were stuck with an obscure (doubtless poorly understood by most Afghans), dysfunctional, and party-inhibiting, single non-transferable vote electoral system.[45] As pointed out by Ben Reilly in chapter 2, this method of proportional representation has been heavily criticized for its disadvantages. The effects in Afghanistan have been further political fragmentation and manipulation along ethnic and tribal lines, preventing rather than enabling a stabilizing multiparty system to emerge.

Following a rushed vetting process by the ECC, 41 presidential and 3,178 provincial council candidates were qualified for the official campaign period that began on 16 June. Most of the latter ran as independents, given the voting system. In any event, these councils have very little power in comparison to the presidentially appointed provincial governors. The main focus of attention was the presidential race, with only one candidate, former foreign minister Abdullah Abdullah, emerging as a serious challenger to the incumbent Karzai. If the campaign was hardly fair, much worse was to come. Polling day itself, 20 August, was the country's most violent day of 2009 to that point, with 300 incidents reported and thirty-one people killed.

In a devastating analysis of the results, the ICG documents the staggering vote-rigging on Karzai's behalf, abetted by the IEC.[46] Even using its preliminary fraud-inflated vote tally released on 16 September, showing Karzai the victor, turnout was dismal – only 38.7 per cent of registered voters, far below the levels recorded in 2004–05. The ECC was flooded with thousands of complaints. Its final audit, published on 18 October, threw out fully 1.2 million of 5.2 million valid votes cast, giving Karzai 48.3 per cent to Abdullah's 31.5 per cent, thereby necessitating a run-off. Although the Karzai camp denied responsibility for fraud and alleged foreign interference in the ECC, the IEC conceded to a second round to be held on 7 November. It never happened, since Abdullah withdrew, citing the impossibility of a fair vote. Hence, on 2 November, Karzai was declared "re-elected."

What is surprising is how muted Afghanistan's international partners were in their criticisms. In fact, senior UN official Peter Galbraith was even fired for being too openly critical. The ICG report cited above is almost as excoriating about the failings of the UN mission and ELECT as it is of the Afghan role in widespread fraud, going so far as to call for the resignation of the then UN Special Representative Kai Eide. It states bluntly: "The international community demonstrated a complete lack of resolve in pressing for a credible electoral process."[47] In this and subsequent reports the ICG makes clear that nothing less than a fundamental reform of the Afghan political system is required.

Even before the electoral debacle, writing about "The Long Democratic Transition," ECC Chair Grant Kippen put the situation bluntly: "If the international community is committed to the democratization process in Afghanistan, then it needs to not only recalibrate its expectations about how long this process will take but also take a hard look at the breadth and depth of the programmatic activities that are needed to indicate a democratization process and culture among the diverse stake-holder communities in the country."[48]

Kippen makes eminently sensible suggestions for moving forward in practice: fewer guns (i.e., finally getting somewhere on the disarmament, demobilization, and reintegration of illegal or extra-legal armed groups); civic education (a big challenge, given over 70 per cent illiteracy, and neglected since the 2004–05 elections); professionalization and cleaning up (starting with the worst corruption abuses) of the civil service, executive, legislative branches, and the courts, the security forces, public institutions, and political parties. He argues compellingly for "a community-focused public-awareness campaign" and for serious international and Afghan coordination with Afghans ultimately taking over responsibilities for their own democratic affairs.[49]

I am not partial to the word "Afghanization." Not only does it sound too much like "Vietnamization" – and look where that got the US – it is open to manipulation by the client regime. While the Karzai regime is highly dependent on international support, in 2010 the president increasingly lashed out at foreign influence. In February, he introduced amendments to the electoral law that would see the respected ECC "Afghanized" – that is, fully subject to his power of appointment with no international or independent commissioners.[50] Two international members did join the ECC in May, including South African Justice John Kriegler.

Canada at least protested publicly; the US gave the impression of tacit acceptance.[51] In late March Afghanistan's lower house, the Wolesi Jirga, which had earlier voted against many of the president's cabinet choices, rejected the amendments. Karzai upped his attacks, now acknowledging that massive electoral fraud had occurred, but bizarrely blaming it on foreigners.

Although there was some improvement in how Afghanistan's much-criticized IEC oversaw the 2010 parliamentary electoral process, the campaign and September 18 voting day were plagued by violence, some 6,000 complaints were received by the ECC, and recounts were ordered in some provinces. Early results indicated that 4.3 million ballots were cast for over 2,500 candidates, the lowest turnout recorded since 2001. That was revised to 5.6 million in the preliminary tally released on October 20; however, 1.3 million of these votes were disqualified.

More delays followed while the ECC did its work. When "final" results were announced by the IEC on November 24, twenty-four winning candidates (almost 10 per cent of the total, including a cousin of President Karzai) were disqualified and results from Ghazni Province were postponed for "technical problems" that were in fact political (no Pashtuns were elected in this majority Pashtun province). The results set off a storm of protests, created new uncertainties, and inflamed ethnic divisions. The Free and Fair Election Foundation of Afghanistan denounced the elections as massively fraudulent. An unhappy President Karzai, seeing his Pashtun base eroded, launched a judicial proceeding aimed at the electoral bodies. As astutely observed by Ahmed Rashid:

> Turnout among the Pashtuns of southern and eastern Afghanistan, who make up some 40 per cent of the population, was very low. The Taliban, who are largely Pashtuns, had threatened the Pashtun voters, telling them to boycott the polls. As a result the Pashtuns lost between 10 and 20 per cent of their seats to ethnic minorities, especially the Tajiks and Hazaras. In the last parliament Pashtuns held 129 seats and now they are down to around 90. All eleven seats in the important province of Ghazni, which has a mixed Pashtun-Hazara population, were won by Hazaras, a result that infuriated both the Pashtuns and Karzai. Ghazni's results were announced after much delay and the eleven Hazaras were declared winners. Earlier the results were challenged by the attorney general, who ordered the arrest of several IEC officials, and there were demonstrations in Kabul for the failure to announce the results ... Karzai is trapped. If he accepts the election results, as he eventually must, he faces a parliament dominated by non-Pashtuns and his political opponents, which could scuttle his talks with the Taliban. Yet if he declares the elections null and void on account of the rigging and orders them redone, he could face open defiance from the ethnic minorities.[52]

According to Grant Kippen, "the silence from the international community is deafening when it comes to the egregious pressure and manipulation tactics being used by the [presidential] Palace on the IEC and the ECC to change results of the Wolesi Jirga election." Tensions reached a dangerous high point in January 2011 when Karzai tried to delay convening the parliament by one month to give his judicial manoeuvres more time. Kippen and another 2009 ECC commissioner Scott Worden issued a strong warning:

> If the extraordinary five-member panel of judges appointed by Karzai to review fraud nullifies the results of the September 2010 vote, it will provoke a constitutional crisis and leave Afghanistan without a legitimate parliament at a time when national unity is urgently needed to fight the insurgency and manage a delicate reintegration process with militants. The delay is also a strong sig-

nal that the international community's $500 million investment in Afghan elections over the past two years, and a fundamental pillar of the rule of law in Afghanistan, is about to fail ... To travel down the path the government of Afghanistan is currently taking will only create future electoral chaos and confusion, further undermining the rule of law and democratic development.[53]

The outcry forced the president to back down within days and newly elected legislators took their seats on January 26. Still, the electoral institutions have been undermined, again, and the outcome remains in dispute, a far from satisfactory situation.

Unsurprisingly, in light of such ongoing machinations and pending real progress on long-term political reforms, many analysts are sceptical about these elections being a step forward in democratization. An important series of studies on Afghan elections and instability that included surveys of Afghans was published by the Kabul-based Afghanistan Research and Evaluation Unit shortly before the September 18 vote. The findings revealed disturbing underlying patterns. As Noah Coburn observed:

> Learning from previous campaigns can also have its drawbacks. In light of fraud in the 2009 elections and minimal reforms by the IEC, it seems likely that fraud will actually increase as successful techniques are spread among the numerous candidates. ... Most respondents felt that the IEC had made no real changes to address issues of fraud and corruption, and that this would favour those who had been successful within the system once before ...
> Violence is viewed as an effective political tool; the country is deeply divided on the question of whether it should be ruled by religious leaders, former commanders or bureaucrats; and there is a deep sense that the current political elite, who most Afghans feel are corrupt and unsympathetic to community needs, are so firmly entrenched that it is impossible to remove them from power.
>
>   The 2010 elections in Afghanistan are likely to be deeply flawed, marred by fraud and, perhaps, violence. Members of the international community who have been disappointed by these faltering steps on what many hoped would be the path toward democracy should not be asking what procedures might address these election flaws. Rather, the question should be: How can a

more transparent, accountable and impartial political culture be encouraged in Afghanistan? Elections by themselves will not necessarily bring stability, or even representative governance, to Afghanistan.[54]

According to another study by the same author:

Recent elections in Afghanistan have created a new set of winners and losers based upon the ability to manipulate a corrupt, non-transparent system. Respondents complained less about the outcomes of elections than about the fact that elections were a part of political processes where they did not always know the rules, and where powerful figures could alter those rules when they desired. Due in part to this lack of predictable outcomes, elections have encouraged decision-making by political leaders that often ignores the needs of local communities and have fuelled community divisions along ethnic, class and tribal lines, without allowing equal access to political resources ideally guaranteed in competitive democracy. In fact, the case of the 2010 parliamentary election sheds doubt on the value of continuing elections in Afghanistan if significantly more is not done to ensure greater equality of access to these resources. More generally, this example demonstrates some of the issues with holding elections quickly in postconflict situations.[55]

The secretary-general's report to the Security Council on the situation in Afghanistan, released a few days before the 18 September vote, and the Canadian government's quarterly report on its Afghan mission released a few days after, as well as a tenth such report released on 8 December, try to put the electoral process in a positive light.[56] But I agree with Francesc Vendrell's argument[57] that donors have yet to make a serious effort to tie their support for elections to meaningful reforms. Moreover, as Anthony Cordesman points out, technical improvements in the conduct of elections may not translate into a better quality of governance that benefits Afghans grown weary of the unfulfilled promises of their quasi-democracy.[58]

Many also question whether the Karzai government can ever be a credible partner for international efforts. At the same time, any sustainable democracy has to be Afghan-led, and building one will be a decades-long process. That brings us to a central question. Does the "international community" generally, and Canada specifically, have the staying power to support a "long democratic transition" in Afghanistan?

CANADIAN CHOICES IN LIGHT OF EVOLVING US AND INTERNATIONAL POLICY

The best we can do is train the Afghans so that they are able to manage the insurgency themselves and create, not a Western liberal democracy, because Afghanistan is not going to look like that any time soon, but at least a government that has some democratic and rule-of-law norms that is moving in a positive direction.

Stephen Harper[59]

When it comes to Afghanistan's democratic prospects, what some welcome as overdue hard-nosed realism could also appear as a calculated deflating of mission objectives, a prelude to scaling down Canadian commitments on the way to an exit. But this leaves some thorny questions hanging. To what extent can outside interveners declare "success" if Afghanistan fails to become a stable *and* rights-respecting democratic state? Is the prevention of future terrorist attacks on the West even possible without long-term support of Afghans in their struggle to achieve full democracy? Are we beginning to lose our nerve at a critical juncture in Afghanistan's history? Were the intervention sceptics right all along?

Beyond the fact that Canada's Kandahar combat role will end in 2011, there is a sense that Canadian public opinion has become increasingly less committed to Afghanistan's future. A February 2009 survey in *Maclean's* magazine revealed a striking contrast: whereas Canadian respondents then gave President Obama an off-the-charts 82 per cent approval rating, when asked "Should Canada stay in Afghanistan if Obama asks?" only 20 per cent said yes.[60] Consistently since then more Canadians oppose than support continued Canadian engagement. Despite the main opposition Liberal party's explicit endorsement of the government's future military training mission, a December 2010 Angus Reid survey found just 44 per cent of respondents in favour. Fewer still, 36 per cent, support the current combat mission.[61]

Although there has been much talk in Canada of the 3Ds (Defence, Development, and Diplomacy) morphing into a "whole-of-government" strategy, and of boosting the civilian mission, the military component has predominated. The number of Canadian civilians working in Afghanistan has steadily increased, but in comparison to the 2,800 Canadian Forces personnel deployed until July 2011, they accounted for only slightly more than 3 per cent of the Canadian contingent. The ballooning costs of the military mission have been a subject of controversy. An October 2008 report by the parliamentary budget officer projected the total costs at up to CAN$18.1 billion over the period 2001–02 to 2010–11 (an annual average of approximately $2 billion).[62] Whatever the final figure, it will be many times the CAN$1.2 billion in Canadian development assistance over that decade. From 2011 to 2014, when military costs are forecast to drop to $500 million annually, development aid will also fall to $100 million annually. The armed forces will remain the largest and most visible Canadian presence in Afghanistan.

Canada's evolving Afghanistan policy should be seen in the context of NATO/ISAF strategies, the actions of the international community through the UN and other forums, as well as the complex interactions of these with what the Afghan government does, or fails to do, combined with volatile circumstances on the ground. In particular, as Canada's superpower neighbour increasingly dominates Western engagement, some discussion is needed of evolving US objectives.

From the moment Barack Obama took the oath of presidential office on 20 January 2009, it was obvious that Afghanistan was going to become his war.[63] Following a two-month sweeping review, the *White Paper of the Interagency Policy Group's Report on US Policy Towards Afghanistan and Pakistan* was released on 27 March 2009 prior to the 31 March International Conference on Afghanistan in The Hague and the early April NATO sixtieth anniversary leaders' summit. There was no comparable process on the Canadian side. Canada was among many countries looking to the direction that would be set by the Obama administration, although the government was tabling quarterly "progress reports" in Parliament as required by the March 2008 motion extending the Canadian mission through 2011.

Calling for "realistic and clear objectives," the US white paper stated: "The core goal of the US must be to disrupt, dismantle, and defeat al-Qaeda and its safe havens in Pakistan, and to prevent their return to

Pakistan or Afghanistan."⁶⁴ Effectively this was an Obama version of the "war on terror" under a less contested rubric, while still putting US national security imperatives first. In terms of governance, the paper called for "promoting a more capable, accountable, and effective government in Afghanistan that serves the Afghan people and can eventually function, especially regarding internal security, with limited international support."⁶⁵

After more months of review and internal debate, the White House had also announced a further major military escalation. President Obama's 1 December 2009 speech at the West Point military academy committed another 30,000 troops to the war effort, even though he indicated that some troops might come home in 2011 and that "America has no interest in fighting an endless war in Afghanistan."⁶⁶ By the summer of 2010, the US had some 100,000 troops in the country, at enormous cost, a tripling of force strength since Obama took office.

Disappointingly, there was no reference to democracy in the Obama administration's 2009 policy statements. The December 2009 speech was even more firmly rooted in US national security imperatives. The sole reference to the failed 2009 elections seems obliquely to legitimize it: "We and our allies prevented the Taliban from stopping a presidential election, and – although it was marred by fraud – that election produced a government that is consistent with Afghanistan's laws and Constitution."⁶⁷

The 2010 London Conference on Afghanistan also confined itself to diplomatic niceties, welcoming "the Government of Afghanistan's commitment to ensuring the integrity of the 2010 Parliamentary elections [postponed by the IEC to 18 September] and to preventing any irregularities and misconduct." As well, they noted that Afghanistan had committed "to work closely with the UN to build on the lessons learned from the 2009 elections to deliver improvements to the electoral process in 2010 and beyond."⁶⁸ As mentioned earlier, what has happened instead is the attempted weakening of the ECC. With regard to political reconciliation and the Karzai government's overtures to insurgent factions, including the notorious Islamist warlord Gulbuddin Hekmatyar, democracy activists are concerned that this not be done at the expense of justice and human rights principles.

International conferences on Afghanistan still regularly uphold liberal-democratic goals. For example, the March 2009 conference in

The Hague "reaffirmed" a collective "determination to fulfil the vision of a democratic, peaceful, pluralistic, and prosperous state based on the Afghan Constitution and the principles of Islam, as set out in the Bonn Agreement of 2001, in the Afghanistan Compact of 2006, and in the Paris Declaration of 2008."[69] The January 2010 London conference, looking ahead to the July 2010 Kabul conference, called for an Afghan government program that "should be based on democratic accountability, equality, human rights, gender equality, good governance and more effective provision of government services, economic growth, as well as a desire to live in peace under the Afghan Constitution."[70]

Are these more than ritual wish lists? What does it mean to help build an Afghan democracy with Islamic characteristics? This is no simple matter. The day after The Hague conference, on 1 April 2009, a furore erupted in Canada's House of Commons over the treatment of some Afghan women under the Shiite Personal Status Law approved by President Karzai, following its passage by the Afghan parliament.[71] Indeed the measure, which violates international conventions binding on Afghanistan, drew widespread condemnation. On 2 April the United Nations High Commissioner for Human Rights, Navi Pillay, stated: "For a new law in 2009 to target women in this way is extraordinary, reprehensible and reminiscent of the decrees made by the Taliban regime in Afghanistan in the 1990s."[72] A female Afghan parliamentarian even described it as "worse than the Taliban" since it was passed by a duly elected legislature (in which 89 of 351 members are women).[73] President Karzai claimed to have no problem with the law but, bowing to international pressure, submitted it to review by the justice ministry and also the conservative ulema. This episode had a significantly negative impact on Western public opinion. Yet the law was in fact promulgated by President Karzai in July 2009. Another controversial law on the books grants blanket amnesty to all perpetrators of atrocities from 1979 to 2002.[74]

An important September 2009 field study also pointed problematically to a declining "acceptance of the current democratization process among [Afghan] citizens":

> Firstly, democracy is increasingly associated with the individual liberal freedoms of the West and thus distanced from Afghan religious and cultural norms. If liberal values continue to be consid-

ered "imposed" in Afghanistan, the result may be widespread disownership of the democratic process entirely, as a reaction against a perceived Western cultural "invasion." Secondly, there is widespread disillusionment with the benefits that "democracy" can bring, due to an expected but lacking improvement in rule of law and economic development combined with a hopelessness brought about by deteriorating security. This is heightened by concerns that encouraging multi-party competition and political opposition could *contribute to insecurity* rather than promote peace and stability. Thirdly, democratic representation is seen as inherently flawed, due to the inefficacy and fraud perceived to infiltrate formal representative processes and the under-performance of elected representatives. Finally, there is a fundamental disconnect between people and government, which has not been addressed by the formation of formal democratic institutions.[75]

CONCLUSION: DETERMINING CANADA'S ROLE

Despite declared Afghan and Canadian commitments to democratic advancement, Afghanistan remains a very troubled state with a government of dubious legitimacy. Recent elections have contributed to the problem rather than consolidating democratic gains. The year 2011 will mark a decade of foreign intervention and the prospect of a much-diminished Canadian presence thereafter. It is unclear how Canada will then exert influence on the Karzai government and political developments in Afghanistan, addressing a deep democratic malaise of which flawed elections are the most visible manifestation.

Significantly, democratic progress is at the core of a March 2010 advocacy report by the Canada-Afghanistan Solidarity Committee:

> Canada's new mission in Afghanistan should be countrywide, long-term, and well resourced, guided by a single overriding policy: The entrenchment, growth, and development of democratic culture in Afghanistan ... The promise of Afghan democracy is a promise the Canadian government has made to the Afghan people – not just to the current occupant of Afghanistan's Presidential Palace. This is also a promise the Canadian government has made to its own citizens. Canadians cannot allow a betrayal of this promise ... The construction of democracy is the one neces-

sary and lasting project Canadians can and should advance in Afghanistan.[76]

That said, there has been very little public debate centred on a sustained Canadian engagement in Afghanistan's long democratic transition. Such engagement is an unlikely prospect in the absence of stronger democratic support among Canadians. Moreover, Canadian assessments of the ongoing dilemmas of democratization in Afghanistan will need to be as rigorously forthright as possible, applying the hard lessons paid for in blood and treasure.

This is not an argument for an unsustainable Afghan dependence on outsiders but rather for Canada to examine and pursue all reasonable options for working with Afghans dedicated to democracy and human rights. The alternative is to be left with a result that fails both Afghans and Canada's best foreign policy traditions.

If Canadians are weary of the Afghan conflict, imagine what ordinary Afghans must feel. Will commitments made to them be followed through with the right kinds of help, including support for democracy building, for as long as they need it?

There will be some tough democratic choices ahead for Afghans and for Canadians. With enough careful attention and resolve, it should be possible to avoid overpromising and under-delivering. That would only invite further disappointments, with serious consequences for them and for us. In democracies, informed, honest choices are best.

Looking ahead without illusions, now is not the time to give up on the goals of supporting Afghans' struggle for democracy, understanding that in the case of Canada and Afghanistan, democratization is still a question in search of an answer.

CONCLUSION

An Ounce of Prevention: Preliminary Implications for Policy and Practice

DAVID GILLIES AND GERALD J. SCHMITZ

As we write this final chapter, the Jasmine and Facebook revolutions in Tunisia and Egypt have come to symbolize the struggle for pluralism, development, and dignity across the Middle East. In a "democracy-free zone" where the imperative of stability has long trumped human rights, the Arab world is going through a profound, and possibly irreversible, transformation. Spikes in food prices, soaring youth unemployment, and growing income inequality have all played a role in breaking down fear of corrupt regimes in the region. So too has "the failure of Egypt and Tunisia's allies and aid donors – including Canada – to take economic and social development seriously and ensure that their assistance really results in more equitable growth rather than just stronger regimes."[1]

Pent-up resentment over repression, flawed elections, and unrepresentative institutions have created the perfect storm now facing autocrats from Tunisia to Egypt, from Jordan to Yemen, to Libya and Sudan. Mubarak's Egypt in particular faced an insuperable legitimacy crisis in the wake of 2010 parliamentary elections. Voter turnout may have been as low as 20 per cent, opposition candidates intimidated by security forces, ballots allegedly stuffed, and yet the ruling National Democratic Party was returned with 90 per cent of the seats to a National Assembly widely seen as lacking in legitimacy and effective oversight of the executive.

The drama now unfolding points to the creation of legitimacy as the most difficult challenge of any political transition. Elections in situations of conflict crystallize the trade-offs between short-term peace and stability and the long-term search for a durable democracy. As

Conclusion: An Ounce of Prevention

Egypt's struggle continues, international opinion appears to be tilting toward the view that "even a messy democracy could eventually be a rich prize" and that the West, which has "damaged its image [in the] pursuit of stability above democracy"[2] has a chance to abandon the "fallacy of myopia" and help win that prize.[3]

What lessons then do our country, regional, and thematic essays provide for international policy and practical action to mitigate violent electoral conflict? In the context of democratic institution building, a key message that emerges is the centrality of the election management body (EMB). Technical efficiency in electoral administration is necessary but not sufficient. Unambiguous political neutrality, what Sara Staino calls "fearless independence," is the litmus test of an EMB's ability to build the confidence of the public, contending political parties, and the international community. Achieving that neutrality is by no means easy as EMBs can be captured by governments. Recent elections in Kenya and Afghanistan underline the vulnerability of EMBs to political manipulation. By contrast, in the DRC an EMB helped assure the integrity of the 2006 election, and in South Africa an EMB co-opted potential spoilers by building links with all political parties in the 1994 election. Equally crucial is the creation of an authentic electoral dispute resolution (EDR) system. The absence of attention to a formal EDR system in Kenya when multiparty politics emerged in the 1990s reverberated in the aftermath of the 2007 election crisis when the lack of a timely and credible EDR mechanism deepened the impasse.

Turning to our country cases, the debacle of the 2009 Afghan presidential election has corroded the legitimacy of the Karzai government, brought the UN into some disrepute, and set back governance. The international community was tepid in confronting the capture of the EMB by the Karzai government and missed opportunities to insist on reform of the election administration and dispute resolution system. Francesc Vendrell is forthright in condemning those external voices that are now willing to lower the bar and accept that international standards should no longer apply to Afghanistan. Unfortunately, our collective failure to help Afghans establish representative and accountable institutions will undermine a faltering counter-insurgency strategy. Some US$500 million was spent on elections that set back democracy in Afghanistan. It is hard to see any clear return on that investment.

Marc Lemieux discerns a modest evolution of the political system in occupied Iraq, aided in part by elections and changes in electoral design. Some lessons appear to have been learned. Compared with the flawed election of 2005, the polls of 2009 and 2010 "rewarded" tendencies for more national, moderate, and even secular ideals. Even Islamic parties have embraced the democratic process. While Iraq, for more than nine months, "miserably failed" Ben Reilly's second function of elections, namely to form a government, the shift to an open list proportional representation system has encouraged greater political choice, transparency, and legitimacy, with the potential to improve the accountability of law makers to voters. In the longer view, Lemieux thinks that the federal model can support democratization in Iraq and that a political culture blending democratic values with the yearning for a traditional strongman is not incompatible.

As Khalid Medani explains, the national elections and South Sudan referendum were the final acts of the "armistice" in Africa's longest conflict and the culmination of the 2005 Comprehensive Peace Agreement between North and South Sudan. The fact that both polls were broadly consistent with international standards and conducted in a relatively peaceful and orderly environment is a testament to the maturity of Sudanese elites and citizens. Paul Collier has shown that it is during the first year after a post-conflict election that countries are at most risk of reversion to war.[4] The next six months will be fraught with potential pitfalls as North and South Sudan negotiate the terms of secession and agreements on contentious issues, such as the border, water, debt, wealth sharing, citizenship, and the status of the oil-rich Abyei area. An independent South Sudan faces a precarious future in the absence of infrastructure, limited human capital, and, at the present rate of extraction, the exhaustion of its oil reserves in about ten years. If the Sudanese can resolve the final steps in a velvet divorce and move in a more democratic direction, that will serve as a heartening "ideal model of change," not just in Africa but also in the Arab world, where events in Tunisia and Egypt represent other promising, albeit as yet fragile and unfinished, harbingers of citizen-led, systemic, democratizing change in deeply autocratic societies.[5]

From the DRC election in 2006 we learn that, while steps were taken by local, national, and international actors to mitigate both pre- and post-election violence, elections have not helped the larger project of democratic consolidation or the creation of stable governance.

Instead, violence and large-scale hostilities have occurred every year since the 2006 election. State authority continues to be absent from large swaths of the country, particularly in the east. Finally, donors and peacekeepers were too quick to judge the election a success. Eugenia Zorbas and Vincent Tohbi underline that aid levels "tapered off precipitously" after 2006, reinforcing the idea that the elections "were indeed little more than an exit strategy." Paul Collier is more blunt, calling the decision to have peacekeepers start leaving one day after the second round "the denial of reality at its most absurd," particularly since Bemba and Kabila loyalists were subsequently involved in a shoot-out.[6]

From the Kenyan election of 2007 we learn that donors were not adequately prepared for the post-election violence, having not fully learned from many past experiences of smaller scale conflicts in and around earlier elections. As Stephen Brown puts it, "Kenya's experiences warn against donor complacency and naivete." More worrying is that what Susanne Mueller calls the "mask of elections" amid a deliberate weakening of institutions, the personalization of power, and the diffusion of violence signals long-term danger to democracy and the integrity of the Kenyan state. Mueller sees limits in a social engineering approach to preventing electoral conflict: "When the rules of the game are to bypass, ignore or undermine the law, why should one [expect] that new ... laws, whether a new constitution or new rules about elections, will change the way politics works?" The latest shenanigans of the Kenyan political class, as it considers repudiating its new constitution to wriggle away from the International Criminal Court, is ample demonstration of the disincentives for playing by the formal rules of the game and of the continued risk of impunity for violent crimes.

The issue of election timing is vexed. Ill-timed elections can be disastrous, generating mass protest, violence, and political instability. The 2010 Côte d'Ivoire election was supposed to advance peace but had the opposite effect. The 2010 Haitian election was held at the worst of times: less than one year after a ruinous earthquake, in the middle of a cholera epidemic, and with citizens at boiling point at the slow pace of reconstruction. Evidence of ballot stuffing and a stolen result was the perfect storm for a wave of violent protest. At the very least, the timing of the Haitian election has destroyed some of the momentum for recovery.

The country situations examined here broadly reinforce Ben Reilly's view that there is no longer agreement about the centrality and timing of elections in political transitions at war's end. While Iraq, on the positive reading of Marc Lemieux, may affirm the value of elections in complex war-to-peace transitions, the massively fraudulent Afghan elections of 2009 and 2010 have given elections there very bad press as keystones of reconstruction or democracy. Simply put, a violent or flagrantly manipulated election is democracy in reverse.[7] When people can perceive that elections are merely a facade or have been stolen from them, whether in Kenya or Kosovo, Egypt, Iran, or Belarus, the electoral process itself becomes a provocation, the antithesis of democratic voice rather than its instrument.

At the same time, we do not want to fall into what Thomas Carothers has called the fallacy of "democratic sequentialism," in which a number of preconditions must be met before elections can even be considered.[8] As he puts it, to suggest that a substantial part of the global third wave of democracy was "merely electoral froth, caused by the West promiscuously pushing for elections all over the world" is to misconstrue it "by underestimating the normative shift in favour of elections that has occurred around the world" and overestimating "the consistency and power of Western support for elections and democracy in developing and post-communist countries."[9] Francesc Vendrell and Gerald Schmitz point out that international donors have given conflicting messages by investing large sums in holding elections in Afghanistan only to respond tepidly to their manipulation by the Karzai regime instead of demanding fundamental electoral reforms.

Carothers argues that a more useful approach to dealing with the complications and risks of democratization is one of "gradualism," which aims at building electoral democracy slowly in certain contexts but not avoiding it or putting it off indefinitely. We agree. And it is because elections are such a necessary, but also insufficient, component of democratization and the consolidation of democracy on a stable basis that it is so important to address the circumstances surrounding them. Especially in conflict and post-conflict situations, everything from the choice of electoral systems to determining the timing of national and subnational electoral processes must take into account the nature of societal divisions – geographic, ethnic, religious, and so on. Otherwise elections are very likely to exacerbate these divisions instead of contributing to conflict resolution.

In short, elections matter because so much can depend on the ramifications of how they do, or do not, support nonviolent democratic evolution in diverse societies. This pivotal role of elections is graphically illustrated in two compelling documentaries about intensely contested electoral processes – one fragile but successfully managed, the other brutally taken over, ending in failure – that had their world premieres at the Sundance film festival in January 2011. *An African Election*, directed by Jarreth and Kevin Merz, a fascinating account of Ghana's tense December 2008 presidential elections and December-January 2009 runoff ballots, provides insights that reinforce our point about the role of EMBs and the importance of building their capacity and integrity. In contrast, writer-director Ali Samadi Ahadi's *The Green Wave* graphically illustrates how Iran's June 2009 elections raised popular hopes for democratic changes only to cruelly dash them against the rock of theocratic intransigence. While the contexts may be very different, what is evident is that understanding the uses and misuses of elections is a key part of pursuing a democratic development agenda.

Elections reflect the problematic character of the states and societies in which they take place. How could they not? A strategy of avoiding them, or making a mockery of them in the interests of regime "stability", leads to an undemocratic dead end that ultimately is likely to become destabilizing. Repression, however much it has been able to thwart and sometimes roll back democratic expression, has shown that it cannot be counted on to prevail indefinitely against the determined force of this fundamental human aspiration. The critical questions therefore revolve around creating the best possible circumstances conducive to the conduct (*not* stage managing) of orderly elections through institutions and processes that build confidence among citizens, enhance state legitimacy, and thereby contribute to the realization of sustainable democratic political systems.

The fact that many democratizing states are conflict-prone should not be an argument against holding elections. Rather, it reinforces the case that conflict prevention matters a great deal to the success of complex democratic transitions. This approach should therefore be a priority for international and domestic actors where the risk of electoral conflict and instability is high. One of the positive messages emerging from the case studies is that coordinated and timely international action can make a difference in mitigating election-related conflict and violence. This was most evident in the DRC in 2006 and in Kenya in the achievement of a National Accord brokered by Kofi Annan in the aftermath of the 2007 election. The DRC elections in 2006 avoided the predicted widespread electoral violence after the brutal civil war. Zorbas and Tohbi discuss four approaches that worked in the DRC. These were: (1) a legislative approach in which electoral laws were applied in an impartial and balanced manner; (2) a technical approach in which the Independent Electoral Commission was equipped with the tools to administer an election and address disputes; (3) a diplomatic approach with regional involvement, a contact group of fourteen countries as friends of DRC, and the use of former African heads of state to mediate disputes; and (4) a community-led approach with local conflict management panels for mediation. Crucially, the interplay of these different approaches proved effective in mitigating conflict in the 2006 DRC election.

It is no accident that this collection features three African case studies: Sudan, the DRC, and Kenya. Africa is a bellwether of the relationship between elections and conflict. The region accounts for 40 per cent of the global peace operations deployment, with large-scale UN actions in the DRC, Sudan, Darfur, Liberia, and Côte d'Ivoire.[10] But alongside persistent conflicts in the Horn of Africa, West Africa, and Central Africa, two dozen elections will be held in Africa in a three-year period. This is both a welcome development and a cause for concern. The good news, as Christian Hennemeyer puts it, is that "most African nations now hold regular, scrutinized elections as a matter of course." It is also good news that African citizens consistently support democratic governance. Notwithstanding backsliding in Niger, Mauritania, and Madagascar, there are signs that elections are replacing coups d'état as a mode of political succession and regime change in Africa. Democratic norms are also being reinforced by African regional organizations, such as the African Union and Economic Organization of West African States (ECOWAS), which roundly condemn military coups and unconstitutional change and can act collectively to prevent or respond to such illegal actions.

The bad news about elections in Africa (and more broadly in conflict-affected countries) is that they are so vulnerable to manipulation, including the use of violence, intimidation, and outright fraud. Manipulation can be orchestrated by incumbents determined to stay in power at all costs, by militarized groups and other spoilers in fragile peace agreements, or by demagogues and their political party supporters facing certain defeat at the polls. Not only has the concept of a loyal opposition not really taken hold in large parts of Africa, manipulated elections from Ethiopia – where opponents to Meles Zenawi won just two of the parliament's 547 seats – to Sudan – where opponents largely boycotted elections – underline just how tenuous competitive politics is in parts of the continent.[11]

IMPLICATIONS AND RECOMMENDATIONS FOR POLICY AND PRACTICE

Many conflict-prone societies or emerging democracies in Africa, Asia, and parts of the Americas rely on international assistance in order to conduct elections. In a policy environment where a number of rich donor countries are facing periods of fiscal austerity and reduced or stagnant aid budgets, it may become more difficult to justify continued large-scale spending to support elections that are violent, stolen, or sterile exercises simply to "tick the box" as part of a tenuous peace agreement. It may be no bad thing if donor governments no longer subscribe to costly support of "good enough" elections in malign environments. Using the prospect of success as a guiding criterion, some donors could instead direct their scarce tax dollars to support elections where there are enabling conditions, such as a strong civil society, an effective dispute mechanism, an independent election management body, and a conflict mitigation program.

The case studies on Kenya and the DRC mention the role of regional institutions in conflict management. Given the upsurge of elections in Africa, it is good news that the African Union and some regional economic communities (RECs) have laid a normative framework to address election-related conflicts as part of the larger African peace and security architecture.

The AU framework is set out in the 2007 African Charter on Democracy, Elections, and Governance. Through its Democracy and Electoral Assistance Unit and associated fund, and by calling on the Panel of the Wise (a group of eminent elders), the AU can provide technical support to EMBs and civil society, and play an election conflict-management role. ECOWAS established a Protocol on Democracy and Good Governance in 2001 and has interceded in electoral and succession crises in Togo and other jurisdictions. Brief mention should be made also of the African Peer Review Mechanism (APRM), which addresses inadequacies of the electoral machinery in countries that have permitted voluntary scrutiny in the wider context of the quality of democratic institutions and practices.

Between 1990 and 2008, the Organization of African Unity and its successor the AU observed more than 200 elections in the majority of its member states.[12] However, if Africans want to take ownership for conflict resolution on the continent and reduce external involvement, it is imperative that the credibility of the AU and the RECs in election monitoring, reporting, mediation, and technical support be enhanced. Professionalism and capacity building must replace politics and lowest-common-denominator exercises. The potential of the AU to act as a conflict manager is illustrated by the effectiveness of the troika led by former UN Secretary-General Kofi Annan in mediating an interim solution to the 2007 post-election political crisis in Kenya. Beyond any technocratic fix, there is the more troubling and less soluble problem of political will where African regional organizations remain inconsistent in their collective action on whether to intercede or turn a blind eye in the case of coups and dubious elections.

Based on the analysis of country situations and discussion of tools and approaches, what follows are a number of broad implications and recommendations for both policy and practice:

1 Democracy is a matter of degree and quality. Democratization is a process through which a society and a system of government moves toward regular political competition, accountability of office holders, independent institutions that limit executive power, extensive public participation, and the enjoyment of a wide range of human rights. The quality and reach of democratic politics in conflict-prone societies may be quite weak.[13]
2 Supporting democracy in conflict-prone societies is an ambitious, complex, and sometimes disruptive transformation, requiring sustained effort and considerable time. It involves a multiplicity of domestic and international institutions and stakeholders. Given the scale and complexity of the agenda, what is perhaps most needed is a shift away from viewing elections as the principal first-order means of achieving a functioning democracy toward approaching elections more critically and cautiously as one component, albeit a necessary one, among many in building a sustainable democracy.

3 In countries emerging from violent conflict or making a protracted political and economic transition, democratization can be destabilizing. Elections are a necessary but not sufficient attribute of democratization. All aspects of democracy promotion are interconnected and should be supported in mutually reinforcing ways. The quality and resilience of constitutions, legislatures, political parties, election administration, judiciaries, and security institutions are linked. Inattention to a weak link in the chain may adversely affect the independence and effectiveness of other public institutions.

4 A single swallow does not signal summer. In conflict-prone and transitional societies, the first "post-settlement" election must be reinforced by successive elections that are viewed as legitimate by citizens and the international community. The case of Afghanistan illustrates the danger of backsliding if robust and independent electoral and democratic institutions are not built between elections. The intrinsic merit of promoting local ownership should never be met at the cost of international electoral standards.

5 Conflict prevention and support for social cohesion and peacebuilding need to be at the centre rather than the periphery of donor support for elections in conflict-prone situations. Practical support must inevitably be context-dependent and based on a sound understanding of the resiliency and vulnerabilities of societies according to whether they are sliding toward violence, already war-torn, nominally post-conflict, or in transition toward stable development and durable democratic governance. That said, the electoral cycle approach is an organizing principle to identify meaningful conflict prevention activities before, during, and after elections.

6 There is a plethora of potential interventions to mitigate electoral conflict and sensitize voters, candidates, EMBs, marginalized groups, donors, civil society organizations, security institutions, the judiciary, and the media. These include conflict mapping, civic and voter education, human rights training, and traditional and alternative electoral dispute resolution. Support for a single sector cannot eradicate violence on its own. Cross-sector programming incorporating conflict analysis, prevention, mitigation, and resolution, all integrated with the electoral cycle, provides a comprehensive road map for addressing conflict-prone election environments.

7 In the context of election timing at war's end, later may often be better by allowing more time for pre-electoral factors to be addressed, including the careful design of electoral systems, voter registries, electoral bodies, accountability and oversight mechanisms, and other aspects of institution building directed at improving the societal and cultural conditions for political liberalization. In some cases proceeding with sub-national elections ahead of national elections can help address citizen participation while enhancing the preparedness for national exercises, which, if rushed, can undermine the overall credibility of electoral democracy. Better a delayed national election than a failed one that invites cynicism and actually sets back the cause of democracy. It should be acknowledged, however, that the timing and sequencing of elections is a profoundly political decision. The influence of external actors may often be quite limited, though that does not let them off the hook. Whatever the circumstances, external actors will still need to assess how best to use their funding leverage (see point 8, below) to improve the chances for positive outcomes. International support for, followed by tacit acceptance of, an electoral debacle as in Afghanistan will throw the whole process into question.

8 The costs of conducting elections in conflict-affected situations can be very high and is often largely borne by the international community. Although international support for elections should decrease over time as local institutions such as EMBs become more capable, predictable funding for elections continues to be a challenge. In Africa, many governments do not want to pay for elections, putting in question the sustainability of democracy and raising the spectre of donor fatigue.

9 There is a potentially unbalanced relationship between the very large resources allocated to peacekeeping as opposed to conflict prevention. The same is true of the large volume of resources given to election management bodies compared with the support given to political party development and civic education. In the pre-electoral phase, more attention can be focused on the precursors of violence through systematic conflict mapping.

10 A regional approach can aid conflict resolution. While international election assistance is often essential, a long-term objective is to nurture domestic and regional capacity and ownership of

conflict resolution. The credibility of regional bodies such as the AU and ECOWAS will be enhanced by scrupulous professionalism and observation and monitoring consistent with their own normative frameworks and the highest international standards. Regional bodies are well positioned to maintain early warning systems and to deploy panels of the wise and other forms of pre-election preventive diplomacy or post-election conflict mediation.

11 One implication for supporting elections in conflict prone situations, such as the DRC in 2006, is the value of effective coordination among local, national, regional, and international conflict management mechanisms. A unity of purpose and understanding of roles and responsibilities can reinforce the impact of both traditional and improvised or alternative dispute resolution.

12 In order to mitigate electoral violence effectively, there must be timely and effective electoral dispute resolution as well as security sector reform. A failure to address the impunity associated with election violence, as in Kenya's inability to establish a tribunal to consider these issues, may reinforce the status quo and help prompt violence in future elections. "Floating" election commissions for countries that lack a capable EMB or recourse to regional judicial mechanisms have been suggested to ensure effective dispute resolution.

13 Electoral system design can in some circumstances support peaceful politics in deeply divided societies. There is a debate between advocates of proportional and majoritarian systems. In some jurisdictions, a shift to forms of proportional representation (PR), which tend to produce multiparty parliaments, appears to have promoted inclusion and mitigated conflict. Elections conducted under UN auspices favour proportional representation. Variants of simple party-list PR systems are being experimented with in various countries, such as Sudan (mixed member proportional) and Iraq (provincial PR). But not all variants of PR are favourable to building national representative institutions of multiparty competition and compromise. On the contrary, the adoption of the single non-transferable vote (SNTV) in Afghanistan has served to increase the powers of an already centralized presidency to rule, unhindered by any party affiliation or platform, over the heads of a highly fragmented and fractious legislature to which many have been elected with only tiny frac-

tions of the votes cast. No stable party system can be built on such a foundation.

14. Political instability can marginalize and worsen discrimination against women.[14] Women are especially prone to an upsurge of sexual violence, intimidation, and physical abuse in conflict-prone elections. As women are not a homogeneous group, care must be given to questions of race, ethnicity, class, and culture in crafting appropriate responses to the gender dimensions of election conflict. The Convention on the Elimination of all forms of Discrimination against Women (CEDAW) and regional instruments such as the APRM are potential entry points to enhance the position of women in political life and safeguard their ability to campaign and vote.

15. Security is fundamental for candidates to campaign and for citizens to vote. Security institutions help deter violence and enforce the law. In conflict-prone elections, confidence-building and coordinated understandings of expectations, roles, and responsibilities need to be systematically encouraged among the security services, judiciary, political parties, traditional leaders, and civil society organizations. Sound operational procedures and human rights training can help the police serve as impartial guarantors of electoral security.

16. Conflict-prone and transitional societies should not be held to a lower electoral standard than other jurisdictions. Judgments on "good enough" elections run the risk of endorsing flawed and controversial events that do not meet the standards of legitimacy and delay or hinder the building of democratic institutions and a civic culture.

17. In conflict-prone elections, aid donors are an important provider of checks and balances in holding governments accountable. As the pre-conditions for conflict may be latent, donors should be careful not to discard the possibility of election-related disputes and violence even in ostensibly stable societies. Donors need to be better versed in understanding recent political histories. More can be done to situate conflict prevention outside the narrow horizon of an election process and link interventions to longer-term development processes, such as the promotion of social cohesion.

18. Elections held in conflict situations just to "tick the box" in complex, externally brokered peace settlements or to satisfy political

cycles in foreign capitals may be a waste of time or run the risk of setting back public order, citizen security, political legitimacy, and reconstruction and development.
19 International actors face difficult choices between diplomatic engagement, technical support, or economic pressure in flawed, controversial, or violent elections. Aid conditionality, international human rights investigations, and targeted sanctions should not be discounted as approaches to help deter and redress the worst forms of electoral chicanery, including the use of violence.
20 International actors concerned with regional stability or the continuity of security alliances can be vulnerable to endorsing sham elections that reproduce autocratic rule. While responses must always be context dependent, violence before, during, and after elections should always be unambiguously and impartially condemned.

What remains to be discovered?

The case studies and thematic issues discussed in this volume point to a series of knowledge gaps in our understanding of the root causes of and practical solutions to electoral conflict. These gaps could form the basis for longer-term research agendas. For example, there is a relatively robust academic literature on the relationship between electoral systems and electoral performance, including conflict management. Ben Reilly (this volume) and others highlight the value of different types of proportional representation in deeply divided societies. Sudan is one example of what looks to be a modest trend toward the adoption of mixed member proportional voting and other kinds of more "representative" electoral systems. However, less is known about the relative merits of power-sharing arrangements brokered as part of peace agreements versus majoritarian systems in conflict-prone societies. A good case can be made that in fragile states a majoritarian system enables clear and effective decision making for weak governments that are profoundly challenged to deliver basic social services, citizen security, and public order.

Similarly, what are the limits of a technical fix or a programmatic approach to election conflict mitigation? Can strategic interventions throughout an election cycle – to train the security institutions, educate voters, promote dialogue among political parties – tilt the balance away from violence? While civic education is seen by many as a key method of mitigating electoral discord, there is insufficient empirical evidence on the efficacy of mass education. Support for civic and voter education seems to have made a difference in areas where it was tried in the 2007 Nigerian election, but these approaches did not prevent conflict in the 2007 Kenyan election. The elections community could do more to understand citizen perspectives about political participation and personal security, including more studies on public opinion, such as those undertaken by the National Democratic Institute in South Sudan. These approaches support local ownership and active citizen engagement in democratic governance. Why did the private sector do so little in the wake of electoral violence in Kenya? In other settings, can the private sector be more proactive in conflict management and resolution?

Susanne Mueller (this volume) asks whether conflict-mitigation and other well-meaning assistance can save the day in a zero-sum, winner-take-all political culture? Instead, she underscores the powerful covert alliances among criminal gangs, militia, and political entrepreneurs prepared to use violence as a means to hold or win power. Highly inflated MPs' salaries can be a potent incentive for recourse to illegal tactics, including violence. In this sense, violence and other forms of electoral shenanigans do pay. Much more needs to be learned about the incentives and disincentives for politicians and others to use violence as an election strategy. As Staffan Lindberg asks, what is the tipping point, in conflict-prone societies, where the costs of electoral oppression – including the use of violence, intimidation, and fraud – outweigh the costs of toleration, tilting the election playing field in a more democratic direction?[15]

Another gap in our knowledge is how insecurity and electoral violence affects historically marginalized groups, such as women, the internally displaced, and ethnic minorities. How can gender equality be mainstreamed in election preparations? Do reforms that introduce quota systems for women improve voter turnout even in situations of conflict or insecurity? Better understanding the incentive structures of political elites to adopt illegal strategies or to play by the democratic rules of the game is an avenue of research worth supporting. Equally interesting is understanding why some countries with characteristics that often predispose them to violence, such as being multi-ethnic, small, poor, or asset-rich, do not necessarily go down that path. In Africa, why have post-conflict countries such as Mozambique, Namibia, and Sierra Leone managed to hold relatively peaceful elections? And how have Botswana, Ghana, and Senegal avoided widespread electoral violence in contrast to say Kenya, Zimbabwe, and Madagascar?

Finally, a closer look at how socio-economic, cultural, and political fault lines between groups play out in elections may shed additional light on the relationship between horizontal inequalities and conflict. Flawed elections in Côte d'Ivoire and Kenya appear to confirm the pernicious, mutually reinforcing effects of deepening inequalities in the status of contending ethnic groups. In Kenya, reduced Luo representation in the last few years of the Kibaki presidency coupled with "rigged" elections in 2007 threatened to create a situation in which neither political nor socio-economic horizontal inequalities "would be corrected by the ballot." In Côte d'Ivoire, economic downturn, reduced state redistribution, the xenophobia of identity (*Ivoirité*), and political exclusion created the conditions for ethnic exclusion as a way to build electoral support. It seems that as a root cause of violence, both socio-economic and political inequalities need to be high and pulling in the same direction.[16]

CONCLUSION

As we close this final chapter, the crisis in Côte d'Ivoire again makes clear that elections in conflict situations can be a lightning rod for violence and instability. The handling of this political impasse could be a bellwether for future electoral conflict mitigation in Africa. Protest and violence erupted when incumbent President Laurent Gbagbo refused to recognize the international endorsement of Alassane Ouattara as winner of the second round vote. Gbagbo's intransigence has led to a remarkable congruence of regional and international efforts to dislodge him. A range of levers is being used or considered, including mediation by the AU and ECOWAS. These regional organizations have dispatched West African heads of government, former South African leader Thabo Mbeki and current Kenyan Prime Minister Raila Odinga. More muscular action has also been taken or discussed, such as freezing the assets and visas of Gbagbo and his inner circle, a credible ECOWAS threat to use force, and potential appeals to the International Criminal Court to investigate electoral violence. A variety of economic sanctions could also be used to end the impasse and pre-empt a descent into civil war. This could include embargoes and export bans on cocoa and coffee, the neighbouring countries sealing their borders, which could prompt mass protest by small traders who cross the border each day, and coordinated "contract sanctions" to dissuade new investment or credit for Gbagbo by refusing to recognize the "odious debt" inherited by an incoming government.

The best of times, the worst of times. Elections in dangerous places can become national projects of peaceful change or periods fraught with conflict and violence. Elections in these supercharged environments matter because they are about real flesh-and-blood people and about national destinies. With the possible exception of Iraq, the countries examined in this collection show that elections in conflict-prone societies typically produce mixed results that are more often negative than positive, becoming impediments to, rather than modes of, transition to democracy. They can produce unintended consequences that may deepen the rifts of ethnic geography, unleash violence, and accelerate the drift toward or the reproduction of autocratic rule. In settings of conflict, governments, international partners, and citizens themselves may benefit from more gradualism in the building of durable institutions as a prelude for political liberalization. Impatience for democracy where it has been long denied is understandable. But there is no case of a stable liberal democracy being achieved without the slow and steady strengthening of its societal foundations. That includes, but is not limited to, a carefully considered, progressive institutionalization and consolidation of elections as both a necessary means for democratic expression and basis of legitimate state authority. Especially in dangerous places, inflated expectations about short cuts to electoral democracy can themselves be dangerous.

Notes

INTRODUCTION

1 In 2009 separate conferences on this theme were organized by The North-South Institute, the Electoral Institute for the Sustainability of Democracy in Africa, and International IDEA. See also Kristine Höglund and Anna K. Jarstad, *Strategies to Prevent and Manage Electoral Violence: Considerations for Policy*, African Centre for the Constructive Resolution of Disputes (ACCORD), Policy and Practice Brief, no. 1 (Durban, 2010).
2 The book builds on a North-South Institute workshop held in Ottawa on 29-30 October 2009. Speakers at the event included David Gillies, Ben Reilly, Christian Hennemeyer, Linda Maguire, Paul Collier, Momina Yari, Hussein Ramoz, Nipa Banerjee, Khalid Medani, Traci Cook, Christina Hartman, Kemi Ogunsanya, Sara Staino, Abbé Apollinaire Muholongu Malumalu, Vincent Tohbi, Thomas Axworthy, Susanne Mueller, and Koki Muli.
3 This figure, provided by George Perlin at Queen's University, is based on estimates of spending by governments, multilateral organizations, and private foundations. There is currently no authoritative reckoning of total spending on democracy assistance, or on global elections support. For a distinction between democracy promotion and democracy assistance, see Peter Burnell, "From Evaluating Democracy Assistance to Appraising Democracy Promotion," *Political Studies* 56, no. 2 (2008): 414–34.
4 These terms mark the intertwining of security and development in the post-9/11 world. They mark situations where governments will not or cannot assure the territorial integrity of the state, ensure public order, and provide key citizen services. For a flavour of the prescriptive side of this agenda, see Seth Kaplan, *Fixing Fragile States: A New Paradigm for Development* (Santa

Barbara, Calif.: Praeger, 2008); Ashraf Ghani and Clare Lockhart, *Fixing Failed States* (Oxford: Oxford University Press, 2007); James Dobbins, Seth G. Jones, Keith Crane, and Beth Cole DeGrasse, *The Beginners Guide to Nation Building* (Santa Monica, Calif.: RAND Corporation, 2007).
5 Larry Diamond, "Building Democracy in Fragile and Conflict-Affected Countries: Some Common Challenges and Policy Directions" (keynote address at the symposium Democracy Dialogue 2009: Democracy in Fragile and Conflict-Affected Situations, Department of Foreign Affairs and International Trade, Ottawa, November 2009).
6 Peter Harris and Ben Reilly, eds., *Democracy and Deep-Rooted Conflict: Options for Negotiators* (Stockholm: International Institute for Democracy and Electoral Assistance, 1998); Stephen Baranyi, ed., *The Paradoxes of Peacebuilding Post 9/11* (Vancouver: University of British Columbia Press, 2008), 18.
7 Roland Paris, *At War's End: Building Peace after Conflict* (Cambridge: Cambridge University Press, 2004).
8 Michael Bratton and Eldred Masunungure, "Zimbabwe's Long Agony," *Journal of Democracy* 19, no. 4 (2008): 41–55.
9 Norma Kriger, "ZANU (PF) Strategies in General Elections, 1980–2000: Discourse and Coercion," *African Affairs* 104, no. 414 (2005): 1–34.
10 Bratton and Masunungure, "Zimbabwe's Long Agony," 51.
11 Larry Diamond and Marc F. Plattner, eds., *Democratization in Africa: Progress and Retreat*, 2nd ed. (Baltimore, Md.: Johns Hopkins University Press, 2010).
12 Notably the UNDP's 2009 guide on *Elections and Conflict Prevention*, available online at http://www.undp.org/governance/focus_electoral_publications.shtml. See also Höglund and Jarstad, *Electoral Violence*.
13 Krishna Kumar, ed., *Postconflict Elections, Democratization and International Assistance* (Boulder, Colo.: Lynne Rienner, 1998); Ben Reilly and Andrew Reynolds, *Electoral Systems and Conflict in Divided Societies* (Washington, DC: National Academies Press, 1999); Terrence Lyons, *Demilitarizing Politics: Elections on the Uncertain Road to Peace* (Boulder, Colo.: Lynne Rienner, 2005).
14 Jeroen De Zeeuw and Krishna Kumar, eds., *Promoting Democracy in Postconflict Societies* (Boulder, Colo.: Lynne Rienner, 2006).
15 These authors focus on inter- not intra-state wars. See Edward D. Mansfield and Jack Snyder, "Democratization and War," *Foreign Affairs* 74, no. 3 (1995): 79-97. See also Mansfield and Snyder, *Electing to Fight: Why Emerging Democracies Go to War* (Cambridge, Mass.: MIT Press, 2005).
16 Mansfield and Snyder, "Democratization and War," 79.
17 Ibid., 97.

18 Paul Collier, *Wars, Guns, and Votes* (New York: Harper Collins, 2009), 81.
19 Ibid., 27.
20 Collier's findings are consistent with other studies indicating that mixed democratic/authoritarian regimes with weak state institutions are most prone to civil wars. For example, the 1993 elections in Burundi were judged internationally as free and fair, but intensified Hutu/Tutsi ethnic division eventually led to 200,000 deaths. See also James Fearon and David Laitin, "Ethnicity, Insurgency, and Civil War," *American Political Science Review* 97, no. 1 (2003): 75–90.
21 Staffan I. Lindberg, *Democratization by Elections: A New Mode of Transition* (Baltimore, Md.: Johns Hopkins University Press, 2009).
22 Ibid., 341.
23 Paris, *At War's End*, 235.
24 Terrence Lyons, "The Role of Postsettlement Elections," in *Ending Civil Wars: The Implementation of Peace Agreements*, ed. Stephen John Stedman, Donald S. Rothchild, and Elizabeth M. Cousens (Boulder, Colo.: Lynne Rienner, 2002), 215–35.
25 George Perlin and David Sully, "Literature Review of Applied Research on Democratic Development" (literature review commissioned by the International Development Research Centre, Ottawa, 2008), 9, http://idl-bnc.idrc.ca/dspace/bitstream/10625/36831/1/127774.pdf. See also National Research Council, Committee on Evaluation of USAID Democracy Assistance Programs, *Improving Democracy Assistance: Building Knowledge Through Evaluations and Research* (Washington, DC: National Academies Press, 2008); Andrew T. Green and Richard D. Kohl, "Challenges of Evaluating Democracy Assistance: Perspectives from the Donor Side," *Democratization* 14, no. 1 (2007): 151–65.
26 International IDEA has developed an assessment framework. See David Beetham et al., *Assessing the Quality of Democracy: A Practical Guide* (Stockholm: International Institute for Democracy and Electoral Assistance, 2005).
27 Ben Reilly, "Post-War Elections: Uncertain Turning Points of Transition," in *From War to Democracy: Dilemmas of Peacebuilding*, ed. Anna K. Jarstad and Timothy D. Sisk (Cambridge: Cambridge University Press, 2008), 157–81.
28 Of which UN projections anticipated the government of Sudan would provide about US$139.5 million. United Nations Development Programme (UNDP) Sudan, Support to Elections and Democratic Processes project, *Project Document* (Khartoum: UNDP Sudan, undated), 1, http://www.sd.undp.org/doc/prodocs/dg16%20elections_PD.pdf.
29 An approach to election support that goes beyond a focus on the election

moment to consider the full range of election laws, regulations, administration, campaigning, civic and voter education, dispute resolution, and post-election period as opportunities to help enhance domestic capacity in all facets of election management.

CHAPTER ONE

1 Krishna Kumar, "Postconflict Elections and International Assistance" in *Postconflict Elections, Democratization and International Assistance,* ed. Krishna Kumar (Boulder, Colo.: Lynne Rienner, 1998), 7.
2 See Jørgen Elklit and Palle Svensson, "What Makes Elections Free and Fair?" *Journal of Democracy* 8, no. 3 (1997): 32–46.
3 Juan J. Linz and Alfred Stepan, *Problems of Democratic Transition and Consolidation: Southern Europe, South America, and Post-Communist Europe* (Baltimore, Md.: Johns Hopkins University Press, 1996), 98–107.
4 Larry Diamond, *Developing Democracy: Toward Consolidation* (Baltimore, Md.: Johns Hopkins University Press, 1999), 158.
5 See Staffan I. Lindberg, ed., *Democratization by Elections: A New Mode of Transition* (Baltimore, Md.: Johns Hopkins University Press, 2009).
6 See Andrew Reynolds, Ben Reilly, and Andrew Ellis, *Electoral System Design: The New International IDEA Handbook* (Stockholm: International Institute for Democracy and Electoral Assistance, 2005).
7 I have discussed this tendency elsewhere. See Ben Reilly, "Post-War Elections: Uncertain Turning Points of Transition?" in *From War to Democracy: Dilemmas of Peacebuilding,* ed. Anna K. Jarstad and Timothy D. Sisk (Cambridge: Cambridge University Press, 2008), 157–81, and idem, "Elections in Post-Conflict Societies" in *The UN Role in Promoting Democracy: Between Ideals and Reality,* ed. Edward Newman and Roland Rich (Tokyo: United Nations University Press, 2004), 113–34.
8 Terrence Lyons, "Peace and Elections in Liberia," in Kumar, *Postconflict Elections,* 182.
9 Joel D. Barkan, "Elections in Agrarian Societies," *Journal of Democracy* 6, no.4 (1995): 106–16.
10 Rafael López-Pintor, *Electoral Management Bodies as Institutions of Governance* (New York: Bureau for Development Policy, United Nations Development Programme, 2000).
11 Ibid., 53.
12 Sue Nelson, "Haitian Elections and the Aftermath," in Kumar, *Postconflict Elections,* 76.

13 See Ben Reilly and Per Nordlund, *Political Parties in Conflict-Prone Societies: Regulation, Engineering, and Democratic Development* (Tokyo: United Nations University Press, 2008).

CHAPTER TWO

1 Kabul Conference communiqué, Kabul International Conference on Afghanistan, 20 July 2010, 9, http://www.mfa.gov.af/FINAL%20Kabul%20Conference%20%20%20Communique.pdf.
2 Sue Pleming, "Biden Says No Plans to Nation-build in Afghanistan," Reuters, 29 July 2010, http://www.reuters.com/article/2010/07/29/us-afghanistan-usa-idUSTRE66S41P20100729.

CHAPTER THREE

1 Adeed Dawisha, *Iraq: A Political History from Independence to Occupation* (Princeton, NJ: Princeton University Press, 2009), 173.
2 Patrick Cockburn, *Muqtada al-Sadr and the Battle for the Future of Iraq* (New York: Scribner, 2008), 119.
3 Janet Wallach, *Desert Queen* (New York: Anchor Books, 2005).
4 Judith S. Yaphe, "The View from Basra: Southern Iraq's Reaction to War and Occupation, 1915–1925," in *The Creation of Iraq: 1914–1921*, ed. Reeva S. Simon and Eleanor Harvey Tejirian (New York: Columbia University Press, 2003), 19–35.
5 Adeed Dawisha, "Democratic Attitudes and Practices in Iraq, 1921–1958," *The Middle East Journal* 59, no. 1 (2005): 11–30.
6 Ibid.
7 The al-Hadba coalition was comprised of the United Mosul Coalition, Iraqi Centrist Coalition, Iraqi Kurdistan Justice and Freedom Party, Democratic Shabak Gathering, Socialist Arab Stream Movement, Tal Afar People's Coalition, Pan-Arab and National Forces Coalition in Ninawa, Movement of Justice and Reform in Iraq Political Council of National Forces, and many independents. See Mariam Aziz, "Ninawa's New Political Competitor," *Niqash*, 30 July 2009, http://www.niqash.org/content.php?contentTypeID=75&id=2234&lang=0.
8 Rajiv Chandrasekaran, *Imperial Life in the Emerald City: Inside Iraq's Green Zone* (New York: Knopf, 2006), 297.
9 The author worked for the UN Transitional Authority in Cambodia (UNTAC) as district electoral supervisor in 1993, Preah Vihear Province.

10 Larry Diamond, *Squandered Victory: The American Occupation and the Bungled Effort to Bring Democracy to Iraq* (New York: Times Books, 2005), 323.
11 A subsequent terrorist attack at the same Samarra mosque in June 2007 destroyed two remaining minarets but failed to re-ignite Iraqi violence.
12 The IHEC website (www.ihec-iq.com) posts the names of thirty-five IECI election officials killed during 2005.
13 The author was Regional Coordinator of the USAID-funded IFES Election Violence, Education and Resolution (EVER) project from October 2004 to December 2005, Erbil.
14 During 2004, twenty-three Iraqi journalists were killed, mostly by insurgents, up from thirteen in 2003, thus making Iraq the most dangerous place for journalists, according to the Committee to Protect Journalists.
15 Diamond, *Squandered Victory*, 321.
16 Mohammed M. Hafez, *Suicide Bombers in Iraq: The Strategy and Ideology of Martyrdom* (Washington: United States Institute of Peace Press, 2007), cited in Frederic Wehrey, Dalia Dassa Kaye, Jessica Watkins, Jeffery Martini, and Robert A. Guffey, *The Iraq Effect: The Middle East After the Iraq War* (Santa Monica, Calif.: RAND Corporation, 2010), 130.
17 Sydney J. Freedberg Jr, "Iraqi Rebels: The New Iraqi Way of War," *National Journal*, 8 June 2007, cited in Wehrey et al., *Iraq Effect*, 130; Rex Brynen, "The Iraq War and (non)Democratization in the Arab World," in *From Desolation to Reconstruction: Iraq's Troubled Journey*, ed. Mokhtar Lamani and Bessma Momani (Waterloo, Ont.: Wilfrid Laurier University Press, 2010), 183.
18 Chandrasekaran, *Inside Iraq's Green Zone*, 264.
19 More than 100 expats working for the Research Triangle Institute (RTI) Local Governance Project, including the author, were ordered to the safety of Kuwait during the first Sadrist assault.
20 Badr units had fought with Iranian forces against Saddam's mostly Shia army in the 1980s.
21 Allawi, *Occupation of Iraq*, 441.
22 David Kilcullen, "Anatomy of a Tribal Revolt," *Small Wars Journal*, 29 August 2007, http://smallwarsjournal.com/blog/2007/08/anatomy-of-a-tribal-revolt/ (accessed 23 May 2009).
23 Faleh A. Jabar, "The Dilemma of Political Uncertainties," in *What Can Europe Do in Iraq? Recommendations for a New US-European Collaboration*, Democracy, vol. 11 (Berlin: Heinrich Böll Stiftung, 2009), 17.
24 Thomas E. Ricks, *The Gamble: General David Petraeus and the American Military Adventure in Iraq, 2006-2008* (New York: Penguin, 2009), 271.

25 Ellen Knickmeyer, "Envoy Faults Militias' Interference in Iraq Vote," *Washington Post*, 17 December 2005.
26 Several Peshmerga units have participated in US-coordinated Iraqi army operations since 2004.
27 International Crisis Group, *Iraq and the Kurds: Trouble Along the Trigger Line*, Middle East Report №88, 8 July 2009, 22.
28 Loretta Napoleoni, *Insurgent Iraq: Al Zarqawi and the New Generation* (London: Constable, 2005), 157, cited in Cockburn, *Muqtada al-Sadr*, 136.
29 Stephen Farrell, "50 Die in Fight Between Shiite Groups in Karbala," *New York Times*, 29 August 2007.
30 Ricks, *The Gamble*, 284.
31 Some 80 per cent of the officer corps and 50 per cent of rank and file were veterans of Saddam's military. See Stephen Biddle, Michael E. O'Hanlon, and Kenneth M. Pollack, "How to Leave a Stable Iraq: Building on Progress," *Foreign Affairs* 87, no. 5 (2008): 1–8.
32 Unlike Saddam's privileged and largely Sunni Arab Republican Guard, the Iraqi Army, whose officer corps was mixed and nationalist, enjoyed significant popular support. See Joost Hiltermann, video documentary interview, *No End in Sight*, International Crisis Group, 2007.
33 The author lost two local staff to targeted insurgent killings in Mosul in 2004 while they worked for a democracy-advocacy campaign funded by USAID and coordinated by Research Triangle Institute (RTI). In the April 2004 Sadrist assault on Najaf, two local RTI staff were kidnapped and held briefly before being released.
34 Chandrasekaran, *Inside Iraq's Green Zone*, 190.
35 United Nations, Security Council, *The Political Transition in Iraq: Report of the Fact-Finding Mission*, annex to the letter dated 23 February 2004 from the Secretary-General to the President of the Security Council, S/2004/140, http://daccess-ods.un.org/access.nsf/Get?OpenAgent&DS=S/2004/140&Lang=E (accessed 6 February 2009).
36 IFES (www.ifes.org) managed two projects in Iraq, one based in Baghdad providing support to Iraq's election commission, the other, called the Election Violence, Education and Resolution (EVER) project, based in three regions monitoring political violence, training Iraqi election observers, and developing a national observation network of some ninety local civic groups.
37 Faleh A. Jabar, "Ethnic and Communal Identities in the Iraqi First Post-Conflict General Elections: The Difficult Search for Centrism," in *La problé-*

matique de la démocratie consensuelle dans les sociétés multiculturelles : Liban et Irak (Beirut: Lebanese Center for Political Studies, 2007), 157.
38 International Crisis Group, *Iraq's Provincial Elections: The Stakes*, Middle East Report №82, 27 January 2009, 15.
39 Ibid., 4.
40 Ibid., 6.
41 In Arabic, *ein* means eye. The network did not survive to observe 2009 polls. In 2010, NDI funded and organized the Sun Network, which conducted a parallel vote tabulation resulting in a compatible showing of actual voter behaviour in 95 per cent of polling stations observed, proving a statistical tie between the top two coalitions. See Leslie Campbell, "Iraq's Election Was Free and Fair," *Foreign Policy*, 30 March 2010.
42 Stephen Farrell, "Election: Preliminary Results," Baghdad Bureau Blog, *New York Times*, 5 February 2009, http://baghdadbureau.blogs.nytimes.com/2009/02/05/election-preliminary-results/ (accessed 10 February 2009).
43 Amnesty International, *Open Letter to Iraq's Political Leaders*, 22 February 2010.
44 United Nations Assistance Mission for Iraq, "Provincial Elections Smoothly Conducted and Well Organized," news release, 31 January 2009, http://www.uniraq.org/newsroom/getarticle.asp?ArticleID=967 (accessed 11 February 2009).
45 US Director of National Intelligence, *Iraq – Provincial Elections Guide 2009* (Washington, DC: DNI Open Source Center, 2009), http://www.fas.org/irp/dni/osc/iraq-elections.pdf (accessed 14 March 2009).
46 United Nations Assistance Mission for Iraq, Public Information Office, "The Independent High Electoral Commission of Iraq Announced the Preliminary Official Results of the Presidential and Parliamentary Elections in the Kurdistan Region of Iraq on 29 July 2009," *UNAMI Focus*, no. 35 (July 2009): 10–12.
47 IHEC statistics were shared with the author by Faleh A. Jabar, Director, Iraqi Institute for Strategic Studies, during a visit to his Beirut office, 23 May 2009. The IHEC website excluded such details.
48 Jonathan Finer, "For Kurds, A Surge of Violence in Campaign," *Washington Post*, 14 December 2005, http://www.washingtonpost.com/wp-dyn/content/article/2005/12/13/AR2005121302119.html (accessed 12 January 2006).
49 *Aswat al-Iraq*, "Kurdistan Islamic Union HQ Attacked in Arbil," 27 July 2009.
50 *Aswat al-Iraq*, "450 Electoral Violations Reported During Kurdish Polls – IHEC," 29 July 2009.

51 United Nations Assistance Mission for Iraq, "Elections in the Kurdistan Region"; Khaled Saleh, "Ramifications for the Kurdistan Region and for Iraq," *Middle East Round Table* 7 (August 2009), http://www.bitterlemons-international.org/previous.php?opt=1&id=284 (accessed 6 August 2009).

52 Tim Cocks, "How Will Kurdistan Poll Results Affect Iraq?" *Reuters*, 29 July 2009, http://www.reuters.com/article/idUSTRE56S4CQ20090729.

53 Timothy Williams and Zaid Thaker, "Killers Stalk Politicians as Iraq Seeks Government," *New York Times*, 30 June 2010.

54 During his 1970s self-exile to London, Allawi, an ex-Baathist, almost fell victim to an axe-wielding assassin. See Oliver August, "Threats to Likely Iraqi PM Iyad Allawi," *The Australian*, 22 June 2010.

55 Steven Lee Myers, "Iraq Suicide Bomber Strikes in Anbar," *New York Times*, 18 February 2010.

56 Institute for War and Peace Reporting, "Kurdish Politicians Raise Civil War Fears," *Report News*, 28 January 2010, http://iwpr.net/report-news/kurdish-politicians-raise-civil-war-fears.

57 United Nations Assistance Mission for Iraq, *UNAMI electoral update – 10 March 2010*, http://www.uniraq.org/documents/ElectoralMaterial/UNAMI%20Electorla%20update%2010%20March%202010%20EN.pdf.

58 Sardar Muhammad, "Tensions rising between PUK and Change Movement," *Niqash*, 8 January 2010, http://www.niqash.org/content.php?contentTypeID=75&id=2581&lang=0 (accessed October 6, 2010).

59 United Nations, *Declaration of Principles for International Election Observation and Code of Conduct for International Election Observers* (New York, 2005), article 12 i, http://www.ndi.org/files/1923_declaration_102705_0.pdf

60 In January 2005, the Kurds' Kirkuk Brotherhood list included some token Arabs, Turkmen, and Christians. Comparatively, in May 2003, US Army officers formed a Kirkuk council comprising six Kurds, six Arabs, six Turkmen, six Christians, and six independents, mostly Kurds. The CPA's pre-departure council refreshing exercise changed the formulation to a forty-member council of thirteen Kurds, twelve Arabs, eight Turkmen, and seven Christians. See Joost Hiltermann, "Spoils of Babylon," *The National Interest*, 16 December 2009, 3, http://nationalinterest.org/articles.

61 Jim Muir, BBC correspondent, 12 February 2009.

62 Leila Fadel, "Mosul Struggles with Ethnic Divides, Insurgency," *Washington Post*, 24 July 2010.

63 Jane Arraf, "Iraq Border Concerns Spur Effort to Integrate Kurdish and Iraqi Army Forces," *Christian Science Monitor*, 23 August 2010.

64 United Nations Assistance Mission for Iraq, "Encouraging Second Round of

Talks between Hadba and Ninawa Fraternity List," news release, 12 May 2010.

65 Denise Natali, "Are the Kurds Still Kingmakers in Iraq?" *Arab Reform Bulletin*, 26 May 2010.

66 Arend Lijphart, "Constitutional Design for Divided Societies," *Journal of Democracy* 15 (April 2004): 100.

67 Pippa Norris, *Driving Democracy: Do Power-Sharing Institutions Work?* (Cambridge: Cambridge University Press, 2008), 17.

68 As a conflict mitigating measure to the peace process in DR Congo in 2002, four new positions of vice-president were created. In 1995, the international community imposed a tripartite rotating ethnically-based presidency for Bosnia. The Iraqi-drafted 2005 Constitution does not specify the ethnic or sectarian identity of the Presidency Council, or the offices of prime minister and parliamentary speaker, unlike in Lebanon's antiquated 1943 straightjacket political framework. See Marie-Joëlle Zahar, "The Dichotomy of International Mediation and Leader Intransigence: The Case of Bosnia and Herzegovina," in *Power Sharing: New Challenges for Divided Societies*, ed. Ian O'Flynn and David Russell (London: Pluto Press, 2005), 123–37.

69 As early as the October 1992 conference of anti-Saddam forces in Iraqi Kurdistan, an elected tripartite leadership council of Shia-Arab, Sunni-Arab and Kurd had been established. See Francke, "The Opposition," 173.

70 Reidar Visser, "Three's a Crowd," *The National*, 18 February 2010.

71 In February of 2008, three key bills on budget, amnesty and provincial powers were passed by parliament in typical US omnibus style in order to assure the government's survival and inter-communal accommodations. See Jason Gluck, "From Gridlock to Compromise: How Three Laws Could Begin to Transform Iraqi Politics," Peace Brief, March 2008, *United States Institute of Peace*, http://www.usip.org/publications/gridlock-compromise-how-three-laws-could-begin-transform-iraqi-politics.

72 Elected on the Allawi ticket in December 2005 and a former Industry Minister under Prime Minister Jaafari, Nujaifi engineered the Sunni-Arab success of the anti-KDP al-Hadba coalition, which won nineteen of thirty-seven provincial seats in January 2009.

73 Including three deputy prime ministers, the cabinet still excludes the three ministers of defense, interior and national security, also delayed by Maliki in 2006. The Council of Ministers includes nineteen members of Maliki's alliance, including eight Sadrists, four Kurds including a Goran minister and the Foreign Ministry, and ten al-Iraqiya seats including Finance to a Sunni Arab. The COR also acquitted three elected Sunni candidates that the

Notes to pages 50–7

De-Baathification Commission had banned, allowing Mutlaq to be named a deputy prime-minister.
74 M. Steven Fish, "Stronger Legislatures, Stronger Democracies," *Journal of Democracy* 17, no. 1 (2006): 17.
75 Iraqi mediation efforts have under-utilised the potential of Articles 48 and 65 calling for the formation of a Federation Council. The May 2007 report of the UNAMI-assisted Constitutional Reform Commission had called for four senators per province plus four extras for Baghdad.
76 Seymour Martin Lipset, "The Social Requisites of Democracy Revisited," *American Sociological Review* 59, no. 1 (1994): 10.

CHAPTER FOUR

1 Richard Soudriette, cited in Ernest Simone, ed., *Foreign Policy of the United States*, 2 vol. (Huntington, NY: Nova Science Publishers, 2000[–2002]), 1:104.
2 Security Council Report, "The Resurgence of Coups d'État in Africa," *Update Report*, no. 3, 15 April 2009, 1.
3 George H.W. Bush, "Remarks Following Discussions with President Mobutu Sese Seko of Zaire," 29 June 2009, *The American Presidency Project*, John Wooley and Gerhard Peters, http://www.presidency.ucsb.edu/ws/index.php?pid=17223.
4 African Union, "The Chairperson of the Commission Condemns the Seizure of Power by Force," news release, Addis Ababa, 19 February 2010.
5 Economic Community of West African States (ECOWAS), "ECOWAS Regrets Interruption of Dialogue and Condemns Coup Attempt in Niger," news release, no. 022/2010, Abuja, 18 February 2010.
6 Margaret Thatcher, press conference at Vancouver Commonwealth Summit, 17 October 1987.
7 Wolfgang Saxon, "Samuel Doe: 10-Year Reign in the Shadow of Brutality," *New York Times*, 11 September 1990.
8 Etannibi Eo Alemika, "Quality of Elections, Satisfaction with Democracy and Political Trust in Africa" (working paper 84, Afrobarometer, Michigan State University, East Lansing, 2007), 1, http://next.pls.msu.edu/index.php?option=com_docman&Itemid=39 .
9 Wole Soyinka, interview by Harry Kreisler, *Conversations with History*, University of California, Berkeley, 16 April 1988, http://conversations.berkeley.edu/content/wole-soyinka
10 Gordon L. Streeb, *Observing the 1997 Special Elections Process in Liberia*, preface and acknowledgments (Atlanta: Carter Center, 1997), 9.

11 European Union Election Observation Mission to Liberia, *Peaceful and Well Administered Presidential Run-off Election Advances the Process of Returning Liberia to a Normal Functioning State,* Statement of preliminary findings and conclusions (Monrovia, 10 November 2005), 1.
12 Afrobarometer, "Popular Attitudes toward Democracy in Liberia: A Summary of Afrobarometer Indicators, 2008," 20 October 2009, http://next.pls.msu.edu/index.php?option=com_content&view=category&layout=blog&id=16&Itemid=43.
13 See https://www.cia.gov/library/publications/the-world-factbook/geos/ni.html.
14 European Parliament, European Parliament resolution on the recent elections in Nigeria, motion for a resolution, 2004-2009 Session document, B6-0201/2007, 15 May 2007, 4.
15 US Department of State, "Examining the US-Nigeria Relationship in a Time of Transition," Johnnie Carson, Assistant Secretary, Bureau of African Affairs, Opening Statement: Testimony before the Senate Committee on Foreign Relations Subcommittee on African Affairs, Washington, DC, 23 February 2010.
16 Steve Freeman, "How to Steal an Election without Breaking a Sweat," *Foreign Policy,* 28 January 2008, http://www.foreignpolicy.com.
17 The Corruption Perceptions Index is available at http://www.transparency.org/policy_research/surveys_indices/cpi.
18 Larry Diamond, "The Rule of Law versus the Big Man," *Journal of Democracy* 19 (April 2008): 138–49.
19 Thomas Carothers, Jean Bethke Elshtain, Larry Diamond, Anwar Ibrahim, and Zainab Hawa Bangura, "A Quarter Century of Promoting Democracy," *Journal of Democracy* 18, no. 4 (2007): 112–26.
20 European Union Election Observation Mission, *Ethiopia Legislative Elections 2005: Final Report,* Brussels, 10 June 2005, 1.
21 International Center for Not-for-Profit Law, "Introductory Overview," in "Sub-Saharan Africa Country Reports," special section, *International Journal of Not-for-Profit Law* 12, no. 2 (2010): 6, 7.
22 Human Rights Watch, *An Analysis of Ethiopia's Draft Anti-Terrorism Law* (New York: Human Rights Watch, 2009), 1.
23 European Union Election Observation Mission, *Ethiopia 2010: House of Peoples' Representatives and State Council Elections,* Preliminary Statement, Adis Ababa, 25 May 2010, 1.
24 "Coup Anniversary – 20 Years of Islamist Rule," *Africa Confidential* 50, no. 13 (2009).

25 Carter Center, Common Market of Eastern and Southern Africa, Communauté économique des États de l'Afrique centrale, Electoral Institute of Southern Africa, Mission d'observation électorale de l'Union européenne, Organisation Internationale de la Francophonie, Southern African Development Community – Parliamentary Forum, and African Union, joint statement, Kinshasa, 2 November 2006.
26 Herbert F. Weiss, "Voting for Change in the DRC," *Journal of Democracy* 18, no. 2 (2007): 138-51.
27 See Transparency International, CPI 2009 Table, *Corruption Perceptions Index 2009*, http://www.transparency.org/policy_research/surveys _indices/cpi/2009/cpi_2009_table.
28 Freedom House, *Freedom in the World 2010: The Annual Survey of Political Rights and Civil Liberties*, Freedom in the World (Lanham, Md.: Rowman & Littlefield and Freedom House, 2010).

CHAPTER FIVE

1 Chaim D. Kaufman, "When All Else Fails: Ethnic Population Transfers and Partitions in the Twentieth Century," *International Security* 23, no. 2 (1998): 120-56.
2 Michael C. Horowitz, Alex Weisiger, and Carter Johnson, "The Limits to Partition," *International Security* 33, no. 4 (2009): 203-10.
3 Nicholas Sambanis, "Partition as a Solution to Ethnic War: An Empirical Critique of the Theoretical Literature," *World Politics*, 52 (2000), 437-83.
4 Carter Johnson, "Partitioning to Peace: Sovereignty, Demography and Ethnic Civil Wars," *International Security* 32, no. 4 (2008): 140-70.
5 Macartan Humphreys, "Natural Resources, Conflict, and Resolution: Uncovering the Mechanisms," *Journal of Conflict Resolution* 49, no. 4 (2005): 508-37; Paul Collier and Anke Hoeffler, "Greed and Grievance in Civil War," *Oxford Economic Papers* 56, no. 4 (2004): 563-95.
6 J. John Mearsheimer, "Shrink Bosnia to Save It," *New York Times*, 31 March 1993; Mary Kaldor, "Balkan Carve-Up," *New Statesman and Society* 9, no. 397 (1996): 24-5.
7 Jaroslow Tir, "Keeping the Peace after Secession: Territorial Conflicts between Rump and Secessionist States," *Journal of Conflict Resolution* 49, no. 5 (2005): 713-41.
8 Saud Choudhry, "The Enduring Significance of Bangladesh's War of Independence: An Analysis of Economic Costs and Consequences," *Journal of Developing Areas* 36, no. 1 (2002): 41-55.

9 Sambanis, "Partition as a Solution to Ethnic War."
10 Tir, "Keeping the Peace after Secession."
11 Johnson, "Partitioning to Peace."
12 Francis M. Deng, "Sudan: A Nation in Turbulent Search for Itself," *Annals of the American Academy of Political and Social Science* 603, no. 1 (2006): 155–162.
13 Deng, "Sudan," 159.
14 Ibid.
15 Collier and Hoeffler, "Greed and Grievance in Civil Wars."
16 Luke A. Patey, "State Rules: Oil Companies and Armed Conflict in Sudan," *Third World Quarterly* 28, no. 5 (2007): 5.
17 It is also important to note that Khartoum was only able to secure the oil-rich areas by exploiting the divisions within the SPLA. Specifically, the Bashir regime forged a tactical alliance with the Nuer breakaway faction of the SPLA. John Harker, "Human Security in Sudan: The Report of a Canadian Assessment Mission" (Ottawa, 2000): 11, 48–9; quoted in Douglas H. Johnson, *The Root Causes of Sudan's Civil Wars* (Bloomington: Indiana University Press, 2003), 163.
18 Paul Collier, *Wars, Guns, and Votes: Democracy in Dangerous* Places (New York: Harper Collins, 2009), 19.
19 Justin Willis, Atta el-Battahani, and Peter Woodward, "Elections in Sudan: Learning from Experience," *Rift Valley Institute, Report Commissioned by the UK Department of International Development* (2009): 1–71.
20 See "Bayyan min far' al-tadammun al-watani al-dimuqrati al-sudani bi Washington" (Declaration from the Branch of the National Democratic Alliance in Washington), pamphlet distributed by the Sudanese National Democratic Alliance (NDA).
21 Ibid.
22 It is worth noting that President Bashir insisted to this author that he considered his assumption to power a revolution (*thawra*) and not a coup (*inqilab*). Omar al-Bashir, interview by the author, Khartoum, November 1989.
23 Interview with former Sudanese Minister of the Interior, Mubarak al-Fadl, *Al-Hayat*, 2–3 September 1989.
24 M. Rafiqul Islam, "Secessionist Self-Determination: Some Lessons from Katanga, Biafra and Bangladesh," *Journal of Peace Research* 22, no. 3 (1985): 211-21.
25 Pablo Idahosa, "Ethics and Development in Conflict (Zones): The Case of Talisman Oil," *Journal of Business Ethics* 39, no. 3 (2002): 227–46.

26 Out of fifteen oil companies in Sudan, the three largest are the China National Petroleum Cooperation, Malaysia's Petronas, and India's ONGC Videsh. Together they own 95 per cent of the Greater Nile Petroleum Company (which accounts for 88 per cent of the total oil production in the country), the remaining 5 per cent being owned by Sudapet, the Sudanese national oil company. Damien Helly, ed., *Post-2011 Scenarios in Sudan: What Role for the EU?* ISS Report No. 6 (Paris: European Institute for Security Studies, 2009), 44.

27 In 2004, China's Deputy Foreign Minister Zhou Wenzhong explained China's Sudan policy succinctly: "Business is business. We try to separate politics from business." Quoted in David Zweg and Bi Jianhai, "China's Global Hunt for Energy," *Foreign Affairs* 84, no. 5 (2005): 32.

28 Donald Rothchild, "Ethnic Insecurity, Peace Agreements, and State Building," in *State, Conflict, and Democracy in Africa*, ed. Richard Joseph (Boulder, Colo.: Lynne Rienner, 1999): 328.

29 Ibid.

30 The existing power-sharing arrangements to be enforced until July 2011 give the south a large measure of autonomy, with its own legislative and judicial branches, while also participating on "equitable" bases in the Government of National Unity (GNU), with the president of the South holding the office of First Vice-President of the Republic.

31 Ngor Arol Garang, "SPLM Slams Calls for War by NCP official," *Sudan Tribune*, 4 October 2010.

32 "Sudanese President Pledges to Protect Southerners Living in the North," *Sudan Tribune*, 4 October 2010, 1.

33 According to the CPA, southerners born after independence (1956) can vote only in the referendum, but those born before have the right to register and vote in the South.

34 There is little indication that the non-Dinka and non-Nilotic tribes of equatorial southern Sudan will be integrated into the political and economic system monopolized by the SPLA following secession. The SPLA has driven thousands of Equatorians from their homes and has generally refused to return their property to them. See Adam Branch and Zachariah Cherian Mampilly, "Winning the War, but Losing the Peace? The Dilemma of SPLM/A Civil Administration and the Tasks Ahead," *Journal of Modern African Studies* 43, no. 1 (2004): 1–20. See also Cherry Leonardi, "Liberation or Capture: Youth in between 'Hakuma,' and 'Home' during Civil War and Its Aftermath in Southern Sudan," *African Affairs* 106, no. 424 (2007): 391–412.

35 John Young, "Eastern Sudan: Caught in a Web of External Interests," *Review of African Political Economy* 33, no. 109 (2006): 594-601.
36 Yasir Arman's withdrawal from the elections is the primary reason that most other opposition parties boycotted the vote. The reason for Arman's withdrawal resulted from the fact that polls were showing him potentially garnering enough votes to force a run-off election against Bashir. In response, the NCP applied pressure on the SPLM to withdraw Arman's candidacy under the threat of delaying the referendum. Yasir Arman, interview by the author, Khartoum, July 2010.
37 Ron E. Hasner, "The Path to Intractability: Time and Entrenchment of Territorial Disputes," *International Security* 31, no. 3 (2006/07): 107–38.
38 Douglas H. Johnson, "Why Abyei Matters: The Breaking Point of Sudan's Comprehensive Peace Agreement?" *African Affairs* 107, no. 426 (2008): 1–19.
39 "Clinton Says Dealing with Khartoum Is 'Difficult,' Status of Abyei Talks Unclear," *Reuters*, 6 October 2010.
40 Paul Collier, *The Bottom Billion: Why the Poorest Countries Are Failing and What Can Be Done about It* (Oxford: Oxford University Press, 2007).
41 International Monetary Fund, Middle East and Central Asia Department, *Sudan: Staff-Monitored Program for 2009–10*, IMF Country Report No. 09/218, Washington, DC, July 2009.

CHAPTER SIX

1 Gérard Prunier, *Africa's World War: Congo, the Rwandan Genocide and the Making of a Continental Catastrophe* (Oxford: Oxford University Press, 2009).
2 "UN Official Calls DR Congo 'Rape Capital of the World,' " BBC News, 28 April 2010, http://news.bbc.co.uk/2/hi/africa/8650112.stm (accessed 30 August 2010).
3 International Rescue Committee, *Mortality in the Democratic Republic of Congo: An Ongoing Crisis* (New York: International Rescue Committee, 2007), http://www.theirc.org/sites/default/files/resource-file/2006-7_congoMortalitySurvey.pdf (accessed 30 August 2010).
4 World Bank, World Development Indicators, available at http://data.worldbank.org/indicator; United Nations Development Programme, Human Development Reports, 2009 statistics available at http://hdr.undp.org/en/statistics/.
5 Instances of election and post-election violence are detailed later in the chapter; large-scale military hostilities have occurred in North Kivu in 2007, 2008, 2009 and 2010.

6 United Nations Security Council (SC), final report of the Group of Experts on the Democratic Republic of Congo, S/2010/596, 2010.
7 Namely, the Independent Electoral Commission (Commission Électorale Indépendante, CEI), the Higher Media Authority (Haute Autorité des Médias, HAM), the Truth and Reconciliation Commission (Commission Vérité et Réconciliation, CVR), the Ethics and Anti-Corruption Commission (Commission de l'Éthique et de la Lutte contre la Corruption, CELC), and the National Human Rights Observatory (Observatoire National des Droits de l'Homme, ONDH).
8 "Bemba Followers Attack Congo Court in Poll Protest," Reuters, 21 November 2006, http://www.alertnet.org/thenews/newsdesk/L21778288.htm (accessed 30 August 2010).
9 The corruption that characterized these indirect elections of senators and provincial governors, including how some disappointed generous candidates asked for their gifts back, is discussed in Noel Obotela Rashidi and Jean Omasombo Tshonda, "De la fin des 'composantes' à l'hégémonie par les elections en RDC" in *L'Afrique des Grands Lacs : Annuaire 2006-2007*, ed. Stefaan Marysse, Filip Reyntjens and Stef Vandeginste (Paris: L'Harmattan, 2008), 157.
10 Reilly notes the great variation of what "free and fair elections" means in practice and the way the international community has "lowered the bar" for certain cases.
11 SC, final report of the Group of Experts.
12 International Crisis Group, *Congo: Consolidating the Peace*, Africa Report N°128, Kinshasa/Brussels, 5 July 2007, i.
13 The Special Representative of the Secretary-General (SRSG), William Swing, called on MONUC and EUFOR-DRC troops to diffuse the situation, and established a joint working group comprised of representatives of the Bemba and Kabila camps, the EUFOR-DRC, and MONUC to establish dialogue and build confidence. But distrust and fear of assassination by the other side ran so high that neither presidential candidate actually attended any campaign events in person after the August 2006 events.
14 The renaming puts emphasis on the UN Mission's "stabilization" mandate as per the DRC government's wish to be seen as a post-conflict State. MONUC/MONUSCO's budget has increased year on year to over US$1.37 billion for fiscal year 2010/11.
15 Claudia Major, "The Military Operation EUFOR-R.D. Congo 2006," in *Election Security and Defence Policy: the First Ten Years (1999-2009)*, ed. Giovanni Grevi, Damien Helly, and Daniel Keohane (Paris: European Union Institute

for Security Studies, 2009), 311–23, http://www.iss.europa.eu/uploads/media/ESDP_10-web.pdf (accessed 30 August 2010).
16 William Swing, UN SRSG for the DRC, and Carlo Filippi, head of the European Commission delegation in the DRC, presentation at the donors meeting on the DRC electoral process, Brussels, 11 July 2005, PowerPoint slide (on file with authors).
17 International Crisis Group, *Securing Congo's Elections: Lessons from the Kinshasa Showdown*, Africa Briefing N°42, Nairobi/Brussels, 2 October 2006, 4.
18 Alan Doss, "The UN Mission in Congo Has Not Signed a 'Pact with the Devil,'" *The Guardian*, 24 February 2010, http://www.guardian.co.uk/commentisfree/2010/feb/24/un-mission-congo-monuc-drc (accessed 30 August 2010).
19 International Crisis Group, *Stalled Democratic Agenda*, 22.
20 Global and Inclusive Agreement on Transition in the Democratic Republic of the Congo, signed in Pretoria, Republic of South Africa, 16 December 2002, Annex IV.
21 Originally, two more members were supposed to join the CIS: President Nicéphore Soglo, former head of state of Benin, and Ambassador Kai Eide, Norwegian ambassador-at-large and later UN SRSG in Afghanistan. Soglo did not participate due to ill health; Eide, a late addition, participated only briefly.
22 International Crisis Group, *Escaping the Conflict Trap: Promoting Good Governance in the Congo*, Africa Report N°114, Nairobi/Brussels, 20 July 2006, 22.
23 The Congolese Rally for Democracy (Rassemblement Congolais pour la Démocratie, RCD) won fifteen seats in the 500-seat Assembly and elected seven senators (out of a 108-seat Senate). Even though elements within the RCD would ultimately regroup under Nkunda's National Congress for the Defence of the People, Ruberwa and most RCD troops did not return to arms to challenge the election results or the new government.
24 Secretariat of the International Committee of the Wise (*Comité international des sages*) "Project Report 2006, Implementation Phase: July-December 2006," 24–5.
25 Filip Reyntjens, "Briefing: Democratic Republic of Congo: Political Transition and Beyond," *African Affairs* 106, no. 423 (2007): 307–17.
26 The Africa Forum (http://www.africaforum.org) brings together former African heads of state and government for unpublicized high-level advisory and mediation missions to newly elected governments in Africa. Kabila was

reportedly approached by the Africa Forum after his inauguration by declined their assistance.

27 The information on EISA Conflict Management Panels is culled from Marcus Nana Kwamie, "Electoral Institute of Southern Africa Conflict Management Panel Model in the Democratic Republic of Congo" (unpublished report).

28 According to CEI decision number 027/CEI/BUR/05 of 14 December 2005 on the creation, organization, and functioning of mediation panels.

29 As mentioned above, EISA documents the work of its Conflict Management Panels in a database and in reports shared with the IEC and other stakeholders. The examples cited here are sourced from EISA, "De la médiation des conflits électoraux à la médiation des conflits sociaux", Kinshasa, 22 September 2010 (report on file with the authors).

30 The crowd had become so violent and out of control that a woman was reported dead of asphyxiation on-site.

31 Séverine Autesserre, "Hobbes and the Congo: Frames, Local Violence, and International Intervention," *International Organization* 63 (spring 2009): 249–80.

32 William Swing, *The United Nations Mission in the Democratic Republic of Congo (MONUC): Experiences and Lessons,* Institute for Security Studies, Situation Report, 23 November 2007, 4.

33 Roland Paris, *At War's End: Building Peace After Civil Conflict* (Cambridge: Cambridge University Press, 2004).

CHAPTER SEVEN

* This revised version of the paper prepared for the North-South Institute workshop Elections and Conflict: Promoting Good Practice in Electoral Conflict Management, held 29-30 October 2009 in Ottawa, has also been published in *Journal of Contemporary African Studies* 29, no. 1 (2011): 99–117. It is reproduced here by kind permission of the publisher, Taylor and Francis.

1 Kimani Njogu, *Healing the Wound: Personal Narratives About the 2007 Post-Election Violence in Kenya* (Nairobi: Twaweza Communications, 2009).

2 Robert A. Dahl, *Polyarchy: Participation and Opposition* (New Haven, Conn.: Yale University Press, 1971). Also see note 3, below.

3 It is beyond the scope of this paper to discuss fully theories concerning democracy and the transition to democracy.

4 Daron Acemoglu, Simon Johnson, Pablo Querubín, and James A. Robinson, "When Does Policy Reform Work? The Case of Central Bank Independence," *Brookings Papers on Economic Activity* (Spring 2008): 353–4.
5 Daron Acemoglu and James A. Robinson, "Persistence of Power, Elites, and Institutions," *American Economic Review* 98, no. 1 (2008): 288–9.
6 Paul Collier and Anke Hoeffler, "Democracy's Achilles Heel or, How to Win an Election without Really Trying" (CSAE WPS/2009–08, Centre for the Study of African Economies, Department of Economics, Oxford University, 2009), http://users.ox.ac.uk/~econpco/research/politicaleconomy.htm.
7 Catherine Boone, "Electoral Populism Where Property Rights Are Weak: Land Politics in Contemporary Sub-Saharan Africa," *Comparative Politics* 41, no. 2 (2009): 183–96.
8 Richard Joseph, "Africa 1990-1997: From Abertura to Closure," *Journal of Democracy* 9, no. 2 (1998): 1–17; Thomas Carothers, "Democracy without Illusions," *Foreign Affairs*, vol. 76 (1997): 22–48; Steven Levitsky and Lucan Way, "The Rise of Competitive Authoritarianism," *Journal of Democracy* 13, no. 2 (2002): 51–65.
9 Francis Fukuyama, Thomas Carothers, Edward Mansfield, Jack Snyder, and Sheri Berman "The Debate on 'Sequencing,'" *Journal of Democracy* 18, no. 3 (2007): 5–22; Daniel Branch and Nic Cheeseman, "Democratization, Sequencing and State Failure in Kenya: Lessons from Kenya," *African Affairs* 108, no. 430 (2009): 1–26.
10 Staffan I. Lindberg, *Democracy and Elections in Africa* (Baltimore, Md.: Johns Hopkins University Press, 2006); Daniel N. Posner and Daniel J. Young, "The Institutionalization of Political Power in Africa," *Journal of Democracy* 18, no. 3 (2007): 126–40.
11 As John Githongo has noted, "Indeed, in a cruel irony the much vaunted middle class, supposed to be the driver of modernity, became and remains the most vociferous of Kenya's new ethnic nationalists." See "Kenya Needs a Reboot: John Githongo," *Newsweek*, 5 October 2009, international edition.
12 William Reno's work is most closely associated with the term "shadow states." He defines a shadow state "as one that is constructed behind the face of laws and government institutions" and "is a form of personal rule," "based on the decisions and interests of an individual, not a set of written laws and procedures." William Reno, "Clandestine Economies, Violence, and States in Africa," *Journal of International Affairs* 53, no. 2 (2000): 434.
13 Susanne D. Mueller, "The Political Economy of Kenya's Crisis," *Journal of Eastern African Studies* 2, no. 2 (2008): 185–210.

14 Kenya. Commission of Inquiry into Post-Election Violence (CIPEV). *Report of the Commission of Inquiry into Post-Election Violence* (Nairobi: Government Printer, 2008) (hereafter cited as "Waki Report"). Available at http://www.kenyalaw.org/Downloads/Reports/Commission_of_Inquiry_into_Post_Election_Violence.pdf.

15 Mueller, "Kenya's Crisis." The first part of this chapter, encompassing the following three subsections, summarizes the main points of the article. The original article includes more theory, analysis, and attention to empirical detail. In some places I have used direct quotes from the paper, but being the author, I have not used quotation marks.

16 Musumbayi Katumanga, "A City Under Siege: Banditry and Modes of Accumulation in Nairobi, 1991–2004," *Review of African Political Economy* 32, no. 106 (2005): 513.

17 Max Weber, *Basic Concepts in Sociology* (New York: Kensington, 2002). For a further discussion of this in the Kenyan context, see Mueller, "Kenya's Crisis." For a discussion of the emergence of "shadow states" elsewhere in Africa, see William Reno, "The Politics of Insurgency in Collapsing States," *Development and Change* 33, no. 5 (2002): 837–58; idem, "Clandestine Economies."

18 For a discussion of how repression in Kenya worked and its continuity with the colonial state, see Susanne D. Mueller, "Government and Opposition in Kenya," *Journal of Modern African Studies* 22, no. 3 (1984): 399–427. The biggest crackdown was after the 1982 failed attempted coup.

19 Kenya. Judicial Commission Appointed to Inquire into Tribal Clashes in Kenya. *Report of the Judicial Commission Appointed to Inquire into Tribal Clashes in Kenya.* Nairobi: Government Printer, 1999.

20 Mueller, "Kenya's Crisis"; Robert Bates, *When Things Fell Apart: State Failure in Late Century Africa* (Cambridge: Cambridge University Press, 2008).

21 Much of the discussion in this section is drawn from articles in Kenyan newspapers the *Daily Nation* and the *Standard* from February 2008 to the present.

22 Kenya National Dialogue and Reconciliation Monitoring Project, *Review Report for October-December 2009* (Nairobi: South Consulting Group, 2010), http://www.dialoguekenya.org/docs/ReviewReport2009.pdf.

23 Kenya National Dialogue and Reconciliation Monitoring Project, *Status of Implementation of Agenda Items 1-4: Fourth Review Report* (Nairobi: South Consulting Group, 2009), http://www.dialoguekenya.org/docs/4th%20review%20report%20(October%2009).pdf.

24 For a discussion about why Kenya had not experienced civil war up to 2005,

see Mwangi S. Kimenyi and Njuguna S. Ndung'u, "Sporadic Ethnic Violence: Why Has Kenya Not Experienced a Full-Blown Civil War?" in *Understanding Civil War: Evidence and Analysis*, 2 vols., ed. Paul Collier and Nicholas Sambanis (Washington, DC: World Bank, 2005), 1:123–56. For a related discussion about rebel groups in the post cold war situation that are able to challenge the state but not confront it directly, see Stathis N. Kalyvas and Laia Balcells, "International System and Technologies of Rebellion: How the End of the Cold War Shaped Internal Conflict," *American Political Science Review* 104, no. 3 (2010): 415–29.

25 Gabrielle Lynch, "Durable Solution, Help, or Hindrance? The Failings and Unintended Implications of Relief and Recovery Efforts for Kenya's Post-Election IDPs," *Review of African Political Economy* 36, no. 122 (2009): 604–10.

26 Private interviews by author with Kenyans and researchers, 2008-9.

27 For discussions and information collected by human rights groups, see http://blog.marsgroupkenya.org/?p=623 (website closed); for the UN's Special Rapporteur, see United Nations, Human Rights Council, Eleventh Session, Report of the Special Rapporteur on extrajudicial, summary or arbitrary executions, Addendum, *Mission to Kenya*, 2009, A/HRC/11/2/Add.6/26, http://www2.ohchr.org/english/bodies/hrcouncil/docs/11session/A.HRC.11.2.Add.6.pdf.

28 Private discussions. See also Johan De Smedt, "'No Raila, No Peace!' Big Man Politics and Election Violence at the Kibera Grassroots," *African Affairs* 108, no. 433 (2009): 581–98.

29 Kenya National Dialogue and Reconciliation Monitoring Project, *Fourth Review Report*.

30 Reports over the past year in Kenya's dailies, the *Daily Nation* and the *Standard*, report an increase in crime. This is supported by surveys in which only half of the respondents feel safer than they did six months ago, and with 27 per cent feeling less safe and another 20 per cent feeling about the same. See Kenya National Dialogue and Reconciliation Monitoring Project, *Fourth Review Report*, 3.

31 Christopher Ksoll, Rocco Macchiavello, and Ameet Morjaria, "The Impact of the Kenyan Post-Election Violence on the Kenyan Flower Export Industry" (iiG Briefing Paper 05, Improving Institutions for Growth (iiG), Centre for the Study of African Economies, Oxford University, 2009), http://www.iig.ox.ac.uk/research/25-contractual-relationships-kenya-flower.htm.

32 Oliver Mathenge, "Kenyans Wary of Violence in 2012 Elections," *Saturday Nation* (Nairobi), 19 October 2010.

33 Kenya National Dialogue and Reconciliation Monitoring Project, *Fourth Review Report*, 5; Stefan Dercon, "Ethnicity, Violence, and the 2007 Elections in Kenya" (unpublished paper, Oxford University, 2008).
34 As of April 2010, the Truth, Justice and Reconciliation Commission was paralyzed with all of its commissioners demanding that its head, Bethwell Kiplagat, resign because of questions concerning his credibility when he was an official under former president Moi. The new constitution, which still awaits the passage of laws to implement it, contains greater checks and balances on the president, a new Senate, and some level of devolution to the county level, with each of the above changes still being contested by parts of the political elite as too little or too much change.
35 Already since the ICC announced its list of perpetrators there has been an apparent realignment of forces with William Ruto, Uhuru Kenyatta, and Kilonzo Musyoka teaming up against Raila Odinga in preparation for the 2012 election in spite of the Ruto and Kenyatta having been identified as alleged perpetrators by the ICC.
36 See Branch and Cheeseman, "State Failure in Kenya," for their discussion of elite fragmentation. For instance, the recent marginalization of William Ruto, who mobilized the Kalenjin vote for Odinga in the 2007 election, by Kibaki and Odinga could either be a precursor to a new Kikuyu Luo alliance in 2012 or a first attempt by key Kibaki stalwarts to strand Odinga in 2012.
37 Kenya, "Waki Report."
38 International Criminal Court, Decision Pursuant to Article 15 of the Rome Statute on the Authorization of an Investigation into the Situation in the Republic of Kenya, ICC-01/09, 2010, http://www.icc-cpi.int/iccdocs/doc/doc854287.pdf. See also Beth Van Schaack, "Seeking Truth, Justice & Reconciliation in Kenya," IntLawGrrls (blog), 7 July 2009, http://intlawgrrls.blogspot.com/2009/07/seeking-truth-justice-reconciliation-in.html. Before receiving permission to begin a formal investigation in Kenya, the ICC's Office of the Prosecutor was doing a "Situation Analysis" of the case. This was the first time the ICC's chief prosecutor had taken up a case on his own volition. Previously, all cases before the court had been referred to him either by a country itself (known as self referral) or by the Security Council.
39 Those named as suspects by the ICC are Uhuru Kenyatta, son of Kenya's first president, a Party of National Unity deputy prime minister and current minister of finance; William Ruto, former deposed Orange Democratic Movement (ODM) minister of agriculture, minister of higher education, and

acknowledged leader of the Kalenjin; Henry Kosgey, chairman of the ODM, key ally of Raila Odinga, and minister of industrialization; Francis Muthaura, the head of the civil service and a close Meru confidant of President Mwai Kibaki; Mohammed Ali, former police commissioner and current postmaster general; and Julius arap Sang, host of the vernacular Kalenjin radio station Kass FM. For the ICC's cases and evidence against these individuals see http://www.icc-cpi.int/NR/exeres/BA2041D8-3F30-4531-8850-431B5B2F4416.htm.

40 Even if the bill is signed by the president, pulling out of the ICC would not affect the current Kenya cases according to Article 127 of the Rome Statute. Also, to pull out, Kenya would have to notify the United Nations secretary-general, with the whole process taking up to a year.

41 Many Kenyans hope and believe that both the ICC's charges against high level perpetrators of the 2007 post election violence and the possibility of some successful prosecutions might be enough to deter future electoral violence.

42 Numerous reports of witness harassment have appeared in the Kenyan press since the Waki Commission finished its work. For recent examples, see Kenya National Dialogue and Reconciliation Monitoring Project, *Review Report for October–December* 2009, 16–17; "Ocampo Writes to Mutula Over Witness Threats," *Standard* (Nairobi), 25 January 2010; Francis Mureithi and Nzau Musau, "Rift Leaders Behind Witnesses Attacks – NSIS," *Nairobi Star*, 15 January 2010; "Too Much Talk but Very Little Action, *Standard* (Nairobi), 10 January 2010; "Ocampo Witnesses Escape Death," *Nairobi Star*, 5 January 2010; Caroline Wafulap, "Imanyara Says More Threats Made on Him," *Daily Nation* (Nairobi), 24 November 2009; Lucas Barasa and Barnabas Bii, "Threats to Kenya Violence Witnesses Increase," *Daily Nation* (Nairobi), 8 March 2010; Benson Amadala and Ouma Wanzala, "Poll Violence: What Does This Man Know?" *Daily Nation* (Nairobi), 20 March 2010; Alisha Ryu, "Theft in Kenya May Be Tied to ICC Probe," voaNews.com, 7 March 2010.

43 Kenya. Independent Review Commission on the General Elections Held in Kenya on 27 December 2007 ("Kriegler Commission"). *Report of the Independent Review Commission on the General Elections Held in Kenya on 27 December* 2007 (Nairobi: Government Printer, 2008). Available at http://www.dialoguekenya.org/docs/FinalReport_consolidated.pdf.

44 Ibid., 24.

45 This point also is discussed Mueller, "Kenya's crisis."

46 Kenya, "Waki Report."

47 Ibid., 445.
48 Ibid., 457.
49 Emmanuel Gyimah-Boadi, "Political Parties, Elections and Patronage: Random Thoughts on Neo-Patrimonialism and African Democratization," in *Votes, Money, and Violence: Political Parties and Elections in Sub-Saharan Africa*, ed. Matthias Basedau, Gero Erdmann, and Andreas Mehler (Uppsala: Nordiska Afrikainstitutet; Scottsville: University of Kwazulu Press, 2007), 21.
50 This quotation is from the invitation to the North-South Institute workshop Elections and Conflict: Promoting Good Practice in Electoral Conflict Management, held 29–30 October 2009 in Ottawa, for which this paper was originally prepared.
51 Peter Burnell, "Political Parties in Africa: Different, Functional and Dynamic? Reflections on Gero Erdmann's 'Party Research: Western European Bias and "African Labyrinth,"'" in Basedau, Erdmann, and Mehler, *Votes, Money, and Violence*, 65–81.
52 Kenya, Report of the Independent Review Commission, 24.
53 A recent commission suggested increasing MPs salaries and perks to around Ksh 14.7 million (US$210,000) a year. See Alphonce Shiundu, "New Pay Hike for Kenyan MPs," *Daily Nation* (Nairobi), 10 January 2010.
54 Among others, see articles in *Journal of Democracy* 13, no. 2 (2002). Also see Roger Southall, "Electoral Systems and Democratization in Africa," in *Voting for Democracy: Watershed Elections in Contemporary Anglophone Africa*, ed. John Daniel, Roger Southall, and Morris Szeftel (Aldershot, England: Ashgate, 1999), 19–36.
55 Mueller, "Kenya's Crisis."
56 Philip Keefer, "Insurgencies and Credible Commitment in Autocracies and Democracies," *World Bank Economic Review* 22, no. 1 (2008): 25–6.
57 Andrew Reynolds, "Constitutional Medicine," *Journal of Democracy* 16, no. 1 (2005): 64.
58 Roger Southall, "Alternatives for Electoral Reform in Kenya: Lessons from Southern Africa," *Journal of Contemporary African Studies* 27, no. 3 (2009): 456–7.
59 Keefer, "Insurgencies and Credible Commitment."

CHAPTER EIGHT

* The author wishes to thank Hervé Maupeu and the Centre de recherche et d'étude sur les pays d'Afrique orientale (CREPAO) at the Université de Pau et des Pays de l'Adour, Pau, France, for hosting him during the writing of this chapter. He is also grateful to various organizations, especially the Social Sciences and Humanities Research Council of Canada and the International Peace Academy, for funding the fieldwork in Kenya in 1998, 2001, 2008, and 2010, upon which this chapter draws.

1 Africa Watch, *Divide and Rule: State-Sponsored Ethnic Violence in Kenya* (New York: Human Rights Watch, 1993), 1, 90.
2 National Council of Churches of Kenya (NCCK), *The Cursed Arrow: Organized Violence Against Democracy in Kenya*, (Nairobi: National Council of Churches of Kenya, 1992); Kenya National Assembly, *Report of the Parliamentary Select Committee to Investigate Ethnic Clashes in Western and Other Parts of Kenya, 1992* (Nairobi: Kenya National Assembly, 1992); Africa Watch, *Divide and Rule*, 28–30.
3 Stephen Brown, "Authoritarian Leaders and Multiparty Elections in Africa: How Foreign Donors Help to Keep Kenya's Daniel arap Moi in power," *Third World Quarterly* 22, no. 5 (2001): 726–8; François Grignon and Hervé Maupeu, "Les aléas du contrat social kényan," *Politique Africaine*, no. 70 (June 1998): 3-21; David W. Throup and Charles Hornsby, *Multi-Party Politics in Kenya: The Kenyatta and Moi States and the Triumph of the System in the 1992 Elections* (Oxford: James Currey, 1998).
4 Joel D. Barkan, "Kenya: Lessons from a Flawed Election," *Journal of Democracy* 4, no. 3 (1993): 92.
5 Brown, "Authoritarian Leaders," 730.
6 Human Rights Watch, *Old Habits Die Hard: Rights Abuses Follow Renewed Foreign Aid Commitments* (New York: Human Rights Watch, 1995).
7 US Department of State, *Kenya Human Rights Practices, 1993* (Washington, DC, 1994), 1, 15, 35.
8 Human Rights Watch/Africa, *Failing the Internally Displaced: The UNDP Displaced Persons Program* (New York: Human Rights Watch, 1997).
9 Grignon and Maupeu, "Aléas du contrat social kényan", 15; Arne Tostensen, Bård-Anders Andreassen, and Kjetil Tronvoll, *Kenya's Hobbled Democracy Revisited: The 1997 General Elections in Retrospect and Prospect* (Oslo: Norwegian Institute of Human Rights, 1998), 43–44.
10 Interviews with Western diplomats and aid officials (names withheld) by author, Nairobi, May 1998 and April–May 2001. For further information, see Stephen Brown, "Quiet Diplomacy and Recurring 'Ethnic Clashes' in Kenya" in *From Promise to Practice: Strengthening UN Capacities for the Prevention of Violent Conflict*, ed. Chandra Lekha Sriram and Karin Wermester (Boulder, Colo.: Lynne Rienner, 2003), 69–100.
11 Brown, "Authoritarian Leaders," 734.

12 Rok Ajulu, "Kenya's Democratic Experiment: The 1997 Elections," *Review of African Political Economy* 25, no. 76 (1998): 285.
13 Institute for Education in Democracy, *National Elections Data Book: Kenya, 1963-1997* (Nairobi: Institute for Education in Democracy, 1997), 186.
14 Election Observation Centre, *Kenya General Elections 1997: Final Report for Donors' Democratic Development Group* (Nairobi: Election Observation Centre, 1998).
15 Judith Geist, "Kenya's 1997 Elections: An Assessment and Recommendations for Improvement" (report submitted to USAID, 14 January 1998), *ii, v,* 18.
16 US Department of State, *Kenya Report on Human Rights Practices for 1997* (Washington, DC, 1998), 5.
17 Bryan E. Burton, interview by author, Nairobi, 27 April 2001. At the time, Burton was the chair of the bilateral missions' Democratic Development Group.
18 Electoral Commission of Kenya, "General Elections Results 2002," http://www.eck.or.ke/general_elections_results_2002.htm (accessed 8 January 2003).
19 Stephen Brown, "Theorising Kenya's Protracted Transition to Democracy," *Journal of Contemporary African Studies* 22, no. 3 (2004): 332–33.
20 David Throup, "The Kenyan General Election: December 27, 2002," *Africa Notes* 14 (2003): 1–9.
21 Prisca Mbura Kamungi, "The Politics of Displacement in Multiparty Kenya," *Journal of Contemporary African Studies* 27, no. 3 (2009): 353.
22 Beth Elise Whitaker and Jason Giersch, "Voting on a Constitution: Implications for Democracy in Kenya," *Journal of Contemporary African Studies* 27, no. 1 (2009): 13.
23 See, for instance, Stephen Brown, "Quiet Diplomacy," 92; Brown, "Transition to Democracy," 337.
24 "Africa's Uncertain Democracies: The 2008 Crisis in Kenya," special issue, *Journal of Contemporary African Studies* 27, no. 3 (2009); "Election Fever: Kenya's Crisis," special issue, *Journal of Eastern African Studies* 2, no. 2 (2008); Jérôme Lafargue, ed., *The General Elections in Kenya, 2007* (Dar-es-Salaam and Nairobi: Mkuki na Nyota, 2008); "Élections et violences au Kenya," special section, *Politique Africaine* 109 (March 2008): 107–66.
25 This section draws significantly on previous work, which analyzes these issues in greater detail: Stephen Brown, "Donor Responses to the 2008 Kenyan Crisis: Finally Getting It Right?" *Journal of Contemporary African Studies* 27, no. 3 (2009): 389–406.

26 Daniel Branch and Nic Cheeseman, "Democratization, Sequencing, and State Failure in Africa: Lessons from Kenya," *African Affairs* 108, no. 430 (2009): 1–26.
27 See Susanne D. Mueller, chap. 7, this volume.
28 Nic Cheeseman, "The Kenyan Elections of 2007: An Introduction," *Journal of Eastern African Studies* 2, no. 2 (2008): 170.
29 Kenya National Commission on Human Rights (KNHCR), *On the Brink of the Precipice: A Human Rights Account of Kenya's Post-2007 Election Violence* (Nairobi: KNCHR, 2008), 61, 70, 184.
30 On four other "steps taken that paint a picture of a well orchestrated plan to ensure a pre-determined result," see Maina Kiai, "The Political Crisis in Kenya: A Call for Justice and Peaceful Resolution," *Review of African Political Economy* 35, no. 115 (2008): 142.
31 International Crisis Group, *Kenya in Crisis*, Africa Report N°137, Nairobi/Brussels, 21 February 2008, 6.
32 On the AU-led mediation process, see Brown, "Donor Responses"; Monica Kathina Juma, "African Mediation of the Kenyan Post-2007 Election Crisis," *Journal of Contemporary African Studies* 27, no. 3 (2009): 407–30; and Gilbert M. Khadiagala, "Regionalism and Conflict Resolution: Lessons from the Kenyan crisis," *Journal of Contemporary African Studies* 27, no. 3 (2009): 431–44.
33 Stephen Brown, "From Demiurge to Midwife: Changing Donor Roles in Kenya's Democratisation Process" in *Kenya: The Struggle for Democracy* ed. Godwin Rapando Murunga and Shadrack Wanjala Nasong'o (London: Zed Books, 2007), 301–29.
34 KNCHR, *On the Brink*; Republic of Kenya, Commission of Inquiry into Post-Election Violence, *Report of the Commission of Inquiry into Post-Election Violence* (Nairobi: Government Printer, 2008).
35 François Grignon, Africa Program Director, International Crisis Group, interview by author, Nairobi, 4 December 2008; Bo Jensen, Ambassador of Denmark to Kenya, interview by author, Nairobi, 8 December 2008; interview with Western embassy official (name withheld) by author, Nairobi, December 2008.
36 Western donor agency official, interview by author and Chandra Lekha Sriram (School of Oriental and African Studies, University of London), Nairobi, January 2010.
37 Gitobu Imanyara, Member of Parliament for Central Imenti, interview by author and Chandra Lekha Sriram (School of Oriental and African Studies, University of London), 20 January 2010.

Notes to pages 147–8   291

CHAPTER NINE

1   For example, "countries in transition, which have experienced transitions from authoritarian or single party-rule to multi-party politics [and] consolidating democracies ... remain susceptible to shocks and require further deepening of democracy to build resilience in the system." See United Nations Development Programme (UNDP), Democratic Governance Group, Bureau for Development Policy, *Elections and Conflict Prevention: A Guide to Analysis, Planning and Programming* (New York: UNDP, August 2009), 8.
2   The International Foundation for Electoral Systems (IFES) is the world's premier independent election assistance organization. IFES promotes democratic stability by providing technical assistance and applying field-based research to the electoral cycle worldwide. Since its founding in 1987, IFES has worked in more than 100 countries.
3   This approach was first presented in Gabrielle Bardall, "A Conflict Cycle Perspective on Electoral Violence: Taking the Long and Broad View on Electoral Violence," *Monday Developments* 28, no. 3 (2010): 15–16, 29.
4   Within this chapter "election violence," "electoral conflict," and "electoral violence" will be used interchangeably. "Elections and conflict" and "conflict around elections" will refer to latent or active conflicts between groups that may or may not be directly related to elections or the electoral process.
5   There are a variety of authors and evidence of this; see in particular, Bardall, "Conflict Cycle Perspective"; UNDP, *Elections and Conflict Prevention*; Chris Fomunyoh, "Mediating Election-Related Conflicts" (background paper, Centre for Humanitarian Dialogue, Geneva, July 2009); and United Nations, Human Rights Council, Fourteenth Session, Report of the Special Rapporteur on extrajudicial, summary or arbitrary executions, Addendum, *Election-Related Violence and Killings*, 2010, A/HRC/14/24/Add.7, 21. Also, the International Criminal Court has issued indictments related to election violence for the first time in relation to the violence in Kenya (see International Criminal Court, "Background Information on the Chamber's Process of Ruling on Summons to Appear or Warrants of Arrest," news release, 16 December 2010, http://www.icc-cpi.int/NR/exeres/C3D48F4D-8132-46AC-A84D-94D87F3C64C4.htm, and International Foundation for Electoral Systems (IFES), "The Kenya Case and the Role of the ICC in Election Violence," 27 January 2010, http://www.ifes.org/Content/Publications/Opinions/2010/Jan/The-Kenya-Case-and-the-Role-of-the-ICC-in-Election-Violence.aspx).
6   Relevant publications include Rakesh Sharma and Lisa Kammerud, "Election Violence: Causes, Trends, and Mitigation," paper presented at the Elec-

toral Symposium, IFES and Ahram Center for Political and Strategic Studies, Cairo, 22 April 2010; Jeff Fischer, "Electoral Conflict and Violence: A Strategy for Study and Prevention," IFES White Paper, 2002; Lisa Kammerud, *Managing Election Violence: The IFES EVER Program*, IFES, October 2009; Ashish Chaturvedi, "Rigging Elections with Violence", *Public Choice* 125, no. 1/2 (2005): 189–202; Paul Collier and Pedro C. Vicente, "Violence, Bribery, and Fraud: The Political Economy of Elections in Africa," working paper, Oxford University, 2009.

7 It should be noted that several research initiatives focusing on election violence are underway, such as those programs at the Department of Peace and Conflict Research, Uppsala University, Sweden (http://www.pcr.uu.se/) and the United States Institute for Peace (USIP). USIP also has a programming side and launched workshops on elections and violence in Sudan in 2009 to generate dialogue (see http://www.usip.org/programs/projects/preventing-electoral-violence-sudan). Though we are in communication with these and similar initiatives, more can be done to increase their interaction with election practitioners.

8 IFES' EVER program began with assessments and research of the forms of election violence and mitigation strategies and identified civil society as an overlooked entry point for engaging the full range of stakeholders in reducing election violence. Mainly focusing on capacity building program for civil society organizations (CSOs) to monitor and mitigate election violence through modules such as conflict monitoring, peacebuilding activities, and public outreach, EVER has been implemented in 13 countries thus far (Bangladesh, Burundi, East Timor, Ghana, Guyana, Indonesia, Iraq, Kyrgyzstan, Liberia, Nepal, Nigeria, Pakistan, and Sierra Leone), and has led to the formation or consolidation of three national networks for elections and democracy work and two early warning projects built on the EVER framework.

9 This definition is based on that of electoral expert Jeff Fischer, who in the first IFES white paper on the topic (see Fischer, "Electoral Conflict and Violence"), defined election violence as "any random or organized act to intimidate, physically harm, blackmail, or abuse a political stakeholder in seeking to determine, delay, or to otherwise influence an electoral process."

10 See the addendum to the Report of the Special Rapporteur on extrajudicial, summary or arbitrary executions, *Election-Related Violence and Killings*.

11 Fischer, "Electoral Conflict and Violence"; Sharma and Kammerud, "Election Violence"; Kammerud, *Managing Election Violence*.

12 Bardall, "Conflict Cycle Perspective."

13 USAID published its *Election Security Framework* in August 2010; see US Agency for International Development (USAID), *Election Security Framework: Technical Guidance Handbook for USAID Democracy and Governance Officers* (Washington, DC: USAID, 2010). International IDEA launched its working group in a fall 2009 workshop; see International IDEA, "Towards a Global Framework for Managing and Mitigating Election-Related Conflict and Violence," International Institute for Democracy and Electoral Assistance workshop report, 27–30 October 2009, http://www.idea.int/resources/analysis/upload/Towards_a_Global_Framework.pdf.

14 International IDEA, *Electoral Justice: The International IDEA Handbook* (Stockholm: International Institute for Democracy and Electoral Assistance, 2010).

15 While this paper focuses on collaborative measures in which the EMB must take the lead, a more comprehensive look at the role of the EMB can be found in Staffan Darnolf, The Role of the EMB in Managing Election Conflict (forthcoming). For the role of EMBs in post-conflict countries, see Terrence Lyons, "Post-Conflict Elections and the Process of Demilitarizing Politics: The Role of Electoral Administration," *Democratization* 11, no. 3 (2004): 36–62.

16 Raquel Fontanes, "Now Online! Uganda's Voter Registry," 23 November 2010, http://www.ifes.org/Content/Publications/Opinions/2010/Nov/Now-Online-Ugandas-Voter-Register.aspx.

17 BRIDGE is a modular professional development program with a particular focus on electoral processes. The five BRIDGE partners are the Australian Electoral Commission, International IDEA, the IFES, UNDP, and the United Nations Electoral Assistance Division. For more information, see http://bridge-project.org/.

18 Much of the on-the-ground knowledge comes from interviews with local electoral and government officials across South Sudan conducted by the IFES's electoral conflict assessment team in March 2009; for a review of the complexities involved specifically with reforming the South Sudan Police Service, see Alfred Sebit Lokuji, Abraham Sewonet Abatneh, and Chaplain Kenyi Wani, *Police Reform in Southern Sudan* (Ottawa: North-South Institute, 2009).

19 Based on interviews with Lt. Gen. Gordon Kur Micah, Deputy Inspector General of Police, South Sudan Police Service, and United States government officials in Juba and Khartoum.

20 Report of the Special Rapporteur on extrajudicial, summary or arbitrary executions, *Election-Related Violence and Killings*.

21 For examples, see Alka Marwaha, "Web Tool Maps Congo Conflict," BBC World Service, 10 December 2008, http://news.bbc.co.uk/2/hi/technology/7773648.stm; Jamillah Knowles, "Remote Control Crisis Management," BBC News, 3 September 2010, http://www.bbc.co.uk/news/technology-11134297; Jami Makan, "When Necessity Invented Global SOS," *Daily Nation* (Nairobi), 14 October 2008, http://www.nation.co.ke/News/-/1056/480528/-/item/1/-/lsupwr/-/index.html; Anand Giridharadas, "Africa's Gift to Silicon Valley: How to Track a Crisis," *New York Times*, 13 March 2010, http://www.nytimes.com/2010/03/14/weekinreview/14giridharadas.html; Megha Bahree, "Citizen Voices", *Forbes Magazine*, 8 December 2008, and online, 13 November 2008, http://www.forbes.com/forbes/2008/1208/083.html.

22 Interviews by author with Odhikar District Coordinators and presentations by Odhikar monitors during refresher training session (Dhaka, December 2006).

23 Many sources discuss the relevance of civic education. Several non-profits exist to promote the importance of civic education in US schools; a set of evaluations can be found on the Center for Civic Education website at http://www.civiced.org/index.php?page=program_evaluation. The World Movement for Democracy used Civic Education for Democracy as its theme for 2003, highlighting the work of its members and advocating for increased global commitment to long-term civic education; see http://www.wmd.org/resources/whats-being-done/civic-education-democracy. For the positive effects of civic education regarding Indonesia, see Kokom Komalasari, "The Effect of Contextual Learning in Civic Education on Students' Civic Competence," *Journal of Social Sciences* 5, no. 4 (2009): 261–70; see also Steven E. Finkel, "Can Democracy be Taught?" *Journal of Democracy* 14, no. 4 (2003): 137–51.

24 Author's conversations with stakeholders in Guyana, Bangladesh Nigeria, and elsewhere.

25 For election assessments, see observer reports such as the *Report of the Commonwealth Observer Group: Guyana General and Regional Elections 28 August 2006* (London: Commonwealth Secretariat, 2006). News coverage includes "EAB Project Aims to Monitor, Prevent Poll Violence," *Stabroek News* (Georgetown), 3 July 2006; "Communities Tense about Potential for Electoral Violence – EVER report," *Stabroek News* (Georgetown), 30 July 2006; "Vote Was Peaceful but a Few Serious Incidents – EAB report," *Stabroek News* (Georgetown), 8 September 2006. PDFs of the articles are on file with IFES.

Other details can be found in Guyana EVER reports, available at http://www.ifes.org.

26 Bardall, "Conflict Cycle Perspective," 29.

CHAPTER TEN

1 John Finn, "Electoral Regimes and the Proscription of Anti-democratic Parties," in *The Democratic Experience and Political Violence*, ed. David C. Rapoport and Leonard Weinberg (London: Frank Cass Publishers, 2001), 52.
2 Larry Diamond, *Political Culture and Democracy in Developing Countries*, (Boulder, Colo.: Lynne Rienner, 1994), 242f.
3 Ibid.
4 This chapter builds on comparative studies carried out by the International Institute for Democracy and Electoral Assistance (International IDEA) and the Organization of Security and Co-operation in Europe (OSCE), as well as on other insights from both peacebuilding literature and democracy research. For the classification of EDR systems, see International IDEA, *Electoral Justice: The International IDEA Handbook* (Stockholm: International IDEA, 2010), 57–80.
5 The "legal framework of elections" generally includes all legislation and pertinent constitutional, legal, and quasi-legal documents that have an impact on elections and/or are related to the administration of electoral processes (such as penal codes and civil rights statutes; political party and media laws; EMB regulations and directives; and, in some cases, codes of conduct of the EMB, political parties, election observers, and the media).
6 International IDEA, *International Electoral Standards: Guidelines for Reviewing the Legal Framework of Elections, Guidelines Series* (Stockholm: International IDEA, 2002)
7 United Nations Development Programme (UNDP), *Elections and Conflict Prevention: A Guide to Analysis, Planning, and Programming* (New York: UNDP, 2009): 37ff.
8 International IDEA, *Electoral Management Design, The International IDEA Handbook* (Stockholm: International IDEA, 2006), 22ff.
9 See also J. Jesús Orozco Henríquez and Raúl Ávila, "Electoral Dispute Resolution Systems: Towards a Handbook and Related Material," paper presented to the EDR expert group workshop held in Mexico City, 27-28 May 2004, http://www.idea.int/news/newsletters/upload/concept_paper_EDR.pdf.

10 The constitution, statute law, international instruments, or treaties and other provisions in force in a country.
11 Its essential purpose is the genuine and effective protection of the right to vote, either to elect (or be elected as) a representative to hold a public or government position – national, local, or even supranational – or to participate directly in some normative or governmental decision by means of a referendum or recall.
12 J. Jesús Orozco Henríquez, "Sistemas de justicia electoral en el derecho comparado" (Electoral justice systems in comparative law), in *Sistemas de justicia electoral: Evaluación y perspectivas* (Electoral justice systems: Assessment and prospects), ed. J. Jesús Orozco Henríquez, (Mexico City: Tribunal Electoral del Poder Judicial de la Federación, 2001); International IDEA, *Electoral Justice*.
13 *ACE Encyclopaedia*, s.v. "Legal Framework – Essential Elements – Electoral Dispute Resolution – Different Systems" http://aceproject.org/ace-en/topics/lf/lfb/lfb12/lfb12a/onePage.
14 *ACE Encyclopaedia*, s.v. "Legal Framework – Essential Elements – Electoral Dispute Resolution," http://aceproject.org/ace-en/topics/lf/lfb/lfb12/default/?searchterm=justice.
15 International IDEA, *Electoral Justice*, 62.
16 David C. Rapoport and Leonard Weinberg, "Elections and Violence," in Rapoport and Weinberg, *Democratic Experience*, 33.
17 Denis Petit, *Resolving Election Disputes in the OSCE Area: Towards a Standard Election Dispute Monitoring System* (Warsaw: Office for Democratic Institutions and Human Rights, 2000): 9.
18 Ibid., 7ff.
19 Ibid., 9.
20 ACE Encyclopaedia, s.v. "Electoral Integrity – Integrity in Election Administration," http://aceproject.org/ace-en/topics/ei/eif/onePage.
21 Petit, *Resolving Election Disputes*, 10.
22 Ibid., 14
23 International IDEA, *Electoral Justice*.
24 International IDEA, *Electoral Management Design*, 205.
25 International IDEA, *Electoral Justice*.
26 *ACE Encyclopaedia*, s.v. "Electoral Integrity – Enforcement of Electoral Integrity," http://aceproject.org/ace-en/topics/ei/eie/.
27 Ibid.
28 Denis Kadima and Susan Booysen, ed., *Compendium of Elections in Southern*

Africa 1989-2009: 20 Years of Multiparty Democracy (Johannesburg: Electoral Institute for the Sustainability of Democracy in Africa, 2009): 16ff.

CHAPTER TWELVE

* This essay was originally presented as a keynote address to the North-South Institute workshop Elections and Conflict: Promoting Good Practice in Electoral Conflict Management held in Ottawa, 29–30 October 2009.
1 Rosie DiManno, "Twisting through Afghan Recount," *Toronto Star*, 23 October 2009.
2 Gerald Schmitz and David Gillies, *The Challenge of Democratic Development: Sustaining Democratization in Developing Societies* (Ottawa: North-South Institute, 1992).
3 Immanuel Kant, *Perpetual Peace: A Philosophical Sketch*, (1795), http://www.mtholyoke.edu/acad/intrel/kant/kant1.htm.
4 A.J.P. Taylor, *The Troublemakers: Dissent over Foreign Policy* (London: Panther Books, 1969), 31.
5 Robert D. Kaplan, "Kissinger, Metternich, and Realism," *The Atlantic* Online, June 1999, http://www.theatlantic.com/issues/99jun/9906kissinger.htm.
6 Benjamin Schwarz, "Globaloney," *The Atlantic*, January/February 2009, 90.
7 Andrei Sakharov, *Alarm and Hope* (New York: Alfred A. Knopf, 1978), 173.
8 Andrei Sakharov, Nobel lecture, 11 December 1975, http://nobelprize.org/nobel_prizes/peace/laureates/1975/sakharov-lecture.html.
9 Andrei Sakharov, *Memoirs* (New York: Vintage Books, 1992), 686.
10 House of Commons, Standing Committee on Foreign Affairs and International Development (SCFAIT), *Advancing Canada's Role in International Support for Democratic Development*, July 2007, 6.
11 Thomas S. Axworthy, Leslie Campbell, and David Donovan, *The Democracy Canada Institute: A Blueprint*, IRPP Working Paper Series no. 2005-02 (Montréal: Institute for Research on Public Policy, 2005).
12 Edmund Burke, *Reflections on the Revolution in France* (London: J.M. Dent & Sons, 1790/1971), 44.
13 SCFAIT, *Advancing Canada's Role*, 26.
14 Government of Canada, *Speech from the Throne*, 19 November 2008.
15 Thomas S. Axworthy, ed., "Creating Democratic Value: Evaluating Efforts to Promote Democracy Abroad – Final Report," (working paper presented at the symposium Creating Democratic Value: Evaluating Efforts to Promote

Democracy Abroad, Ottawa, 25–26 February 2008), http://www.queensu.ca/csd/publications/Creating_Democratic_Efforts-Final.pdf.
16 For conference summary, see ibid.
17 Michael McFaul, Amichai Magen, and Kathryn Stoner-Weiss, "Evaluating International Influences on Democratic Transitions: Concept Paper," (working paper, Program on Evaluating International Influences on Democratic Development, Center on Democracy, Development, and the Rule of Law, Freeman Spogli Institute for International Studies, Stanford University, 2008), 10.
18 Andrei Sakharov, quoted in Richard Lourie, *Sakharov: A Biography* (London: Brandeis University Press, 2002), 412.

CHAPTER THIRTEEN

1 Freedom House, *Freedom in the World 2011: The Authoritarian Challenge to Democracy; Selected Data from Freedom House's Annual Survey of Political Rights and Civil Liberties* (Washington DC: Freedom House, 2011), http://www.freedomhouse.org/images/File/fiw/FIW_2011_Booklet.pdf. The annual survey examined 194 countries and fourteen territories.
2 Economist Intelligence Unit, *Democracy Index 2010: Democracy in Retreat* (London: Economist Intelligence Unit, 2010), 1–2, www.eiu.com/public/topical_report.aspx?campaignid=demo2010 (registration required).
3 Ibid., 13, table 4. In both the 2008 and 2010 rankings Afghanistan is placed among "authoritarian regimes." In the Freedom House survey, Afghanistan is listed as "not free" with highly negative ratings on both political rights and civil liberties and "a downward trend arrow due to fraudulent parliamentary elections in September 2010." See Freedom House, *Freedom in the World 2011*, 19.
4 *Virtual JFK: Vietnam if Kennedy Had Lived,* prod. and dir. Koji Masutani, 80 min., Global Media Project/Sven Khan Films/Watson Institute for International Studies, 2008.
5 A prime case in point is the *National Post* editorial, "Realism in Afghanistan," 3 March 2009.
6 Paul Fitzgerald and Elizabeth Gould, *Invisible History: Afghanistan's Untold Story* (San Francisco: City Light Books, 2009), 60.
7 Office of the Chief Electoral Officer, *A History of the Vote in Canada*, 2nd ed. (Ottawa, 2007), http://lpintrabp.parl.gc.ca/lopimages2/bibparlcat/16000/Ba411638.pdf.
8 Fitzgerald and Gould, *Invisible History*, 62 ff.

9 Ibid., 90 ff. Fitzgerald and Gould offer a richly detailed account in the section "Afghanistan's 'Experience' with Democracy," 104–36.
10 *Examined Life*, dir. Astra Taylor, 87 min., Sphinx Productions and National Film Board of Canada, 2008.
11 Gerald Schmitz and David Gillies, *The Challenge of Democratic Development: Sustaining Democratization in Developing Societies* (Ottawa: North-South Institute, 1992), 16.
12 "Report of the "Democracy Dialogue 2009: Democracy in Fragile and Conflict-Affected Situations," Department of Foreign Affairs and International Trade, Ottawa, 2010.
13 The organization has been described as "in crisis" and "dysfunctional" in hearings before the Standing Committee on Foreign Affairs and International Development.
14 Prime Minister of Canada, Speech from the Throne, "Protecting Canada's Future," 19 November 2008, http://www.sft-ddt.gc.ca/eng/media.asp?id=1364.
15 Minister Cannon's exact words were "Hopefully it is done in much the same way as at IDRC, which is I think not only world renowned but certainly something of whose work Canada can be extremely proud." See House of Commons, Standing Committee on Foreign Affairs and International Development, *Evidence*, no. 2, 10 February 2009, 10, http://www2.parl.gc.ca/content/hoc/Committee/402/FAAE/Evidence/EV3663799/FAAEEV02-E.PDF.
16 Lee Berthiaume, "Full-Steam Ahead on Spreading Democracy," *Embassy*, 18 February 2009, 1, 4.
17 Privy Council Office, *Advisory Panel Report on the Creation of a Canadian Democracy Promotion Agency*, November 2009, 8, http://www.pco-bcp.gc.ca/docs/information/publications/promotion/docs/promotion-eng.pdf.
18 Ibid., 10.
19 Thomas S. Axworthy, "Liberty and Order Are Not Natural Allies," *Ottawa Citizen*, 5 February 2011.
20 Out of 1,707 coalition military fatalities, the US toll stood at 1,032 at the time of writing.
21 According to a report by the Kabul-based Afghanistan Rights Monitor, at least 2,421 Afghan civilians were killed and more than 3,270 injured in "conflict-related security incidents". US/NATO and Afghan government forces were accused of responsibility for a third of reported deaths. Afghanistan Rights Monitor (ARM), *ARM Annual Report: Civilian Casualties of War January–December 2010* (Kabul: Afghanistan Rights Monitor, 2011), 2.

22 Calotta Gall, "Taliban's 2 Branches Agree to Put Focus on an Offensive," *New York Times*, 27 March 2009.
23 "The Soldiers Get It," *Ottawa Citizen*, 14 February 2009.
24 For extracts from the interview broadcast on March 1 see "NATO Can't Beat Afghan Insurgents Alone: Harper," Canadian Press, 1 March 2009; Bradley Bouzane, "Afghan Insurgency Will Never Be Defeated: Harper," CanWest News Service, 1 March 2009.
25 Michelle Collins, "Afghan Nerves Rattled by Harper Defeatism: Samad," *Embassy*, 11 March 2009, 1, 9; Khorsheid Samad, "Why Afghanistan Needs Democracy," *Ottawa Citizen*, 7 March 2009.
26 White House, Office of the Press Secretary, "Overview of the Afghanistan and Pakistan Annual Review," news release, 16 December 2010, http://www.whitehouse.gov/the-press-office/2010/12/16/overview-afghanistan-and-pakistan-annual-review.
27 "An Open Letter to President Obama," http://www.afghanistancallto reason.com/.
28 Independent Panel on Canada's Future Role in Afghanistan, final report, Ottawa, January 2008, 33.
29 Sima Wali, "Introduction," in Fitzgerald and Gould, *Invisible History*, 3–7. Wali was the sole female US delegate to the 2001 Bonn talks that led to Afghanistan's first post-Taliban interim government, headed by Hamid Karzai.
30 Waillullah Rahmani, "A Message from Kabul Center's CEO and founder, Waliullah Rahmani," *Kabul Center for Strategic Studies*, http://kabulcenter.org/?page_id=2. Message from the founder and CEO of the Center. The Center was established as an Afghan initiative in 2007, "dedicated to building democracy in Afghanistan," with a primary goal "to erect a state that will guarantee the rights and liberties of all Afghan citizens."
31 James F. Dobbins, *After the Taliban: Nation-Building in Afghanistan* (Washington, DC: Potomac Books, 2008), 83. The book as a whole provides an indispensable account of the Bonn negotiations.
32 Steve Coll, *Ghost Wars: The Secret History of the CIA, Afghanistan, and Bin Laden from the Soviet Invasion to September 10, 2001* (New York: Penguin Books, 2005), 299. The book won the Pulitzer Prize.
33 Malalai Joya, *A Woman Among the Warlords: The Extraordinary Story of an Afghan Woman Who Dared to Raise Her Voice* (New York: Scribner, 2009); see also Nick Grono and Candace Rondeaux, "Dealing with Brutal Afghan Warlords Is a Mistake," *Boston Globe*, 17 January 2010.

34 J. Alexander Thier, ed., *The Future of Afghanistan* (Washington, DC: United States Institute of Peace, 2009), 7.
35 Rory Stewart, "The Irresistible Illusion," *London Review of Books* 31, no. 13 (2009): 3–6.
36 Constitution of Afghanistan, 3 January 2004, http://www.supremecourt.gov.af/PDFiles/constitution2004_english.pdf.
37 John R. Schmidt, "Can Outsiders Bring Democracy to Post-Conflict States?" *Orbis* 52, no. 1 (2008): 108. Emphasis in original.
38 Ibid., 120, 122.
39 Ali Jalali, "Is There Hope for Peace in Afghanistan?" presentation, University of Ottawa, 14 November 2008. Jalali is a former Minister of the Interior in the government of Afghanistan.
40 Marc André Boivin, cited in House of Commons, Standing Committee on Foreign Affairs and International Development, *Canada in Afghanistan: Report of the Standing Committee on Foreign Affairs and International Development*, July 2008, 86.
41 Grant Kippen, *Elections in 2009 and 2010: Technical and Contextual Challenges to Building Democracy in Afghanistan* (Kabul: Afghanistan Research and Evaluation Unit, 2008).
42 Peter Goodspeed, "Karzai May Call Snap Elections," *National Post*, 28 February 2009; Ben Farmer and Dean Nelson, "Karzai's Backers Frown on Idea of Snap Election," *National Post*, 27 February 2009.
43 International Crisis Group, *Afghanistan's Election Challenges*, Asia Report N°171 (Kabul/Brussels: International Crisis Group, 2009), ii and passim.
44 Grant Kippen, e-mail to author from Kabul, 25 March 2009.
45 For a detailed examination and analysis, see Andrew Reynolds, "Electoral Systems Today: The Curious Case of Afghanistan," *Journal of Democracy* 17, no. 2 (2006). Although this is supposed to produce a form of proportional representation, as an indication of the perverse results in practice, Reynolds observes that of the about 50 per cent of eligible Afghans who voted in the 2005 parliamentary elections (voter turnout was below 35 per cent in Kabul and below 30 per cent in Kandahar Province), fully 68 per cent voted for candidates who lost.
46 International Crisis Group, *Afghanistan: Elections and the Crisis of Governance*, Asia Briefing N°96 (Kabul/Brussels: International Crisis Group, 2009).
47 Ibid., 9.
48 Grant Kippen, "The Long Democratic Transition," in Thier, *Future of Afghanistan*, 36.

49 Ibid., chapter 4 and passim.
50 The 2009 ECC members comprised three UN-appointed experts, one chosen by the Afghanistan Independent Human Rights Commission, and one by the country's Supreme Court.
51 Canada's minister of Foreign Affairs, Lawrence Cannon, issued a statement on 23 February that "a strong and independent ECC is vital for the future of a democratic Afghanistan, and any efforts to weaken this body are disturbing." See "Canada Troubled Over Reported Revisions to Afghan Electoral Law, news release, 23 February 2010, http://www.afghanistan.gc.ca/canada-afghanistan/news-nouvelles/2010/2010_02_23.aspx?lang=eng. According to US Department of State spokesperson Philip J. Crowley on 24 February: "We are supportive of the Afghan government stepping up and assuming its responsibilities for its own [election] processes." See "Remarks to the Press," news release, 24 February 2010, http://www.state.gov/r/pa/prs/ps/2010/02/137263.htm
52 Ahmed Rashid, "The Way Out of Afghanistan", *New York Review of Books*, 13 January 2011.
53 Grant Kippen and Scott Worden, "Election aftermath and the rule of law in Afghanistan," *Foreign Policy*, 21 January 2011, http://afpak.foreignpolicy.com/posts/2011/01/21/election_aftermath_and_the_rule_of_law_in_afghanistan.
54 Noah Coburn, *Afghan Election, 2010: Alternative Narratives*, (Kabul: Afghanistan Research and Evaluation Unit, 2010), 4, 7, 8.
55 Noah Coburn, *Parliamentarians and Local Politics in Afghanistan: Elections and Instability II* (Kabul: Afghanistan Research and Evaluation Unit, 2010), 1-2. See also Anna Larson, *The Wolesi Jirga in Flux: Elections and Instability I* (Kabul: Afghanistan Research and Evaluation Unit, 2010).
56 See United Nations, Security Council, *The Situation in Afghanistan and Its Implications for International Peace and Security*, S/2010/463, 2010; Department of Foreign Affairs and International Trade, *Canada's Engagement in Afghanistan: Quarterly Report to Parliament for the Period of April 1 to June 30, 2010*, Ottawa, 22 September 2010.
57 See chapter 2.
58 See Anthony Cordesman, *The Afghan Elections: Another Milestone on the Road to Nowhere?* (Washington DC: Center for Strategic & International Studies, 2010).
59 Cited in Craig Offman, "We Cannot Defeat the Taliban, Harper Says," *National Post*, 2 March 2009.

60 Charlie Gillis, "Canada's Love Affair with Obama," *Maclean's*, 23 February 2009, 16–17.
61 Jill Mahoney, "Canadians Divided on Afghan Training Mission: Poll," *Globe and Mail*, 13 December 2010.
62 Parliamentary Budget Officer, "The Fiscal Impact of the Canadian Mission in Afghanistan," statement, 9 October 2008, http://www2.parl.gc.ca/Sites/PBO-DPB/documents/2008-10-09%20Statement%20-%20Afghanistan.pdf.
63 See Peter Goodspeed, "Obama's War," *National Post*, 14 February 2009.
64 White House, *White paper of the Interagency Policy Group's Report on US Policy toward Afghanistan and Pakistan*, Washington DC, 27 March 2009, 1, http://www.whitehouse.gov/assets/documents/Afghanistan-Pakistan_White_Paper.pdf.
65 Ibid.
66 White House, Office of the Press Secretary, "Remarks by the President in Address to the Nation on the Way Forward in Afghanistan and Pakistan," news release, 1 December 2009, http://www.whitehouse.gov/the-press-office/remarks-president-address-nation-way-forward-afghanistan-and-pakistan.
67 Ibid.
68 *Afghanistan: The London Conference; Communiqué*, London, 28 January 2010, 7, http://afghanistan.hmg.gov.uk/en/conference/london-conference/communique/.
69 *Chairmen's Statement of the International Conference on Afghanistan*, The Hague, 31 March 2009, http://www.afghanistan.gc.ca/canada-afghanistan/2009-03-31.aspx?lang=eng&highlights_file=&left_menu_en=&left_menu_fr.
70 *Communiqué*, 1.
71 Mike Blanchfield, "Afghan Bill Draws Fury Over Women's Rights," *Ottawa Citizen*, 2 April 2009; "Afghan Travesty," *National Post*, 2 April 2009.
72 United Nations, Office of the High Commissioner for Human Rights, "UN Human Rights Chief Says Afghan Law Restricting Women's Rights Is Reminiscent of Taliban Era," news release, 2 April 2009, http://www.ohchr.org/EN/NewsEvents/Pages/DisplayNews.aspx?NewsID=8634&LangID=E.
73 Interview from Kabul, *As It Happens*, CBC Radio, 2 April 2009.
74 See "Afghanistan: Human Rights under Pressure," *RAWA News*, 25 March 2010, http://www.rawa.org/temp/runews/2010/03/25/afghanistan-human-rights-under-pressure.html.

75 Anna Larson, *Towards an Afghan Democracy? Exploring Perceptions of Democratisation in Afghanistan* (Kabul: Afghanistan Research and Evaluation Unit, 2009), 27.

76 Canada-Afghanistan Solidarity Committee, *Keeping Our Promises, Canada in Afghanistan Post-2011: The Way Forward* (Vancouver: Canada-Afghanistan Solidarity Committee, 2010), 3, 11–12, http://afghanistan-canada-solidarity.org. On the case for long-term support to help Afghans fulfill their democratic aspirations, see also Richard Kraemer, "Towards State Legitimacy in Afghanistan," in "Democracy Assistance," ed. Christopher Sands, special issue, *International Journal* 65, no. 3 (2010): 637–51.

CONCLUSION

1 Joseph K. Ingram, "Egypt Demonstrates Need to Get Serious about Development," *National Post,* Full Comment, 7 February 2011. Joseph Ingram is president of The North-South Institute.

2 "The West Should Celebrate, Not Fear, the Upheaval in Egypt", The Economist, 3 February 2011.

3 The phrase is from Timothy Sisk in Anna K. Jarstad and Timothy D. Sisk, eds. *From War to Democracy: Dilemmas of Peacebuilding* (Cambridge: Cambridge University Press, 2008), 257.

4 Paul Collier, *Wars, Guns, and Votes: Democracy in Dangerous Places* (New York: Harper, 2009), 81.

5 See Rami Khouri, "Three Paths to Change in the Arab World", *Globe and Mail,* 18 January 2011.

6 Collier, *Wars, Guns, and Votes,* 82.

7 Schmitz observes that following the two aforementioned elections, Afghanistan's score on the Economist Intelligence Unit's Democracy Index dropped significantly at the end of 2010 compared to what it had been in 2008.

8 Thomas Carothers, "The 'Sequencing' Fallacy," *Journal of Democracy* 18, no. 1 (2007): 12–27.

9 Ibid., 20.

10 Center on International Cooperation, *Annual Review of Global Peace Operations 2009* (Boulder, Colo.: Lynne Rienner, 2009).

11 "Africa's Year of Elections," *The Economist,* 22 July 2010. Future African election hotspots include Nigeria, Burundi, and Guinea.

12 I am grateful to Gilbert Khadiagala for discussion of the AU as a conflict

management body. See also African Union Panel of the Wise, *Election-Related Disputes and Political Violence: Strengthening the Role of the African Union in Preventing, Managing and Resolving Conflict,* African Union Series (New York: International Peace Institute, 2010).

13 In the tradition of democratic theorist Robert Dahl, this understanding of democracy is essentially one of "expanded polyarchy." See Staffan I. Lindberg, ed., *Democratization by Elections: A New Mode of Transition* (Baltimore, Md.: Johns Hopkins University Press, 2009) for further discussion.

14 A proposed chapter on women and elections in situations of conflict was to have been prepared by Sheila Bunwaree of the Center for Conflict Resolution in Cape Town. Instead, this section is drawn in part from her presentation at the 4th annual EISA Symposium held in Johannesburg, 17–18 November 2009.

15 Lindberg, *Democratization by Elections*.

16 Frances Stewart, "Horizontal Inequalities in Kenya and the Political Disturbances of 2008: Some Implications for Aid Policy," *Conflict, Security and Development* 10, no. 1 (2010): 133–60; and Graham K. Brown and Arnim Langer, "Horizontal Inequalities and Conflict: A Critical Review and Research Agenda," *Conflict, Security and Development* 10, no. 1 (2010): 27–56.